Classroom Based Assessment

Classroom Based Assessment

Bonnie Campbell Hill
Cynthia Ruptic
Lisa Norwick

Christopher-Gordon Publishers, Inc.
Norwood, Massachusetts

Credits

Every effort has been made to contact copyright holders for permission to reproduce borrowed material where necessary. We apologize for any oversights and would be happy to rectify them in future printings.

All student work used with permission.

Form 5.5 from *Spelling in Use,* by Lester Laminack & Katie Wood, NCTE, 1996.

Form 6.1 adapted from *An Observation Survey of Early Literacy,* by Marie Clay, Heinemann, 1993.

Forms 7.11A, 7.13B, and 7.13C based on the six-trait writing assessment model fom the Northwest Regional Educational Laboratory.

Form 9.2 and Form 9.19 adapted from *Literacy Assessment: A Handbook of Instruments,* by Lynn Rhodes, Heinemann, 1993.

Form 9.22B adapted from *Highlight My Strengths,* by Leanna Traill, Rigby, 1993.

Christopher-Gordon Publishers, Inc.
1502 Providence Highway, Suite #12
Norwood, MA 02062
(800) 934-8322

Printed in the United States of America

10 9 8 7 6 5 4 3 02 01 00

ISBN: 0-926842-84-6
Library of Congress Catalogue Number: 98-071523

Contents

List of Forms

Chapter 1

Framing the Puzzle

Four years ago, when we wrote *Practical Aspects of Authentic Assessment: Putting the Pieces Together* (Hill and Ruptic, 1994), we had no idea that our voices would be heard around the world. We were amazed by how many teachers told us that our book provided practical ideas that they could use in their classrooms. Encouraged by this enthusiastic response, we started on what we thought would be a simple revision of the book. A year later, we found that our revision had grown into a four-part assessment series! As we thought about our puzzle metaphor, four key components of assessment emerged: classroom based assessment, developmental continuums, student portfolios, and reporting student growth. We decided to structure our assessment series around these four corner pieces (Figure 1.1).

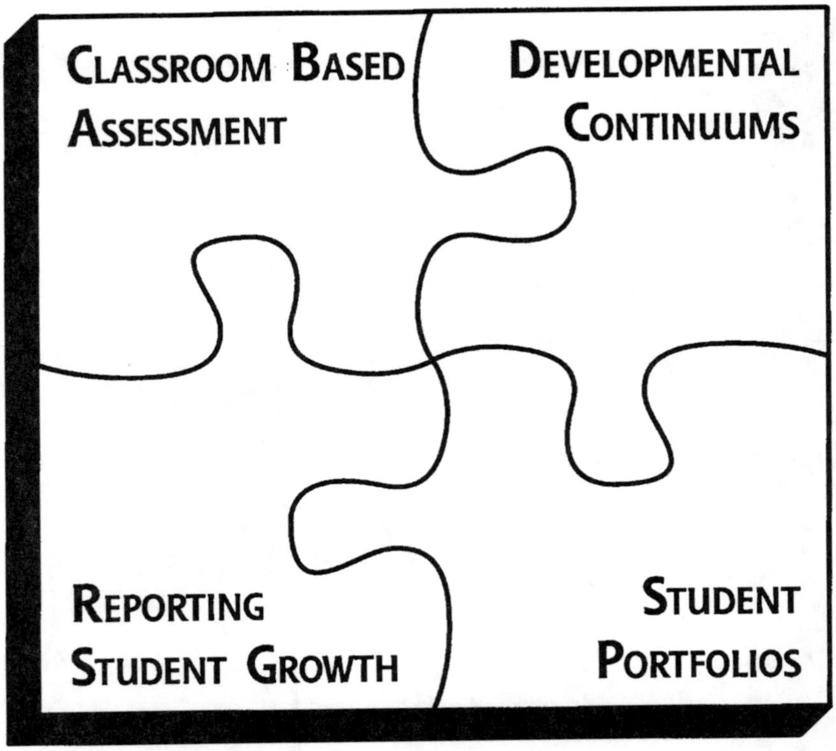

Figure 1.1: Corner Pieces

Corner Pieces Assessment Series

In this first volume (*Book One: Classroom Based Assessment*), we'll examine manageable and practical ways to collect information about young learners. You'll hear the voices of many elementary teachers at various grade levels discussing how they weave assessment into their daily routines. We've also included many assessment forms in this book and on the accompanying CD-ROM.

The next book in the series (*Book Two: Developmental Continuums*) explores the relatively new concept of developmental continuums and how teachers use these benchmarks to document student growth. We will provide examples of books by continuum levels, parent support documents, and student self-evaluation checklists. We'll also address how some districts are incorporating continuums into their report cards. Since there is very little published information on this topic, we'll provide information about how continuums are being used at the classrooms, school buildings, and district levels, along with some helpful resources.

The third book (*Book Three: Student Portfolios*), will focus on the challenges and rewards of portfolios. How can you organize and manage student portfolios in your busy classroom? How can you help students reflect on their own growth? We'll review the many recent ideas and books about portfolios with a focus on student ownership.

The final book in the series (*Book Four: Reporting Student Growth*) will offer some alternatives for sharing the information we collect through classroom based assessment, continuums, and student portfolios. What information should be passed along to next year's teacher? Could students keep anchor pieces, key work samples, video clips, and reflective letters in a Learner Profile that would paint a broader picture of their growth over time? We'll also discuss the challenges of creating a report card that actually matches what students are learning and include some innovative examples. In addition, ideas about goal setting and student-led conferences will be explored.

Four years ago, we had read most of the books and articles on assessment and portfolios. Now we can't keep up with the piles of new books on these topics avalanching on our desks and bedside tables. The recent emphasis on state and national standards has heightened public awareness, media coverage, and educators' concerns about assessment and accountability. Yet, despite the inundation of literature and rhetoric, we still find missing pieces at the classroom level. No matter how excited we get about an idea we read or hear about at a conference, it's at the classroom level that those ideas are put to the test. At the same time, we want our practices to be based on current research. How can you blend theory and practice? How can assessment match instruction? How can you keep from being overwhelmed by all you should be doing? Rather than viewing assessment as "one more thing to add," it helps to see assessment as a way to prioritize, organize, and integrate what you already do in the classroom. Effective assessment should make your job easier. It also helps when you see how all the pieces fit together. We hope that our discussion of the four corner pieces in this series will provide a framework to help you build a clearer picture of the assessment puzzle.

Structure of This Book

Putting the Pieces Together: Chapters 1 to 3

When you start to put together a puzzle, you first look at the picture before you start turning over the pieces. The first two chapters provide the big picture of how assessment and evaluation should align with your philosophy, goals, standards, and curriculum.

Are your file cabinets and drawers overflowing with forms and handouts you've collected from workshops, classes, and professional reading? Have you collected a few assessment tools that work well, but then have trouble using them consistently? In Chapter 3, we address such practical concerns as we discuss Teacher Notebooks and ways to organize and manage classroom based assessment.

Observing and Assessing Students: Chapter 4 to 10

One of the most important tools for assessing student learning is observing students. Over the summer, do you develop a method for jotting down notes that you begin in

September but then abandon by October? Do you change your method of note taking every year? In Chapter 4, we present some realistic techniques for observing students and keeping anecdotal records.

Are most of the assessment workshops you attend still hovering at the theoretical instead of the practical level? Do they leave you frustrated and yearning for assessment tools you can actually use in your classroom? Chapters 5 to 10 include a wide range of assessment tools for spelling, writing, reading, and the other content areas.

Continuums and Conclusions: Chapters 11 and 12

Even when you share report cards, assessment tools, and student portfolios, do some parents still ask, "So how's my child *really* doing?" In Chapter 11, we'll briefly show how developmental continuums can provide standards or benchmarks for both the diagnostic information you collect and the work that students gather in their portfolios. In the next book in this series (*Book Two: Developmental Continuums*), we'll examine these topics in greater depth.

We're excited about the collection of assessment ideas we gathered for this book. At the same time, we still question how much is feasible in the everyday world of the classroom. We continue to search for ways to become more organized in order to use our time well. As each state develops standards in each content area, we wrestle with how to align them with our teaching and assessment practices. How can we reconcile the idea of standards with a developmental philosophy of learning? We still struggle with how to give students and families a more powerful voice in the process. The book ends with some of these lingering questions and areas of concern.

Assessment Forms

We decided to include our assessment forms in the Appendix at the end of this book. However, we placed a thumbnail sketch of the forms discussed in each section to make it easier for you to keep track of all these forms and decide which ones might work best for you. The forms in this book were developed by teachers and have been used in many classrooms. They evolved through multiple drafts as teachers read and shared ideas with students and colleagues. We tried to make the forms clear and easy to use. The List of Forms on page ix lists the forms included in the Appendix. In addition, there are additional variations of the forms on the companion CD-ROM.

The CD-ROM

Changing the ways in which we assess students takes a great deal of energy, time, and hard work. Making forms, especially on the computer, is also very time consuming, so we included a CD-ROM along with each of the books in this series so you can easily reproduce and modify our forms to meet your needs. The information on the CD-ROM can be read on either a Macintosh or a PC. All of the forms were created using Microsoft Word and all you need is a word processor to modify the forms. Simple instructions for using the CD-ROM are included on the CD-ROM itself. You are welcome to copy and adapt the forms in this book and on the CD-ROM for classroom use. If these forms are included in other publications, however, credit must be given and permission granted by Christopher-Gordon Publishers.

Professional Growth

Change can be both exciting and exhausting. As teachers, we often feel pulled in too many directions. Sometimes it seems like our schools and districts have tackled major changes in too many areas and most of us are on far too many committees. It's an ongoing challenge to balance our personal and professional lives. We have to keep reminding ourselves that change takes time. We have to recognize that in-depth change is most successful when we prioritize potential areas for professional growth, set reasonable goals, and tackle one issue at a time. We're also more apt to follow through with new ideas when we work with friends and colleagues. At the end of each chapter, we've listed some suggestions for professional growth that we hope you will find helpful.

Recommended Readings

We've included an extensive list of references at the end of the book, but realize that such a long list can be overwhelming. Keep in mind that these references are an accumulation of books read by several teachers who authored various sections of this book. No one has time to read all of those books. Sometimes we may feel if we simply buy them, we've read them! So where should you start? When colleagues or presenters "booktalk" resources they have found helpful, we're more apt to know which books we want to read first. At the end of each chapter, we've highlighted the books we've found pivotal in our thinking for particular areas of assessment and instruction. We hope these recommendations provide a focus for your professional reading.

Using This Book

Some of you reading this book may be university students, eager for a classroom of your own. Others may be classroom teachers, reading specialists, curriculum directors, or administrators. Just like students, you are all at various places on a learning continuum. You all differ in terms of your education, years of experience, and comfort level in each content area. How familiar are you with current assessment practices? Are you getting started, expanding your skills, or fine-tuning your assessment program?

Getting Started

Those of you who are just getting started in the area of assessment may find it easiest to first focus on one particular area, such as writing. Others may wish to choose three or four assessment forms or techniques as a starting point for change. It is important that your choices are consistent with your philosophy and that they reflect activities your students are already doing. Stop there! Work on implementing those techniques until you and your students feel comfortable with both the forms and the criteria for evaluation. Adapt the forms to fit your needs. You may wish to skim the first three chapters again, before adding another piece to your assessment program. Take it slowly so that neither you nor your students become frustrated or overwhelmed. Remember, significant change takes time!

Expanding Your Skills

Some of you may already be using various assessment tools and may feel affirmed as you read along. You may have read other books and articles on assessment, attended workshops, or taken assessment coursework. Compare the forms in our book to the ones you're already using. You may want to develop new forms by combining ideas from several sources. We recommend that you revise each form by using it with students a few times before tackling additional forms and techniques. A word of caution: it's easy to start drowning in forms at this point, so be selective.

Fine-Tuning

A few of you may have been experimenting with portfolios and classroom based assessment for quite some time. As you develop your own techniques and forms, we invite you to join our professional dialogue by sending your ideas and forms to: Dr. Bonnie Campbell Hill, c/o Christopher-Gordon Publishers, 1502 Providence Highway, Suite 12, Norwood, MA 02062. Please include your name, school, address, and phone number so we can respond. You can also contact us on the Christopher-Gordon website at www.Christopher-Gordon.com.

Note to Administrators

As principals, reading teachers, and language arts specialists, you work with teachers with a variety of backgrounds and levels of expertise. Somehow you need to validate these teachers, yet also nudge and invite them to grow as professionals. There is a fine line between encouraging and mandating change! It's helpful to become involved alongside teachers in reading, learning, and reflecting so that you can provide the support necessary for change to take hold. What are other ways a staff can explore new ideas and improve instruction? We hope the recommended readings and activities for professional growth at the end of each chapter spark ideas for fostering inquiry and improving instruction and assessment in your building or district.

This book provides practical information for all elementary teachers, whether they are just getting started, getting comfortable, or fine-tuning their assessment program. As an instructional leader, we hope the book will also help you clarify issues and provide exciting directions for improving classroom based assessment.

Innovation in assessment and evaluation is part of a long-term process that requires time and thrives best with well-informed and visionary leadership.

Contributors

The idea for our first book, *Practical Aspects of Authentic Assessment: Putting the Pieces Together* (Hill and Ruptic, 1994), evolved during a series of assessment courses on Bainbridge Island in Washington state. Six of the thirteen teachers from the original group were involved in creating this book and one other contributor was added. For readability purposes, whenever we mention Bainbridge Island, we're referring to that district outside of Seattle, Washington.

Bonnie Campbell Hill teaches in Seattle at local universities and works with students, teachers, schools, and districts around the world in the areas of writing, children's literature, and assessment. Cynthia Ruptic originally taught in a multiage primary class on Bainbridge Island. Six years ago she moved to Japan, where she now teaches multiage intermediate students at Osaka International School and works with schools throughout Asia in the area of assessment and evaluation. Lisa Norwick became an invaluable co-author for this book. Four years ago, Lisa taught sixth grade and then a third/fourth multiage intermediate class in Redmond, Washington. She now teaches second grade in Bloomfield Hills, Michigan.

Roz Duthie taught kindergarten and first grade for the past several years and is currently taking a year's sabbatical to sail and write for children. Jan Peacoe was a resource room teacher when the first book was written and is now teaching first grade at Ordway Elementary on Bainbridge Island. Mary Hadley teaches fifth grade at the same school. Sandi Sater teaches fifth grade at Wilkes Elementary on Bainbridge Island. Cindy Fulton taught a multiage primary class on Bainbridge Island five years ago and currently teaches first grade at Ridgecrest Elementary in the Shoreline District north of Seattle.

Ideas from other Bainbridge Island teachers, as well as from teachers at other schools around the world, are sprinkled throughout the text. We often mention Christy Clausen, who has been a first-grade teacher in Woodinville, Washington for ten years and is our resident early years expert. This year Christy is working as a Reading Recovery teacher for the Northshore School District. Megan Sloan, a primary multiage teacher in Snohomish, Washington, also gave us feedback on drafts and contributed many forms and ideas. Anne Klein, a fourth/fifth grade teacher in Edmonds, Washington, provided many valuable samples and ideas about teaching intermediate students. The teachers from Brighton School in Lynnwood, Washington also let us use some of the forms and assessment tools they've developed. We truly appreciate the willingness of all these teachers to share their ideas.

We tried to acknowledge the original source of assessment ideas or forms. When teachers adapt forms and share techniques with colleagues, however, it's sometimes hard to trace the original source. The changing nature of the forms is one of the reasons why we included a CD-ROM with this book. We hope that you will give credit when possible, but adapt the techniques and tools to fit your own teaching situation.

Starting the Puzzle

As this book evolved, it was interesting to see how much our ideas and forms had changed in four years. We certainly do not claim to have "solved" the entire puzzle. We're certain our ideas and assessment tools will continue to change as we learn more. Our hope, however, is that this book will spark professional sharing of ideas about assessment. As you read this book, we encourage you to try out some ideas, modify others, then read some more. The ideas, the assessment forms, and the accompanying CD-ROM are intended to be used flexibly, based on your needs and your particular group of students.

What are your personal beliefs about teaching and learning? What are your goals for your students? Based on your philosophy and curriculum, how can you best measure what students are learning? These are the questions that should precede any discussion of assessment. In the next chapter, we explore how changes in philosophy and curriculum lead to changes in assessment and evaluation.

Chapter 2

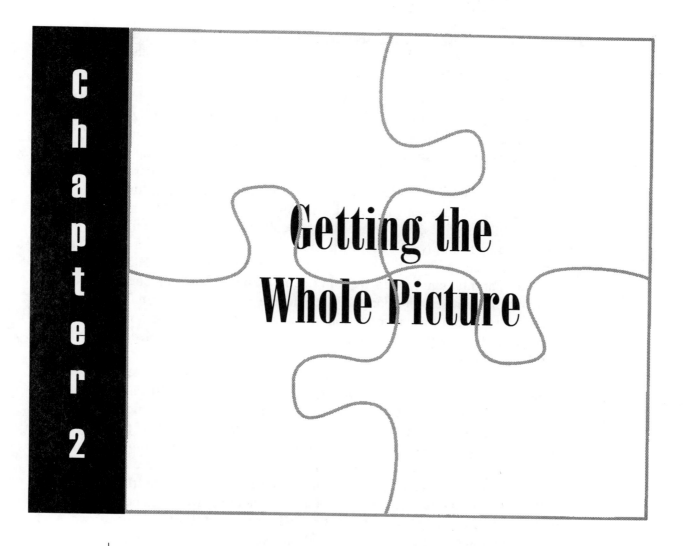

Getting the Whole Picture

Michael's mom requests a special conference. Pam arrives, clutching an article she has read in *Parent Magazine* about how teachers aren't providing enough instruction in phonics. She shows you the phonics workbooks she bought at the bookstore and asks how you teach phonics in first grade. How can you share what you know about this issue in a ten-minute conference? How can you assure Pam that phonics is indeed part of your program? How can you assuage her fears and yet not appear defensive? How can you explain to Pam, and to others in the community, that there is no one quick fix, one perfect program, or one simple test?

As teachers, it's our responsibility to share what we know about teaching and learning. Reggie Routman, in *Literacy at the Crossroads* (1996), claims that one of the best responses to the emotionally charged plea for better education is meaningful assessment:

> If you want to make "back to basics" a nonissue with parents, move to more meaningful assessment practices. When parents "see" what students are learning, producing, thinking and evaluating—as well as what the expectations are—

> in spelling, math, phonics, science, all areas, they stop asking for "the basics" because they know firsthand it underpins all that is happening in the teaching-learning process. (pp. 157–158)

In addition, parents become even more respectful when they see their own children involved in setting high standards, evaluating their own growth, and setting their own goals. Students can become our best advocates for change.

Change in assessment has lagged behind innovation in teaching. Parents, teachers, and students all recognize that end-of-the-unit quizzes, standardized tests, and little columns of boxes on report cards do not fully reflect what children are learning or need to learn. Students need to learn how to gather and synthesize information from multiple sources, read critically, work collaboratively, and think creatively. We can no longer simply test recall of facts. So why is changing a report card so emotionally charged? Why is it so hard to move away from standardized tests? Why do parents panic when we don't send home a list of ten spelling words to hang on the refrigerator? For many people, these are the only remaining recognizable artifacts from their recollection of school. If we change or remove these last vestiges of the past, parents need to know why they have been replaced and what we are doing differently.

It's not only the community that finds change difficult. As teachers, we are usually open to new ideas. However, we understandably resist change when it's mandated without our input. We also need to know what we are doing differently and why. For instance, in one district, a superintendent "mandated" portfolios without consulting teachers and without providing any staff development. In another district, teachers were told to implement writing portfolios in their classrooms without any training in teaching writing. In both cases, teachers were frustrated and rebellious. This "cart before the horse" approach naturally results in negative feelings and misunderstandings about portfolios and assessment. Problems occur when administrators and teachers hear about ideas like portfolios or running records and decide to jump in without having spent considerable time thinking about how assessment fits within the bigger picture of the school's beliefs and curriculum. If a philosophy and framework are firmly established before leaping into changes, teachers have a common language and reference point so that decisions about materials, curriculum, and assessment don't appear whimsical or random.

Let's examine the metaphor we used to structure this book. It's hard to put a puzzle together unless you've seen the complete picture. It helps when you keep the box propped up in front of you in order to keep looking back and forth between the individual pieces and the whole picture. Figure 2.1 illustrates how changes in assessment and evaluation are part of a larger perspective. Authentic assessment is based on a constructivist, responsive, child-centered philosophy and curriculum. We placed the learner at the center of the figure since your decisions will be affected by the developmental needs of your particular group of students. The arrows extend in both directions because students' responses should impact decisions about curriculum, assessment, and evaluation. Student learning, rather than curriculum or lesson plans, should be at the heart of education. We also want to emphasize the recursive nature of the process; changes in any one arena may affect other areas. In the next section, we briefly discuss each of these seven educational components.

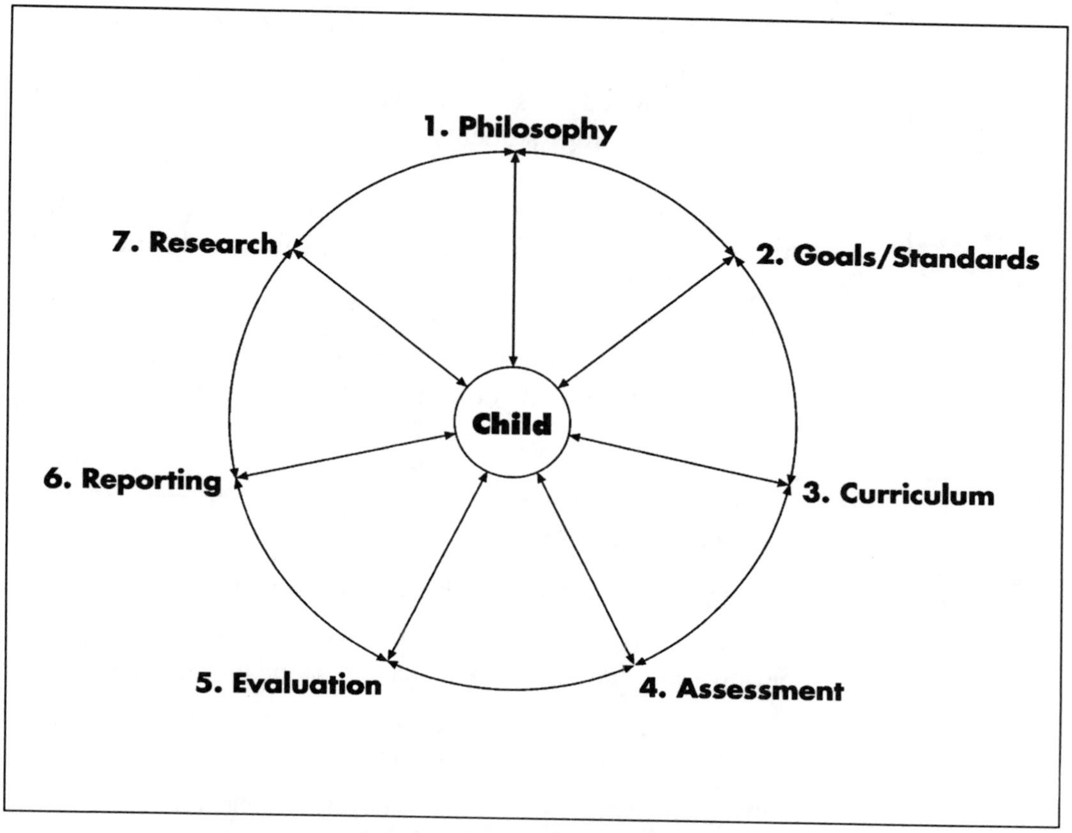

Figure 2.1: Seven Educational Components

Seven Educational Components

1. Philosophy

Before you begin to assess and evaluate students, it's crucial to articulate, review, and continually revise your beliefs about teaching and learning. These beliefs should be grounded in current research about learning and literacy acquisition. Whether you are working individually, as a school, or as a district, the process of clarifying your philosophy is a crucial first step.

Ideally, your decisions about curriculum and assessment should match your philosophy. What are your deeply held beliefs about teaching and learning? If you believe that people learn in many different ways, you may want to allow students to decide how to show what they have learned. In reading, for example, students may choose to include written journal responses or reading logs as evidence of reading growth. Other students may want to show their understanding as readers through art, drama, or the use of technology. When you provide models and opportunities for students to demonstrate what they have learned in a variety of ways, the range and depth of their responses can be astounding.

Let's take another example. If your primary goal is to nourish independent thinkers who view learning as interactive and collaborative, then traditional report cards and standardized tests are inadequate. You may want to incorporate assessment tools that encourage students to share ideas and work together to solve problems.

Some schools have articulated their values and beliefs in a formal way. Teachers at Audubon Elementary in Redmond, Washington developed a philosophy statement (Figure 2.2) that the staff uses to anchor any decisions about new curriculum or materials. This philosophy statement is printed on the back of their report card and in their school handbook. The process of drafting and revising a philosophy statement helps a staff clarify common values that can guide curriculum and assessment.

- All children can learn.
- Teaching decisions should be based upon what is best for students.
- All learning (including academics, life skills, etc.) is accomplished through partnership involving students, parents, teachers, and the community at large.
- Appropriate teaching environments foster students' creative thinking and success, which contribute to their self-esteem.
- Learning and independent thinking develop continuously throughout one's life.
- Given a diverse student population, children learn and grow at their own rate and in their own way.
- We expect students to be responsible for their own behavior and learning.
- Modeling is a powerful teaching tool.
- Curriculum should be relevant and integrated.
- Learning happens in a developmentally appropriate, stable, consistent, and supportive environment.
- Appropriate teaching environments foster student success and self-esteem.
- As abstract, collaborative systems thinkers, children develop skills necessary to enter the work force of the future.

NOTE: If we believe the first four statements, then the remaining statements are true; the rest are simply an elaboration.

Figure 2.2: Philosophy Statement of Audubon Elementary

2. Goals and Standards

Once you articulate your philosophy, the next step is to define your specific goals as a teacher, school, or district. What are your goals for your reading or writing program? Are there local, state, or national standards to consider? Write down your own beliefs on the Philosophy and Goals page (Form 2.1) in the Appendix. Be specific and focus on your most important values. Try to keep this list to one page that you can share with parents and your principal.

The larger the group of teachers, the more important it becomes to develop a common framework from which to build curriculum. Clearly articulated goals also provide a framework for consistency. For example, if some teachers in a school emphasize computation in mathematics, while others stress problem solving and mathematical reasoning, conversations about goals can help a school create a balanced mathematics program. Discussions can focus first on what we want children to be able to do as mathematicians, rather than starting with teaching methods and materials.

In the past few years, there has been a tremendous push to articulate standards. Broad local, state, or national standards can provide a focus for your curricular goals. As an example, we have listed Washington State's Learning Goals, called the Essential Learnings (Figure 2.3), which are spelled out in more detail in documents from the Washington State Commission on Student Learning (1998). These goals were developed by teachers and community members outside education and can help create a common language and set of goals. For more information about the Washington State Essential Learnings, the web site address is: http:\\csl.wednet.edu and the email address is csl@inspire.ospi.wednet.edu or call (360) 664-3155.

Goal 1

Read with comprehension, write with skill, and communicate effectively and responsibly in a variety of ways and settings.

Goal 2

Know and apply the core concepts and principles of mathematics; social, physical, and life sciences; civics and history; geography; arts; and health and fitness.

Goal 3

Think analytically, logically, and creatively, and integrate experience and knowledge to form reasoned judgments and solve problems.

Goal 4

Understand the importance of work and how performance, effort, and decisions directly affect career and educational opportunities.

Figure 2.3: Washington State Essential Learnings

We're so often caught up in the daily whirlwind of teaching that we don't step back to examine our direction and our path. Regie Routman (1996) warns that "As professional educators, we must clearly understand and articulate our beliefs and practices. Otherwise, we are at the mercy of non-educators and the media who make public statements that can set our teaching back" (p. 41). The public is more likely to trust us as educators when we show that we are professional and thoughtful practitioners.

Routman advises that we also examine the language we use in education. For instance, she suggests that when we use the term, "mini-lesson," it sounds as if we barely teach! With her advice in mind, we've used Routman's term, "focus lesson," in our classrooms and in the remainder of this book. The more thoughtfully we clarify our language and articulate our beliefs and curricular decisions, the more clearly we can communicate with families and the wider community.

3. Curriculum

After you've defined your philosophy and goals, then you can focus on the specifics of your curriculum. All three components should mesh. It's frightening that curriculum development and materials adoption often takes place in seven-year or even ten-year cycles. Curriculum reexamination should be ongoing. Curriculum revision should also be responsive to new research in education, current children's literature, as well as changes in technology. Changes in one content area should ripple through other subject areas. In addition, the curriculum must be adaptable to the particular needs and interests of each year's new group of students. Regie Routman (1996) suggests that we view curriculum more as a dialogue than as a static document.

Let's look at a specific example. One of the goals in Washington state is for students to read a wide range of materials for a variety of purposes. This goal is having an impact on curriculum, staff development, and material selection across the state. Margaret Mooney, an educator from New Zealand, has been working with the Washington State Commission on Student Learning. She has helped teachers question the balance between fiction and nonfiction in their classrooms. Sparked by this new goal, teachers are trying to provide a wider range of materials, such as schedules, maps, lists, brochures, menus, magazines, manuals, and letters, as well as well-written informational books. In addition, teachers are beginning to spend more time explicitly teaching students how to read and write in different genres.

What are your primary goals for reading? Writing? Mathematics? Science? You may want to begin by listing the specific activities that help you reach each goal. How do you teach writing? For instance, your writing program may include a writing workshop structure with focus lessons, daily time to write, and time for sharing. How do you teach reading? The activities in a literature-based reading program may involve reading aloud, silent reading, literature circles, guided reading, shared reading, dialogue journals, and response projects. We need to articulate where we're headed and how we plan to get there.

Families need to know our goals and plans for teaching their children. Most schools sponsor a curriculum night in the fall for parents. Consider how powerful it would be for families to hear about your philosophy, your goals for their children, and the activities that will help students reach those goals. It would also be helpful at the beginning of the year to explain to parents how students will be assessed and evaluated and how that information will be shared.

Christy Clausen uses some of the ideas from *Getting It Together* (Morrison, 1994) at her Curriculum Night in the fall. She likens the process of learning to read to that of learning to talk. She leads parents through a series of reading activities to demonstrate what researchers have learned in the past few years about reading. Christy also explains her philosophy and goals for the year.

At her Curriculum Night, Megan Sloan shows parents a range of writing samples from previous years to show how students develop as writers. She also shares student work that exemplifies the specific writing traits she will be teaching and assessing during the year.

We also need to discuss curriculum with the wider educational community. Some of you may be in schools or districts that are involved in the arduous process of aligning goals and curriculum with new state and national standards. This opportunity to talk about the values of a community and to re-examine curriculum and assessment can be both exciting and time-consuming.

In the past, evaluation has been an externally imposed method of sorting and ranking students. Rarely has evaluation guided teaching or involved students. In contrast, we hope to convey how assessment, evaluation, and reporting can be linked closely with instruction in a way that helps teachers, parents, and students define standards, measure growth, and set new goals. In Figure 2.4, we've defined the terms that we'll explore further in the next three sections.

4. Assessment

Assessment is the process of gathering evidence in order to document learning and growth. This daily, ongoing collection of data is often inseparable from instruction. We make professional decisions based on observations, conferences, and data from surveys, as well as from samples of student work. Assessment helps us know our students and guides our instruction.

How do you know what to teach unless you first assess what students know? Assessment and instruction are inextricably intertwined, as we try to show with the Möbius strip in Figure 2.5.

Rather than scrambling to collect information about students the week before report cards and parent conferences, assessment becomes much more manageable when data are collected on a regular basis during the normal cycle of teaching and learning. Assessment becomes much more feasible and valid when you assess children's reading as they read and assess progress in writing during writing time. However, before you decide *what* and *when* to assess, you need to examine *why*. What is your primary purpose for assessment?

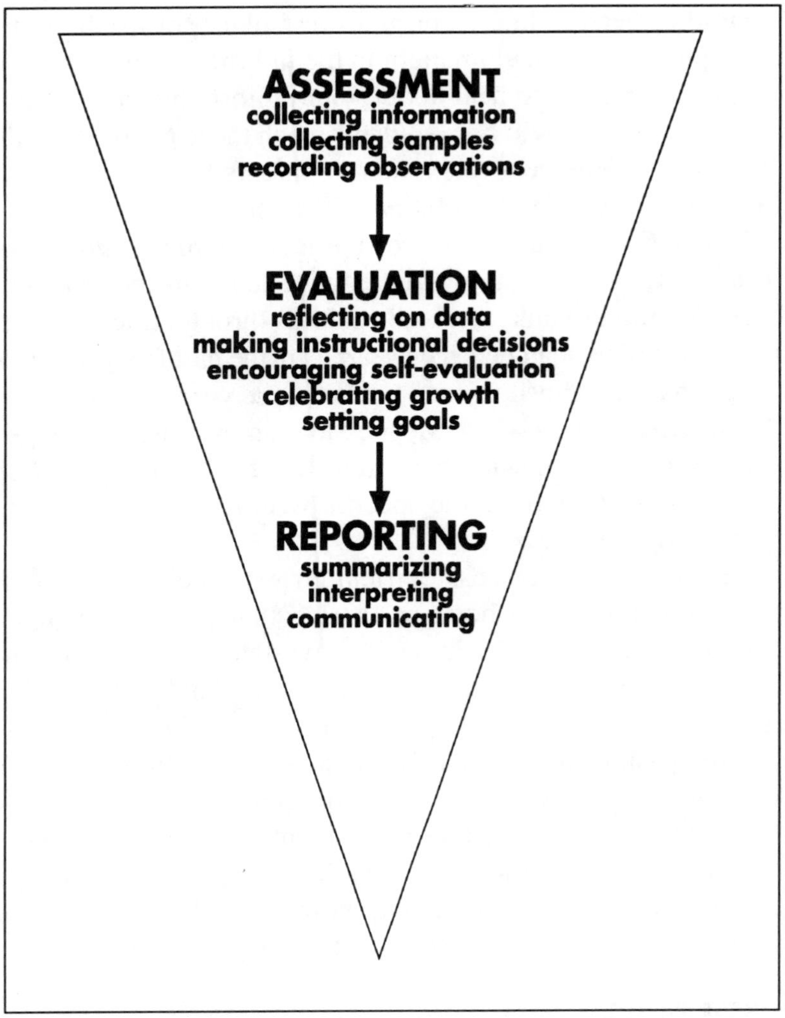

Figure 2.4: Assessment, Evaluation, and Reporting

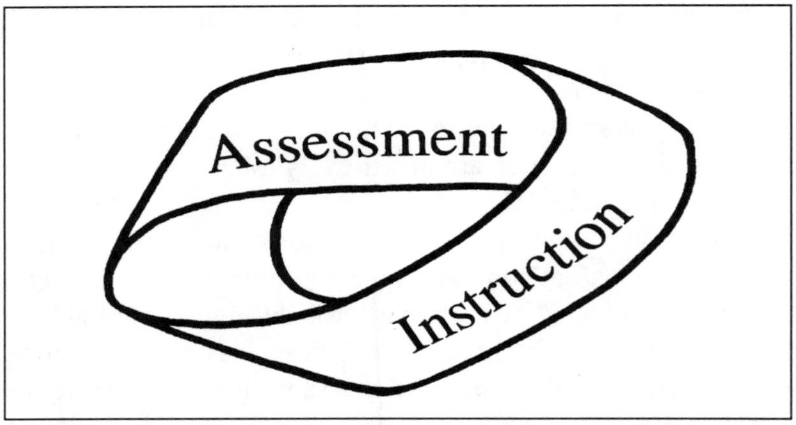

Figure 2.5: Assessment and Instruction

Edward Chittenden (1991) suggests four purposes for assessment: keeping track, checking up, finding out, and summing up. He states that assessing in order to "find out" what students know forms the framework for responsive teaching. The more we know about our students, the better teachers we become. Like Chittenden, we place a heavy emphasis in this book on observing and talking with students, as well as involving them in the assessment process.

Once you've thought about your purpose, the next step is to decide what you want to assess. You may want to make several copies of the Curriculum and Assessment page (Form 2.2) in the Appendix. At the top of the page, write one of your goals for a particular subject, such as writing. On the left-hand side of the box, list the activities that comprise your program. At this point, you may want to brainstorm a list of possible assessment tools. Next, opposite each activity, note the specific assessment tools or techniques you plan to use. We have provided an example in Figure 2.6. The Curriculum and Assessment form may help you see the connection between instruction and assessment more clearly. You may want to complete this form at the beginning of the year and refer to it periodically. You could also share this form with families and your administrator.

Goal: Students will acquire the ability to communicate through writing.	
Curricular Activities	**Assessment Tool**
Writing Workshop	Writing continuum
Writing conferences	Writing conference form
Daily Oral Language	Checklist or student graph of performance
Writing portfolios	Self-evaluation and goal-setting forms
Learning logs	Self-reflection
Research reports	Rubric
Math journals	Rubric
Literature journals	Assessing response to literature form

Figure 2.6: Curriculum and Assessment

5. Evaluation

Evaluation is the process of reflecting upon all the data we have collected. We should evaluate students based on both their own individual growth and in comparison to widely held expectations for their particular age group or grade level. In addition, we should help students learn how to evaluate and celebrate their own growth as learners. This "stepping back," in order to value or reflect upon learning and progress, is what separates evaluation from assessment.

How do you know when a student is not progressing at an appropriate rate? What is the normal developmental range that you expect for the ages you teach? When should you become concerned about a child? How do you meet the needs of the student who is flying along at a faster rate than others in the classroom? The choices you make about evaluation will depend a great deal on school and district policies. The nature of student evaluation will be determined to some extent by whether or not you are required to give grades, by the nature of your report card, and by your system for parent conferences.

As you collect information about student learning, you will also be evaluating your own teaching. What focus lessons were successful? How well did the students understand a particular math concept? How can you deepen your students' understanding? The better you become at assessing students' learning, the more you can fine-tune your instruction. As you involve students in self-evaluation, they can begin to celebrate growth and set goals for their next steps.

6. Reporting

You can report student growth by showing evidence of learning and by communicating your insights to students, parents, and administrators. Traditionally, report cards and standardized test scores have been the only information parents have received regarding their children's learning. What other means can you use to help parents understand their children's progress? What information can you provide for parents about how you teach and what their children are learning? In most schools, the only window into the classroom occurs at Back to School Night or once or twice a year during parent conferences. If student work is kept in the classroom in work folders and portfolios, how can parents know what their children are learning in class? Throughout this book, we suggest other ways for teachers and students to demonstrate learning to families on an ongoing basis.

As curriculum and assessment change, you may find that the traditional report card, with letter grades or checks in columns of little boxes, does not adequately reflect what your students are learning. As you begin to involve students more actively in goal setting and self-evaluation, the structure, schedule, and length of time for conferences may need to change. In *Book Four: Reporting Student Growth* of this assessment series, we will discuss alternatives to traditional report cards and parent conferences.

7. Research

The information you report to parents is based on observations, student work, and your expertise as a teacher. Your instruction, assessment, and evaluation should also be shaped by current research in education. Teaching *is* research as you fine-tune your methods and incorporate new ideas. In turn, you can share your insights by contributing to the growing body of qualitative, classroom based research.

Over a decade ago, educators such as Donald Murray, Peter Elbow, Donald Graves, and Lucy Calkins documented how writers revisit their work to increase the power of their writing. Teachers began to help students reexamine their writing through conferences. They incorporated focus lessons on revision, modeled their own writing strategies, and tried to assess both writing products and writing process. Teachers encouraged students to write reflections about their process and to include rough drafts as well as published writing in their portfolios. In these ways, teachers wove what they learned from research into the fabric of their classrooms. New research should impact your philosophy, instruction, and methods of assessment in a continual interaction between these seven educational components.

Turning Over the Pieces

All of this reading, thinking, and re-designing of education is hard work. It requires time and support from administrators, colleagues, and even your families. Significant change is a long-term process and cannot occur during occasional half-day workshops or after-school meetings. To be successful, teachers need time to meet and share ideas, observe colleagues, and read and write together. Teachers also need time to reflect and plan in order to implement meaningful changes.

In this chapter we focused on how philosophy, goals, curriculum, assessment, evaluation, reporting, and research can all fit together. We hope these working forms and ideas provide a way for you to strengthen your professional voice as you share your expertise with students, colleagues, and the wider community. Articulating your beliefs, goals, and plans will help you create a framework with the larger picture in mind before you begin turning over the individual pieces of the puzzle.

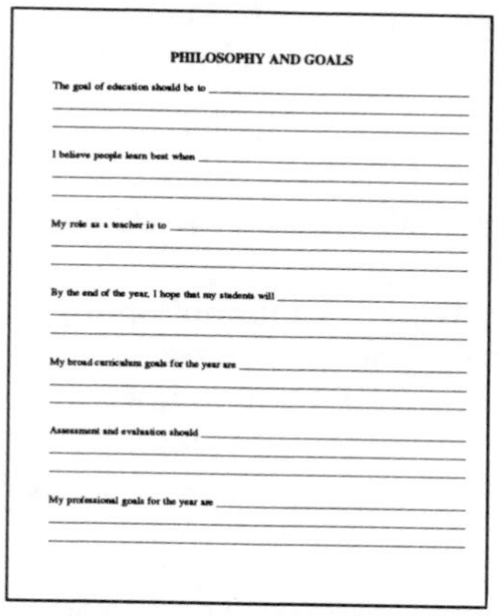
PHILOSOPHY AND GOALS

The goal of education should be to ____

I believe people learn best when ____

My role as a teacher is to ____

By the end of the year, I hope that my students will ____

My broad curriculum goals for the year are ____

Assessment and evaluation should ____

My professional goals for the year are ____

Form 2.1: Philosophy and Goals

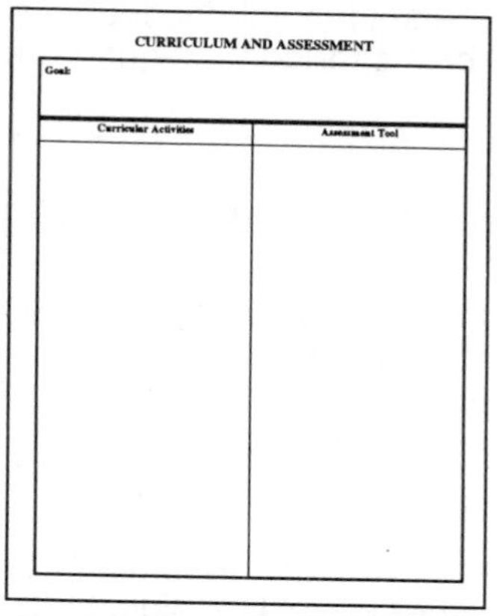
CURRICULUM AND ASSESSMENT

Goal:

Curricular Activities	Assessment Tool

Form 2.2: Curriculum and Assessment

Professional Growth

In some schools, teachers write their philosophy statement and set two or three professional goals at the beginning of the year as part of a professional growth plan. Principals, in turn, provide support in terms of materials, release time, further training, or visits to observe other classrooms. Teachers work together on curriculum projects that can be shared with the staff. Evaluations are linked to their professional goals when teachers meet with the administrator once or twice each year. In Cynthia Ruptic's school, the teachers receive formal written evaluations based on their progress toward goals they set in the fall during a conference with their administrator. Teachers appreciate personalized evaluations that are tailored to their individual needs.

Teachers are constantly presented with new curriculum, standards, and research. In many schools, the same group of dedicated teachers work on multiple committees and take on curriculum projects that demand a great deal of time and energy. These are often the same teachers who attend workshops and perhaps do some consulting themselves. With all this enthusiasm and hard work, however, comes the danger of burning out and becoming overwhelmed. As a staff or individually, however, you may want to step back and list possible areas for professional growth. Could you prioritize the list and develop a focus for the year? How can you ensure depth of learning in one or two areas? Would the most effective method be grade level sharing, ongoing inservice, classroom visits, peer coaching, or a work session?

Teachers at many schools are looking at scheduling in creative ways in order to build in more time for professional dialogue and sharing. Some schools lengthen the school day by a few minutes in order to have early release days once every week or month. Other schools plan back-to-back specialists so teachers have longer chunks of time for planning. In team teaching or multiage classrooms, this collaborative time is invaluable. Check with neighboring districts to see what other schools in your area have tried.

What about looking at staff meetings in new ways? Shelley Harwayne is an innovative principal in a New York City public school. Her forthcoming book, *Spirits on High: Lessons in Literacy,* and *Leadership from the Manhattan New School,* challenges conventional ideas and raises intriguing possibilities for principals and schools. Her superintendent suggested that faculty meetings should be so good that they could be televised. At Shelley's school, they took that challenge seriously. Mundane issues are dealt within written notes. Faculty meetings are reserved for research and focused professional growth. For instance, teachers might all bring their reading logs to post around the faculty room as a springboard for a discussion about new books. At other times the staff might choose a year-long focus such as struggling readers.

Which of these ideas might work in your school? How can you start making changes

Recommended Readings about Assessment Issues

We'd recommend that every educator read Regie Routman's book, *Literacy at the Crossroads: Crucial Talk about Reading, Writing, and Other Teaching Dilemmas* (1996). This book addresses the current backlash against education and what we all need to do in response if we want to maintain our voice and choices in what and how we teach. We refer to this excellent resource throughout this book. It's a call to action and an affirmation of why we teach.

Expanding Student Assessment (1991), edited by Vito Perrone, also raises some interesting issues about teaching and assessing learning. The chapters are written by leading authorities in the field and provide helpful definitions and issues to ponder.

Shelley Harwayne's forthcoming book, *Spirits on High: Lessons in Literacy and Leadership from the Manhattan New School,* challenges our notion of what a principal and school can be. Steven Bialostok, in his book *But Will She Read?* (1996), re-thinks conventional ideas about Back to School Night and report cards. These two books present intriguing, revealing interesting possibilities for innovative educators.

Some of you May have offered a workshop on a particular topic in your school or district. Other readers may be university professors or staff developers who often give presentations for teachers. *The Presenter's Fieldbook: A Practical Guide* by Robert Garmston (1997) is a delightful book full of tips and insights about giving workshops.

Chapter 3

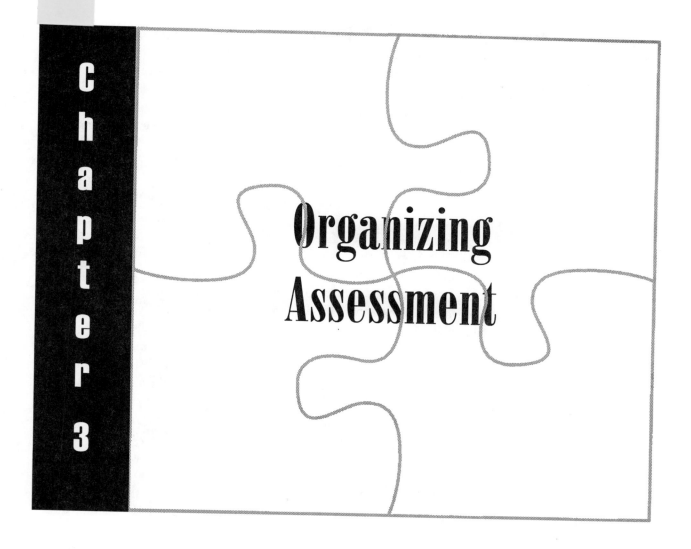

Organizing Assessment

When you put a puzzle together, do you first construct the border? Then do you sort by color or shape? Do you start with the most recognizable parts of the picture, the sections that stand out, or your favorite color? The way you begin putting the assessment puzzle together depends on your needs, experience, and personal style. Whatever your approach, it helps to devise a system. In this chapter, we describe several ways of organizing classroom based assessment.

Teacher Notebooks

Do you keep information about students in many different places in your room? The week before parent conferences and report cards, do you lug home writing folders, literature logs, and math journals? Are the assessment forms you want to use buried in stacks on your desk or lost somewhere in your file cabinet? Wouldn't it be great to have everything in one place?

We've developed an organizational strategy to keep all your classroom based assessments in one Teacher Notebook. First, you'll need a large three-ring binder. You'll need a section divider for each of your students. Write the students' names on both sides of the tabs so you can locate each child's section quickly. The Teacher Notebook contains all the information that you, as the teacher, collect about your students. Most primary students wouldn't be very interested in your running records or anecdotal notes. Those pieces are for your information as you assess students, report progress, and plan instruction. Other assessment pieces might be collected by students and housed in their portfolios. We delve more into portfolios in the third book in this series (*Book Three: Student Portfolios*). For now, let's start with the evidence you can collect.

What might go into your Teacher Notebook? Many of you may already give students an attitude survey at the beginning of the year or take some form of anecdotal notes. At the beginning, you might include only three items in your Teacher Notebook, such as an attitude survey, anecdotal notes, and some type of reading assessment. As you become more comfortable with these tools, you may wish to add assessment strategies in other areas. For instance, if you teach primary-age students, you may want to add a developmental spelling checklist, running records, and a writing conference form. The choices you make will depend on your goals and curriculum, your experience with classroom based assessment, the size of your class, and the ages of your students.

It's easy to become overwhelmed by all the things you're *not* doing! What's important is to start slowly and add assessment pieces over time. Use the Assessment Planning page (Form 3.1) in the forms section to list those assessment tools you currently use in the "Now" column. As we describe other techniques and assessment forms that appeal to you and would be easy to incorporate into your repertoire, jot them down in the "Next" column. There may be other assessment ideas that you would like to research and try down the road. Write these down in the "Later" column as a reminder. We've found that this page can become a launching point for staff development.

Assessment Tools for Primary Grades

We asked several primary teachers to list the six classroom based assessment tools they felt provided the most information about their students. They suggested six invaluable tools: a parent survey, running records, the reading continuum, "Words I Know" (Clay, 1993), the writing continuum, and anecdotal notes (see Figure 3.1). These six tools provide a solid basis for teachers' first steps in collecting assessment information about students. Each month these primary teachers collect information from one or two of these assessment tools.

TEACHER NOTEBOOK: PRIMARY GRADES

FIRST STEPS	ADDING ON
Parent Survey	Student Interest Survey
Running Record	Spelling 10 Words
Reading Continuum	Writing Conference Form
Words I Know (Clay)	"Fix-it" Strategy
Writing Continuum	Assessing Written Response
Anecdotal Notes (ongoing)	Writing Names
	Draw Me/Draw a Tree
	Story Scramble
	Retelling
	Concepts of Print (Clay)
	Spelling Development Form
	Emergent Writing Development Form
	Spelling Continuum

Figure 3.1: Teacher Notebook: Primary Grades

The teachers told us that if they had enough energy, an easy class, and hadn't changed grade levels three times in three years, they might add one or two other assessment tools such as the Spelling 10 Words or Retelling techniques from the second column in Figure 3.1. Most primary teachers said they add or change one or two assessment tools each year. Three or four assessment tools per month seem to be the most any teacher can reasonably handle. Some tools, like the parent survey, are quite simple. Others, such as running records, are more time-consuming and need to be woven into regular classroom routines.

Assessment Tools for Intermediate Grades

We gathered a similar list (Figure 3.2) from intermediate teachers. As you can see, the list of assessment tools that intermediate teachers might first include is very similar to the primary list, with the addition of the Student Interest Survey and the "Fix-it" strategy. In the second column, labeled "Adding On", we listed additional assessment tools that you may want to incorporate into your classroom. It's important to begin with a reasonable number of tools that provide helpful information and add or modify only a few each year.

TEACHER NOTEBOOK: INTERMEDIATE GRADES

FIRST STEPS	ADDING ON
Parent Survey	Spelling 10 Words
Student Interest/Attitude Survey	Writing Conference Form
Reading Conference Form	Assessing Response to Literature
Reading Continuum	Reading Strategies Assessment
Fix-it Strategy	Story Scramble
Writing Continuum	Rubrics
Anecdotal Notes (ongoing)	Spelling Strategies Form
	Spelling Survey
	Cloze Procedures
	Retelling
	Informal Miscue Analysis

Figure 3.2: Teacher Notebook: Intermediate Grades

Organizational Grid

Once you've decided *what* information to collect, the next challenge is to decide *when* to use each assessment tool. Teachers always agree that the greatest obstacle to effective assessment is time. Somehow, we feel that if we were better organized, we might use our time more wisely.

Cynthia Ruptic developed an Organizational Grid where teachers can visually see which assessment tools they plan to collect each month. As an example, we took the list of six assessment tools from Figure 3.1 and put them on an Organizational Grid (Figure 3.3). If you tuck the Organizational Grid in the front of your Teacher Notebook, then the first of each month you can flip to the chart as a reminder of what you want to collect. We left blank boxes only under the months where you plan to collect that particular assessment tool. Check or date the blank rectangle when you've collected the data.

On the sample (Figure 3.3), you can see that the parent survey is collected just once in September. The "Words I Know" (Clay, 1993) samples are collected in October and again in May to show growth over time. The reading and writing continuums are completed once each grading period and running records are taken four times a year. Anecdotal notes are an ongoing assessment technique that would be used all year long.

Of course, you will need to decide your own time frame for each assessment tool. For instance, Lisa Norwick listens to most of her second graders read and completes a running record once every two weeks. She takes weekly running records on the students about whom she is more concerned. Lisa finds that taking running

ORGANIZATIONAL GRID: PRIMARY GRADES

Assessment Tool/Strategy	SEPT	OCT	NOV	DEC	JAN	FEB	MAR	APR	MAY	JUN
Parent Survey										
Running Records										
Reading Continuum										
Words I Know (Clay)										
Writing Continuum										
Anecdotal Notes (ongoing)										

Figure 3.3: Organizational Grid (Primary Grades)

records on a more ongoing basis helps her see the patterns and document growth in each child's reading.

We next took the list of eight assessment tools from the intermediate list in Figure 3.2 and created a similar example for intermediate teachers. Figure 3.4 shows the one or two assessment tools an intermediate teacher might collect each month.

ORGANIZATIONAL GRID: INTERMEDIATE GRADES

Assessment Tool/Strategy	SEPT	OCT	NOV	DEC	JAN	FEB	MAR	APR	MAY	JUN
Parent Survey										
Student Interest/Attitude Survey										
Reading Conference Form										
Reading Continuum										
Fix-it Strategy										
Writing Continuum										
Anecdotal Notes (ongoing)										

Figure 3.4: Organizational Grid (Intermediate)

Take a minute now and look back at the Assessment Planning sheet (Form 3.1) we described at the beginning of this chapter. Which assessment tools do you plan to use this year that you listed in the "Now" and "Next" columns? When will you collect each one? You can transfer the tools you've listed onto the blank Organizational Grid (Form 3.2) in the Appendix as you develop a plan for which assessment tools you will use on a regular basis. Throughout the rest of this book, we'll explain each of the assessment techniques we've listed in this chapter and discuss how teachers use these tools in their classrooms.

Just a warning. Many teachers start the year with ambitious plans, but by winter break find they collected only a small portion of the information they had intended to collect. As you list the assessment tools on the chart, try to find a balance so you're only collecting a few things each month. Remember, it's not a matter of "He (or she) who dies with the most tools wins!" The most effective teachers are not those who use the most tools, but those who select the tools that best match their philosophy, curriculum, and students.

Adapting Teacher Notebooks

You will need to constantly re-evaluate your system for collecting data. Like your students, you are continually growing and refining your work to reflect what you learn. Your assessment program needs to be flexible and responsive to issues that arise in your classroom. For instance, last year when Mary Hadley on Bainbridge Island worked with her fifth graders on persuasive writing, they developed a rubric specific to that genre. She found it helpful and added it to her repertoire of assessment tools.

In addition to their Organizational Grid, many teachers also keep class checklists in the front of their Teacher Notebook for recording test scores, returned homework, and completed projects. You may also want to include a section for notes about contact with parents and emergency numbers. Some teachers also include their Philosophy and Goals statement (Form 2.1) and Curriculum and Assessment plan (Form 2.2) described in the previous chapter, along with lists of focus lessons and generic substitute plans.

Some teachers have adapted the idea of a Teacher Notebook to suit their teaching styles. Lisa Miller, a fourth-grade teacher in Tacoma, Washington, keeps two separate Teacher Notebooks, one for reading and another for writing. Cindy Fulton, a first-grade teacher in Seattle, also keeps two Teacher Notebooks, as well as a hanging file for each student where she keeps parent surveys, math screening, and other assessment tools. Several teachers at Brighton School in Lynnwood, Washington use hanging files instead of a notebook. On Bainbridge Island, Roz Duthie keeps four separate Teacher Notebooks lined up on her desk in which she records information about reading, writing, mathematics, and social interactions.

Assessment Files

What do you do with the hefty notebooks or pages of notes you collect at a workshop or conference? Most of us stick them on our already-avalanching piles by our bed or desk, fully intending to go through the material and sort it into neatly labeled files. Somehow, it never happens despite our good intentions and New Year's resolutions to our spouse about The Piles. How can we create a system for the flood of professional materials we receive?

Some of us have created an Assessment File in a three-ring binder with sections for each content area. This notebook houses new ideas and forms we might want to incorporate into our classroom. When you return from a conference or workshop (preferably that night or weekend), you can toss the materials you know you will never use and pull out one or two forms or assessment ideas that you might want to try for your Assessment File. For instance, after attending a state reading conference, one of the presenters might share a reading attitude survey you really like. You might decide to tuck the survey and the notes you took during the keynote speaker's presentation into the reading section of your Assessment File. As you read along in this book, you could copy the forms you might want to use in your classroom and place them in your Assessment File as well. Some teachers keep a new notebook for each year, while others have created separate notebooks for each content area. You might want to have a section for favorite quotes you find in your professional reading that you could use in newsletters or your own presentations. Like a toolbox, the Organizational Grid, Teacher Notebooks, and Assessment Files provide an organizational structure. In the next seven chapters, we'll provide a large collection of tools from which to choose as you create an organized system for classroom based assessment.

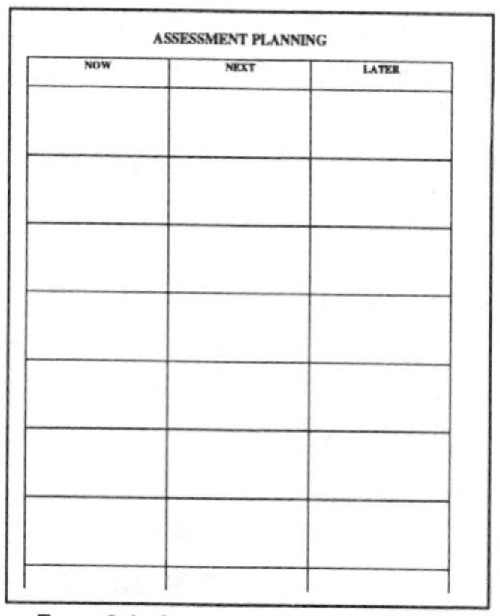

Form 3.1: Assessment and Planning

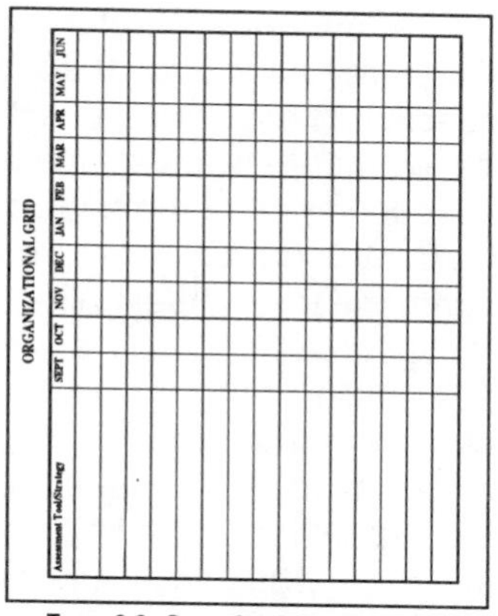

Form 3.2: Organizational Grid Plan

Professional Growth

Several schools allocate a half-day or three-hour workshop after school for teachers to actually put together their Teacher Notebooks. Teachers collect all the forms and handouts they've received in the last few years from their closets, file cabinets and boxes in the basement. Before they come to the meeting, teachers toss out pieces they will never use and file the ones that apply to other grade levels (in case they end up teaching that grade at some point!). The teachers then bring in a tub or box of only the forms they might consider using.

In grade level teams, the teachers spread these forms out on tables and on the floor. (As you read, you may want to put "Post-it" notes on two or three forms you are considering using from this book.) The goal for the three hours is for each grade level to narrow their list to 3–6 assessment tools they plan to use during the year. Toward the end of the workshop, each grade level can share the assessment tools they selected in order to look for common tools that are being used throughout the school. Finally, teachers can use the Organizational Grid to outline which month they will collect each piece of evidence of student learning. Individual teachers may decide to use more tools than others; however, the purpose of the activity is to foster dialogue about assessment within and among grade levels and to develop a degree of consistency and shared expectations.

So often teachers come back from conferences or workshops full of wonderful ideas, but have no time to talk to colleagues, develop forms, or think about how to weave the new ideas into the classroom. As professionals, we need time to work and share ideas. As a staff, you may want to meet periodically to share your Assessment Files. The ensuing discussions among the staff might also lead to plans for further professional growth and reading.

Recommended Readings about Assessment Tools

One of the newest and most helpful books on assessment is Bill Harp's book, *The Handbook of Literacy Assessment and Evaluation* (1996). The first half of the book includes a collection of assessment techniques, an explanation of how teachers use the techniques, advantages and disadvantages, and then more references for further readings. The second part of the book describes published assessment and evaluation tools. This book is a must for any professional library.

We recommend three other collections of assessment tools. The most comprehensive book of assessment tools is *Windows into Literacy: Assessing Learners K-8* (Rhodes and Shanklin, 1993). This 500-page book looks rather daunting, but can be used as a resource rather than a book to read from cover-to-cover. This extensive book covers information about everything, from miscue analysis to retellings and portfolios. The accompanying spiral-bound book, *Literacy Assessment: A Handbook of Instruments* (Rhodes, 1993) is a collection of ready-to-reproduce assessment forms. Similarly, *The Whole Language Catalog: Forms for Authentic Assessment* (Bird, Goodman and Goodman, 1994) also includes reproducible forms with brief descriptions of each technique.

Chapter 4

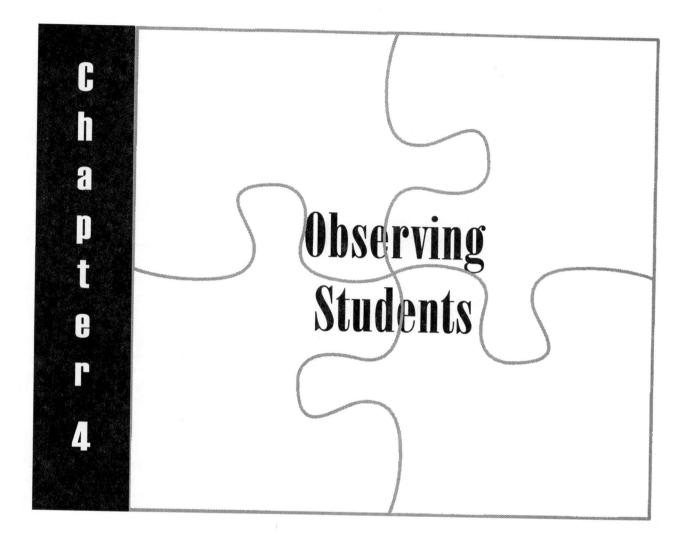

Observing Students

One of the delights of parenting and teaching is watching children grow. Lucy Calkins writes, "Wise teaching, like wise parenting, begins with watching and listening and delighting in the learner" (1994, p. 54). You can learn so much by watching students solve math problems or listening to children argue about why dinosaurs became extinct. One way to record learning steps and poignant incidents that occur in the classroom is to capture these moments by writing brief notes. Regardless of your class size, however, watching closely and recording observations of students is a real challenge. Yet if you don't record those special moments, your insights and the wonderful things your students say are often lost. Have you heard a student say something delightful in the morning, and by the end of the day you can't remember exactly what it was? Our challenge is to find a method for taking anecdotal notes that is informative, yet efficient and manageable.

Anecdotal Notes

Anecdotal records are brief written notes based on observations of students. "It's November and Randy still cries when his mother leaves him at school." "Gloria will be out another week with strep throat." "Nathan shared his poem at author's chair today and explained the revisions he made." Do you keep notes like these on bits of paper or "Post-it" notes, but never really know what to do with your written comments? What is a practical system for taking anecdotal notes and how can you use the information you collect?

Why Use Anecdotal Notes?

Marie Clay says, "Educators have done a great deal of systematic testing and relatively little systematic observation of learning" (Clay, 1993, p. 7). Teachers also spend a great deal of time monitoring rather than assessing children. In *Learning to See: Assessment through Observation* (1994), Mary Jane Drummond observes:

> Teachers are expected to have eyes in the backs of their heads, to see accidents before they happen, fights before they break out and difficulties with learning before pupils begin to fail. For the purposes of classroom management and control, teachers have risen to the challenge of seeing everything, with only one pair of eyes, by developing a modified radar technique; the busy teacher scans the horizon of the classroom from time to time, watching for any blips of disturbance that might require intervention. If the radar sweep reveals nothing amiss, the teacher will probably refrain from looking any more closely. If classroom events seem to be progressing smoothly, or even according to plan, the teacher is temporarily released from the need to see everything, and can concentrate on a smaller segment of classroom like: work with an individual or a small group perhaps—until it is time for the next global classroom scan. (p. 24)

Drummond later suggests that when teachers move from scanning the room to purposefully watching for student learning, they have taken a huge pedagogical leap. She suggests that the process of watching children's learning "is the only certain safeguard against children's failure, the only certain guarantee of children's progress and development" (p. 10).

The systematic and intentional use of anecdotal records enables teachers to become what Yetta Goodman calls "kidwatchers." Keeping anecdotal notes also helps you get to know individual students. Your observations can then help you develop instruction to meet each child's needs. In addition, anecdotal notes provide a focus for reading and writing conferences. Written records provide information that can be used to:

- evaluate students' learning
- make instructional decisions for individual students
- make instructional decisions for the whole class
- determine which students need extra assistance

- give feedback to students on what you notice
- look for patterns in student behavior
- prepare for report cards and conferences
- provide documentation
- evaluate your own teaching

You will find that the better you become at taking anecdotal records, the more you notice about your students and the easier it becomes to recognize patterns of student growth.

> Anecdotal records readjust the teacher's vision of who and where the student is and sharpens teachers' insight into how each student travels along his or her own path to learning. Only when we look as if with a magnifying glass can we see and hear individual and idiosyncratic child-based standards of growth, accomplishment, and failure. (Matthews, 1992, p. 169)

Systematic anecdotal records can help you document student behavior and learning. They can also help you define the specifics of what to look for as you confer with students. Anecdotal records can also capture the personal insights and vignettes that make teaching so rewarding. In addition, it is your very specific narrative comments on report cards and at conference time that help parents feel you really know their child.

What Information Do You Record?

It's important that you decide your purpose for taking anecdotal notes and whether you will keep your notes private or share them with others. Either way, you should be careful to record observations rather than make judgments. For instance, "Jessica often leans her head on her desk and closes her eyes during the day" is more accurate than "Jessica needs more sleep," which is an assumption that may or may not be true. You can always add an opinion or question to your observations: "Mario most often seems to be alone at recess. I wonder why?" In her book, *Taking Note: Improving Your Observational Notetaking* (1996), Brenda Power suggests recording student's actual words whenever possible. These actual quotes help give voice to your narrative comments on report cards.

It's helpful to record information during different activities, such as recess, quiet reading, literature circle discussions, writing workshop, or math centers. You may want to record some of the following information:

- specific behaviors in different contexts
- choices of activities
- choices of friends
- skills/strategies students use
- notes to yourself about ways to support learning
- records of conversations

- records of skills/strategies taught
- breakthroughs
- incidents of students teaching each other
- funny comments

Three important things to remember: Date everything! Be specific! Be brief! You shouldn't spend more than a minute or two jotting down a note about a child. Lengthy descriptions aren't necessary, just words that capture the moment.

Your students may be curious about what you are writing. For instance, one day during writing workshop, Cynthia Ruptic's second-grade student, Julia, inquired, "What are you always writing on those 'Post-it' notes?" Cynthia opened her Teacher Notebook to Julia's section and, pointing out examples, explained how she needs to write things down in order to recall specific details during parent conferences. She told Julia how she uses her notes to keep track of what strategies she had taught during conferences and what students were learning. Ever since that conversation, Cynthia has made a point of explaining her Teacher Notebook and anecdotal notes to her class at the beginning of the year. Regie Routman (1991, 1994) suggests that we should feel comfortable if students ask to see the anecdotal notes we've written about them. Sometimes just seeing that you're taking notes keeps your students on task and shows that you care enough to watch their learning closely.

How Do You Get Started?

Brenda Power (1996) suggests two times to take anecdotal notes: "in the midst" and "after the fact." Some teachers write down comments as they talk with students, while others prefer to step aside afterwards and jot down notes "after the fact." One way to begin using anecdotal records is to focus on only one content area at a time. For instance, you may want to keep notes only in the midst of writing workshop or during math center time. Another method is to focus on only two or three students each day and observe them throughout the day. The best time to observe students is when they are busy. Keep your clipboard handy and write just a few notes every day during literature discussions, writing time, or while students are working independently in math or science.

We've found the section on anecdotal records (pages 309–317) in Regie's book, *Invitations* (1991, 1994), particularly helpful. She cautions that some teachers take several years to become comfortable with this form of ongoing assessment. "As you begin to make taking anecdotal records a part of your teaching, eventually, the task will no longer seem like an extra encumbrance, and you will feel as though you know your students a lot better" (p. 317).

Creating a System for Anecdotal Notes

Your system for taking anecdotal records must be simple or you won't keep it up. Do you take notes on any handy scraps of paper and intend to copy them into a legible form when you have time? Somehow, it never happens! You need a simple system for recording and storing information. Many of you have developed systems that work for you. We'll describe one system in detail, but recognize that the same concepts and structure would work equally well using a notebook, file cards, or mailing labels. At the end of this chapter, we discuss some alternate methods teachers find useful.

"Post-it" notes are one of the most wonderful inventions of the last twenty years! We've created an Anecdotal Notes Grid (Form 4.1) to fit the size of 1 ½" × 2" "Post-it" notes. Cynthia Ruptic writes the names of all of her students in the small rectangles on the anecdotal note form. She places a blank "Post-it" note in each of the spaces and tucks the form in a clipboard with a pen attached. At specific times during the day, Cynthia takes anecdotal notes as she observes students. Since the names are on the grid, she only has to write the date and a brief comment (these are very small "Post-it" notes!). As the week progresses, she can scan the chart and see at a glance which students she has missed (Figure 4.1).

Figure 4.1: Anecdotal Clipboard

To get started, first, write your students' names in the appropriate rectangles on the Anecdotal Notes Grid (Form 4.1), then place blank "Post-it" notes below each name. You'll probably need two pages to have enough spaces for your whole class. Others may want to use the legal-size version of this form we included on the CD-ROM. Some teachers laminate the class grid once they've written the students' names. Others like to keep a blank piece of paper over the top of their anecdotal notes both for confidentiality and to keep the "Post-it" notes from falling off.

When Cynthia has collected anecdotal notes on all her students, she transfers the notes into her Teacher Notebook (Figure 4.2). In each child's section in her notebook, Cynthia has placed a blank copy of the Anecdotal Notes Grid (Form 4.1). She moves the "Post-it" note from her clipboard onto each child's section. The notes are placed in chronological order and she hasn't had to copy them over! The other advantage of the "Post-it" note system is that you can stack several notes on top of each other on your clipboard until you find time to transfer them to your notebook. Some teachers prefer to transfer the notes into individual assessment folders. What's important is having a place to store your comments.

Figure 4.2: Teacher Notebook and Anecdotal Notes

In addition to where the notes are stored, another important consideration is how often to take anecdotal notes on each student. Most teachers find it reasonable to take anecdotal notes on two or three students each day. This means it would take you two or three weeks to complete anecdotal notes for your whole class in one subject area, such as writing. Many teachers find that once their system is established, it only takes one or two weeks.

Figure 4.3 is an example of anecdotal comments from Cynthia Ruptic's reading/writing workshop at Osaka International School in Japan. On Figure 4.4, you can see how she transferred her comments about Allen onto his individual page in her Teacher Notebook. Notice how you can learn quite a bit about Allen just from these few anecdotal notes. Cynthia uses her anecdotal notes when she writes narrative comments on report cards, fills out continuums, and prepares for parent conferences.

Adapting Anecdotal Notes

Specialists who see large numbers of students may want to keep a clipboard for each class or group of students. If you see many students each day, your goal may be to record one anecdotal comment about each student for each grading period.

Principals can adapt this method by creating a Principal Notebook with a section for each teacher. In each section would be three types of documentation. The

ANECDOTAL RECORDS for Reading Writing Workshop

Allen	**Artiom**	**Gage**	**Hiroaki**
9/17 Consulting book for evidence to support contributions Active listening, thoughtful responses/insights	9/16 Forgot his folk tale log at home, Telling of "Lazy Jack" w/out notes—remembering all main points of the story,		9/20 As moderator read the entire schedule and most of the jobs with no assistance. Tremendous growth since the first day of school!
Jimmy	**Julia**	**Jyongri**	**Karin**
9/18 Writing folktale—trickster tale about how rabbit became so timid Needs to expand lead-up to ending from one sentence to at least a ¶—too abrupt right now	9/18 Writing folktale about how elephant got big. Very imaginative and clever story line. All elements of folktale—working on dialogue and illustrations	9/17 Really "with it" already selected topic (Bats) for her report and went to library to find and check out books (some too difficult?)	9/20 Telling Lon Po Po to group w/out looking at her notes for the most part. Eye contact only w/ Jyongri
Lindsay	**Meelad**	**Megat**	**Ryu**
9/20 "I'm trying to write a story like Roald Dahl and make up special creatures and use outrageous words"	9/16 Assisted with brainstorming elements for his folktale, esp. characters (inc. stock) setting details, problems and solutions/morals Began writing.	9/17 Long conference about how to make his folktale come alive—showing not just telling, rearrange to create interesting lead, use dialogue	9/16 Ming Lo Moves Mountain Forgot to bring log, using classroom extra copy of book. During others' retellings/sharings tuned out/not really listening
Satomi	**Sonya**	**Tatsuhiko**	**Teman**
9/17 Retelling of The Goose Girl "storytelling" voice adding dialogue and details fr. story w/ very concise picture notes	9/16 Writing original folk tale about why parrot is more colorful than owl interesting plot. Has included all elements of folktale. Now working on "said" replacements.	9/18 Writing Three Trolls story w/ all elements of folktales. Suggested adding a little refrain for trolls to say; also to make it sound more "long ago..."	9/17 Very difficult time choosing his book and settling in for SSR. Finally chose Monster Manners (blue/easy reader) well below instructional level
Tejas	**Tran**	**Ville**	**Yuko**
9/17 Comment from Mom (on phone) "Tejas likes to be in front where he is sharp and to be in shadow where he is not so confident."		9/20 Telling Anansi tale using notes (great short summary statements) from which he built an extensive story.	9/20 Asking Karin (and me) about meanings of: approaches, regurgitates, wound/clot, valuable. Nudge to also try using a dictionary

Figure 4.3: Class Anecdotal Notes

ANECDOTAL RECORDS for Allen

9/4 Attempting to take home 3-4 books w/out checking them out. Not understanding rules?	9/4 Maths "Hanging out" to wait for Ryu! Artiom before choosing color tiles/collapsing wall	9/11 calling names in PE - Beth dealt with it as a whole class issue ART - OK Computer ok MUSIC - often disruptive	9/11 Maths wrestling w/ Gage on carpet. After redirect
9/5 Moved away from Ryu at calendar today - disrupting Later "Should I be hearing your voice?" during SQW	9/5 Maths - building a long train "to the wall" w/ Ryu Artium Gage	9/12 Redirects/workshop/calendar 8:30 ||| > C&ML 8:45 | 9:00 | > SSR 9:15 | 9:30 | 9:45 | > SQW 10:00 || 10:15 || 10:30 ||| AC	9/12 Conference - Allen does understand - needs help focusing to stay on task especially when reading/writing; will use "1-2-3" w/ call parents at 3. specialist will use too. Called parents re: system 8PM
9/6 Off-task at calendar again "Where can you sit so that you can pay better attention"?	9/6 Maths Train card - able to extend pattern independently, but unable to build his own	9/13 (1) Turning up volume at listening center (2) "Please choose a place where you can work w/out disrupting others' SQW 3) ——— rest of day ok!	9/16 (1) Late (9:05) in computer lab w/out checking in first (2) SSR changing books every 3 minutes - "stick with one" (3) "skipped out" on making up time @ lunch recess 2:10 Called home
9/9 Reading buddies w/ Jyongri side-by-side but not invested in reading w/her. Re-direct about reading book together	9/9 Maths - 2nd time!!! Redirect about doing graphing incorrectly not understanding directions? or choosing own way?	9/17 (1) SQW: "stop playing game and get back to your writing plans for the day" Finished Super Hero working on more drawings to illustrate 2) N/A 3) N/A	9/17 Consulting book for evidence to support contributions + Active listening, + thoughtful responses/insights
9/10 Directed to leave room during read aloud talked to him privately about doing a better job or my calling home	9/10 Osako-sensei concerned about his not working up to ability in [illegible] Set up 4 way conference w/ Osako-sensei, Dr J, Allen & I check w/ other specials	9/18 (1) calendar SSR - OK Owl Moon Jolly Postman Nine O'Clock Lullaby SQW (2) "What is your plan?" 3) N/A. Esp. helpful during science today - materials w/ Gage	9/19 Note sent home re: improved behavior and cooperation

Figure 4.4: Individual Anecdotal Notes

first page could be blank paper for formal observations and goal setting. The second page would be for less formal interactions. The principal could keep a clipboard handy with a "Post-it notes" on an Anecdotal Grid with names of the faculty and take one or two notes during the day. The notes could be transferred to the blank grid in each teacher's section of the Principal Notebook. Finally, each teacher's section could also contain a class grid with the names of all his or her students. The principal could then keep anecdotal notes about student interactions in the lunchroom, on the playground, or parent contacts under that teacher's section.

You could also involve students in contributing anecdotal comments about their own breakthroughs or insights. Brenda Power (1996) suggests having one student record the homework assignment, as well as what was learned or discussed that day in class. Those anecdotal notes could be placed in your planning book at the end of the day as a review. This information would be helpful to substitutes and students who were absent, and would also provide the teacher with an ongoing learning log.

Managing Anecdotal Notes

Lisa Norwick suggests five things that have made her anecdotal notes more effective: start slowly, schedule time to take notes, organize your notes, connect your notes to instruction, and focus your observations. Let's take a look at these suggestions in more detail.

Start Slowly

At the beginning, you may want to take notes in only one content area until you get into a routine. Some kindergarten and first grade teachers decide to focus on social interactions during the first few weeks of school before concentrating on academic areas. Some teachers write anecdotal notes only during writing workshop for the first two months of school. In November and December, they take notes during quiet reading and focus on math after winter break. Other teachers focus on one or two children throughout the day in all of the content areas. Here are several ways to begin taking anecdotal notes:

- Focus on one content area at a time
- Focus on one or two children throughout the day
- Take anecdotal notes when working with small groups
- Focus on one group/team per day in all content areas (all 5 in a week)
- Take anecdotal notes during independent work time

Once your system is in place, it's easier to branch out and take anecdotal notes throughout the day. As Lisa became more comfortable with taking anecdotal notes, she placed three clipboards around the room: one for mathematics, one for reading, and one for writing. She now takes notes in all three areas at different times during the day.

Schedule Time to Take Notes

It's important to plan specific times for taking anecdotal notes. Lisa finds it's fairly easy to take anecdotal notes on two or three children "in the midst" of math time when students are working independently. She takes anecdotal notes for reading during literature circle discussions, focusing on one group each day. Writing is more challenging with her primary students, so she pulls out two writing folders each day after school and writes notes about those two students' growth in writing "after the fact" (Power, 1996). Lisa also takes anecdotal notes when her students share their writing during author's chair (Graves and Hansen, 1983).

Megan Sloan finds anecdotal notes most manageable during individual reading and writing conferences. As she chats with students, she simply writes down one or two observations. Like exercising, it's getting into a routine that's the biggest challenge! Once the routine is part of your daily life, it becomes less overwhelming. Anecdotal notes are manageable only when you select specific times throughout each day to write a few comments.

Organize Your Notes

The first few years she took anecdotal notes, Lisa transferred her comments about reading, writing, and mathematics from her clipboards to a blank grid in each child's section in her Teacher Notebook. More recently, she has organized each child's notes by running off the blank Anecdotal Notes Grid (Form 4.1) on three different colored sheets and placing all three grids in each child's section of her Teacher Notebook. She sorts her anecdotal notes, placing reading comments on a green page, writing comments on a blue page, and comments about mathematics on a yellow page. That keeps all her notes about one content area together, which is helpful when she writes narrative comments on report cards and fills out the reading and writing continuums. It also becomes immediately apparent if there are gaps in knowledge about a child that Lisa can fill in with further observations.

Brenda Power (1996) suggests using a simple code to show the context for your interactions with students. For instance, you might use WW for writing workshop, LC for literature circles, C for notes during conferences, and MC for math centers. These simple organizational tips can help make anecdotal notes more efficient and manageable.

Connect Your Notes to Instruction

Lisa's anecdotal notes are closely tied to her focus lessons and the reading/writing continuums. For instance, as Lisa was taking anecdotal notes and conferring with students during writing workshop, she noticed that many of the children were writing stories that were very broad and general. Over the next few days, she did several focus lessons on narrowing topics. Lisa began by writing a draft of a story and sharing it with her students on the overhead. She told her students that she wanted them to help her find the heart of her piece. As they read the story together, she had the children listen for key words and phrases. She explained that the heart of the story could be found in the sentences that grab the reader's attention and make you want to hear more. Lisa and her students chose three key sentences from her draft, which Lisa marked with a highlighter. The next day she explained to her students that the highlighted sentences were going to become the starting point for her new draft. Lisa expanded on the highlighted sentences, adding description and details. Over the next few days, Lisa wrote the new story with the highlighted sentences embedded in the text. Lisa encouraged students to experiment with this strategy to find the heart of their stories. She took anecdotal notes about their progress as students worked on narrowing their topics.

For example, one of Lisa's second-grade students, Julie, decided to delete her first three sentences ("Today is Friday. Tomorrow is Saturday. I have skating to do.") and wrote a more grabbing lead ("I'm going to be a figure skater when I grow up."). The sentence she highlighted ("Last week I twirled like an angel.") became the title for her piece and the heart of her story. Julie's new draft was more focused and her voice was evident. Lisa captured Julie's new steps as a writer on her anecdotal notes and on the writing continuum.

In Carl Braun's thoughtful book, *Looking, Listening, and Learning: Observing and Assessing Young Readers* (1993), he suggests that careful observation can help teachers fine-tune their instruction:

> Ongoing, intelligent observation is a proactive move on behalf of children. It is driven by the belief that taking preventative action makes more sense than waiting for children to flounder, and then trying to extricate them from their learning problems—which are so often intensified by low self-esteem. Day-to-day observation provides a framework for learning and instruction and invites on-the-spot adjustments (p. 17).

Focus Your Observations

When Lisa first began taking notes, they were often very general and didn't provide much useful information. She decided to brainstorm lists of focus questions for her observations in each content area. Lisa keeps these lists on the top of her anecdotal clipboards to help focus her observations. She picks one focus question and tells her students what she will be looking for during the next week or two.

For instance, at the beginning of the year she might say, "Now that writing workshop is underway, I'm going to be looking to see who has been able to find a topic and stick with it." At the end of each writing period, she might share general observations with the students. She might mention how several students used the "topics list" they brainstormed during the first week of school, while other students gathered ideas from the books they were reading or things that happened in their lives. The next week Lisa might pick a new focus for her anecdotal notes.

Lisa Norwick and Cynthia Ruptic developed primary and intermediate versions of the lists for anecdotal notes about writing which are included in Chapter 7. The lists of focus questions about reading are included in Chapter 9. These lists are tied directly to the reading and writing continuums described in Chapter 11. They also created similar primary and intermediate lists for taking anecdotal notes about mathematics and science which are included in Chapter 10. You may want to begin with these lists, then revise the questions to match your specific goals and curriculum.

Other Ways of Organizing Anecdotal Notes

There are other ways to organize anecdotal records that you may want to use instead of "Post-it" notes.

Mailing Labels: Anne Klein, an intermediate teacher in Edmonds, Washington, prefers mailing labels to "Post-it" notes. Ahead of time, she prints the names of all her students on a sheet of mailing labels on the computer. Anne keeps the sheets of labels on a clipboard. When she has taken notes on all her students, she transfers the mailing labels to a blank page in each child's sections of her Teacher Notebook. One advantage of mailing labels is that you can type the names on the computer and run the sheet of blank mailing labels through your printer. Mailing labels also adhere better than "Post-it" notes.

Flip Folders: Those of you who see many students (such as reading teachers, special education teachers, librarians, or music teachers) may prefer a separate folder for each of your classes. On the two sides of the folder, you can layer index cards by attaching them with clear tape along the top of each card to create a flip folder (Figure 4.5). The cards can be layered so you can see each student's name. Some specialists keep a clipboard with an anecdotal grid for each class. Others keep one clipboard with a legal-size grid for each class. You could write notes about one or two students during or after class. At the end of the month or grading period, the sticky notes can be transferred from the grids onto the index cards in the flip folders. Some teachers write directly on the index cards, but it's more difficult to tell which students you've missed. These anecdotal notes can make narrative comments on report cards more personal.

Computer: Teachers with expertise in technology who have access to a notebook or hand-held computer might wish to keep anecdotal records on the computer. If a word processing program is kept active throughout the day, you can record comments immediately. Using "cut and paste" editing functions, you can transfer the comments to individual student files. You then can use these comments to produce a "pen portrait" or narrative comments for conferences or report cards. Programs that integrate word processing, spreadsheets, and databases allow an even greater range of capabilities for sorting and classifying information.

Tape Recorder: If you find it difficult to write notes during the day, you might want to purchase a small hand-held tape recorder for dictation. You may prefer to record a few observations on the tape recorder, play the comments back at the end of the day, then write a short summary in your Teacher Notebook.

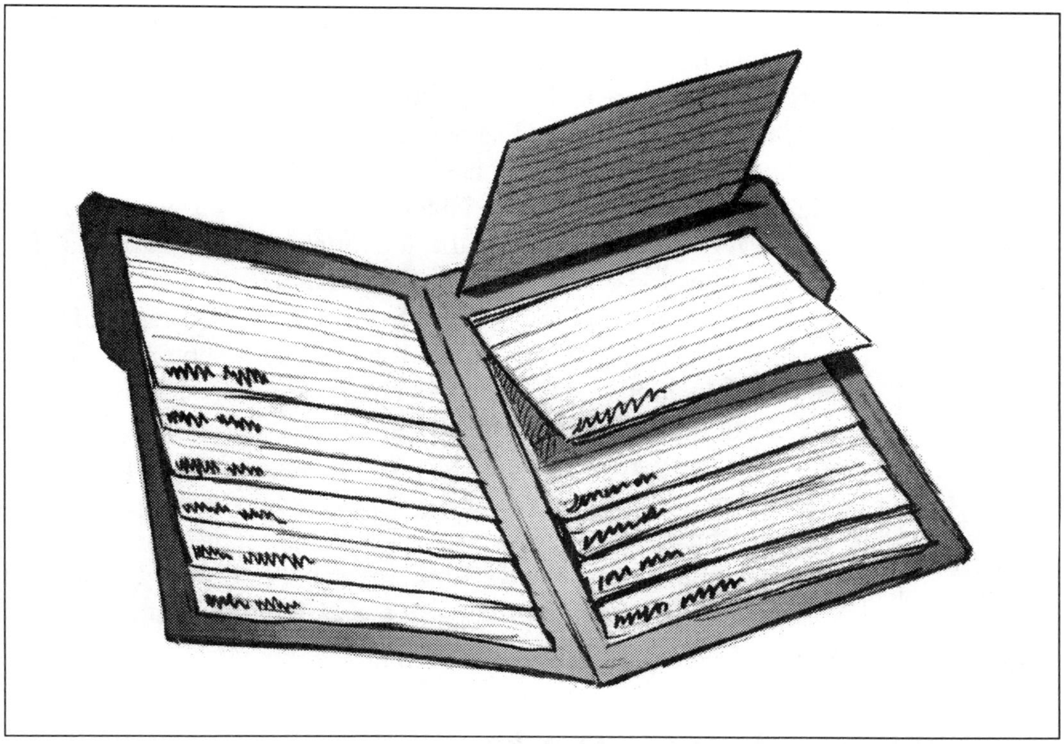

Figure 4.5: Flip Chart

Three-Ring Binder: Some teachers don't like to transfer "Post-it" notes from one place to another and prefer to take anecdotal notes in a separate thin three-ring notebook. You could simply flip to a child's section in the notebook and write anecdotal comments directly into the notebook. You could use different-colored paper for each content area and one for behavioral issues and parent contacts. At the end of the grading period, these sheets could be transferred into the child's section of your Teacher Notebook.

Anecdotal Notes by Others

Other adults and even the students in the classroom can also take anecdotal notes. For instance, Megan Sloan has parent volunteers who read with individual students. Megan asks these parents to take anecdotal notes about the child's choice of book, fluency, expression, and what the child did when faced with an unknown word. At University Child Development School in Seattle, teachers encourage parents to write comments on "Post-it" notes about things that happen at home, such as a sick grandparent, an upcoming trip, or the death of a pet. You might even invite students to write comments on "Post-it" notes about breakthroughs or new learning to include in your Teacher Notebook. Similarly, in *The Whole Language Catalog: Forms for Authentic Assessment* (1994), Lois Bird and her colleagues describe how one group of multiage teachers asked parents to take anecdotal notes during class research field trips. The form in their book (p. 56) contains rows for comments in five areas: questions children asked, comments children made, whether students seemed focused, whether or not they listened, as well as general comments.

Patti Kamber involved parents in documenting student learning in her fifth-grade classroom on Bainbridge Island, Washington last year during literature circles. After her focus lesson about quality literature circle discussions, the students talked about "fat questions" and "skinny questions." They described "skinny questions" as ones that could be answered with a "yes" or "no," such as, "Did you like this book?" On the other hand, "fat questions" were ones that could spark ten minutes of engaged conversations. The students listed examples, such as "If you could take any character in the book out to dinner, which one would you pick? Tell us why." Patti then asked the parent volunteers to record any "fat questions" they heard during literature circle discussions that day. These higher-level questions were then added to the class chart of "Questions to Spark Quality Discussions."

You could also ask the Reading Specialist or ESL or Resource Room teacher to take anecdotal notes when they work with individual students or small groups in your classroom. Sometimes another perspective on a child can be very helpful.

From Anecdotal Notes to Checklists

We believe that observing students and taking anecdotal notes are extremely valuable. Anecdotal notes help us get to know our students and plan instruction. Your system for taking anecdotal notes will probably change as you experiment with what works best for you and your particular style. Some teachers try to "keep everything in their head"; however, with so many student interactions each day, it's very difficult, if not impossible to recall specific incidents, conversations, poignant remarks, and funny stories. Anecdotal notes also help you keep track of those "invisible" students who often "slip between the cracks."

Do you ever find that you're writing the same anecdotal notes over and over? If that is true, you may want to develop a checklist and save your anecdotal notes for more specific types of observations. Of course, the forms you will find most useful are the ones you adapt or develop yourself. As Edward Chittenden (1991) said, "One person's favorite rating sheet is another's income tax form" (p. 25). We hope our ideas will serve as a starting place as you develop your own techniques and forms.

In the last four chapters on assessment, we've used broad brush strokes. In the next six chapters, we'll begin adding the details for specific assessment ideas for spelling, writing, reading, and other content areas.

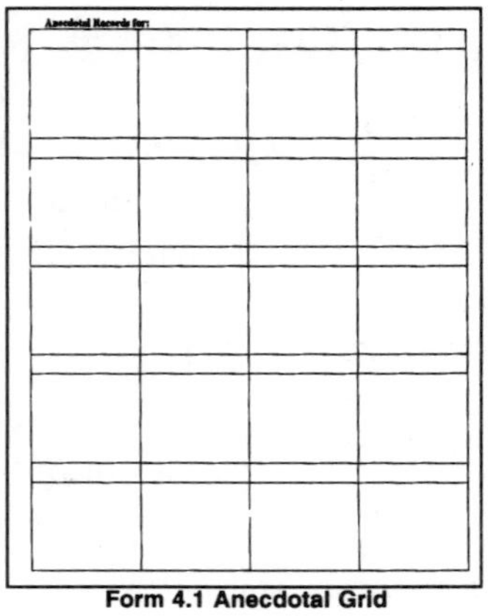

Form 4.1 Anecdotal Grid

Professional Growth

You might want to form a study group at your school using *Taking Note: Improving Your Observational Notetaking* (Power, 1996) as the focus. She begins the book with the suggestion that teachers need a personal life outside of school! She presents ideas for taking anecdotal notes that are practical and efficient. At the end of each chapter are activities and forms designed for a study group.

In some schools, teachers have each chosen one or two students as "case-studies" for a term. Some have chosen students about whom they are concerned or students they don't know well. They collect anecdotal notes and bring the student's work to monthly meetings. Teachers have really valued these sharing sessions and find that looking closely at one child changes how they view all their students.

Cynthia Ruptic uses the anecdotal notes about Allen included in this chapter and asks teachers to try to write a few sentences about this student. What patterns can they see? Where do they see improvement? What might be some instructional directions for this child? After teachers write a bit individually, she has them pair up to share observations. This activity helps teachers build their confidence and see how easy it is to move from anecdotal notes to narrative comments.

Another idea would be to commit to using a system for taking anecdotal notes as described in this chapter. During monthly meetings, you could share your methods, concerns, and successes. You may also want to revise the anecdotal focus questions to match your specific curriculum and standards.

Recommended Readings about Anecdotal Notes

We've found an excellent new book about taking anecdotal records. *Taking Note: Improving Your Observational Notetaking* (Power, 1996) is short, practical and informative and would be an excellent study focus for teachers on this topic. The section on anecdotal notes in Regie Routman's book, *Invitations: Changing as Teacher and Learners K-12* (1991, 1994), is also very helpful.

A less practical but very thought provoking on the topic is *Learning to See: Assessment through Observation* (Drummond, 1994). The author includes classroom examples and stories that will challenge your assumptions about teaching, learning, and observing students.

Chapter 5

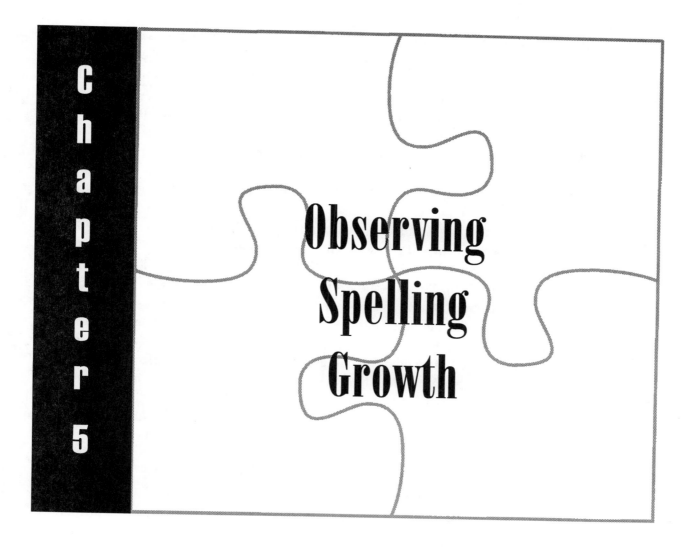

Observing Spelling Growth

Do some of your students get 100 percent on their spelling post-test on Friday morning but misspell the same words in their journal that afternoon? Do other students, despite lists on the wall and countless focus lessons, still misspell "they" as "thay"? Teaching and assessing spelling is a true challenge. In this chapter, we first describe the stages of spelling development. Then we explore seven assessment tools that can be used in the primary and intermediate grades. The spelling assessment forms we describe can be found in the collection of forms in the Appendix.

Developmental Stages of Spelling

Most children first experiment with writing by scribbling or ***pre-writing.*** They make marks on paper that do not yet resemble letters, but their writing is clearly not drawing. They are playing with written language just as babies experiment with spoken sounds.

Children next explore written language by using random strings of letters in the *pre-phonetic* stage. Gentry and Gillet (1993) call this phase "precommunicative." Children at this point recognize that writing is made up of letters, but don't yet realize that letters represent specific sounds.

Most writers at the *semi-phonetic* stage first use only initial consonants, then start to use both beginning and ending consonants. One way to assess spelling development is to observe that many children at this stage must actually say the sounds aloud as they write. You can see (and hear) this in many kindergarten and first grade classrooms as children voice the sounds they are writing. Writing at this stage is seldom silent!

Teachers and parents can usually read a child's writing at the *phonetic* stage. Children begin incorporating some middle consonants with a few vowels sprinkled in. The words students write often bear little resemblance to English, but most adults can decipher them. Students move from relying on their mouth to relying on their ears as they write. During this phonetic stage, writers often "stretch out the words" and write every sound they hear. For example, the word "human" might be spelled "hyoomen" or "eagle" spelled as "eeaggoll." Students use their "invented" spelling in order to write independently. Laminack and Wood (1996) prefer to use the term "constructed" spelling to highlight the constructive nature of learning. Others use the term "temporary" spelling to emphasize the fleeting nature of this stage.

Transitional spellers begin to use the patterns of language, although not always correctly. Gentry and Gillet (1993) note that "The transitional stage is one of the most important stages of invented spelling because it signals readiness for more direct spelling instruction" (p. 34). In the transitional stage, children rely on visual as well as auditory memory as they recall what a word "looks like" and "sounds like." Susan Sowers (1982) suggests that teachers observe the change in the locus of control: "First, the mouth dominates, and then the ears and eyes, and finally knowledge of words" (p. 51). Students spend several years at this transitional stage, consolidating their spelling skills as they become increasingly fluent readers and writers.

By the end of elementary school, most students can correctly spell the majority of the words they use in writing. Writing and reading can help students progress more quickly toward conventional spelling. Research has shown clearly that most of the words we know how to spell have been learned through reading (Wilde, 1996). The more often students see a word, the more readily they can recognize the correct spelling. Even as adults, if we're not sure how to spell a word, when we write it two or three ways, we can usually spot which one "looks right." The more students read and write, the more they can rely on their visual memory of words. In fact, Gentry (1997) notes that "The ability to visualize words is the hallmark of an expert speller" (p. 46). It takes many years for students to truly learn to spell accurately. According to Gentry and Gillet (1993), "Expert conventional spelling requires time, instruction and effort. Conventional spellers develop over years of word study, reading and writing" (p. 34).

The fact that spelling is a developmental process does not mean, however, that we can abdicate our role as teachers. Regie Routman (1996) states,

> I welcome and accept that learning to spell is developmental and that learners develop spelling competency gradually and need lots of time and encouragement to practice and take risks through daily reading and writing experiences. However, I do not accept misspellings that occur because of carelessness, lack of teaching, or low expectations . . . We need to continue to celebrate children's invented spelling while keeping our expectations for students reasonable and high. (p. 110)

As mentioned earlier, one of the things parents cling to from their own school experience is the list of words on the refrigerator door. It's vital that you inform parents about current research on spelling and spelling instruction. If they feel that you don't teach spelling or that spelling doesn't matter in your classroom, they may worry that their children won't learn how to spell. "Unless we inform parents of the developmental nature of learning to spell—along with the strategies and activities we are employing to teach spelling—parents are unsupportive of what they view as nontraditional, questionable practice" (Routman, 1996, p. 109).

Roz Duthie developed a chart (Figure 5.1) to help parents understand the developmental stages of spelling. On the left-hand side of the chart, she listed the commonly used terms for the spelling stages. Roz next noted the characteristics of each stage, along with an example of how children at various stages might spell "word." In the right-hand column, she listed the corresponding stage on the writing continuum described in Chapter 11.

Spelling Stage	Characteristic	Example	Continuum
Pre-writing	Letter-like marks	WORD = [illegible]	Preconventional
Pre-phonetic	Random strings of letters	WORD = BMTYZ	Preconventional
Semi-phonetic	Letter sounds, initial & end	WORD = WD YD	Emerging
Phonetic	Letter sounds, distinct words	WORD = Wad	Developing Beginning
Transitional	Vowels, letter patterns	WORD = Werd	Expanding Bridging
Conventional	Spells most words correctly	WORD = WORD	Bridging Fluent

Figure 5.1: Developmental Stages of Spelling

At Curriculum Night, Roz shows examples of the range of spelling in first grade. She draws an analogy to oral language. She asks parents to remember the first words their child spoke. Parents would never drill toddlers on isolated sounds before allowing them to use whole words. Babies learn to speak by immersion, approximation, and modeling. Roz explains that, in her classroom, she responds to early attempts at writing in the same way. She immerses children in reading and writing, values their early attempts to write, and provides models and demonstrations.

Cynthia Heffernan and Megan Sloan model some of these stages on the first day of school in their multiage primary classroom in Snohomish, Washington. As an example, they demonstrate how to write, "I am six" with pre-writing ("scribble writing"), pre-phonetic random strings of letters ("pick a letter"), phonetic approximations ("hear the sound, pick the letter"), and conventional spelling ("book print"). They laminate examples of each of these four types of spelling and display them in the room as a way to validate all students as authors. The teachers emphasize that getting ideas down on paper is the first step in the process; later they can help students put their writing into "book spelling." In this way, these first and second graders feel like they can write on the first day of school. As Megan and Cynthia teach spelling rules and strategies throughout the year, they can "up the ante" and hold students accountable for conventional spelling of basic words, which they call "red flag words" or "everyday words."

Spelling Assessment Forms

One of the great joys of teaching young students is watching them blossom as writers. Rather than correcting spelling in first drafts, you can celebrate a child's developing concepts about written language at the same time you teach awareness of spelling patterns and strategies at a developmentally appropriate level. As students develop competence as writers, you can raise the expectations for conventional spelling, particularly in published work and final drafts. Our goal is for students to take pride in their work. It's important to clearly communicate that you expect students to use their very best spelling and consistently spell the words they know correctly. Then, and only then, does spelling assessment reflect students' true abilities and use of spelling strategies. Let's now look at specific ways to assess spelling growth.

1. Spelling Continuum

When the reading and writing continuums were initially developed, the teachers decided not to create a separate spelling continuum. They viewed spelling as a tool for writing, rather than a separate subject. Spelling was therefore woven into the writing continuum. In many communities, however, spelling has become the topic of public scrutiny. In response, several schools have decided to include a spelling continuum to show that spelling is valued and taught, as well as the fact that it is developmental.

Some teachers place a copy of the spelling continuum (Form 5.1) in each student's section of their Teacher Notebook. Once each grading period, they look through the students' writing folders and record the descriptors they see used consistently. Some teachers mark the spelling continuum with highlighters (yellow in the fall, blue in the winter, and pink in the spring). Others simply check or date the descriptors on each student's spelling continuum. For instance, let's look at Lianne's Christmas poem (Figure 5.2).

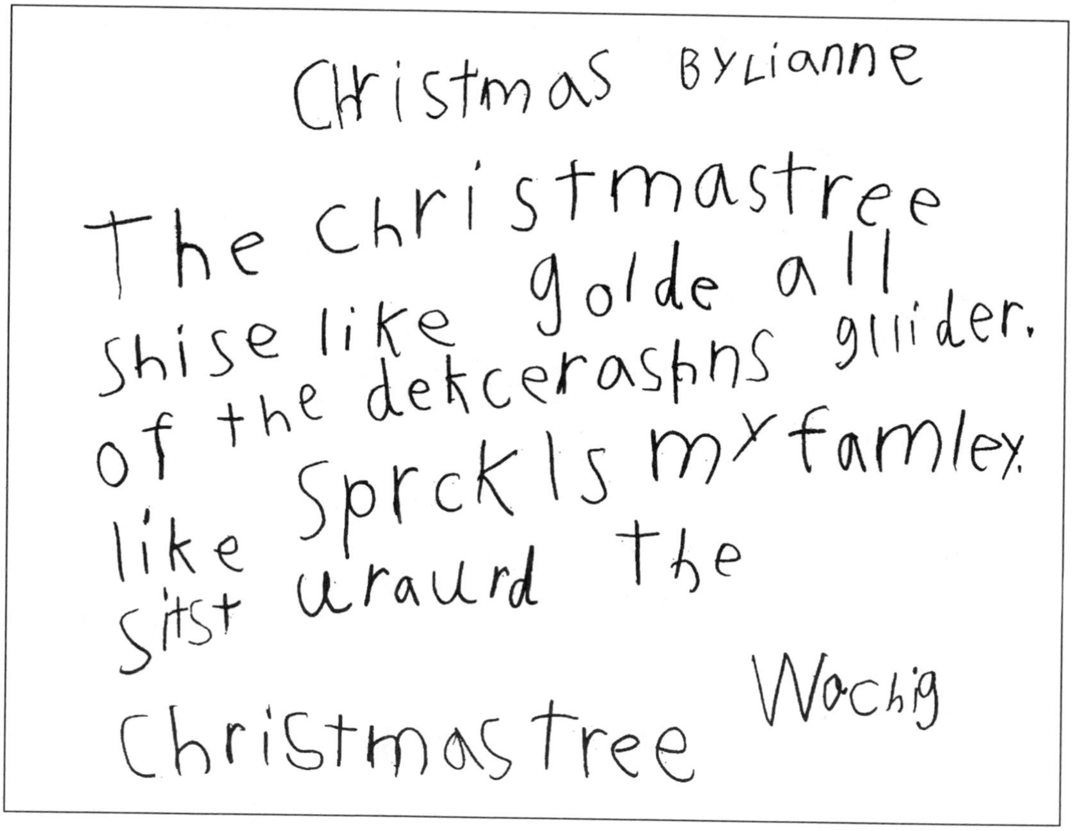

Christmas ByLianne

The christmastree
shise like golde all
of the dekcerashns glider.
like Sprckls myfamley
sitst uraurd the
Christmastree Wochig

Figure 5.2: Lianne's Poem

Lianne spelled some sight words correctly, such as "like" and "of," so her teacher checks that descriptor from the phonetic stage of the continuum. Her spelling of the challenging word, "decoration," shows that Lianne is still relying primarily on the sounds of words to spell independently. She's a pretty solid phonetic speller, although Lianne's poem also shows that she is beginning to incorporate vowels in most syllables. Her teacher wouldn't mark this descriptor until she saw it consistently. Of course, her teacher would want to look through more samples, but you can see how the continuum can provide specific information about spelling growth over time.

It's important to keep in mind, however, Sandra Wilde's (1992) caveat that describing children's spelling in terms of discrete stages is an oversimplification: "Individual spellings can perhaps be categorized, but any one child's spelling taken as a whole is usually too varied to be pigeonholed" (p. 47). What's important is to look at multiple samples of writing over time and to talk about what children are discovering about how words are spelled.

2. Spelling Development Form

Roz Duthie created the Spelling Development Class Profile (Form 5.2A) to use with beginning writers and their families. On the left-hand side, Roz lists the names of all her students. The developmental stages from the spelling continuum are listed across the top of the form with examples of how children at each stage would spell "word." Once each grading period, Roz places a date by the appropriate stage as she assesses each student's writing. This information about the range of spelling development in her classroom is helpful at parent conference time and helps guide her instruction.

Instead of including the spelling continuum in each child's section of your Teacher Notebook, you might wish to use the Spelling Development Individual Profile (Form 5.2A). You may wish to complete the form once each grading period by scanning through two writing folders at the end of each day. The last column on this form includes room for you to add notes or list a few words from the child's writing. The result is a graphic picture of each student's spelling growth over time. By marking each child's stage of spelling with the date or a dot in the fall and an X in the spring, the Spelling Development: Class Profile (Form 5.2B) enables you to capture a portrait of the range of spelling levels and spelling growth in your classroom. After covering up the students' names, you can share this evidence of spelling growth with parents at Curriculum Night.

3. Spelling Strategies I Use

Cynthia Ruptic begins spelling instruction in her class with a discussion about why it's important to use standard spelling as much as possible. Cynthia assures her children, especially third graders who are new to her class, that she wants them to continue to "use the sounds" efficiently as they compose, but also points out that it's important to remember the reader's need for standard spelling. She uses examples from emergent writers to show her third and fourth graders that, although the text is readable, it's much easier to use what she calls "conventional spelling."

Cynthia created a spelling strategies form based on an article by Diane Snowball (1996) in *Instructor Magazine*. Her students keep the Spelling Strategies I Use page (Form 5.3) in their writing folders. She asks everyone to focus only on the first four spelling strategies for a few weeks. Gradually she introduces the other spelling strategies through her focus lessons and class discussions.

Cynthia develops her spelling instruction around her students' needs and inquiries, as well as her school's curriculum. For example, at Osaka International

School, students in third grade are held accountable for the first 300-most-frequently used words and her fourth graders for the first 400 words. However, what's most important to Cynthia is that her students understand that conventional spelling *is* important and that they learn to assess their own growth in spelling.

4. Spelling 10 Words

The Spelling 10 Words technique (Form 5.4) can be used to assess spelling growth over time for primary students. Cynthia Ruptic developed the primary version (Form 5.4A) using ten words from a K–2 spelling list in *Teaching Kids to Spell* (Gentry and Gillet, 1993). You may wish to develop your own list of words. They should be challenging enough so that only a few of your students will spell them conventionally. The words you pick should not be ones that you formally teach during the year. The list should include words that cannot be spelled phonetically but address common spelling patterns or rules in order to analyze a student's strategies. If you make up your own list of 10 words for your grade level, you might refer to Richard Gentry's list in *My Kid Can't Spell!* (1997), pages 36–41, for the spelling patterns students should be learning in each grade.

Dictate the ten words to your class in the same you would a "spelling test." This technique, however, is more like a "dipstick" into their growth as writers and spellers, rather than a test. Students can write directly on Form 5.4A or 5.4B. In the winter, you can simply fold over the previous list so only the blank columns are showing. You can then examine the fall, winter, and spring samples side by side.

Christy Clausen uses the Spelling 10 Words strategy in her first grade classroom. When she gives the second test in the winter, she folds the paper under so the students can't see the list they wrote in the fall. She then asks the children to unfold the paper and write a reflection about what they noticed. Notice Blake's changes in spelling as well as his self-evaluation from the winter of first grade (Figure 5.3). The critical step of self-reflection helps students recognize and celebrate their own growth.

Spelling 10 Words for Older Students

Spelling growth is not quite as dramatic in the intermediate grades as it is at the primary level. As a grade level team, you may want to decide on a list of 10 words to give students just twice a year. You might want to refer to the Professional Growth section at the end of this chapter and also refer to *My Kid Can't Spell* (Gentry, 1997) for developmentally appropriate words. For example, depending on your grade level, you may want to include some common word endings such as "-tion," letter combinations such as "-ight," and words with silent letters. Even in the fifth or sixth grade, you will see changes in students' abilities as they fine-tune their spelling skills. We included an intermediate version of the Spelling 10 Words (Form 5.4C) to use with more proficient writers, as well as a sample from a fourth-grade student (Figure 5.4).

DEVELOPMENTAL SPELLING: 10 WORDS

Student Name Blake **Grade/Age** ______

FALL	WINTER 2-13-98	SPRING
MOSTR	monstir	
YOUNITED	United	
DRAS	dress	
BOTEM	botem	
HOICTE	hiked	
HEYOUMAN	heumen	
EGOLE	EEgolle	
COSD	Closde	
BAMT	bugeat	
TiC	tipe	

I noticed...

I forGot the L in CLosde.

IAlso forot the n in Monstir.

Figure 5.3: Spelling 10 Words Sample and Self-Reflection

Name Erin	Name Erin
Date 11-7-94	Date 4/7/95
Spelling--10 Words	**Spelling--10 Words**
1. tomarow	1. tomorrow
2. would'nt	2. would'nt
3. nallige	3. knowlage
4. Particular	4. particular
5. Presher	5. presure
6. aqudingle	6. acordinglly
7. experenc	7. experinced
8. community	8. community
9. binethe	9. beneath
10. therfor	10. therefore

Figure 5.4: Spelling 10 Words (Intermediate Sample)

5. Index of Control

Some teachers may want to periodically tabulate the percentage of words that students spell correctly in their writing. In *Spelling in Use* (Laminack and Wood, 1996, pages 46–62), the authors describe this technique, which they call an "Index of Control." You may want to collect samples of each student's writing once each grading period.

Use the Index of Control page (Form 5.5) to record all the *different* words in the sample. If the word is used more than once, simply place a tally mark by the word. Place the words in the appropriate column to show whether it was written with conventional or constructed (invented) spelling. You can easily calculate the number of different words spelled correctly. It's important, however, to look at more than the number of words spelled correctly.

What types of words do students misspell? For instance, in Lianne's poem in Figure 5.2, she correctly spells developmentally appropriate words such as "like" and "tree." Her misspellings are for words we wouldn't expect a first grader to spell correctly, such as "decorations," "around," and "glitter." Lianne's writing would be far less powerful if she only used the words she could spell correctly.

Lester Laminack and Katie Wood suggest looking for an increase in the total number of words used, an increase in the total number of *different* words used, and an increase in the writer's index of control. If you're interested in using this technique, you may want to read the section in *Spelling in Use,* which includes wonderful examples and a more detailed explanation of scoring. Although time-consuming, this technique can provide a powerful way to examine primary students' writing growth over time.

6. "Have a Go" Spelling Form

The "Have a Go" Spelling (Form 5.6) was based on the section on spelling in Linda Crafton's book, *Whole Language: Getting Started . . . Moving Forward* (1991). Many other books on process writing describe a technique called "Have a Go" or "Guess and Go." Students are encouraged to write the word they are unsure about in several different ways. Students, as well as adults, often find that they can pick the correct spelling, given several choices. This instructional tool encourages students to discuss spelling options. The form also provides diagnostic information, since the types of words that students spell and their approximations reveal much about students' strategies and understanding of written language.

7. Spelling Survey

Are you a good speller? How do you figure out words that you're not sure how to spell? Do you think of similar words you know and spell by analogy? Do you use the spell checker on your computer? Do you ask a friend or spouse to look something over before you send it off? If you want to use a word that you're not sure how to spell, do you use a different word rather than look it up? As adults, these are a few of the many spelling strategies in our repertoire. You can encourage students to share their spelling strategies during focus lessons and class discussions.

When asked on a spelling survey, the majority of students in Cindy Flegenheimer's third-grade class responded that correct spelling was important "to get 100% on your spelling test." Cindy realized she needed to talk more with students about the need for conventional spelling in our society. You can gain valuable information through spelling interviews. Intermediate students can complete the

Spelling Survey (Form 5.7) independently. If you teach primary students, parents could interview students and transcribe their responses.

Spelling Concerns

The few years when young students use invented spelling is such a fleeting period. Rather than becoming anxious about their errors, teachers and parents should celebrate growth and appreciate how spelling provides a glimpse into how students are constructing language. This certainly doesn't mean you shouldn't teach spelling! Sandra Wilde (1992) suggests five essential spelling strategies that she describes in Chapter 6 of her book, *You Kan Red This!* Her latest book, *What's a Schwa Sound, Anyway?* (1997) provides an informative and humorous look at linguistics, phonics, and spelling. One of the most practical parts of her book is Chapter 6, entitled, "What Does Invented Spelling Tell Us About Kids' Knowledge of Phonics? (And What Should We Do About It?)." Additional suggestions for teaching spelling in a writing workshop context can be found in *Spelling in Use* (Laminack and Wood, 1996). Learning to spell correctly is a long process, but there are many things you can do as teachers to help students. The more you know about research on spelling, the better you can understand students' patterns of mistakes and provide appropriate spelling instruction. The best methods of assessment are to look at authentic writing samples over time and to ask students about their spelling growth.

Sandra Wilde (1996) also warns, "When trying to get a handle on a student whose spelling we're concerned about, we always need to think about spelling in the context of her general literacy development. In particular, how much reading does she do? It's so easy to focus first on spelling because it's more visible than just about any other aspect of language" (p. 38). It's important to remember that spelling development is closely tied to reading and writing growth.

In this chapter, we discussed seven ways to assess spelling. Which one form or tool is most informative at your grade level? How can you weave it into your classroom routines? You might want to take a minute to look over this chapter and write the spelling assessment tools you plan to use on the Organizational Grid (Form 3.2).

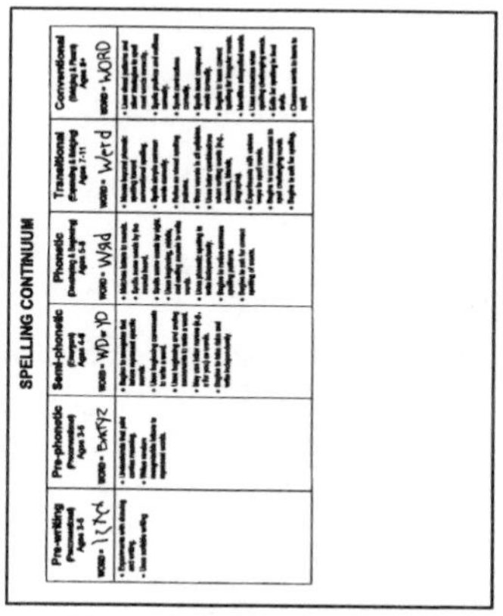

Form 5.1: Spelling Continuum

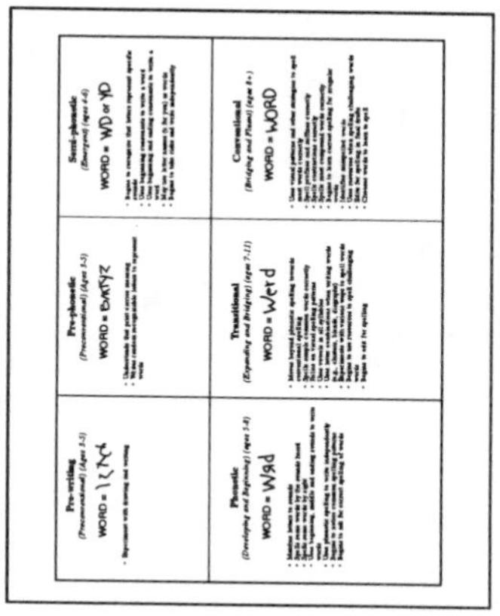

Form 5.2: Spelling Development

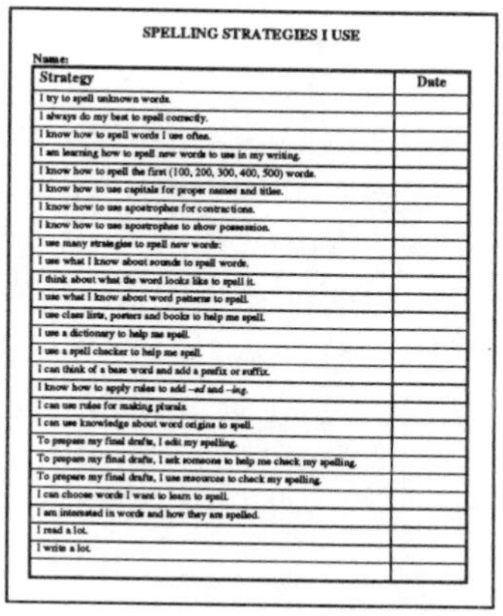

Form 5.3: Spelling Strategies I Use

SPELLING 10 WORDS

Name: Grade/Age:

FALL	WINTER	SPRING

I noticed

Form 5.4: Spelling 10 Words

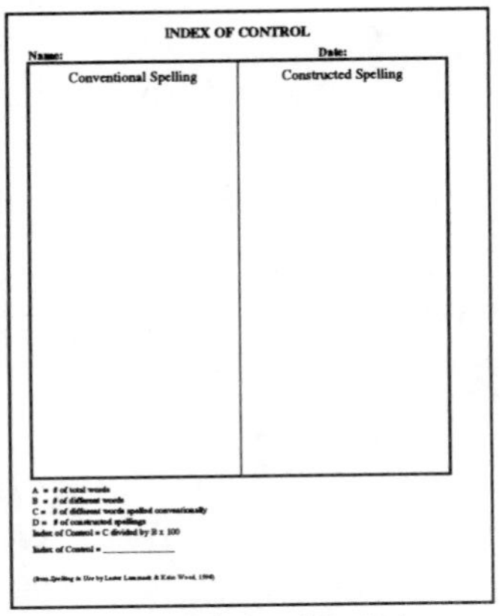

INDEX OF CONTROL

Name: Date:

Conventional Spelling	Constructed Spelling

A = # of total words
B = # of different words
C = # of different words spelled conventionally
D = # of constructed spellings
Index of Control = C divided by B x 100

Index of Control = ___________

Form 5.5: Index of Control

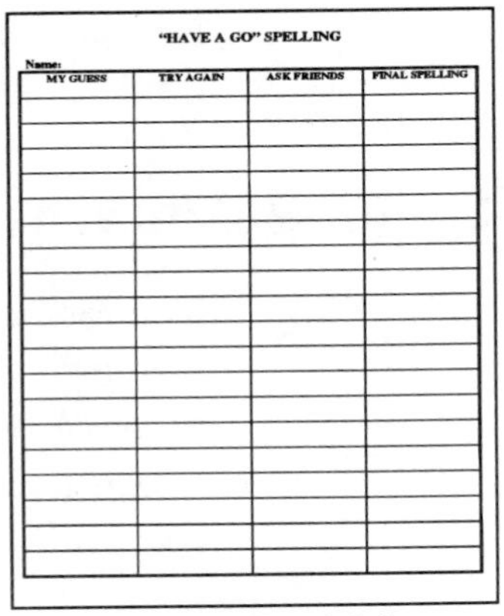

"HAVE A GO" SPELLING

Name:

MY GUESS	TRY AGAIN	ASK FRIENDS	FINAL SPELLING

Form 5.6: "Have A Go"

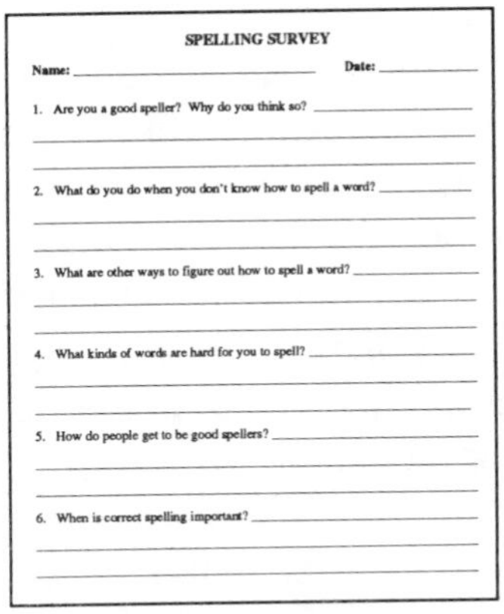

SPELLING SURVEY

Name: ___________ Date: ___________

1. Are you a good speller? Why do you think so? ___________
2. What do you do when you don't know how to spell a word? ___________
3. What are other ways to figure out how to spell a word? ___________
4. What kinds of words are hard for you to spell? ___________
5. How do people get to be good spellers? ___________
6. When is correct spelling important? ___________

Form 5.7 Spelling Survey

Professional Growth

You may want to use either *Spelling in Use* (Laminack & Wood, 1996), *Teaching Kids to Spell* (Gentry & Gillet, 1993), or You *Kan Red This!* (Wilde, 1992) as a text for a study group. The group could bring questions about the text and examples of student spelling to discuss. As a group, you may want to create an index of control for one student, as described on pages 47–66 in *Spelling in Use* (Laminack & Wood, 1996). What did you learn from the process? What surprised you? How could you adapt this technique to use in the classroom? The elementary section of the National Council of Teachers of English can provide help if you want to form a local study group on spelling. For more information, call NCTE at 1-800-369-6283, ext. 271.

An idea for a one-time workshop is to bring samples of student writing without any indication of age or grade level. In small groups, try to ascertain the student's developmental stage on the spelling continuum. Keep track of issues that arise during the process. Were there any surprises about the ages of students? Would the assessment be more accurate with multiple samples from each child? Will the results be affected if the work is edited or not? Does knowing more about the child or context affect your judgment? Sandra Wilde has a similar activity in "Where Should Kids Be As Spellers?" on page 25–27 of the November, 1996 issue of *Primary Voices.*

Prepare a parent workshop on spelling. During the workshop, explain the stages of spelling development, using Figure 5.1. Do a sample focus lesson and activity. Collect student samples and ask parents to ascertain their stage of spelling development. Prepare a simple handout and bring spelling books to share. You might even have copies of *My Kid Can't Spell* (Gentry, 1997) to sell or check out. You might give parents a "spelling test" using very challenging words very few people are likely to spell. Ask the parents to list the strategies they used to tackle these hard words. Leave their chart of spelling strategies they create for their children to see the next day at school.

As suggested earlier in this chapter, you may want to meet in grade level teams and develop a list of 10 Spelling Words as an assessment tool. Richard Gentry's book, *My Kid Can't Spell,* would be helpful in developing appropriate lists. Grade level teams might then meet to compare lists and rationale. The data collected would be very helpful in looking at a broad picture of spelling development at your school. Regie Routman, in *Literacy at the Crossroads* (1996), suggests developing a core list of words for which students will be held accountable at each grade level. She states that these lists show parents your expectations for correct spelling at developmentally appropriate levels.

Some teachers may decide to each use a different spelling assessment form during the year and meet periodically to share results and discuss what they are learning about their students and spelling growth.

Recommended Readings about Spelling

For further reading, we recommend five particularly excellent books on the topic: *Spel . . . is a Four-Letter Word* (Gentry, 1987), *Teaching Kids to Spell* (Gentry & Gillet, 1993), You *Kan Red This! Spelling and Punctuation for Whole Language Classrooms, K-6* (Wilde, 1992), *Learning Phonics and Spelling in a Whole Language Classroom* (Powell and Hornsby, 1993) and *Spelling in Use: Looking Closely at Spelling in Whole Language Classrooms* (Laminack & Wood, 1996). Many teachers also find Rebecca Sitton's materials helpful for developing a spelling program and effective focus lessons.

Richard Gentry's new book, My *Kid Can't Spell* (1997) is an excellent resource for parents as well as teachers. He answers parents' questions, talks about appropriate spelling practices, and outlines the spelling rules worth teaching.

We've also found three additional helpful sources of information on spelling. Chapter 7 in Regie Routman's book, *Literacy at the Crossroads* (1996), is excellent. Another useful resource is the first article in the November, 1996 issue of *The Reading Teacher* by Theodore Clymer. His article lists 45 spelling rules and the percentage of instances those rules actually work. Finally, the entire issue of *Primary Voices* in November of 1996, edited by Sandra Wilde, provides many practical suggestions for classroom teachers. You can subscribe to the journal or you can order single issues by writing to Primary Voices, National Council of Teachers of English, 1111 W. Kenyon Road, Urbana, IL 61801-1096. These books describe the stages of spelling growth in detail and provide excellent strategies for incorporating spelling into writing programs at all levels.

Chapter 6

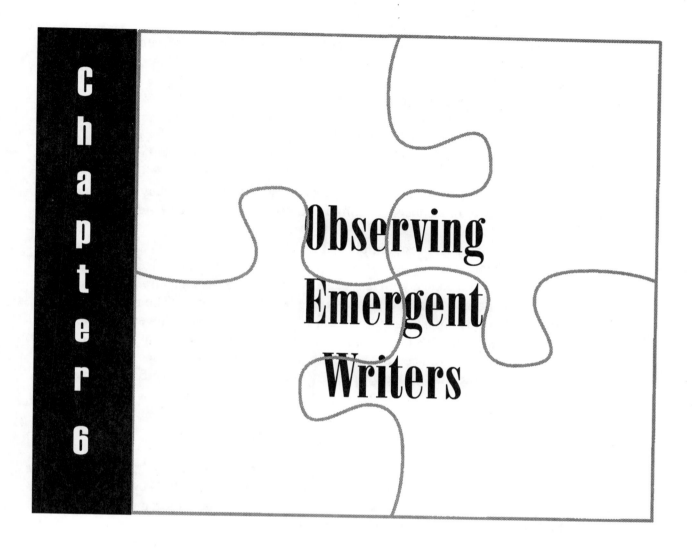

Observing Emergent Writers

Jerry shares his story about dinosaurs at author's chair. He uses invented spelling that only he can read. Randy and Carmen use the notepad in the home center to take orders as they play restaurant. Lindsey makes a sign for the gerbils' cage that warns others, "SHH!!! NU BBS!" These children are in a kindergarten classroom that successfully launches students into reading, writing, and the world of school. For some children, learning to read unlocks the world of written language. For others, writing is the avenue into literacy. Some children may find the more active, kinesthetic nature of writing inviting. Others become engaged because they can write about people and things that matter in their lives. This is particularly noticeable in classrooms where children are encouraged to write daily, even in kindergarten.

In this chapter, we explore writing in the primary grades. If you are an intermediate teacher, you may want to skim over this section. We begin with a discussion of the issues and challenges involved in assessing emergent writing. We then explore four techniques designed specifically for assessing beginning writers.

In the past fifteen years, researchers in the field of emergent literacy (Hall, 1987; Harste, Woodward and Burke, 1984; Morrow, 1989; Newkirk, 1989; Teale and Sulzby, 1986) have documented how writing and reading develop in the first years of life. The term "emergent literacy" was first used by Marie Clay in her doctoral dissertation in 1966 and describes children's developmental process of becoming literate. Primary teachers must build upon the understanding of language that children bring to school. However, our role must move beyond diagnosis. We need to create an environment that invites children to experiment with writing. Lucy Calkins observes, "Once children regard themselves as writers, they go through their lives like vacuum cleaners, sucking up knowledge of written language" (1994, p. 72).

Pencil and paper tests simply cannot capture young children's developing language and their growing understanding of the world around them. To assess children's developing competence with language, we must observe students, analyze samples of their work, and talk with these young readers and writers. The use of anecdotal records described in Chapter 4 is one way to assess children. However, for teachers of primary students, it's particularly challenging to find time to stop and write extensive notes! What we need are some simple and manageable assessment tools that capture the dramatic growth young children make during their first few years in school.

Art and Writing

For young children, writing and drawing are often intertwined. Writing and drawing are both symbol systems (Armstrong, 1987, 1994; Campbell, 1994; Vygotsky, 1978). Lucy Calkins describes how kindergarten and first-grade children use both the actual picture and the process of drawing as scaffolding for early forays into writing. At this point, most of the child's meaning is carried in the picture. "In early first grade, then, the goal is to have writing catch up to drawing; by second grade the goal is often to have writing catch up to talking" (Calkins, 1994, p. 88). With primary students, it is important to examine both their writing and artwork. Susan Bridge (1982) says, "Sometimes I think that writing teachers who only consider the writing part of the child's story are like people who squeeze from the middle of the toothpaste tube. They only get part of what's in there" (p. 75).

Art plays an important role in the classrooms of older students as well. Howard Gardner (1983), in his work with Project Zero at Harvard University, explored the value of including the arts in a well-balanced school program that taps the multiple intelligences of learners. In the Recommended Readings section at the end of this chapter, we list several books about connecting writing with art. For many people, art is a powerful way of making meaning. Drawings can reflect the interest, creativity, and themes in young people's lives. Ruth Hubbard (1989) states,

> Drawing is not just for children who can't yet write fluently, and creating pictures is not just part of rehearsal for real writing. Images *at any age* are part of

the serious business of making meaning—partners with words for communicating our inner designs. (p. 157)

Process and Product

You can learn a great deal about young writers by observing them at work. As adults, we seem to focus on products. We like colorful children's work to hang in the hallway. For young children, however, the process is often more important than the product. As an example, Allen is a first grader from Boston who has been fascinated by the Revolutionary War. When he proudly presented a drawing to his mother, all she saw was a piece of paper, covered with black crayon. He described how he had carefully drawn the British and American soldiers with accurate uniforms, down to the brass buttons. However, Allen explained, the battle took place at night, which he showed by coloring over his drawing with black. His mother would have preferred the original drawing of the soldiers; Allen was more content with his process.

Assessing Emergent Writing

1. Writing Names

Linda Johnson, a kindergarten teacher at Brighton School in Lynnwood, Washington, has a simple assessment technique that provides a glimpse into her students' developing writing skills. Before the school year begins, Linda makes a laminated 4" × 8½" sign with each kindergartner's name printed on the top line and a blank line below the name. As students come in the door on the first day of school, they locate the strip with their own name. Depending on their writing skills, the students trace, scribble-write, or copy their names with erasable felt markers. Each day these "sign-in" sheets are washed off so they can be re-used. Once during each grading period, Linda substitutes regular paper in place of the laminated sheets and the students write their names on the paper. These are dated, clipped together, and placed in her Teacher Notebook to show growth over time. You can see an example below (Figure 6.1).

2. Draw Me, Draw a Tree

Linda Johnson also uses another assessment idea we've called "Draw Me, Draw a Tree" that she gained at a workshop in 1988 with Barbara Rothman. Linda folds large 11" × 17" paper into four vertical columns. On the first of each month, she gives each of her kindergarteners a new piece of paper. Students draw all the shapes they know in the first column on the left. In the next column, the children draw a picture of themselves and on the third part they draw their favorite tree. In the last column, they draw a picture of another person. On the back of the paper, the students write their name and as many numbers and letters as they can. At the end of the year, these sheets are stapled together in chronological order to create a flip book that

Figure 6.1: Writing Names

shows each child's development in drawing and writing. This technique also reveals a great deal about each child's fine motor skills. Each month, students are able to complete the task more quickly and with greater ease. Linda notes, however, that in the spring, some children actually take longer to do their drawings and writing as they begin to take pride in adding more detail. These books are given to parents at the end of the year. We reduced an example here to fit in the book (Figure 6.2) but did not make a form, since you simply have to fold 11" × 17" paper into four columns.

Note on Bruce's drawing that the adult has no head. When asked, Bruce explained very logically, "Well, here's me and my Dad's really tall, so he wouldn't fit on the picture." We learn a great deal about children by asking about their work in order to understand their perspective of the world.

3. Words I Know

One of the techniques Marie Clay developed was to have young children write as many words as they can in ten minutes. When this activity is repeated over time in kindergarten and first grade, it's easy to see writing growth. This technique is describe more extensively in *An Observation Survey of Early Literacy Achievement* (Clay, 1993) along with specific directions for scoring this task, based on tests of large numbers of children.

Christy Clausen modified this technique in her primary classroom. She first reminds students how to find words "in the room" (like "exit"), words they already know (like "mom" and "cat"), and how to "sound out" words on their own (like "hi" and "me"). She next hands out paper cut in half vertically to look like a list or uses the Words I Know sheet (Form 6.1). Christy asks the children to write as many words as they can, starting with their names. As they begin, she uses her clipboard to

Figure 6.2: Draw Me, Draw a Tree

take anecdotal notes about their behaviors and strategies. Some children may only write a word or two, while others write many words. Christy keeps extra paper on hand for enthusiastic children who fill up their lists.

After about ten minutes, Christy asks her students to place a line under their last word. She then allows them to move around the room to look for more words to add to their lists. As she watches the children looking at charts, labels, and books, she can sometimes observe strategies she wouldn't see if they were at their desks. By using the same technique again in the spring, Christy and her students can clearly see changes by placing fall and spring samples side by side.

Roz Duthie has adapted Clay's technique for her first-grade class on Bainbridge Island. In September, she asks her students to list all the words they know as described above. Then, in November, when they focus on Pilgrims, she reads *Sarah Morton's Day* (Waters, 1989) and *Samuel Eaton's Day* (Waters, 1993). As a class, the students compare the daily life of children almost 400 years ago to their own lives. Roz models list making on the board. Next, each student then lists all the things they do during a typical day. In June, Roz reads *Frog and Toad Together* (Lobel, 1971), in which Toad keeps a list of "Things to Do Today." For their final writing sample, she asks the first graders to again list things they do during the day. At the end of the year, she places the three lists side-by-side and asks students what they notice. Since her first graders make such gains in writing proficiency during the year, these increasingly challenging lists reflect her students' growing competence as thinkers and writers. Here you can see the dramatic growth in Benjamin's samples (Figure 6.3).

4. Emergent Writing Development Form

Sue Ondriezek, a teacher in Mukilteo, Washington, wanted to modify the Spelling Development form from Chapter 5 (Form 5.2) to differentiate development within the early stages of writing. The Emergent Writing Development page (Form 6.2) allows you to note whether children are making squiggly shapes for letters, letter-like marks, or actually writing random strings of letters.

Another piece of helpful information is whether children can actually read what they have written. On the right-hand side of this form, there are three columns. In the first column, you can check whether children can only vaguely tell you about the pieces they have written. In the next column, you can note if children proudly hold their paper and pretend to read the piece, not even looking at the words! In the last column, you can record when students get to the point where they can touch each word as they read, matching their spoken words to the print.

As a primary teacher, which of the following four assessment ideas might you want to try? Remember, there are no forms for two of the techniques, so you may want to add the ideas to your Organizational Grid (Form 3.2).

Writing Names
(no form)

No Form: Writing Names

Draw Me, Draw a Tree
(no form)

No Form: Draw Me, Draw A Tree

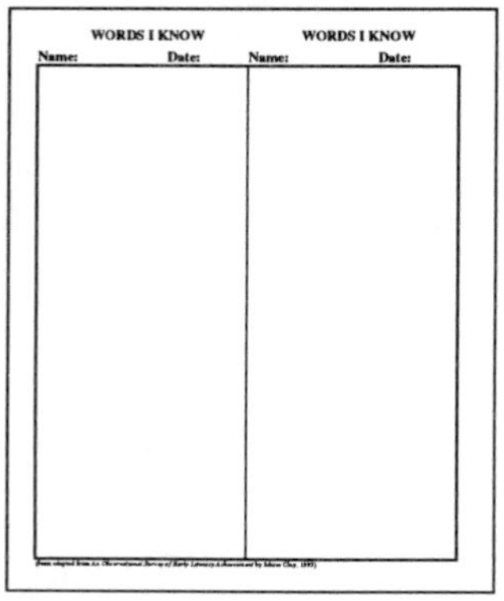

Form 6.1: Words I Know

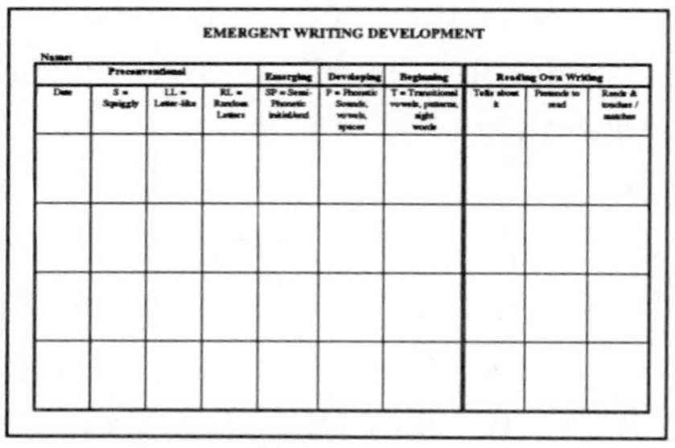

Form 6.2: Emergent Writing Development

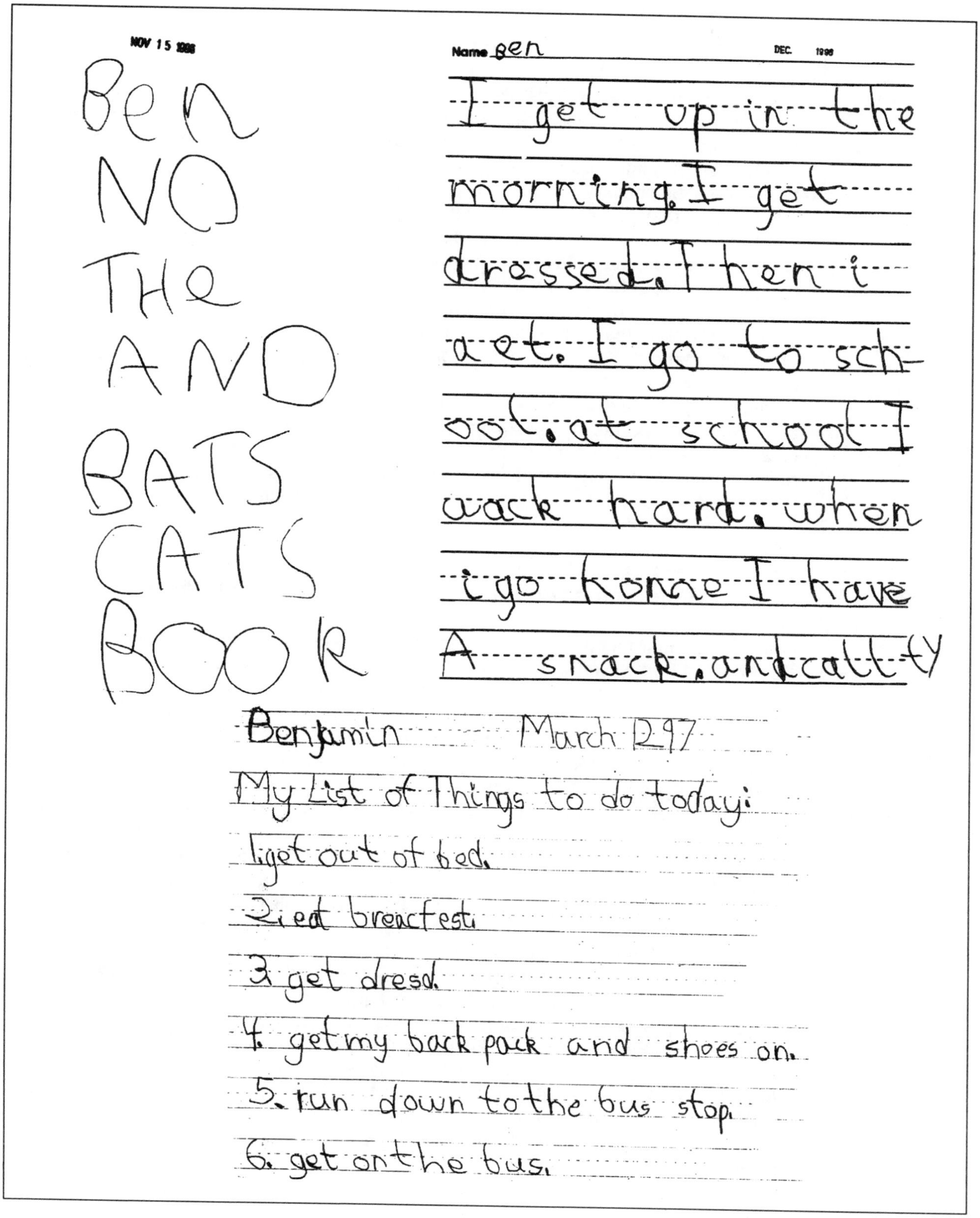

Figure 6.3: Words I Know Samples

Professional Growth

Make an overhead of a child's piece of art and/or writing. In a workshop, ask participants what they can guess about the child. Then show transcriptions of a conversation in which you ask the child about their writing. What could workshop participants add to what they know about this child? Next, show a photograph and your anecdotal notes about the child. What more could the teachers in your group tell you now? What questions do they have? Show a videotape of the child reading and writing. Let teachers add more to the list of understandings and questions. Then share your Teacher Notebook entries, the child's continuums, and the student's portfolio. Talk about how each piece deepens your understanding about the child.

Take a day to observe another primary teacher. If possible, go with a colleague. Take anecdotal notes and write down new ideas and questions that arise. Be sure to bring your camera. You might want to bring a children's book to read to the students and let them interview you. Offer to bring the teacher a sandwich so you can talk during lunchtime. Take the afternoon to talk with your colleague about what you learned and plan to incorporate in your classroom. You might want to send the teacher and the class a thank you note after your visit. Send another note to the principal. It's far too rare that we are publicly thanked or praised! You might want to take some time after your visit to write some reflections and questions for yourself.

Recommended Readings about Emergent Writing

One of the most helpful books on assessing primary students is Marie Clay's *An Observation Survey of Early Literacy* (1993). Although this text is challenging to read, it's an excellent resource for understanding early reading and writing. This book should be in every professional library.

Kindergarten teachers love Bobbi Fisher's book, *Joyful Learning* (1991), which deals specifically with the issues and challenges of teaching two rounds of kindergarten. Likewise, first grade teachers have been delighted with the practical nature of Carol Avery's book, *And with a Light Touch* (1993). We have found two other particularly helpful books for primary teachers, *The Author's Chair and Beyond* (Karelitz, 1993) and *Young Writers in the Making* (Preece and Cowden, 1993). This last book has great information about early writing, which you can share with parents, including ready-to-reproduce pamphlets. Dorothy Strickland and Lesley Morrow's book, *Emerging Literacy: Young Children Learn to Read and Write* (1989) provides a good review of research in this area as well as some helpful suggestions for teaching young children. *Managing Literacy Assessment with Young Learners* (Weeks and Leaker, 1991) is a book specifically geared to assessing primary students.

Five helpful books that examine children's artistic development are *First Drawings: Genesis of Visual Thinking* (Fein, 1993), *Heidi's Horse* (Fein, 1993), *Authors of Pictures, Draughtsmen of Words* (Hubbard, 1989), *Picturing Learning: Artists and Writers in the Classroom* (Ernst, 1994), and *New Entries: Learning by Writing and Drawing* (Hubbard and Ernst, 1996). In these books, the authors discuss artist's workshops and keeping sketchbooks, as well as the connections between drawing and writing.

Chapter 7

Observing Writing Growth

In September, Melissa struggled to write a few lines in her journal. By March, she was deeply involved in writing a book about the rain forest. In June, she published a detective story and her classmates clamored for a sequel. Writing samples collected over time are interesting and demonstrate growth. Samples alone, however, are not an assessment tool. It's what you do with students' writing samples that moves mere appreciation or concern to the level of diagnosis and evaluation.

What are your hopes and expectations for the writers in your classroom? What aspects of writing are important to teach at your grade level? What are the standards for writing in your district, state, or country? Because this chapter is quite long, we've divided it into three sections. In the first section, we focus on ways to assess students' writing strategies, range, and content through the use of writing folders and conference forms. In the second section, we explore how to assess students' knowledge of the writing process, including their ability to revise and edit. The third section will address ways to involve students in self-evaluation.

Section One: Assessing Writing Content and Strategies

When many of us were in school, teachers assigned a writing topic at the beginning of each week. We dutifully handed in our papers on Friday, having received little help during the composition process. As Lucy Calkins (1994) notes, writing was assigned rather than taught. In a workshop approach, writing is viewed as an ongoing process that involves pre-writing, drafting, revising, editing, and sometimes publishing pieces. The most significant change in how writing is taught in a workshop approach is that teachers have a very active role during class time. At the end of this chapter, we've listed some excellent books that provide more information on the teaching of writing.

In *Writing: Teachers and Children at Work* (1983), Donald Graves posits that children come to school ready to write. Our job is to nurture that positive attitude, encourage risk-taking, and demonstrate effective writing strategies. Graves describes a predictable structure in which students write on a daily basis. The workshop approach to writing is now widely used in classrooms around the world.

Writing workshop usually begins with a focus lesson on a particular topic or strategy. Teachers often model their own writing or share a technique on the overhead projector. Three or four times a week, students have blocks of time to write about topics they choose. At other times, teachers provide specific models and guidance for writing in particular genres. As students write, the teacher moves around the room observing and talking with students. This is the perfect time to take anecdotal notes as described in Chapter 4 or to hold one or two individual writing conferences.

In the 1980s, when the concept of writing workshop was new, teachers focused heavily on students' choice of topic and writing personal narrative. Both Lucy Calkins (1994) and Donald Graves (1994) now suggest that teachers model writing strategies and provide practice with a wide range of text types, such as lists, brochures, letters, editorials, research, and poetry, in addition to personal narratives and fiction. Calkins sees writing as a way of viewing and understanding the world, rather than a search for topics. She describes writing as a way of finding significance in our ordinary lives and encourages each student to keep a writer's notebook to use throughout the day for drafting, jotting down ideas, and collecting seeds for later writing.

Our job as teachers is to take young writers seriously, provide models and guidance, and become better observers of our students. We need to purposefully assess students in order to plan effective focus lessons and help our students improve the quality of their writing. Two ways to assess the range and quality of student writing are through writing folders and writing conferences.

Writing Folder Forms

Students need a place where they can keep their daily writing. Some teachers prefer notebooks, while others like having file folders for student work. The writing folder forms in the Appendix can be adapted to suit whatever method you choose. These forms can become assessment tools when students use them to measure growth and set goals. Let's look at five writing folder forms: Topics, Pieces I've Written, Writing Genres, Strategies I Use, and Goals.

1. Writing Topics

On Form 7.1, students can record possible writing topics. Lucy Calkins (1994) describes how you can model topic selection the first day of writing workshop by using your own writing. You can also model topic and genre choices through the books you read aloud. These topic lists are most useful when students revisit them regularly and add to their lists throughout the year. You may want to start the year by providing writing folders that include only this one form.

2. Pieces I've Written

Once students have accumulated several pieces of writing in their folders, you can introduce Pieces I've Written (Form 7.2), so writers can list the titles of pieces they've written. We've purposely used the term "pieces" to emphasize that writing may include nonfiction, lists, poetry, letters, and other types of writing besides fiction. Students can note the dates when pieces were started and finished. They can also use an asterisk to indicate published writing. The form then reveals both how much a child has written and how long the student worked on each piece. It can also serve as a table of contents to a child's writing folder.

3. Writing Genres

Think of the types of writing you do every day. How often do you write an animal report or fairy tale? You may have jotted down a grocery list and left a note for your spouse in the morning, dashed off a quick email or a memo at work, then written an overdue thank-you note after dinner. Just as students need exposure to a wide range of genres in reading, they need experience with many types of writing. We've included a primary Writing Genres list (Form 7.3A) and an additional form for more proficient writers (Form 7.3B) so students can keep track of the types of writing they produce during the year. As students record titles, the form becomes a simple bar graph that visually reflects the balance of a student's writing. The form could be enlarged into a Writing Genres chart for the classroom.

4. Writing Strategies I Use

Teachers use the next writing folder form to document their students' growing grasp of writing strategies. We'll briefly describe five versions of writing strategies forms.

The first Writing Strategies I Use version (Form 7.4A) is blank so that you can list writing skills you notice during either formal or informal conferences with children. You can document a child's writing strategies and ability to revise and edit. You can also use these lists when you help students set writing goals. The advantage of the blank form is that it's flexible and won't be intimidating to students. Students can add strategies to reflect their own unique path of growth.

For instance, Cynthia Ruptic held a writing conference with one of her third graders, Meelad. At the end of the conference, they agreed that he should write on his Strategies I Use form that he was able to organize his ideas in a logical sequence. The following week, Meelad's peer writing group suggested that his action-packed comic book needed more details. Meelad revised it, adding description and even some dialogue. He brought both his draft and the reworked piece to Cynthia as evidence and asked if he could add the following to his Strategies I Use list:

> I add description and details when I revise
>
> I write realistic dialogue to make my writing interesting.

Cythia agreed, but noted that Meelad did not consistently punctuate dialogue correctly. She took this opportunity to show him various ways to use quotation marks. Meelad recorded examples in his Writer's Notebook and added "Learn to use quotation marks correctly" to his list of fall goals. Cynthia will continue to monitor Meelad's use of these strategies.

In this way, the blank Writing Strategies I Use form serves as a record of each child's unique journey toward writing competence. Since students may also suggest strategies to add to their lists, the blank form encourages students to think actively about their own learning and helps them set their own writing goals.

In the next version of Writing Strategies I Use (Form 7.4B), Cynthia Ruptic included specific descriptors of the strategies she teaches in her multiage primary classroom. Rather than simply dating each skill, the form includes a scale to record whether students used the skill with guidance or independently. We've also included an intermediate adaptation (Form 7.4C) that Cynthia now uses in her intermediate multiage classroom.

5. Writing Goals

During individual conferences, students and teachers can use Form 7.5 collaboratively to record students' writing goals. Progress toward these goals can then be assessed at the end of the term. The forms can be stapled to students' writing folders or tucked in their writer's notebooks. These goals can be tied directly to portfolios and student-led conferences.

Could you use some of these writing folder forms with your students? Are there ways you might modify them for your class? How will you introduce each form and concept to your students? The writing folder forms provide a practical way to help students document their growth as writers.

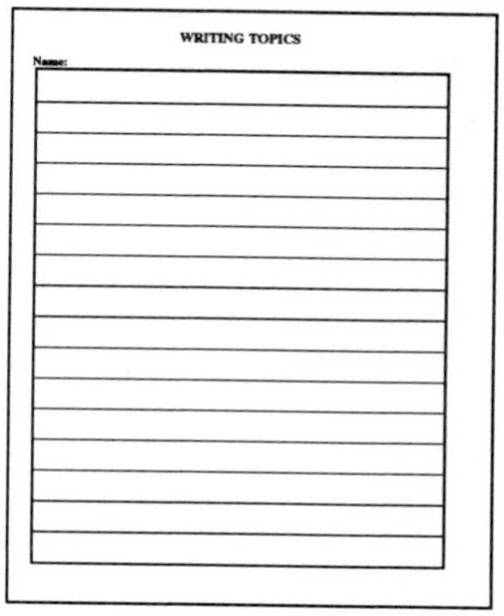

Form 7.1: Writing Topics

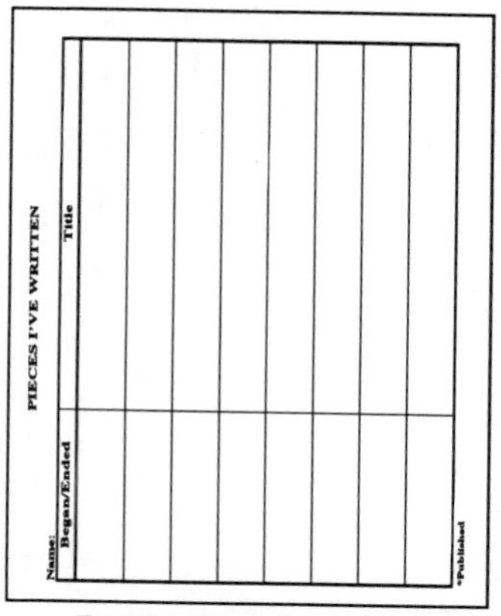

Form 7.2: Pieces I've Written

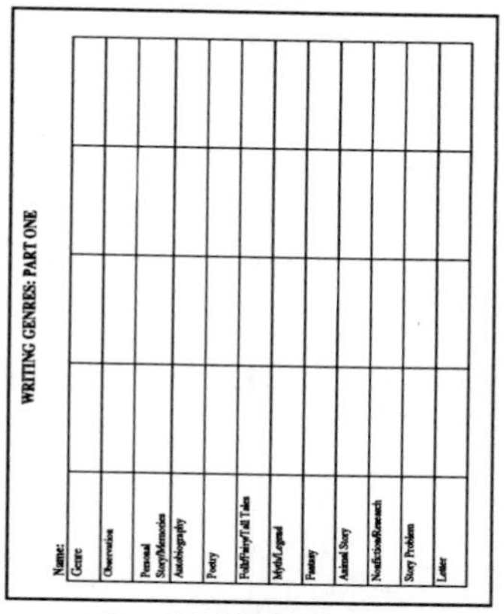

Form 7.3: Writing Genres

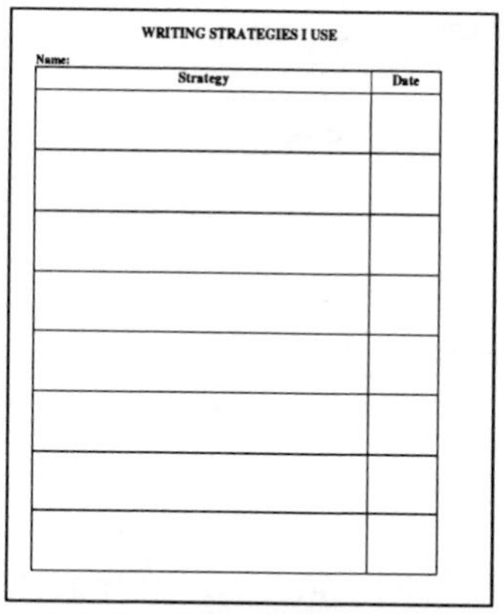

Form 7.4: Writing Strategies I Use

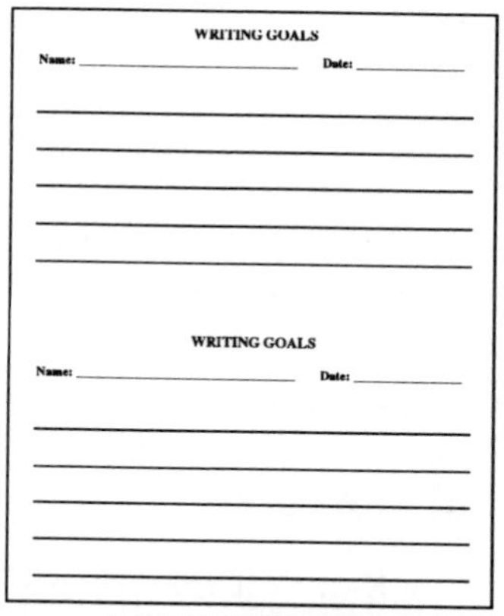

Form 7.5: Writing Goals

Writing Conference Forms

In *The Art of Teaching Writing* (1986), Lucy Calkins claims that "Teacher-student conferences are at the heart of teaching writing; it is through them that students learn to interact with their own writing" (p. 21). Teaching individual children within the context of their own writing can be effective and powerful. Learning to confer effectively with students takes practice and a great deal of intuition. You must have a good grasp of the stages of writing development in order to build on each child's strengths. It's also important to understand the specific characteristics of quality writing and the revision strategies that will help students along the path to effective writing.

The writing continuum, which will be described more fully in Chapter 11, provides a guide for writing development. Although we will discuss the continuum more fully in Chapter 11, we wanted to mention it here, since many of the writing assessment forms use the terminology and developmental progress from the continuum. Here in Figure 7.1 are a list of the ten stages on both the writing and reading continuum.

Preconventional
Emerging
Developing
Beginning
Expanding
Bridging
Fluent
Proficient
Connecting
Independent

Figure 7.1: Continuum Stages

Of course, no child's behaviors fall neatly into one stage, but rather in a range of two or three stages. The writing assessment forms we describe in this chapter can provide you with the information necessary to complete the writing continuum.

6. Anecdotal Notes

When Lisa Norwick taught intermediate students, she was able to take a few anecdotal notes each day during writing workshop. As mentioned in Chapter 4, she found that her observations were more meaningful when she had a specific focus for anecdotal notes. Her assessment aligns with evaluation since her list of focus questions for writing (Form 7.6.) match the descriptors on the writing continuum. We've provided a list of Focus Questions for Anecdotal Notes for writing at the primary level (Form 7.6A) and intermediate level (Form 7.6B). Lisa's anecdotal notes also provide a bridge between her instruction and assessment. For instance, if she has just introduced webbing as a pre-writing strategy, she can use her anecdotal notes to record instances when students use webs independently to organize their ideas.

In the primary grades, Lisa found it was more challenging to take anecdotal notes during writing time. Instead, each afternoon after school, Lisa looks at the writing folders of two students and takes a few anecdotal notes. She finds that when she builds this daily check into her routine, she doesn't end up toting twenty-five journals home before report cards. As she glances through the two children's writing folders, she can record new learning on her "Post-it" notes and jot down notes to help her plan instruction.

7. Writing Observations

Roz Duthie created the Writing Observations sheet (Form 7.7) for taking anecdotal notes as she confers with her first graders during writing workshop or when students share their writing during author's chair. She writes the child's name and date, then jots down information about the child's writing process and products. Roz also records goals for each child. She has found it helpful to note whether or not the student takes risks and is on task during writing time. Roz keeps these forms on a separate writing clipboard.

8. Writing Conversations

Patti Kamber on Bainbridge Island asks her fifth graders to complete the Writing Conversations sheet (Form 7.8A) before she meets with them for a writing conference. She asks students to think about both what's working well and areas of concern. Students note what they have learned and what they will do next. These questions help students prepare for upcoming writing conferences. Students save the completed forms in their writing folders.

Patti fills out her version of the Writing Conversations form (Form 7.8B) during the actual writing conference. She uses the first column when students are in the planning stages for a new piece. She jots down notes in the second column when students share drafts with her. When students are ready to publish their writing, Patti writes their answers to questions in the last column. The conversations provide her with information about individual students, directions for instruction, and data for evaluation.

9. Writing Celebration

As parents, wouldn't you like to hear more often about what your son or daughter is learning? Wouldn't you be thrilled with an occasional personal note celebrating a breakthrough or progress? The Writing Celebration form (Form 7.9) was designed for teachers to periodically to share information about student writing growth with families. This half-page form provides just enough room for you to note the title of the piece and make one or two comments. For example, you might comment about a student's use of vivid language, similes, or revision strategies in a particular piece of writing. Julie Ledford, a fourth-grade teacher, at Brighton School in Lynnwood, Washington, wrote the following Writing Celebration note for one of her students:

> Laura has written a fantastically creative story! She has used strong verbs and lots of dialogue to add interest and variety to her story. Also, she volunteered to publish it at home and did an outstanding job. Congratulations!

Since student writing is often kept at school, this form provides parents with an occasional peek at their child's writing growth and changes. You might want to write the students' names on the forms ahead of time and keep them with your writing clipboard or writing conference forms. A reasonable goal might be to send a Writing Celebration note home for each child once during each grading period.

Whenever students in Lisa Norwick's classroom publish a piece of writing, she makes a copy and sends it home to their parents. You could send home the published writing, along with the Writing Celebration form. Which of these writing conference forms that we've described might work in your classroom?

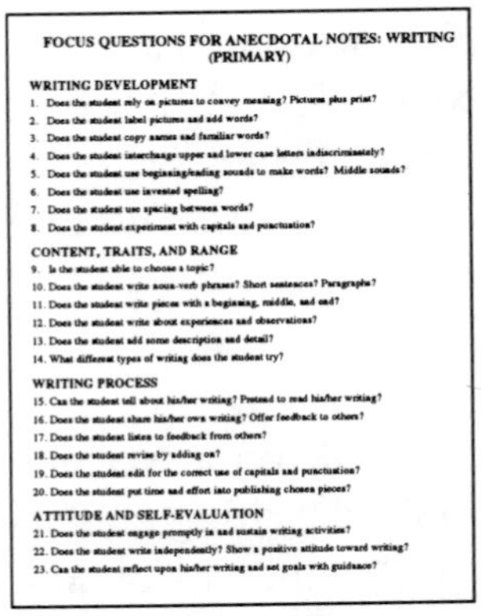
FOCUS QUESTIONS FOR ANECDOTAL NOTES: WRITING (PRIMARY)

Form 7.6: Focus Questions for Anecdotal Notes

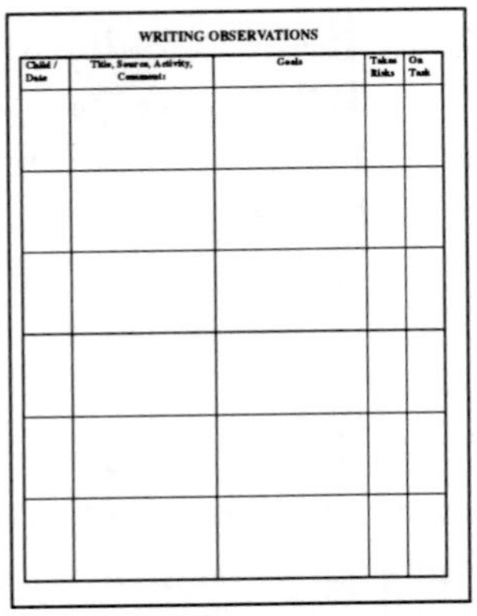
WRITING OBSERVATIONS

Form 7.7: Writing Observations

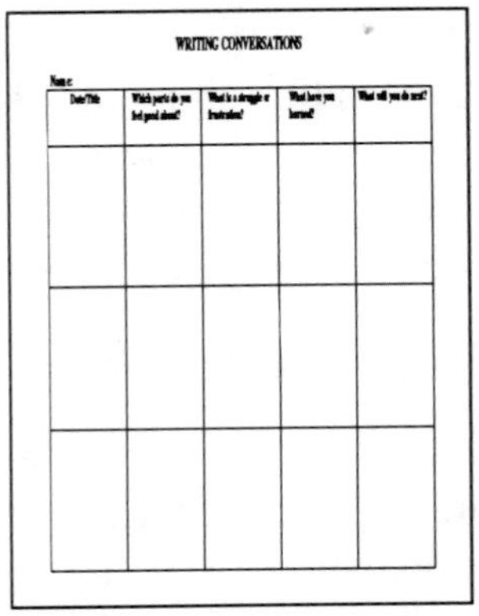
WRITING CONVERSATIONS

Form 7.8: Writing Conversations

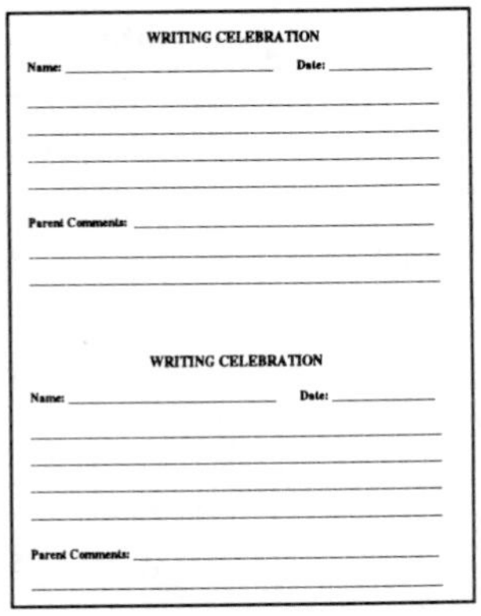
WRITING CELEBRATION

Form 7.9: Writing Celebration

Section Two: Assessing Writing Process

With a room full of students all at various stages in the writing process writing on different topics, how can you keep track of each child's growth and needs? In this section, we'll talk about some practical ways to assess the writing process, including revising and editing.

1. Status of the Class

In her landmark book, *In the Middle* (1987, 1998), Nancie Atwell describes a reading/writing workshop approach in junior high. Within a predictable structure, students become engaged as members of a reading/writing community. She developed a technique called "status of the class." She places a form on her clipboard with the students' names listed down the left-hand side. Her form has five columns, one for each day of the week. Each day she begins writing workshop by calling out students' names. They tell her the titles of pieces they're working on and where they are in the writing process. She uses a key to note whether students are drafting, prewriting, meeting with a peer for a conference, or doing a final edit. This technique takes about five minutes and launches students for the day with a clear purpose and plan.

Cindy Fulton adapted this technique and modified the Status of the Class (Form 7.10) for use in her second-grade classroom. In Figure 7.2, you can see how she lists her students along the left-hand side and uses a key to indicate what each child is doing each day. After her introductory focus lesson for the day, Cindy makes sure all her second graders have started writing. She then takes five minutes to make a sweep of the room, touching base with each student and noting where they are in the writing process. Who needs a conference with a peer? Who is ready to publish? Who is starting a new piece? Cindy also uses a circle to indicate when a student is off task. A quick glance at the week's chart can highlight consistent problems. She might decide to take more focused anecdotal notes on that child or make time for an individual conference. The status of the class helps Cindy decide which students to

STATUS OF THE CLASS

Student	Monday	Tuesday	Wednesday	Thursday	Friday
Allison	P	P	P/AC*	PP(TC)	PP
Anthony	PP(TC)	D1 (TC)	D1 *	R/E	E/PC
Bethany	D1	D1 *	D1 (TC*)	D1	R/E
Cari	D1	D2	R	R*	E
Garrett	P	P	P	AC* PP	PP/AC*
Heather	R (Adding on)	R (Another chapter!)	E	E/PC	P
Holden	E(TC*)	E/PC	P	P	P
Jaime	AC* PP	RR (rocks w/Josh)	PP/D1	D1	R/E
Jennifer	D1	Absent	Absent	D1	R/E
Jordan	P/AC*	PP/(TC)	D1/R	E/PC	P
Josh	PP	PP/D1	D1/(TC)	D1	R/E/P
Julia	AC*(TC)	RR (rocks w/Josh)	PP/D1	D1	R/E
Karla	RR	RR/(TC)	RR/PP	PP/D1	D1/(TC)
Kindra	D1	D1	D1 (needs TC)	D1 (TC)	R/E
Loren	D2	D2	R/E/P	P	Absent
Matthew	D1	D1	D1/R/E	P	P
Marisha	P	AC*/PP	PP	D1	D1
Marika	D1	D2	D2	R	R*
Nathaniel	P	AC*/PP	PP	D1	D1
Nicholas	RR (whales)	RR (whales)	PP(TC)	PP	D1
Patrick	D2	D2	R/E	P	AC*
Ryan	RR/PP	PP	D1	D1(TC)	D2
Sara	AC *	PP	RR	RR(TC)	D1
Steven	PP	D1	D2	D2 (needs TC)	R(TC)

PP = Pre-planning
D1 = First Draft
D2 = Later Drafts
R = Revision
E = Editing
RR = Reading/Researching
P = Publishing
TC = Teacher Conference
PC = Peer Conference
AC = Author's Chair
* = See Anecdotal Notes
◯ = Off-task Behavior

Figure 7.2: Sample Status of the Class

confer with that day. She may also find a few children wrestling with similar problems and pull them together for a small group focus lesson. Cindy can also see which students are ready to share their writing during author's chair.

2. Writing Process Chart

When Melissa Breen, a special education teacher in San Francisco, introduces the writing process to her fifth graders, they construct a wall chart to depict each step. As she and the students discuss each phase of the process (pre-writing, drafting, revising, editing, and publishing), Melissa gains an overview of what her students understand about writing. Working in small groups, the students add small drawings for each stage on the chart. The drawings are displayed and used in the classroom all year.

Each day, at the beginning of writing workshop, Melissa gives students a "Post-it" note. On it they record their name, the date, and the title of their current piece of writing. Children then place the "Post-it" note in the appropriate row on the chart. During the week, when students move to a new stage during writing workshop, they simply move their sticky note. By glancing at the chart, Melissa can easily ascertain which students are at each stage in the writing process and who might be ready for a writing conference. At the end of writing workshop each Friday, Melissa asks students to remove their "Post-it" notes from the chart and write on the "Post-it" note where they are in the writing process. Melissa then adds these brief notes to each student's anecdotal grid in her Teacher Notebook.

Julie Ledford uses a variation of this idea in her fourth grade classroom at Brighton School in Lynwood, Washington. Each child's name is written on a magnet. Julie uses tape on her metal cabinet to form seven columns: pre-write, draft, student conference, revise, edit, teacher conference, and publish. Students all begin with their magnet in the pre-writing column and move their magnets as they move through the writing process. At a glance, Julie can see who is ready to confer, edit, or publish their writing (Figure 7.3).

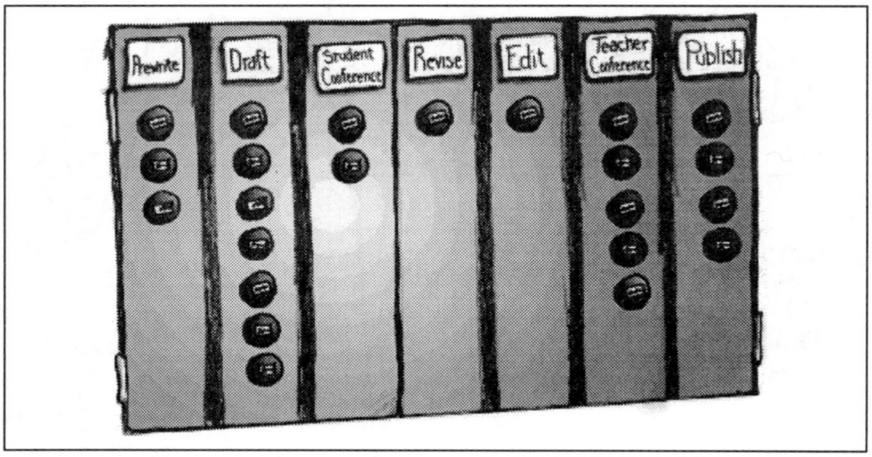

Figure 7.3: Writing Process Chart

3. Pre-writing

Jan Peacoe, on Bainbridge Island, Washington learned the value of talking with students about their writing strategies several years ago. While she was listening to Michael read aloud from *Mossflower* (Jacques, 1988), Jan scanned the room. She saw another student, Ralph, with paper and pencil in front of him, staring off into space. Thinking Ralph's mind was at recess or elsewhere, she gently but firmly asked him to get back to work. He said, defensively, "But I am working! Do you want to hear what I am doing? I'm listening to Michael read and noticing how the author is describing that scene. I'm trying to figure out how I can use words like that in my story." A great portion of learning is underground and invisible; how lucky we are when we catch glimpses of children's connections and insights.

Megan Sloan often uses drama as a form of pre-writing with her multiage primary students in Snohomish, Washington. She has found that children who engage in story theatre, reader's theatre, role-play, or creative drama have a great deal to draw from when they sit down to write. Listening, talking, drawing, drama, and even dance can provide the scaffolding necessary to begin writing. It's also important to find topics and audiences that engage students. You need to help them broaden their topic horizons beyond writing about their summer, pets, trips, and family. At the same time, students must learn to narrow their topics and see how moments can become stories and poems. You can furnish powerful examples by using read-alouds and your own writing. In addition, as students share their writing, they are providing models for each other. Introducing techniques like brainstorming, webbing, and free writing can also help students. We can assess students' strategies by taking anecdotal notes as they talk about pre-writing during class discussions, author's chair, focus lessons, and individual conferences. We've included a sample list of pre-writing ideas in Figure 7.4, but encourage you to develop your own list with your students. What else might you add?

Brainstorm	Use a Venn diagram
Web	Take Notes
Talk	Read
Draw	Outline
Look at examples	Think quietly
Doodle	Act it out

Figure 7.4: Pre-writing Ideas

4. Drafting

Most young children write only single drafts. A second draft for many of these young writers may entail simply re-copying the first version more neatly. However, as students develop as writers and develop a sense of audience, they begin to craft their writing through multiple drafts.

Each writer has a unique approach to drafting. For example, in Cynthia Ruptic's classroom, Johanna begins with brilliantly colored pictures about a topic. Like children's author Allen Say, she thinks visually. As she writes, she constantly refers back to her artwork to evoke vivid, descriptive language.

Karin expresses her ideas initially in rough form with no paragraphs or sequence. Next, she goes back and uses a set of colored highlighters to mark the sentences that belong together. She then re-shapes them into another draft with paragraphs that flow together in a logical sequence. Later, she adds details and effective language to her draft by using arrows and circles.

Tatsuhiko uses his reading as a basis for writing nonfiction pieces. For instance, when he wrote a book about insects, he read for a period of time, paused to think, then read some more. Then he put the book aside and drafted his ideas on paper. He returned to several books to search for specific information to add to his draft. He retains a logical ordering of ideas in his head and does very little revision.

As you can see from these three examples, drafting and revision are inextricably linked. Your anecdotal notes can help capture each writer's method of composing. One effective teaching technique is to show students multiple drafts from your own writing, from people who write in the business world, as well as from published authors. It's fascinating for students to see how a text (like this book!) evolves through multiple versions.

5. Feedback and Advice

In first grade, it's quite challenging to have students give constructive feedback to each other. Christy Clausen devised a very tangible way to foster productive peer conferences with her young writers. The conference table has a laminated sign that reads, "You said . . ." and "I like . . ." At the beginning of the year, she asks two students to model for the class how to give feedback to another writer. One student reads, then the partner reflects back the content of the writing and makes one or two positive comments, then they reverse roles. In the fall, Christy is there to nudge and encourage these early forays into peer conferencing. As the year progresses, the response groups meet without Christy.

How often do you hear students say at author's chair, "I liked your story," over and over again? In Jan and Jerry Miller's multiage primary classrooms in Lacey, Washington, students give more specific feedback to each other at author's chair by using the following statements:

"I remember . . ."

"I noticed . . ."

"I wondered . . ."

Students then take the suggestions of their peers and incorporate them into their goals the next day for writing workshop. These prompts and lots of modeling help students move away from making vague comments to learning how to give specific and constructive feedback.

Even young students who are familiar with the writing process can meet independently with partners or small response groups to get feedback on their writing. Lisa Norwick's second-grade authors ask their audience for specific feedback on a particular aspect of writing before sharing a story or poem at author's chair. The comments and discussions encourage the children to think about criteria for quality writing on a daily basis.

For example, Ben shared his story about a trip to an amusement park with his family. He told the children that he wanted suggestions about word choice. He asked them to listen for the interesting words he used, as well as boring words he could replace. Ben's request helped focus the attention of the audience and enabled them to give specific feedback.

Cynthia Ruptic's intermediate students meet with partners or in small groups at the perimeter of the room. As the author reads a piece of writing, the listeners discuss the most effective parts of the work, raise questions, or make suggestions. Writers often weave the suggestions into their drafts, then return to the same people for further feedback. Some students immediately seek a writing partner when they have completed a piece of writing. Others are not ready for feedback until their second or third draft. Drafting and revision are recursive processes that will differ from writer to writer.

It's important that students learn at an early age that writing is not a solitary activity. Writers need feedback during the writing process in order to be sure that their writing communicates just what they intend to say. Once students learn how to give and accept constructive suggestions, they can begin to internalize the advice they hear from others.

6. Revising

All too often writing instruction and testing have focused on editing skills. As any writer will affirm, revision is far more difficult than editing. A secretary or word processor can help with editing; only the author can revise. Revision is about clarifying meaning. It's the process of trying to match what is in your heart and mind with what ends up on the paper. Whether we write a poem, a letter to the editor, a three-paragraph essay, or directions to a friend's house, our goal is to communicate clearly.

Writing is most effective when it is done for authentic purposes and audiences. Our challenge is to help students find real reasons to engage in the difficult but satisfying struggle to make their writing better. Children's author Mem Fox (1993) comments about her own writing: "The more I admire my potential readers, the more carefully I write and the more often I revise" (p. 9).

As we've worked with students on revision strategies, we've found the work by the Northwest Regional Educational Laboratory in Portland, Oregon (Culham and Spandel, 1998; Culham and Spandel, 1993; Spandel, 1994; Spandel and Stiggins, 1997) very valuable. These resources have been particularly helpful in teaching and assessing six traits of effective writing: ideas, organization, voice, word choice, sentence fluency, and conventions. We've provided information about their materials in the sections on Professional Growth and Recommended Readings at the end of this chapter.

Revision in the primary grades may simply mean adding a bit more to a story. For some first graders, just adding a word or two can be a significant step. Megan Sloan developed a Six-Trait Guide to Revision (Form 7.11A) based on the six-trait model. At the beginning of the year, she makes a version with only one or two revision questions. For instance, with her beginning writers, she might use the question, "Did you use any interesting words?" and have the students revisit their work for that specific quality. As she teaches revision techniques, Megan adds more questions to the Six-Trait Guide to Revision form. By the end of the year, many of her second graders are able to use the entire form. Remember learning how to play tennis? It's incredibly difficult to focus on your ball toss, the follow-through with your racquet, and your footing, all at once. In the same way, it's easier to focus on one writing trait at a time. Learning how to revise for specific elements helps students realize the qualities of powerful writing and the concrete steps they can take to strengthen their own work.

By second or third grade, students can begin to exchange "worn words" for more powerful ones and learn to organize their writing into a logical flow. As writers become more accomplished, they may talk with adults or other students, read their writing aloud, and make notes on drafts. Megan Sloan and her colleagues in Snohomish, Washington, Izi Loveluck and Denise Ohlson, created the Six-Trait Revision Checklist (Form 7.11B) to use with later primary or intermediate students. The top half of the form includes a checklist to help students revise for one specific writing trait. On the bottom half of the form, students revise for a writing trait with a partner. Depending on their confidence and competence, some students may complete the whole form, while others may use only the top half.

How would revision in third grade be different from revision in sixth grade? What types of revision strategies are developmentally appropriate in elementary school? Lisa Norwick found that revision was one of the hardest parts of the writing process to assess. She decided to make a form with the developmental progression of revision strategies, using the descriptors from the writing continuum. The Revision Checklist (Form 7.11C) begins with the early steps in revision, such as adding information and revising for clarity, building to more sophisticated strategies such as incorporating suggestions from others and revising for specific writing traits. This form would be quite helpful in assessing students' ability to revise their writing.

7. Revising and Editing

After students have revised their writing, they can switch gears and check for correct punctuation, grammar, and spelling. Your goals will change depending on the age and proficiency of your students. As you teach new skills, you can raise the level of expectations. In addition, having authentic purposes, real audiences, and genuine response helps students see the reason for revision. Mem Fox (1993) laments, "I wish I could discover what sorts of things my students care enough about to make them weep with worry as they try to get their writing right" (p. 8).

The next series of editing forms (Form 7.12A–D) were designed several years ago by Babs Brownell and Cynthia Ruptic when they taught a multiage primary classroom together on Bainbridge Island. The Revising and Editing Guidelines (Form 7.12A) could be used in the fall with primary students. The form is very simple, with only a few requirements. After discussing and modeling new skills, you can gradually increase your expectations. Form 7.12B was created for use in the winter and each successive form includes more sophisticated requirements. The final revising and editing version (Form 7.12C) could be used in the spring to reflect students' growing confidence and skills. We've included all three versions of the primary Revising and Editing Guidelines here, as well as a spring adaptation for intermediate students (From 7.12D). You could use the form on the CD-ROM to modify the forms for your particular group of students at different times during the year. Finally, we've added an editing checklist specific to writing nonfiction (Form 7.12E).

Lisa Norwick also created a Revising and Editing Checklist series for her second graders. At the beginning of the year, her students are primarily rereading their writing to make sure it's readable and makes sense. We've included a very basic fall and winter version (Form 7.13A and 7.13B) that helps students as they first learn to revise. During her focus lessons, Lisa and her class talk about writing traits and examine examples of quality writing. By spring, Lisa can incorporate the six traits on the Revising and Editing Checklist (Form 7.13C). She also "ups the ante" by including more editing skills on the form as she teaches students more about spelling and punctuation.

The idea of flexible editing forms came from Jan and Jerry Miller, teachers in Lacey, Washington. It makes sense to change your forms and expectations as your students develop as writers. Changing the content of a form as the year progresses helps bridge the gap between instruction and assessment. You can also give individual children different forms, depending on their levels of proficiency. We want to stress, however, that the vocabulary and strategies must be modeled and explained to students (sometimes over and over) before you can expect them to use these forms successfully and independently.

8. Publishing and Celebrating Writing

Writing this book was a challenging experience. We learned a great deal as we struggled to articulate our ideas. Editing the final galleys and seeing the book in print was a joyful experience for all of us. However, the highlight has been hearing from readers, especially the specifics of which ideas and forms have been most helpful. Response is the reward that comes from sharing our writing. We need to provide our students with authentic audiences so that they can experience the genuine thrill that comes when listeners and readers respond to their writing.

Do you remember writing to pen pals in elementary school? It was fun to get their school picture and first letter, but once you wrote your response, it usually took months to receive a reply. Now there are many opportunities for children to share their writing through the Internet. Cynthia Ruptic's students in Osaka wrote a series of reports about Japanese culture that were published on Scholastic's Kid Network on the Internet. They received questions and comments from students all over the world. Cynthia feels that the response from this project did more to spark excitement about writing than any other activity in all her years of teaching. The key was having a real purpose and audience for writing, seeing their work published and receiving an immediate response from readers. All it takes is one such experience and students become what Frank Smith (1988) calls "a member of the literacy club."

9. Writing Process Form

Do you use a web or an outline before you write a paper, or do you just plunge in? Do you prefer drafting on paper or on the computer? Do you prefer oral or written feedback? We developed the Writing Process Evaluation form (Form 7.14) so students can record their strategies for each stage of the writing process that we've described in the last few pages. You might want to use this form once each grading period. Students' responses will become more sophisticated as they internalize the strategies you've presented during focus lessons. The Writing Process Evaluation form would also be helpful for filling out the writing process strand on the continuum and setting writing goals.

Which of the forms or ideas we've described would best help you assess your students' understanding and use of the writing process?

Form 7.10: Status of the Class

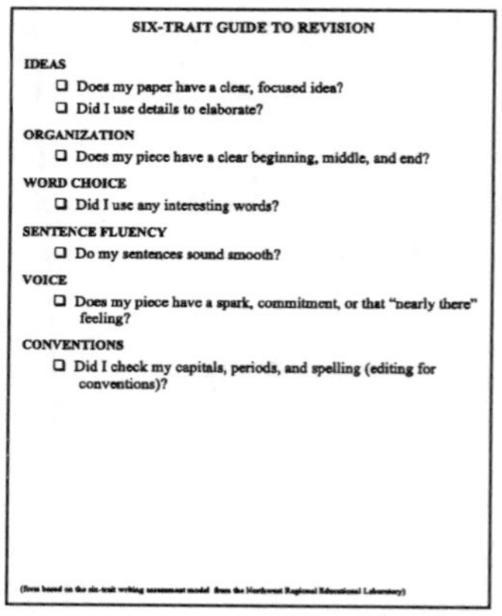

Form 7.11: Six-Trait Guide to Revision

Writing Process
Wall Chart
(no form)

No Form: Writing Processing Wall Chart

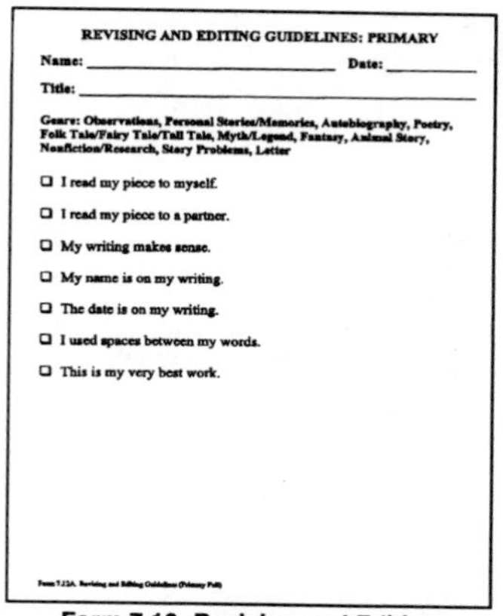

REVISING AND EDITING GUIDELINES: PRIMARY

Name: ______________ Date: ________

Title: ______________

Genre: Observations, Personal Stories/Memories, Autobiography, Poetry, Folk Tale/Fairy Tale/Tall Tale, Myth/Legend, Fantasy, Animal Story, Nonfiction/Research, Story Problems, Letter

- ❑ I read my piece to myself.
- ❑ I read my piece to a partner.
- ❑ My writing makes sense.
- ❑ My name is on my writing.
- ❑ The date is on my writing.
- ❑ I used spaces between my words.
- ❑ This is my very best work.

Form 7.12: Revising and Editing Guidelines

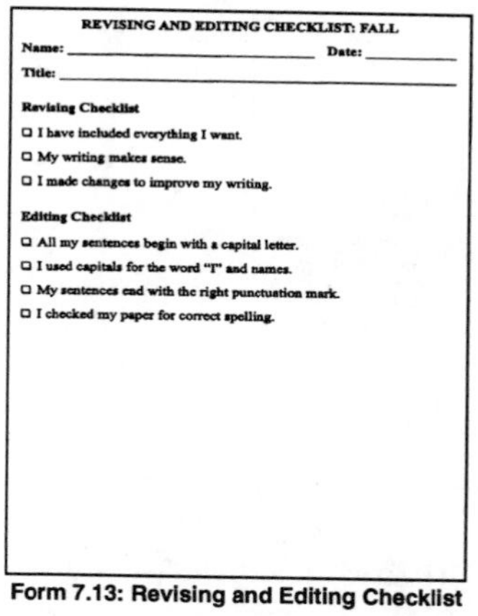

REVISING AND EDITING CHECKLIST: FALL

Name: ______________ Date: ________

Title: ______________

Revising Checklist

- ❑ I have included everything I want.
- ❑ My writing makes sense.
- ❑ I made changes to improve my writing.

Editing Checklist

- ❑ All my sentences begin with a capital letter.
- ❑ I used capitals for the word "I" and names.
- ❑ My sentences end with the right punctuation mark.
- ❑ I checked my paper for correct spelling.

Form 7.13: Revising and Editing Checklist

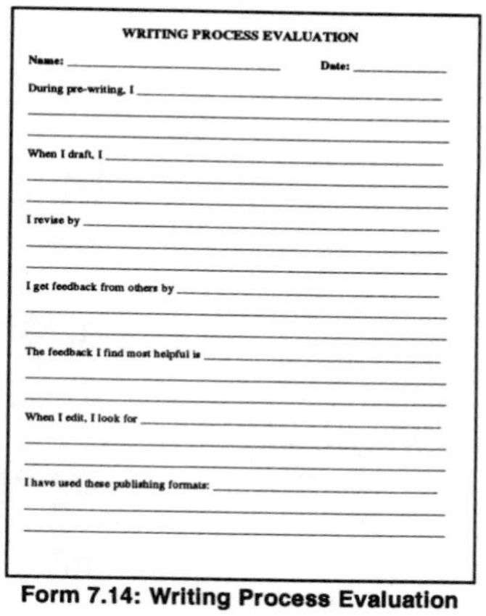

WRITING PROCESS EVALUATION

Name: ______________ Date: ________

During pre-writing, I ______________

When I draft, I ______________

I revise by ______________

I get feedback from others by ______________

The feedback I find most helpful is ______________

When I edit, I look for ______________

I have used these publishing formats: ______________

Form 7.14: Writing Process Evaluation

Section Three: Self-Evaluation

1. "Fix-it" Strategy

A child's writing growth is very dramatic in the elementary grades. One simple technique that demonstrates writing growth is the "Fix-it" strategy. Photocopy or save one writing sample from each of your students early in the fall. Be sure to date the samples and store them where you can find them easily. Lisa Norwick finds it helpful to tuck the fall sample into a clear acetate slip-sheet in her Teacher Notebook. If your students keep a writing folder or writer's notebook, you may want to let them select a piece that shows who they are as writers in the fall.

During individual or small group writing conferences in the spring, show students their writing sample from the fall. Tell them, "You wrote this quite a while ago. Show me what you've learned since then." Students can write on the original draft or rewrite the piece, incorporating all the new strategies and skills they've learned over the year. You could also place the two pieces of writing side by side and ask students to write a brief reflection about what they notice.

We've included a "Fix-it" sample from one of Lisa Norwick's third-grade students. In September, Lisa's students each wrote a paragraph on a topic about which they were an "expert." Some students wrote about skateboarding, sports, or taking care of younger brothers and sisters. T. J. wrote the following paragraph in September:

> Me and my mom and dad talked about it. And I took my first class, it was fun. Then I practiced and practiced. What did I do? I made it to the fifth annual championship. I did not win. But I felt good.

When Lisa handed this piece back to T. J. in May, he rolled his eyes and exclaimed with disgust, "I didn't even have a topic sentence! People wouldn't even know what I was talking about!" Here are the changes T. J. made to the sample from the fall (Figure 7.5):

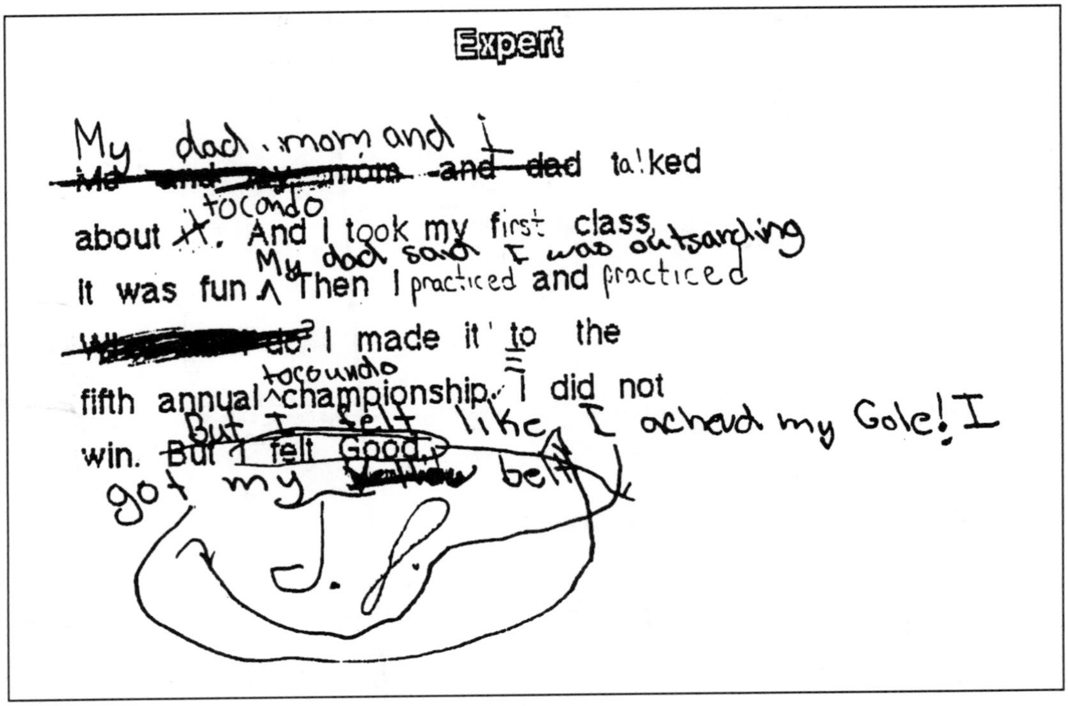

Figure 7.5: "Fix-it" Changes

> My dad, mom and I talked about Taekwondo. And I took my first class, it was fun. My dad said I was outstanding. Then I practiced and practiced. I made it to the fifth annual Taekwondo championship. I did not win. But I felt like I achieved my goal! I got my yellow belt. I felt good.

What are the differences in the two examples? In the second version, T. J. now has a clear topic and his grammar and punctuation are better. His organization and sentence fluency have improved. He varies his sentence structure, includes more details, and his writing has more voice. Some of these changes can be attributed to maturation; however, many can be traced directly to Lisa's focus lessons on specific writing traits. We transcribed these examples so you could see the changes more clearly. Most teachers simply save or photocopy a writing sample from the fall and have students mark their changes directly on the fall copy or rewrite the piece by hand.

Cindy Fulton used a variation of this technique with her first graders. In the spring, she asked if Ingrid would be willing to help with a focus lesson. They made an overhead of one of Ingrid's stories from the beginning of the year. Ingrid then told the class what changes she would make if she were writing the first piece now, such as adding detail or more information, using different words, and correcting the spelling and punctuation. Cindy marked the changes with a pen on the overhead as they talked. Next, Cindy gave each student a "Post-it" note to mark a writing piece from the fall. The students then worked on their rewrites for several days in order to show how much they had learned about writing. They took the original fall sample and the

"Fix-it" revision home to show their families as part of the end-of-the-year celebration.

There is no form for the "Fix-it" technique, so if you plan to use this assessment strategy, you might want to note it on your Organizational Grid (Form 3.2).

2. Checklists

In this chapter, we've discussed several ways to examine writing growth. What about writing quality? What is an effective poem in fifth grade? What does a persuasive letter look like in third grade? Many teachers and students have developed specific criteria for writing. Some are simple checklists, while others are more formal rubrics.

Checklists can be used for authentic assessment when they specify the criteria to be evaluated. Students can hold the targets in mind as they work on a project. The descriptors are very specific to a writing project or genre. Rather than time-consuming narrative feedback, checklists give students important specific feedback on each aspect of a project.

Cynthia Ruptic and her students developed a checklist specific to folktales. As her third and fourth graders read folktales from around the world, they noticed certain common elements. At a class meeting, they constructed a chart listing the elements of folktales. They identified stock characters (villains, witches, heroes), traditional settings (forests, villages), and phrases such as "once upon a time" and "long, long ago." When it came time to write their own folktales, Cynthia constructed the Folktale Checklist (Form 7.15) from their chart of characteristics. They added literary conventions (such as punctuation, paragraphing), as well as elements specific to folktales. They used the checklists as a tool for pre-writing and later for revision. Near the end of the process, the class constructed a rubric (Form 7.16) based on their checklist. Cynthia and her students used this rubric for self-evaluation. When each folktale was published in book form, readers also used the rubric to evaluate each tale.

3. Rubrics

Checklists and rubrics clarify expectations and guide students' writing, since the criteria for evaluation are spelled out before a project begins. In addition, during class discussions, you can discover if students are confused about specific criteria. You will then have to decide if the criteria should be deleted, modified, or further support provided. Expectations are clear since everyone has agreed upon the targets. Rubrics have a higher level of specificity than checklists, since the focus is on quality. There are two types of rubrics: holistic and analytic. Holistic rubrics are used to provide a single score for a finished product. Holistic assessment often involves giving students a writing prompt and then assigning papers one overall score on a scale of 1–3, 1–4, or 1–5. Some rubrics include four levels of proficiency: novice, apprentice, practitioner, and expert (Figure 7.6). Of course, these levels and descriptions could be applied to rubrics in any content area.

Novice

The novice is beginning to work with the skill.
There is inconsistency in form, structure, or parts.
The novice will grow with continued practice and effort.

Apprentice

The apprentice has some experience with the skill.
There are some errors in form, structure, or parts.
The apprentice will become a practitioner with consistent effort.

Practitioner

The practitioner demonstrates knowledge of the skill.
There are fewer errors in form, structure, or parts.
The practitioner will become an expert with continued effort.

Expert

The expert demonstrates a high level of skill.
The form, structure, and parts are accurately done.
The expert demonstrates greater complexity and depth.

Figure 7.6: Rubric Levels

Analytic rubrics, on the other hand, rate specific aspects of a piece of writing, according to a predetermined set of standards. For instance, a report might receive scores for each of the following four categories: organization, content, mechanics, and creativity. Analytic rubrics include a scale, along with descriptors for each level of proficiency.

How do you determine the level of a student's performance? In assessment workshops, Grant Wiggins (1993) suggests that we ask, "What would an expert performance look like?" By starting with exemplary work, students can then define the other levels. It's important to be as specific as possible so that students can clearly differentiate between levels of proficiency. Without defining the specific criteria, the rubric becomes subjective and loses its power.

Both holistic and analytic rubrics can be used to evaluate writing. Chapter 6 in *Windows into Literacy* (Rhodes & Shanklin, 1993) provides a helpful description of these two techniques as they are used for large-scale analysis of writing. Both types of rubrics focus solely on written *products*. It's important to balance this perspective with information about a student's writing *processes* and *attitudes*. A rubric provides a framework for examining finished products. It is simply one piece of a well-rounded assessment program. When teachers begin using rubrics, they generally start in one area of the curriculum and build a level of comfort and confidence before moving on to another area.

Rubrics can be a helpful starting point for young writers to begin examining the qualities of effective writing. We do worry, however, about applying rubrics too heavily with young learners at a time when we're trying to foster fluency and a positive attitude toward writing. Too much emphasis on standards can inhibit risk-taking, confidence, and creativity. Some primary teachers, therefore, provide samples and talk about criteria, but have the students simply evaluate their own work without giving a written score.

Another problem occurs when rubrics are over-used with intermediate students. It's easy to become buried in an ever-increasing pile of paperwork. The key is to use rubrics thoughtfully and sparingly as one piece of your assessment program, perhaps as a way to evaluate only major projects.

We've found that more proficient writers appreciate clear criteria as well as focused and specific feedback on their work. One of the most beneficial aspects to developing scoring criteria is that it nudges you to think more deeply about your assignments. What are you trying to teach? What are the most important features of a particular type of writing? In addition, there are several other advantages. Rubrics can:

- support and enhance student learning
- help students and teachers clarify the purpose of a task or activity
- clarify targets or goals
- provide a focus for instruction
- keep evaluation specific and measurable
- provide guidelines for peer evaluation
- provide guidelines for self-evaluation and goal setting
- involve students in identifying the characteristics of quality writing

Rubrics can also be helpful if you are required to give letter grades at your school. When Lisa taught at a school where grades were required, she and her class decided that one-third of their grade would be based on growth over time. Students could demonstrate growth with their writing folder forms, "Fix-it" pieces, as well as other writing samples and reflections from their portfolios. Another third of their grade was based on how well the student used his/her class time. Lisa used her anecdotal notes (Form 4.1), the Status of the Class (Form 7.10), and the student's Goals (Form 7.5) to assess productivity and attitude. The final third of the students' grade was based on one or two selected writing samples. Lisa had different criteria for the two pieces each quarter, depending on the focus for the quarter. For instance, in the fall Lisa might require students to submit one personal narrative and one poem for evaluation. The next quarter she might require a persuasive piece and a nonfiction report. Each piece submitted was evaluated based on a rubric the class developed for the specific type of writing. Expectations were clear and students had a voice in the evaluation process since they helped create the rubric and set the criteria for grading.

Let's take a closer look at how you can develop specific rubrics, whether in writing or in other content areas. First, you must decide the primary focus for the project or assignment. Next, you must explain the targets and teach the necessary skills to your students. Remember waiting to get back your first paper from a college class, having no idea if you were on track or way off base? Letting students know the goals ahead of time is a radical change from traditional evaluation. If you've collected student samples from previous years, you can show examples in order to make the targets specific and tangible. During writing workshop, you can reinforce target points through focus lessons and individual conferences. We've included a series of rubrics in the Appendix from several teachers.

Trilby Cohen, Heidi Hanson, and Melissa Sargent, a team of second-grade teachers at Syre Elementary in Shoreline, Washington, have created a very simple set of rubrics that can be used with primary students. They developed their rubrics after seeing similar ones at Jackson Elementary in Everett, Washington. As the teachers and students talk about a particular type of writing, the class generates the criteria for each rubric. Of course, this means the rubrics will change each year. Form 7.17A is a generic primary rubric that could be applied to any content or project. The next versions are used to help young students focus on the quality of their Drawing (Form 7.17B), Fiction (Form 7.17C), and Nonfiction (Form 7.17D) writing. The teachers explain the rubric descriptors as they begin a new assignment and refer to concepts as students are working. These teachers feel strongly that the form should *not* be used as a grading sheet. These rubrics are simply posted in the room as a guide for students beginning their work or getting ready to present a project. The class also creates rubrics for the specific projects, such as insect reports. The class has developed a "kid language" version of the rubric levels: 4 = Wow! Terrific! 3 = You've Got It! 2 = Not Yet, and 1 = Try Again (Figure 7.7). You could also use the more conventional levels (Above Standards, At Standards, Below Standards, and Far Below Standards).

Lisa Norwick and her third/fourth graders created three more extensive writing rubrics: one for fiction (Form 7.17E), one for poetry (Form 7.17F), and one for nonfiction (Form 7.17G). Lisa first immerses the students in a genre by reading examples for several weeks. Next, the class lists key characteristics of that specific form of writing. The list is modified as the students continue to read and write. Eventually the class constructs a rubric, organized around the six writing traits. Lisa ties her focus lessons directly to these traits and rubrics. Students keep the criteria in mind as they write and revise their writing, then use the rubric to self-evaluate their work. Lisa uses these rubrics sparingly; her emphasis is on exploring new genres and building fluency. However, quality examples and discussions about the traits of good writing give students a handle on how to improve their own writing.

Let's look at an example of how a rubric works in a fifth-grade classroom. Sandi Sater's students on Bainbridge Island use a rubric to evaluate most of their final projects. The scoring is very specific. For instance, Claire did an excellent job meeting the descriptive paragraph criteria, but did not do as well at creating a well-

NONFICTION RUBRIC

4 WOW! TERRIFIC!	• All sentences written in own words • Pictures add new facets to writing • Exceptional printing and drawings • Capitals and periods used correctly • Correct spelling in final draft
3 You've Got It!	• Most sentences written in own words • All the pictures match the information • Neat printing and drawing • Capitals and periods used correctly most of the time • Most of the spelling in final draft is correct
2 Not Yet	• Few sentences written in own words • Few pictures match the information • Printing and drawings are often incomplete or messy • Capitals and periods used incorrectly • Many spelling errors
1 Try Again!	• Few sentences written • Pictures don't match the information • Printing and drawings are incomplete or messy • No capitals or periods • Many spelling errors

Figure 7.7: Primary Nonfiction Rubric

edited finished product. During their evaluation conference, Sandi talked about ways to help Claire with editing on her next writing activity. After the conference, Claire wrote a brief reflective note about her next goal and what she had learned while completing this project.

One of the reasons for using rubrics is to enable students to evaluate their own work. During the first trimester in Sandi's classroom, she provides sample rubrics she has created and explains how she developed them. By the second trimester, her students are able to give Sandi input on the rubrics and begin to assess their own finished work. Students can design their own rubrics by the end of the year as they develop self-assessment strategies.

Sandi also encourages her students to evaluate each other's work. For example, students may design a rubric for a project and have their partner fill out the scoring criteria. If students are doing an oral presentation, such as reader's theatre or poetry, peers can write comments that are given to the presenter. Needless to say, Sandi spends quite a bit of time up front talking about how to give helpful comments and suggestions rather than criticism.

All of the rubrics in this chapter were developed with input from students. Teachers anchored the rubrics with actual samples of student work from previous years. We hope our examples will provide the scaffolding for you to create your own rubrics with your class. Start slowly with one project or assignment. Exchange rubrics and anchor papers with colleagues. Creating rubrics gets easier with practice and is much more fun when developed collaboratively with colleagues.

Interesting discussions can ensue when students begin to examine the qualities of effective writing and apply that knowledge to their own work. The process of setting performance criteria with your students can also help you analyze your goals and priorities, whether in writing, reading, or other content areas as well. Patti Kamber, writes:

> Such discussions have helped me, as the teacher, to clarify instructional goals and expectations. Because students are part of the process, they feel more powerful and seem more motivated to make improvements in their work. At first, they seemed almost nervous about being allowed such responsibility. There were even a few children who thought I was not doing my job; that I should be the evaluator. A few teachers wondered if I was creating monsters, that children these days have too much power as it is. I believe that the criteria set to evaluate another person's work, however, should not be private information. In fact, the criteria should be clear, written in large letters, and open to public scrutiny. Helping students set the criteria for evaluation can show students how to improve their work and grow as learners.

How might you use the "Fix-it" technique, checklists, or rubrics? How will these tools help your students learn to evaluate the effectiveness of their own writing and set goals for their next steps as writers?

In the last three chapters, we've given you a smorgasbord of ways to assess spelling and writing growth. No one could possibly use more than a handful of these ideas. Think about when you go out to eat at a restaurant. No matter how hungry you are, you never order everything on the menu! Take a moment and look through the spelling and writing assessment tools we described. What two or three things do you want to add to your "plate" before we take a look at reading and content area assessment? You might want to record these on your Organizational Grid (Form 3.2) as you plan when you'll collect each piece of evidence.

As teachers, you will be collecting and analyzing a great deal of information about your students' writing. What about the students' role in the assessment process? With all the information we've included in this book, we decided to save ideas about student portfolios and how to involve students more deeply in reflection and goal setting for another book. In *Book Three: Student Portfolios*, we'll explain how your assessments and student reflection together can demonstrate writing growth more effectively and increase the power of your writing program. For now, you can involve students by using forms for the writing process, writing folders, conference checklists, the "Fix-it" technique, and rubrics. Remember; don't get so caught up in forms and tools that you lose sight of your students. After all, you are teaching writers rather than teaching writing. Your best assessment tool is to listen well. Lucy Calkins writes, "As writers, what we all need more than anything else in the world is listeners, listeners who will respond with silent empathy, with sighs of recognition, with laughter and tears and questions and stories of their own. Writers need to be heard" (1994, pp. 14–15).

Fix-it Strategy
(no form)

No Form: Fix-It Strategy

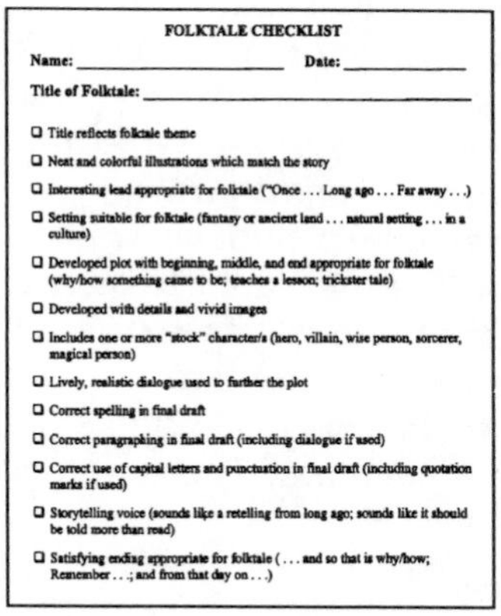

FOLKTALE CHECKLIST

Name: ______________ Date: ______________

Title of Folktale: ______________

- ☐ Title reflects folktale theme
- ☐ Neat and colorful illustrations which match the story
- ☐ Interesting lead appropriate for folktale ("Once . . . Long ago . . . Far away . . .)
- ☐ Setting suitable for folktale (fantasy or ancient land . . . natural setting . . . in a culture)
- ☐ Developed plot with beginning, middle, and end appropriate for folktale (why/how something came to be; teaches a lesson; trickster tale)
- ☐ Developed with details and vivid images
- ☐ Includes one or more "stock" character/s (hero, villain, wise person, sorcerer, magical person)
- ☐ Lively, realistic dialogue used to further the plot
- ☐ Correct spelling in final draft
- ☐ Correct paragraphing in final draft (including dialogue if used)
- ☐ Correct use of capital letters and punctuation in final draft (including quotation marks if used)
- ☐ Storytelling voice (sounds like a retelling from long ago; sounds like it should be told more than read)
- ☐ Satisfying ending appropriate for folktale (. . . and so that is why/how; Remember . . .; and from that day on . . .)

Form 7.15: Checklists Form

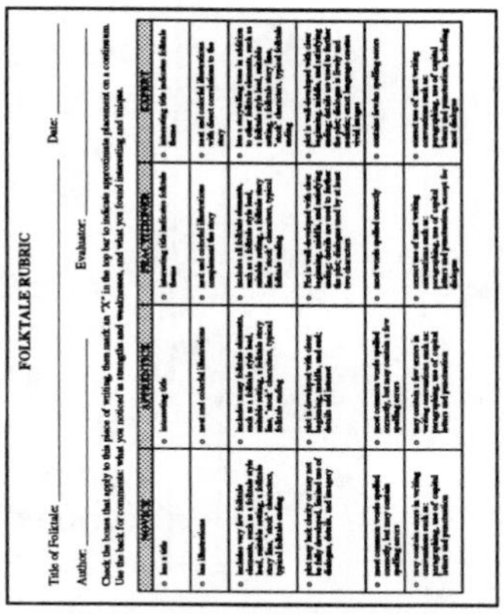

Form 7.16 and 7.17: Rubrics

Professional Growth

One of the most successful ways to explore writing is to write yourself. Many large cities have Writing Projects in which teachers write and share ideas during summer workshops. You might want to find out if there is a National Writing Project connected with a nearby university by calling 1-510-642-0963 or visiting their web site at http://www-gse.berkeley.edu/research/nwp/nwp.html. Another option is to form a writing group with a few friends or colleagues and meet on a regular basis. Almost everyone feels intimidated and self-conscious in the beginning, but by the third or fourth week, people's self-confidence and excitement begin to bloom. We are all writers!

Some of you may want to form a study group around one of the books about writing mentioned in this chapter. *The Art of Teaching Writing* (1994) by Lucy Calkins works well for this purpose. Teachers often comment, "I can't believe I stayed up to midnight reading a professional book!" Her book is well-written and practical.

Another suggestion is to do a case study of one student. It's amazing how much you'll learn by focusing on one child and how it will affect how you view all your students. In some schools, teachers meet on a regular basis and bring writing samples to share and discuss. They raise questions and share assessment tools and forms.

It takes a great deal of time to create focus lessons. In some schools, teachers use release time or meetings after school to create focus lessons tied to an aspect of six-trait writing. They connect the focus lesson with a specific children's book, note if it would be a single lesson or a series of lessons, and leave space for comments. Teachers then exchange focus lessons and try them out with their students. The partners add feedback, student samples, and extensions. They also add ideas for adaptations in other grades, connections to other content areas, and suggestions for other books to use. *After the End* (Lane, 1993), *Crafting a Life in Essay, Story, Poem* (Murray, 1996), and *What a Writer Needs* (Fletcher, 1993) are excellent resources for creating focus lessons on writing.

In order to help students write well, it's important to show them what good writers can do. You may want to start an ongoing hanging file of student writing that illustrates specific qualities in different genres. Of course, you'll need to ask the students for permission to share their work. You may want to organize your hanging files by the six traits. You could add student samples, your own writing, as well as examples from literature. These samples could be tied directly to the focus lessons you've created.

Recommended Readings about Writing

If you want one great book about the teaching of writing, we'd recommend Lucy Calkin's new edition of *The Art of Teaching Writing* (1994). Her chapters on each grade level ring true and her sections on the challenges of conferences, revision and editing are filled with practical ideas. Even if you own the 1986 edition, this new one is worth reading. Calkins continues to grow and her insights are deeper and more thoughtful. We'd also highly recommend Donald Graves' new book, *A Fresh Look at Writing* (1994).

There are two books that are a MUST for intermediate teachers. Barry Lane's *After The End* (1993) is about how to make revision and editing joyful in your classroom. His book is filled with practical suggestions for helping writers re-visit their work. Ralph Fletcher's book *What a Writer Needs* (1993), includes examples from his own published writing, student samples, and writing by children's authors that touch the heart. His chapters on the art of specificity, creating believable characters, and using unforgettable language are rich with ideas to use in your classroom. This book is a delight. A third book that provides helpful information about revision is *Helping Students Revise Their Writing*, by Marianne Tully (1996).

To learn more about writer's notebooks, we recommend Lucy Calkin's book, *Living Between the Lines* (1991) and Ralph Fletcher's *Breathing In, Breathing Out: Keeping a Writer's Notebook* (1996). These books present writing as a way of viewing the world, rather than merely a subject in school. Christine Duthie's book, *True Stories: Nonfiction Literacy in the Primary Classrom* (1996), is one of the only books about weaving nonfiction into your classroom. Her book is full of resources and classroom examples. If you read Georgia Heard's book *For the Good of the Earth and Sun* (1989), you will fall in love with teaching poetry. Her book is about how you have to marinate children in poetry so that they feel at home with the genre. She describes how she shares her passion for poetry with students of all ages.

The *Northwest Regional Educational Laboratory* in Portland, Oregon has developed some helpful materials for involving students in setting criteria and evaluating writing. You might want to call the Northwest Regional Educational Lab at 1-503-275-9519 or look at their web site at http://www.nwrel.org for more information about their books and training. Their books by Vicki Spandel, Ruth Culham, Richard Stiggins, and colleagues have been extremely helpful in teaching and assessing the six writing traits. Some of you might want to purchase their charts of the six writing traits to hang in your classroom.

Chapter 8

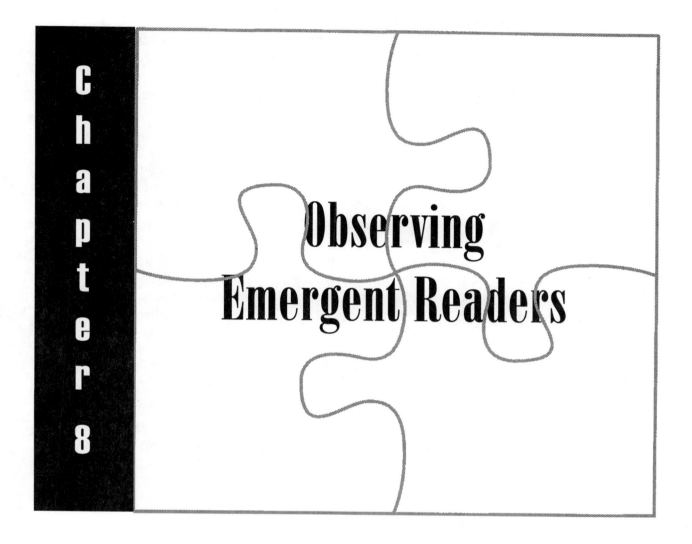

Observing Emergent Readers

In Linda Johnson's kindergarten class, Lianne and Sabrina take turns with the pointer as they follow the words to "Mary Wore Her Red Dress" while Charles and Patrick sprawl on the floor with the big book version of *The Napping House* (Wood, 1984). Chloe flips through the phone book in the home center and reads a number as she dials on the play phone. Which children are "pretending to read" and which ones are "really reading"? What we imagined thirty years ago as reading readiness is now understood as a continuum of approximation. Marie Clay (1993) notes:

> I strongly support the abandonment of the readiness concept in its old form. All children are ready to learn; it is the teachers who need to know how to create appropriate instruction for where each child is. To do this effectively, they need to observe a wide range of literacy behaviours throughout the first years of school. (p. 6)

Children's understanding of reading deepens with each interaction around print. This almost magical process, however, happens silently as children turn the pages of books. How much do children know about print and reading? What connections are they making between the stories and their own lives? What strategies do they use when they encounter unknown words? How are they growing as readers? Standardized tests for young children certainly can't reveal the answers to these questions. How can we observe and assess young readers in a meaningful, yet manageable and organized way?

Although we devoted an entire chapter to observing students, we wanted to reiterate the importance of taking anecdotal notes in the primary grades. One of the best ways to assess reading behaviors is to watch children during quiet reading time. Do they read the book from front to back? Can they point to the print? Do they choose familiar books that you have read aloud? Do they select nonfiction or fiction? Do they read alone or with a friend?

In many kindergarten and first-grade classrooms, teachers write songs and poems on large chart paper. As the teacher or a student follows with a pointer, the class chants along with these familiar texts as part of shared or guided reading instruction. When individual children choose to read these charts during quiet reading time, it's a perfect opportunity to take anecdotal notes. Some children happily wave the pointer down the lines while reciting the poem from memory, while others match each spoken word to the written text.

Another context for observing authentic reading is during writing workshop. As mentioned in Chapter 6, some children can only provide a general description of what they have written, while others can read a few words or even the whole text. The process of learning to read and write is so complex and mysterious that we can only catch small glimmers of the incredible intellectual connections that young children are making. Anecdotal notes can help us focus our observations and record our insights.

Early Literacy Development

Young learners are always searching for generalizations to help them make sense of their world. With repeated experiences, children's theories are confirmed, refined, or readjusted. For instance, a child who is given time to play in the bathtub with different kinds of objects begins to understand that some objects sink while others float. Even a very young child can begin to generalize about what objects will do in the water and make fairly reliable predictions about what will sink and what will float.

In a similar way, children begin to construct tentative theories of how written language works in their early explorations with reading, writing, and letter play. Generalizations are fortified with each language-learning experience. Their conversations and decisions reveal much about their stage of development. Children's development is also affected by their early introduction to reading and writing at home and at school.

For the past decade, Roz Duthie, a primary teacher on Bainbridge Island, Washington, has been fascinated by early literacy. She has observed that a child's generalizations about letter-sound relationships are indicative of early development in reading. In the United States, young children learn the names of the letters of the alphabet before being introduced to the sounds the letters represent. Roz suggests that it's important to recognize common cultural practices as you analyze children's reading and writing development. Preschoolers first learn the names of letters because parents often introduce letter play by teaching children the "alphabet song" and reading them alphabet books that emphasize letter names. Young children may play with magnetic letters on the refrigerator, draw letters (mostly illegible), and identify letters in environmental print ("Yes, that's a 'K' on the cereal box."). As children memorize all or most of the letter names, adults expect they will soon begin to identify letters in print as they labor to decipher the written word.

The next step along the path to reading is the recognition that a word is made up of letters and that letters represent particular sounds. This discovery is a necessary precursor to learning to read. Since children are such strong auditory learners in the early years, it's not long before a youngster begins to understand that the letter "B" (pronounced "bee"), represents the sound "buh." This is an easy connection to make since both the letter name and corresponding sound begin with "buh." Children easily learn that "B" says "buh" and "T" says "tuh." They then begin to generalize. Since "B" says "buh" and "T" says "tuh," they guess that "H" would say "ay" and "F" would say "eh." They use the beginning sound of the letter name to indicate the letter sound for all letters. After all, it worked with "B" and "T."

If you work with young children, you'll see this common mistake as children over-generalize this rule. Unfortunately, their theory only works part of the time because the "code," based on their limited experience, is not as comprehensive as they assume. Until they learn all the simple letter-sound associations, they consistently make these errors. They will not be ready to read until they broaden their understanding of letter-sound relationships. Their generalizations provide a valuable predictor of when a child is ready to move to the next stage of development. Let's now explore four methods for assessing early reading development.

1. Duthie Index (Letter Recognition/Sound Association Form)

Roz Duthie developed a form where she could note each child's grasp of letter names and sounds. She found that her students in the preconventional, emerging, and developmental stages on the reading continuum could be grouped into three categories:

1. Children who can identify most letters by name but do not understand that the letters represent separate and distinct sounds apart from letter names.
2. Children who are beginning to grasp some letter-sound correlations based on their knowledge of letter names. These children apply a very limited understanding of letter-sound correlations.
3. Children who know most of the letter-sound connections. The specificity with which these children identify letter sounds indicates when they have

moved to a more sophisticated level of understanding and are ready for more formal reading instruction.

The Duthie Index (Form 8.1) is a form that you can use to track children's understanding of letter-sound correlations. Roz divided the alphabet into three sections. Each section represents a distinct level of difficulty and sophistication in letter-sound association. Form 8.1A uses upper case letters and Form 8.1B includes the more challenging lower case letters. Form 8.1C contains the directions for administering the Duthie Index.

As you can see in Figure 8.1, Section One on the left side of the form includes letter sounds that children grasp most easily. The initial sound we speak when we say each of these letter names is directly linked to the corresponding sound each letter represents. A child who is successful with this section, but has difficulty with the next two columns, is in the emerging stage on the reading continuum.

Section Two includes more challenging letter sounds. Most of the letters in this section represent two or more sounds. This complicates learning the letter/sound correspondences in English. Most of the vowels appear in this section, with both long and short vowel sounds as part of the assessment. This section also includes both the hard and soft sounds for "C" and "G." Students at the emerging and developing stages who can correctly identify these sounds have developed a more sophisticated understanding of the sounds of the English language.

Section Three requires that children understand the idea that a letter sound is sometimes quite different from the letter name. These are the letters that give emerging and developing readers the most difficulty. Many of the sounds these letters represent are the sounds that are heard *last* when the letter name is spoken. For example, the *letter sound* that "M" represents is a short, clipped "muh" but the *letter name* is the final sound of "ehm." A child who can successfully tell you the letter/sound associations for this section is most likely in the developing stage of the reading continuum. Roz has found that students who are successful with all three stages of the upper and lower case version of the index are usually ready to move into the beginning stages of the reading continuum.

Roz nicknamed this tool the "Eh-Duh" form, after the consistent letter-sound *mis-associations* children make at this early stage of reading development. For example, children at the emerging stage will tell you that "M" and "S" both make the sound of "eh" because that's the first sound they hear when they say the letter names. Continuing their generalization, children will also tell you that "W" makes the "duh" sound since that's what they hear first when they pronounce "dubble-yoo."

The Duthie Index is a variation on the standard letter/sound identification screening common in most kindergarten classrooms. This form can be used to assess a child's understanding of letters, to note progress over time, and to inform instruction. We've included directions for administering the Duthie Index on Form 8.1C. You may find this form helpful to use two or three times a year in kindergarten or first grade to monitor when students are ready to plunge into reading words.

Duthie Index: Letter Recognition/Sound Association

Child's Name: ______________________ Birthdate: ______________

Date: Fall: ______________ Observer: ______________

Winter: ______________ ______________

Spring: ______________ ______________

1	Fall		Winter		Spring	
	R	S	R	S	R	S
B						
K						
P						
T						
V						
Z						
D						
J						

2	Fall		Winter		Spring	
	R	S	R	S	R	S
R						
H						
C s						
C k						
O ˘						
O ¯						
G j						
G g						
U ˘						
U ¯						
I ˘						
I ¯						
Q						
A ˘						
A ¯						

3	Fall		Winter		Spring	
	R	S	R	S	R	S
E ˘						
E ¯						
W						
F						
M						
X						
N						
S						
L						
Y						

[R] Recognizes Letter [S] Sound Association

[✓] Correct Response

[ ] Incorrect Response

[ag] Incorrect Response Indicated by What Child Actually Said

Comments: ______________________________

____

____

____

Figure 8.1: Duthie Index

2. Concepts about Print

In *An Observation Survey of Early Literacy Achievement* (1993), Marie Clay describes a tool for assessing student's emerging concepts about reading using one of two small booklets (*Sand*, 1972; *Stones*, 1972). The adult reads the book to the child, asking specific questions about the text. For example, at one point the teacher asks the child to point to where she (or he) is reading. Many three- and four-year-olds point to the illustration! They have yet to develop the concept that print carries meaning.

Many assessment books have adapted Clay's technique so that it may be used with any text (Bird, Goodman, and Goodman, 1994, pp. 104–117; Harp, 1996, pp. 47–49; Rhodes, 1993, pp. 122–123, 137–138). This technique is best done individually when you have a few minutes to talk about reading and writing with each child. The information you glean from these conversations will be helpful as you plan instruction.

Lynne Rhodes's book, *Literacy Assessment: A Handbook of Instruments* (1993), has other helpful strategies for assessing early reading and writing. She created a series of activities in which you ask a child to draw a picture, then tell you about the drawing while you transcribe the child's words. When you ask the student to read back what you have written, you can assess a child's early understanding of the reading/writing connection. Rhodes also describes techniques for assessing students as they read predictable books.

3. Reading Words

Information about a child's growing recognition of sight words can easily be assessed by parent helpers or assistants. Two or three times a year, an adult can ask a child to read from a list of sight words to note developing reading skills. The student holds one list that is typed in a large font. On a separate list, the adult highlights words that the child reads correctly, using a different color pen for each trimester. For instance, each fall, you can highlight the words the child recognizes in yellow. Use a blue highlighter in the winter and a pink one in the spring to mark the new words a child can read. Teachers find the different colors help parents and students visually see a child's growth in reading. You can gather additional information by asking parents to write down the child's attempts after each word. Of course, this does not mean that you would explicitly teach these words in isolation; the record merely provides one measure of reading growth. Children often can identify words in context that they do not recognize in isolation. You should supplement this reading of words with data gathered during actual reading, using tools such as anecdotal notes, running records, or reading conference forms.

Analyzing Miscues

We can learn a great deal by analyzing the mistakes or miscues a reader makes. A miscue is something said or read in place of the printed text. Ken Goodman (1973) first defined miscues as "windows on the reading process." He described children's deviations from the text when reading aloud as "miscues," rather than the more pejorative term, "mistakes." We don't expect readers to read with 100 percent accuracy, even as adults. The types of miscues a person makes and whether the reader self-corrects, reveal significant information about how the reader processes a text.

In many reading texts, you'll see a diagram of four circles for semantic, syntactic, grapho-phonemic cueing systems, along with other cues, with "meaning" at the intersection. However, the diagram is deceptive, since readers never use one cueing system in isolation. For instance, if you see the word "read," you might first use the sounds of letters to decode the word. But is the word past or present tense? You must use the meaning and grammar of the rest of the text to determine the correct word. We may use one tack initially, but add other cues to confirm or modify our initial choice. Imagine Figure 8.2 as a three-dimensional model where one circle could be stacked on top of another to show the interactions of the cueing systems.

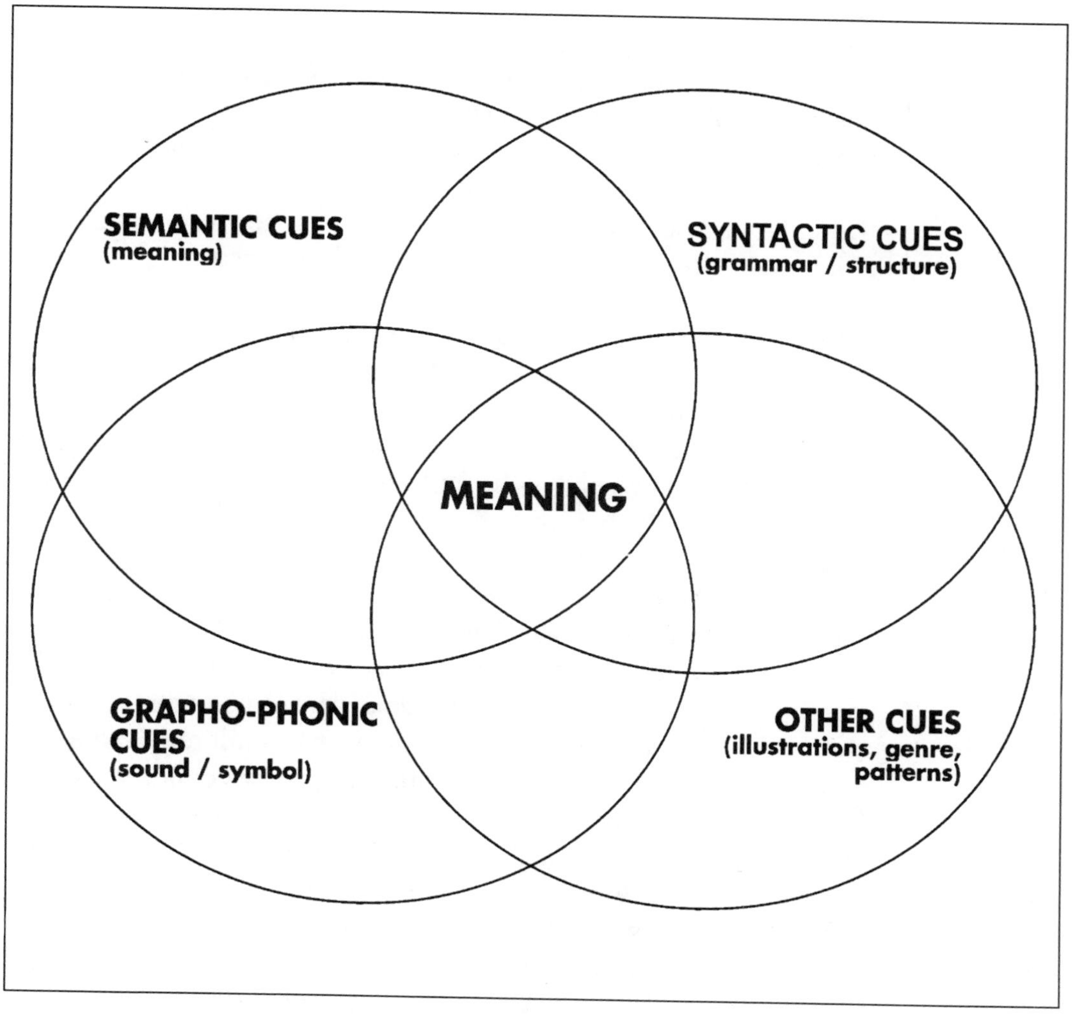

Figure 8.2: Cueing Systems

This orchestration of cueing systems happens silently in the fraction of a second. How can we determine which reading strategies a child is using?

4. Running Records

Many primary teachers feel that running records are the most useful reading assessment tools they use. If you've never tried this technique before, you may want to refer to the resources we've listed at the end of this chapter. Marie Clay's book, *An Observation Survey of Early Literacy Achievement* (1993), provides a detailed description of how to administer and score running records. She states:

> You set yourself the task of recording everything that a child says and does as he tries to read the book you have chosen. Once you begin such recording, and after about two hours of initial practice, no matter how much you might be missing, you have made a good start. The more you take the records, the more you will notice about children's behavior. (p. 24)

Running records are traditionally based on a child's reading of 100 to 200 words. Of course, with kindergarten and first graders, the text they read will be much shorter. During an individual reading conference, a student reads aloud from a book. Most teachers don't have time to make a copy of the actual text, so you can use a blank piece of paper or a running record form. Make a check for each word the student reads correctly. You also need to note any mistakes or errors the student makes. If the child reads a different word from the one in the text, simply record the word the child read. Most teachers develop a code for marking repetitions, deletions, omissions, insertions, substitutions, and self-corrections. By counting up the number of words in the text the child read and the number of miscues, you can get a percentage of accuracy. That information can help you determine the appropriate reading level for instruction for the child. The rule of thumb is that 90–94 percent is instructional level and 95 percent and above is an independent level. More importantly, you can analyze the types of errors the child made. Most teachers also ask students a few questions about the passages they read in order to ascertain comprehension as well as fluency and accuracy.

Lisa Norwick adapted the running record form from Marie Clay's book (1993) and created an Informal Running Record (Form 8.2.). She made boxes on the form where she can tally the number of times the student uses meaning (M), sentence structure (S), and visual (V) cues. The shaded columns allow Lisa to record the numbers of errors and self-corrections made by children. At the bottom of the form, there is a space to record the total number of times children use meaning, sentence structure, and visual cues for both errors and self-corrections. This makes it easier to see at a glance which strategies children are using and the areas where they need help.

For instance, looking at Figure 8.3, you can see how, early in the year, Sheila relied heavily on visual cues when she encountered an unknown word. She would stop and make several attempts to sound out the word. While listening to her read, Lisa had a strong hunch that Sheila was not cross-checking one cueing system against another when she encountered difficult unknown words. For instance, when Sheila

INFORMAL RUNNING RECORD

Name: Sheila **Title:** Henry And Mudge And The Wild Wind **Page(s):** 23-25 **Date:** 9/19

On each line, make a check for each word read correctly in that line or record miscues as read.

Text Line	Words	Errors M	Errors S	Errors V	Errors #	Self-corrections M	Self-corrections S	Self-corrections V	Self-corrections #	Comments / Strategies Taught
1	✓									Shows
2	✓✓✓✓									dependence
3	✓✓✓✓✓✓									on visual
4	✓ sw-swit/switched ✓✓✓			1	1					information.
5	✓✓✓✓✓✓✓									She is
6	✓✓✓✓✓✓ c-co/couch			1	1					beginning to
7	✓✓✓✓✓ ca-can-cand/candles			1	1					pay attention
8	✓✓✓ fi-fif-fih/fifth ✓			1	1					to meaning
9	✓✓✓									and sentence structure.
10	✓✓✓✓✓									Strategy
11	✓✓✓✓✓									Taught:
12	✓✓✓✓✓✓✓✓									Reread when
13	✓✓✓ thunderstorm/thunder	1	1	1	1					the text doesn't make
14	✓✓✓✓✓✓									sense.
	TOTAL	1	1	5	5					

Figure 8.3: Running Record, Fall Sample

read *Henry and Mudge and the Wild Wind* (Rylant, 1993), she unsuccessfully tried to sound out the words "switched" on line 4, "couch" on line 6, "candles" on line 7, and "fifth" on line 8. After two or three unsuccessful attempts with each of these words, she continued reading without trying a different strategy. On line 13, Sheila substituted "thunderstorm" for "thunder." The author used "thunderstorm" earlier in the text and Sheila was familiar with the word. This substitution was a meaning, sentence structure, and visual match. Lisa learned that Sheila was just beginning to use multiple cueing systems with familiar words and she now needed instruction and encouragement to try alternative meaning and sentence structure strategies with challenging unfamiliar words. Sheila also needed encouragement to go back and reread when the text didn't make sense.

By spring (Figure 8.4), Sheila had made progress with cross-checking and using all three cueing systems. As she read from *Stone Fox* (Gardiner, 1980), she read more fluently than in the fall and she included explicit and inferred information in her retelling. Although *Stone Fox* is a more challenging text than *Henry and Mudge and the Wild Wind*, Sheila was also using meaning and structure cues more often. For instance, on lines 1, 2, and 3, Sheila's miscues were meaning and structural matches. On lines 4, 8, and 11, her miscues were meaning, sentence structure, and visual matches. Young readers will often rely on one cueing system when encountering an unknown word, so it's important to prompt them to cross-check one cueing system against another. Once a child is able to cross-check consistently, look for when the child's miscues integrate all three cueing systems. For instance, Sheila was cross-checking and three of her miscues demonstrated meaning, sentence structure, and visual matches. Then, after a child is able to make all three cueing systems match, you can prompt the child to use visual cues to make self-corrections. This self-correcting strategy was the next step for Sheila.

Repetition with the use of all three cueing systems helped Sheila self-correct. For instance, on lines 6 and 10, she reread and used meaning and sentence structure to self-correct. On line 13, Sheila reread again and used the sentence structure to correct her miscue. She was rereading and successfully self-correcting more often when the text didn't make sense, which is a new skill for many beginning readers.

The information recorded on these two running records documents Sheila's growth over time. By taking running records as she listens to children read, Lisa can gather information to help her plan instruction for guided reading and communicate more clearly with parents.

One of the greatest challenges for primary teachers is finding the time to confer with individual students while keeping an eye on the rest of the class. Christy Clausen does two running records every day during silent reading time. At the beginning of the year, Christy discusses two or three reading choices her first graders can make while she conducts reading conferences. For instance, in the fall, children can read the books at their desk, read from the box of laminated poems, or read a Big Book with a partner. As the year progresses, Christy adds other choices to the class list. She finds that when she explains how important it is for her to be able to read with students without being interrupted, most students use their time well.

INFORMAL RUNNING RECORD

Name: Sheila **Title:** Stone Fox **Page(s):** 77-78 **Date:** 5/14

On each line, make a check for each word read correctly in that line or record miscues as read.

Text Line	Words	Errors M	Errors S	Errors V	Errors #	Self-corrections M	Self-corrections S	Self-corrections V	Self-corrections #	Comments / Strategies Taught
1	✓✓✓ loudly/madly ✓✓✓✓	1	1		1					Rereads and
2	✓✓✓✓✓✓✓✓✓✓ the/Main ✓	1	1		1					self-corrects
3	✓✓✓ loudly/madly ✓✓✓✓✓	1	1		1					more often. Using meaning
4	✓✓✓✓✓ trail/tail	1	1	1	1					and sentence
5	✓✓✓									structure cues
6	✓ f-for/forged ✓ R SC ✓✓✓✓			1		1	1		1	to cross-check.
7	✓									Strong retelling-
8	✓✓✓✓✓ called/cried ✓	1	1	1	1					Explains Willy's
9	✓✓✓✓✓✓✓									thoughts, actions
10	✓✓✓ hun-hund/hundred ✓✓✓✓✓ R SC ✓			1		1	1		1	and feelings. Strategy
11	✓✓ broke/burst ✓✓✓✓✓✓	1	1	1	1					Taught:
12	✓									Read to the
13	✓✓✓✓✓ tum-tumble/tumbled ✓✓ R SC ✓	1		1			1		1	end of the word. Look for
14	✓✓✓✓✓✓✓✓✓✓✓✓									familiar word
	TOTAL	7	6	6	6	2	3		3	endings.

Figure 8.4: Running Record, Spring Sample

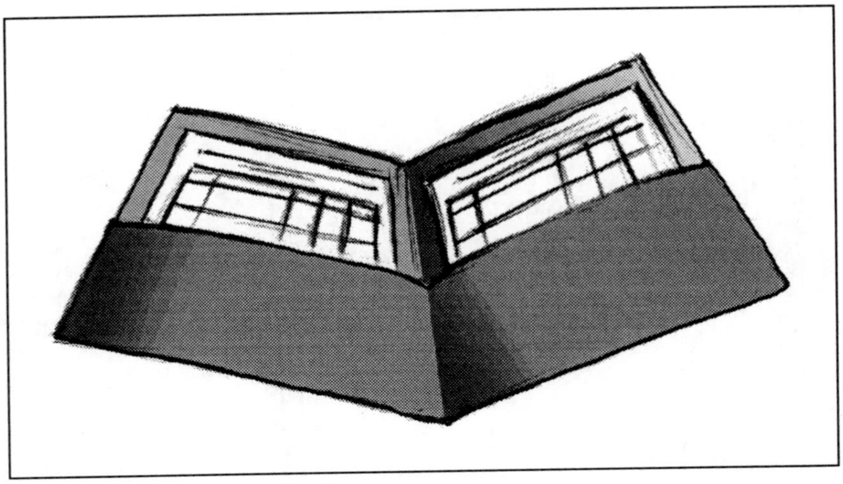

Figure 8.5: Running Record Folder

Christy has a Running Record folder with pockets on both sides (Figure 8.5). She keeps several blank Informal Running Record forms for each student in the right-hand side. Each day, Christy reads with two students and transfers the two completed forms from the right pocket to the left side. When all the forms are on the left side, she moves the stack back to the right pocket and starts another round of conferences. It takes Christy about 5–7 minutes to do a running record and confer with each child, depending on the length of the text.

Immediately after she reads with each student and fills out the running record form, Christy takes a brief moment to complete a Running Record Summary (Form 8.3). On this form, she records the date, title of the book, whether the book was familiar or new, and the number of self-corrections. Christy usually adds a comment about the child's reading. The Running Record Summary is paper-clipped to each child's running record forms in Christy's reading conference folder.

Figure 8.6 shows Lisa Norwick's Running Record Summary for Sheila. Lisa finds it's important to record whether the student is reading a familiar (seen) or unfamiliar text (unseen). For instance, Sheila had read several of Arnold Lobel's *Frog and Toad* books, so she could read with more fluency and make more self-corrections because she was familiar with the story. The types of miscues children make depend on both their reading strategies and the difficulty and familiarity of the text.

The hardest running records to take are your first ones! You'll find the technique becomes natural very quickly and soon you'll develop a "miscue ear" as you listen to students read. While running records may seem time consuming, the information documented provides valuable information about the cueing systems readers use, as well as information about fluency and comprehension. This, in turn, can help you provide intentional and appropriate instruction for your students. Carl Braun (1993) suggests that, with practice, children can even learn to record and analyze their own reading. He created a simplified form on which children record whether their miscues made sense or not, note how they've improved, and set goals.

RUNNING RECORD SUMMARY

Name Sheila

DATE	TITLE	SEEN OR UNSEEN	SELF-CORRECTS	COMMENTS
9/19	Henry And Mudge And The Wild Wind	unseen	0	Relying on visual Goal: Reread to enhance meaning
10/25	Frog and Toad	Seen	3	Read more fluently and with expression
12/17	Marvin Redpost	unseen	2	Difficult text, relied on visual information
2/10	Kate She and the Midnight Express	unseen	4	Reread more often, used meaning cues
3/5	Chalk Box Kid	Unseen	3	Read fluently, good retelling
5/14	Stone Fox	unseen	3	Using meaning and sentence structure to cross-check

Figure 8.6: Running Record Summary

Those of you working with primary students know the challenge of finding time during the day to assess students individually. Some of you may prefer taking anecdotal notes informally as you read with your students. Others may want to incorporate one of the four methods of assessing emergent readers that we've described in this chapter. In the next chapter, we'll suggest additional assessment tools that can be used with readers at all levels.

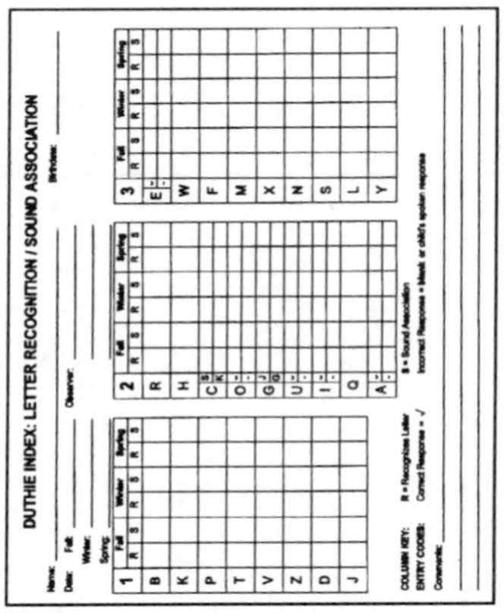

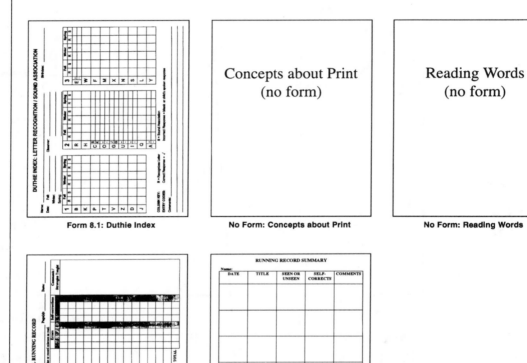

Form 8.1: Duthie Index

Concepts about Print
(no form)

No Form: Concepts about Print

Reading Words
(no form)

No Form: Reading Words

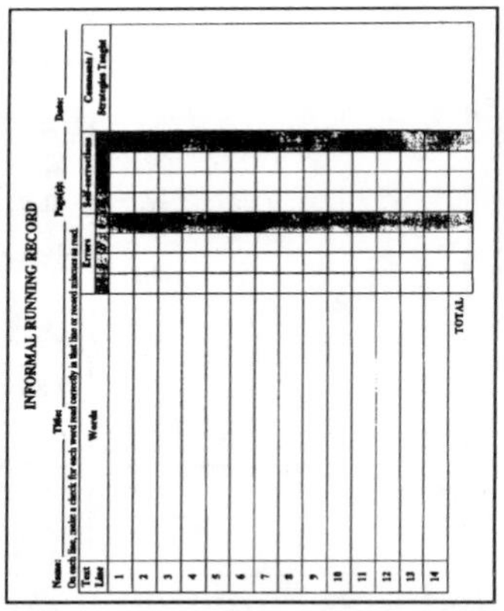

Form 8.2: Informal Running Record

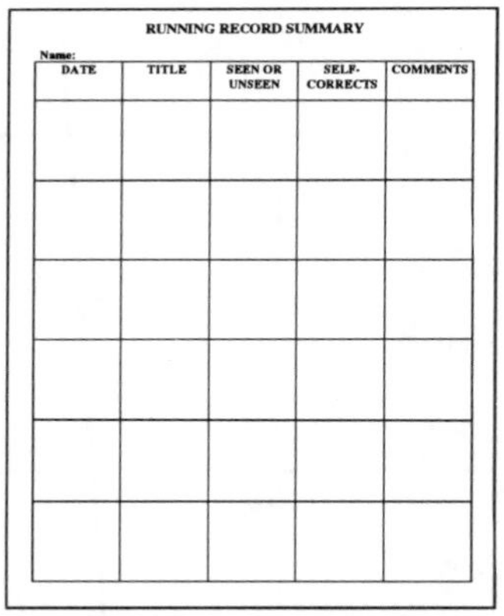

RUNNING RECORD SUMMARY

Name:

DATE	TITLE	SEEN OR UNSEEN	SELF-CORRECTS	COMMENTS

Form 8.3: Running Record Summary

Professional Growth

Primary teachers may want to plan a series of parent workshops about early reading and writing. In *Getting It Together* (1994), Ian Morrison suggests that teachers begin by praising parents for the wonderful work they do in preparing their children for school. He outlines a series of activities you can have parents do to help illuminate the cueing systems and the developmental nature of learning to read. He then presents recommendations for how parents can help with reading at home.

But Will She Read? by Steven Bialostok (1996) also suggests key points to include in parent presentations. He includes a series of parent newsletters in the appendix, as well as overheads that are ready to use for parent workshops.

You and/or your colleagues may want to offer a series of workshops on running records for other teachers. Reading Recovery teachers are well trained in this assessment method and are often willing to share their expertise. Bring in videotapes of students reading with copies of the text and practice taking running records. Try taking running records with each other using a medical text or challenging scientific article. You might find it helpful to meet every week or two to share insights and questions as you try this technique with your students.

Recommended Readings about Emergent Reading

There are several books that we'd highly recommend about assessing early reading. As mentioned earlier, Marie Clay's book, *An Observation Survey of Early Literacy Achievement* (1993), is a landmark book for strategies such as running records and assessing concepts about print. One of the most accessible introductions to running records is in Ian Morrison's little book, *Getting It Together: Linking Reading Theory to Practice* (1994). Bill Harp's *Handbook of Literacy Assessment and Evaluation* (1996) also has a helpful section on this technique.

Guided Reading: Good First Teaching for All Children by Irene Fountas and Gay Su Pinnell should also be on every primary teacher's reading list. This book is about teaching and assessing reading strategies, organizing for instruction, and keeping records. The authors also include a helpful section on running records. Chapters 21 and 22 on running records in *Knowing Literacy* (Johnston, 1997) were co-authored by Peter Johnston and Marie Clay. These chapters are well written and include many helpful examples.

Literacy Assessment: A Handbook of Instruments (Rhodes, 1993) is another book on emergent literacy we would add to a professional library. The surveys and series of activities for assessing early reading and writing are particularly useful. *Highlight My Strengths* by New Zealand educator Leanna Traill (1993) is another favorite of primary teachers. The clear forms and timeline for assessment are easy to understand and implement.

Chapter 9

Observing Reading Growth

Bruce chuckles over the humor in *Commander Toad in Space* (Yolen, 1980). A very precise and focused child, he seldom makes errors as he reads. Bruce waited longer before starting to read than his brother and sister did, then zipped through the early stages of reading. He is delighted when he finds a series of books by an author he likes. His very favorite books are nonfiction, especially the Magic Schoolbus books by Joanna Cole. Like many boys his age, he gravitates to books about space, dinosaurs, and how things work.

His sister, Laura, took a very different path to reading. She memorized books as a toddler, read early, and clamored to have her parents read to her. She read with delightful expression, and preferred fairy tales, poetry, and fiction. Now, as a fourth grader, she devours books and her favorite authors are Jane Yolen, Eve Bunting, Patricia Polacco, and Brian Jacques. Laura reads in the car on the way to school, during any free moments at home, and with a flashlight under her blankets at night.

Bruce and Laura's older brother, Keith, was an inveterate reader of Matt Christopher's sports stories in elementary school. He seldom read fiction other than sports stories unless prompted, but loved pouring over Calvin and Hobbes cartoons, *Sports Illustrated* magazines, and the *Guinness Book of Records*. As a high school student, Keith's reading now consists primarily of texts and required reading from school. However, he has become a devoted email correspondent and spends hours reading messages from friends and downloading guitar lyrics and information about musicians from the Internet.

These are three very different readers from one family; the range of readers in your classroom will be even greater. How can your assessments capture the uniqueness of each reader? How can you build on each child's strengths and interests? We've divided this chapter into three sections. In the first section, we examine ways to assess students' reading strategies. We explore the challenges of assessing comprehension in section two. The third section addresses ways to document the range of students' reading. Aspects of self-evaluation are woven into the discussions in all three sections.

Section One: Reading Strategies

Cooper is a fifth grader who reads at the primer level. When Nicole reads an article she finds on the Internet, she stumbles over many words. John has solid comprehension despite the many mistakes he makes as he reads aloud. How can you learn more about these students in order to help them become more proficient readers?

We want to pause here for a moment to define the difference between reading skills and reading strategies. Curriculum guides and published programs often outline specific skills to be taught at a particular grade level. Word attack skills, vocabulary drills, and specific tasks such as alphabetizing a list of names are often taught in sequence and practiced in isolation. A skill, however, becomes a strategy only when the student can apply and generalize the task to new situations. Regie Routman states, "In other words, a skill—no matter how well it has been taught—cannot be considered a strategy until the learner can use it purposefully and independently" (1991, p. 135). When teachers focus on strategies rather than skills, they encourage students to question, make connections, and form generalizations. Unlike skills instruction with a predetermined scope and sequence, strategy instruction requires responsive teaching and intentional assessment. In order to provide the support learners need, you have to provide the scaffolding between what children already know and new learning. Teaching and assessing effective reading strategies occurs during focus lessons, shared reading, guided reading, literature circles, individual conferences, and informal conversations with students.

We can learn a great deal about children's reading strategies when we listen to them read aloud and talk with them about the texts. Running records, described in the previous chapter, are another way to learn about the strategies of beginning readers. You could also take anecdotal notes about reading strategies, but without a system and focus, there is simply too much information to record. In this section, we'll discuss three methods for assessing reading strategies: self-evaluations, reading conferences, and miscue analysis.

Self-Evaluation: Reading Strategies

1. Reading Tools

When Pam Galloway was a reading specialist in Auburn, Washington, she needed a way to help her students talk about their reading strategies. She and her students made a list of the reading strategies they use to figure out words. Pam often modeled these reading strategies as she read aloud in class. After compiling a list of reading strategies, her students then drew the outlines of tools (a wrench, hammer, saw, screwdriver, etc.) and Pam typed one reading strategy on each tool (Figure 9.1).

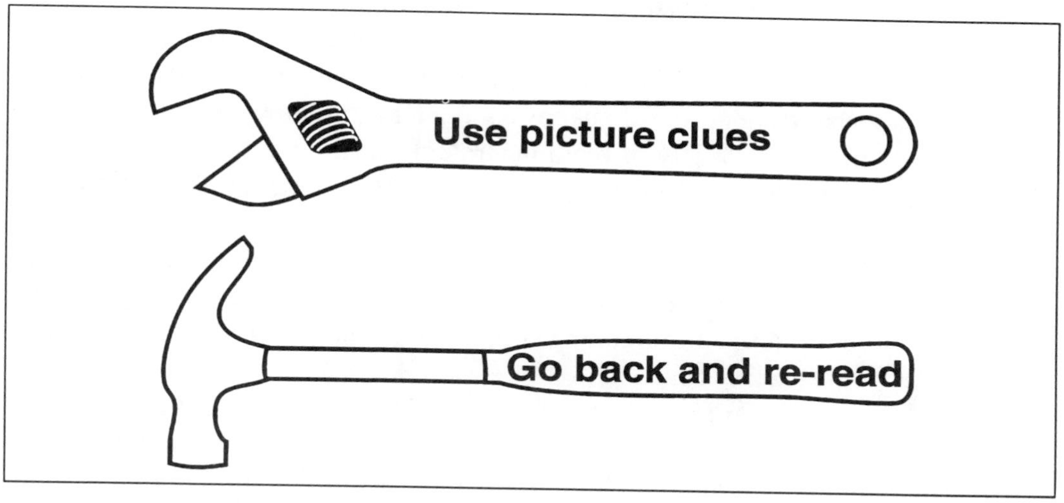

Figure 9.1: Reading Tools

The tools were laminated and cut apart and each student received a set on a metal ring. Periodically, Pam asked her students during silent reading to set out the tools for the reading strategies they used that day. As they discovered more strategies, the class continued to add to their "toolbox." Your students might want to design their own reading tools to share with other classrooms. We've included 10 word identification strategy tools in the Appendix (Form 9.1). Some possible reading strategies are listed in Figure 9.2.

• Use the words around it	• Ask a friend
• Use the sound of the first letter	• Look it up in the dictionary
• Use picture clues	• Guess and go on
• Go back and reread	• Put another word in its place
• Skip the word and keep going	• Think of a word that makes sense

Figure 9.2: Reading Strategies

You could create a similar list for more complex comprehension strategies. Students might also want to interview older students and adults about the strategies they use when reading. How many strategies were the same ones the students listed at school? Once children develop the metacognitive language for talking about what they do as readers, it becomes easier for students to demonstrate growth and set their own reading goals.

2. Word Strategies

Based on the Word Strategy form in Lynn Rhodes's book, *Literacy Assessment: A Handbook of Instruments* (1993), Lisa Norwick created a modified version (Form 9.2) to learn more about the ways in which students figure out new or challenging words. She first introduces the Word Strategies form with a class discussion about what students do when they encounter an unknown word. Over several months, Lisa models a variety of reading strategies using the class read-aloud book. She begins by introducing one reading strategy to her students. This new strategy is posted on a chart in the room and the students practice using it in a variety of settings. Lisa and her students practice and discuss the strategy during guided reading, literature circles, individual reading conferences, and content area reading. Every two weeks, she introduces a new reading strategy to her students and it is added to the "Word Strategies" class chart.

When students have discussed and practiced several reading strategies, Lisa models how to complete the Word Strategies form using the novel she is reading aloud to the class. The students then have a few days to fill out the sheet, describing their approaches when faced with challenging words. For instance, one of her students, Brynne, listed four strategies she used while reading: "Skip the word I didn't know. Read on. Sound out the word. Look for clues." Lisa finds that the discussions sparked by the Word Strategies form have helped increase her students' repertoire of effective reading strategies.

3. Reading Strategies I Use

In Chapter 7, we described the form for Writing Strategies I Use (Form 7.4) that students keep in their writing folders. Similarly, students might want to keep a parallel form in their reading folder for Reading Strategies I Use. The first Reading Strategies I Use version (Form 9.3A) is blank so you can note a child's reading strategies, comprehension, or attitude during formal or informal conferences. Older students can list the strategies that reflect their own strengths as readers. The advantage of the blank form is that it's flexible and won't be intimidating to students.

You may find, however, that you're recording the same comments over and over and may prefer a checklist. In the next variation, we included a primary (Form 9.3B) and intermediate (Form 9.3C) version of Reading Strategies I Use. This checklist allows you to fill out a form as you confer with students, or they can date and check the forms themselves. The placement of the date in the right-hand column reflects whether the student used the strategy independently or with some nudging. We find these lists also provide helpful reminders of the strategies we need to teach and assess.

4. Reading Goals

During individual reading conferences, students and teachers can record reading goals collaboratively on Form 9.4. Goals become most effective when they are developed by the student and re-visited often in order to celebrate growth. You may want to ask students to reflect on their reading goals when you meet for individual reading conferences. You can touch base with where they are, record progress, and provide support for their next steps as readers.

Progress toward these goals can also be assessed at the end of the term. Some students may want to improve reading strategies, while others may focus on reading more challenging texts, reading more widely, or improving the quality of their response journals or literature discussions. The forms for Reading Goals can be stapled to the students' reading folders or included in portfolios. These goals can be tied directly to portfolios and student-led conferences. We'll discuss these connections in more depth in *Book Three* and *Book Four* of this series and provide examples of goal setting from a variety of classrooms.

Reading Conference Forms

As adults, we do most of our reading silently. We read more quickly and efficiently when we read silently. For elementary students, however, oral reading provides an invaluable source of information about students' reading development. You can assess each child's fluency, comprehension, reading strategies, and attitude during individual reading conferences. The challenge is finding time during the day to meet individually with each student. Some teachers conduct one or two reading conferences every day at the beginning of quiet reading time. Other teachers confer with a few students while the rest of the class is involved in independent reading activities or centers. Most primary teachers try to listen to each student read once every two or three weeks. In the intermediate grades, you'll probably want to read with each of your students once a month. In both cases, you'll want to read more often with those students about whom you are concerned. What's important is to create a predictable schedule that's built into your reading program.

5. Anecdotal Notes

Anne Klein holds reading conferences with a few students each day during silent reading time. Each conference lasts about five minutes and she finds it takes about three weeks to meet with all of her students. She confers more often with new students, children who are struggling, or students with specific needs. Anne takes anecdotal notes on mailing labels about the students' reading strategies, comprehension, and book choices. These ongoing conferences enable Anne to get to know each student as a reader, fill out the reading continuum, and help students set individual goals.

Anne also enlists the help of parents for reading conferences. She usually trains one or two parents each year to listen to students read on a regular basis. Anne first models how to conduct a reading conference while the parents watch and ask questions. When the adults feel comfortable, Anne gives them a clipboard with the students' names printed on mailing labels. The adult records the title of the book the student reads, then checks for fluency and expression. In order for parents to know what strategies to record, Anne gives them a copy of a list of effective reading strategies the class developed. With 30 or more students in her room, Anne can gain a great deal of information about her readers with the help of these volunteers. Of course, not everyone has parents who have the time or desire to record this type of information. You may want to recruit college students or community members to help with this task as a supplement to your own reading records.

In Chapter 4, we explained how anecdotal notes are far more informative when your observations are focused and intentional. We developed a list of Focus Questions for Anecdotal Notes for reading at the primary level (Form 9.5A) and intermediate level (Form 9.5B). The focus questions are linked to the strands on the reading continuum described in Chapter 11. Of course, you'll want to modify these lists to match your curriculum and instruction, as well as your particular group of students.

6. Reading Conference Record

The next challenge is how to devise a manageable way to record all the information you learn during reading conferences. Some teachers prefer to assess reading by using anecdotal notes on a clipboard, as Anne Klein does. Others feel that they write the same comments over and over and prefer a checklist for common reading strategies, comprehension, and oral fluency, with room for a few comments. The checklists can then serve as a structure for watching and recording children's reading development. In addition, the forms provide concrete evidence of growth when you contrast your notes from the beginning and end of the year. The next series of reading conference forms provide valuable information about a student's:

- level of fluency
- attitude toward reading
- use of reading strategies
- degree of comprehension
- connections to other books, authors, and experiences

In addition, the structure of the forms allows you to:

- comment positively on areas of growth
- track specific skills/strategies you've taught

- help students with book selection
- encourage self-evaluation
- establish reading goals

Lisa Norwick developed the first Reading Conference Record (Form 9.6A) to document primary students' reading strategies, degree of fluency and inflection, reading level, and comprehension. In addition, there is room for you to write comments and record any new strategies you introduce during the conference. We've included a sample of a completed Reading Conference Record from a third-grade student in Figure 9.3.

Name Megan **READING CONFERENCE RECORD**

Reading Strategies	**Date:** 9-94 **Title:** Mr Fox	**Date:** 9-94 **Title:** The Twits	**Date:** 10-94 **Title:** Taste of Blackberries	**Date:** **Title:**
Rereads		|||	|||||		
Skips/Returns				
Uses Context Clues			✓ +	
Decodes				
Knows Sight Words	✓	✓	✓ +	
Replaces Unknown Words				
Miscues Preserve Meaning	✓	✓	✓ +	
Appropriate Level	yes	yes		
Reads Fluently	✓		✓ +	
Literal Comprehension	+	+	+	
Interpretive Comprehension	✓	✓	✓	
Strategy Taught	using context clues	Rereading		

Key: + consistently ✓ sometimes

Comments:

9/94 appears to read word by word

9/94 Discussed rereading + using context when text doesn't make sense

10/94 Reading was more fluent, retelling more complete

Figure 9.3: Reading Conference Record

In September, when Lisa listened to Megan read from *Fantastic Mr. Fox* (Dahl, 1986) she noticed that when Megan encountered a word she didn't know, she kept right on going. Megan read word by word and did not focus on making sense of the story. Lisa did a brief lesson about using context cues. During the next conference, when Megan read from *The Twits* (Dahl, 1981), Lisa used tally marks to show how she was beginning to reread and self-correct. By October, Megan read *A Taste of Blackberries* (Smith, 1973) and you can see in Figure 9.3 how her fluency and retelling improved as she learned to read for meaning.

In elementary grades, teachers generally ask students to read aloud as they listen for oral fluency and assess reading strategies. Most teachers then ask a few questions to assess comprehension. We developed a primary Reading Conference Record (Form 9.6A) and an intermediate version (Form 9.6B) to provide a record of students' goals and growth over time.

As students become more independent readers, however, we can't learn as much from their oral reading. Janine King asks her sixth graders at St. Joseph's School in Seattle to read a few passages silently as she reads along. After a page or two, Janine may ask a comprehension question or ask about a challenging word. She can check for oral fluency and expression by asking the student to read a section aloud or by evaluating oral fluency during literature circles or oral presentations in other content areas. Janine and her colleagues developed a third version of the Reading Conference Form (Form 9.6C) to use with their more proficient middle school readers. All three versions of the form have room for you to add comments and record the strategies you've taught. Many teachers have told us that the Reading Conference Record is their favorite reading assessment tool.

Let's look at two different systems for organizing Reading Conference Records. Some of you may want to keep the conference forms in each child's section of your Teacher Notebook. Simply flip open your Teacher Notebook and fill out the form during the reading conference. All the information will be in one place and you won't have to transfer information. You'll need a checklist of names to ensure that you meet regularly with each student.

Another method of organizing reading conference forms is to adapt the system Christy Clausen uses for Running Records described in Chapter 8. Keep the Reading Conference Records in a folder with pockets on each side. As you read with one or two students each day, transfer the completed forms from the right pocket to the left pocket. When you have met with all your students, simply move the stack back to the right-hand side. After four conferences, when the form is full, you can move the Reading Conference Records into each child's section in your Teacher Notebook in time for report cards and parent conferences. Let's now take a look at several other versions of reading conference forms.

7. Reading Conference Notes

As Cynthia approaches, eight-year-old Lindsey looks up, exclaiming, "Ms. Ruptic, listen to this!" and expressively reads a description of the Grand High Witch. "I just love the way Roald Dahl makes his characters so outrageous! I'm going to try to use that style for my next story." Such conversations provide rich information about how children are making connections between their reading, writing, and personal lives.

In an effort to capture such varied information on paper, Cynthia developed the more complex Reading Conference Notes (Form 9.7) to use with her more proficient readers during conferences. Although there are many boxes on this form, Cynthia does not make an entry in every section during one conference. For instance, in Figure 9.4 you can see how after a conversation about *The Witches* (Dahl, 1983), Cynthia recorded Lindsey's comment about the writer's craft and her wish to emulate Dahl's style in her own story, as well as her intention to read all of his books. For several weeks, the class had been talking about the difference between books students could read independently and books that were at their instructional level where they could read 90 percent of the words with good comprehension. After asking her opinion, Cynthia checked that the difficulty of the book was between Lindsey's instructional and independent level. She also checked a few strategies and recorded a few comments.

Lindsey's next conference centered on a nonfiction book she was reading as research for a book she was writing about dolphins. In the miscue analysis section of the form, Cynthia noted that Lindsey self-corrected all miscues in order to make sense of the reading. The entry under "Focus Lesson Application" shows that Lindsey was making use of the glossary, a skill that had recently been introduced in class. In the box labeled "Future Focus/Goals," Cynthia recorded Lindsey's intent to include a glossary in her dolphin book.

Cynthia's goal is to hold a reading conference with each student every two weeks and more often with students who are struggling. She carries these Reading Conference Notes on her workshop clipboard, filing them in her Teacher Notebook when she has conferred with a child four times. Since she runs the forms "back to back," Cynthia can see the information from four consecutive conferences and easily track progress over time. We've included a completed sample (Figure 9.4) so you can see how she uses this form.

8. Group Observation: Reading

Whether you meet with students individually or in a group, it's important to find some way to record your observations. Roz Duthie and Jan Peacoe on Bainbridge Island developed a form to use with groups of first graders during shared and guided reading. The Group Observation (Form 9.8) provides a place to record miscues and add comments as you work with small groups of children. We constantly remind ourselves of Regie Routman's comment that any time we work with students, we should be teaching something. This form provides a place to record the strategies you introduce, as well as notes about student learning.

9. Reading Celebration: Home Connection

As a parent, did you ever know if your child's teacher read with your son or daughter? Parents rarely know how often you read with their child or what you learn from a reading conference. We've provided a form that can help you inform families and

READING CONFERENCE NOTES FOR Lindsey **YEAR** 96-97

DATE	TEXT/AUTHOR	GENRE	PAGE(S)	STRATEGIES/COMMENTS	Additional comments:
10/30/96	The Witches/Dahl	Fantasy	84	✓ Uses sentence structure ✓ Uses context ✓ Uses phonics ✓ Knows most words on sight ✓ Retells plot ✓ Retells character Relates to personal experience ✓ Relates to other literature ✓ Comments on author's craft Notes specific literary devices	Chose a part that is so visual, I can just imagine her drawing it. "Roald Dahl makes his characters so outrageous" "He's my favorite author right now." "I'm going to try to use that style for my next story."
LEVEL ☐ Independent ✓ Instructional ☐ Frustrational	**MISCUES/ANALYSIS** Very expressive reading - no miscues magnificent - a little painstaking, but worked it out			**FOCUS-LESSON APPLICATION**	**FUTURE FOCUS/GOAL(S)** Reading/re-reading all of Dahl's books
RESPONSE PROJECT					

DATE	TEXT/AUTHOR	GENRE	PAGE(S)	STRATEGIES/COMMENTS	Additional comments:
11/20/96	Sea World of Dolphins	Non-fiction	104-5	✓ Uses sentence structure ✓ Uses context ✓ Uses phonics ✓ Knows most words on sight ✓ Retells plot Retells character Relates to personal experience Relates to other literature Comments on author's craft Notes specific literary devices	Excellent understanding! Lindsey was amazed at the fact that the dolphins' "sounds" can stun or kill prey.
LEVEL ☐ Independent ✓ Instructional ☐ Frustrational	**MISCUES/ANALYSIS** rifles (rivals) sc echolocation - sounded out Aristole (Aristotle) sc schoolers (scholars) sc anchent (ancient) sc entering (entertaining) sc consistently self-corrects to make meaning			**FOCUS-LESSON APPLICATION** using glossary	**FUTURE FOCUS/GOAL(S)** wants to include a glossary at end of her own non-fiction book
RESPONSE PROJECT Writing non-fiction book @ dolphins					

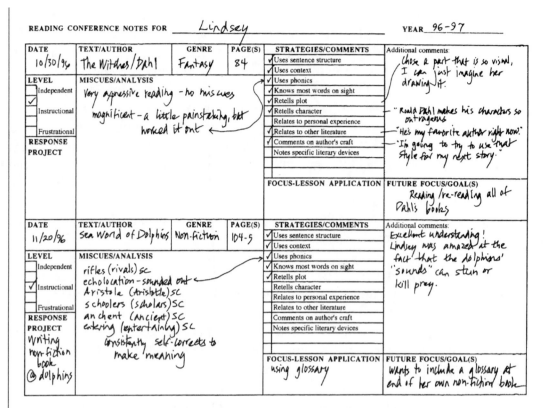

Figure 9.4: Reading Conference Notes

celebrate reading growth. The Reading Celebration (Form 9.9) includes room to record the title and author of the book the student read, as well as space to write a few comments. You can note ways in which the student has shown growth and perhaps suggest ways that parents can help their children at home. We've included a sample from Bruce (Figure 9.5), the first reader described at the beginning of this chapter.

Bruce's teacher at Brighton School, Linda Johnson, received very positive feedback about this form from parents. The Reading Celebration form can provide specific information, invite questions, and set a positive tone. All too often, notes that go home are about problems or concerns. Most parents are thrilled to know you took the time to read with their child. It's not realistic to write a note to parents after every reading conference, but it might be worth doing once each grading period. This very specific and ongoing type of informal parent communication can help supplement more formal means of assessment.

READING CELEBRATION

Name Bruce Hill Date 4/10/97

~~Book~~ Story "The Mechanical Man" Author Collection of Stories p. 193–200

Bruce chose this robot story and read the first 4 pages beautifully! He sounded out several words such as "flash," "speak," "metal," and his new favorite one "chrome" with the silent "h"! He added these words to his "new" word packet! (Sandwich bag with word cards! ☺)

Parent Comments:

Figure 9.5: Reading Celebration

Miscue Analysis

We've saved our discussion of miscue analysis for the last since it's the most technical and perhaps the most challenging technique for assessing reading strategies. Like running records, miscue analysis is a practical, diagnostic assessment technique that complements any reading curriculum. This technique provides detailed information about the strategies that a reader uses when processing written texts.

Several miscue inventories are available, from commercially published ones to simple teacher-made versions. Some inventories are too complex and time consuming for classroom use. However, there are a few versions that you might want to use with the students in your class who are still struggling with reading. The chapter by Dorothy Watson and Janice Henson in *Assessment and Evaluation for Student Centered Learning* (Harp, 1994, pp. 67–96) contains a short but helpful explanation of how to mark substitutions, omissions, insertions, repetitions, and self-corrections on a copy of the text. This level of analysis is quite time consuming and they recommend using this technique only with your less-proficient readers. Another helpful reference is the November, 1995 issue of *Primary Voices*, which is devoted specifically to miscue analysis and includes specific suggestions for adapting the technique for classroom use.

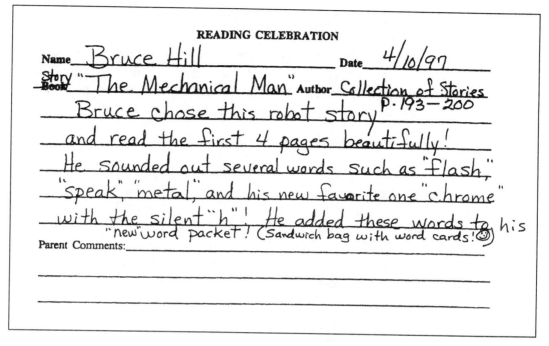

When taking running records, you make a check mark on a form or blank piece of paper for every word the student reads correctly and record each of the reader's miscues. However, as the students become more capable readers and increase their speed and fluency, you simply can't make check marks quickly enough. In a true miscue analysis, you photocopy the text or retype the passage in order to have a copy for recording data, then use a coding system to mark the reader's miscues. You can then analyze the miscues to determine how a child is using various cueing systems and processing the text. You should also ask the student questions about the passage in order to determine comprehension.

10. Informal Miscue Analysis

We wanted to create a version of miscue analysis that was simple to administer and did not require special training. A few years ago, Jan Peacoe, a special education teacher on Bainbridge Island, Washington developed an Informal Miscue Analysis (Form 9.10A) to use without making a copy of the text. In the first column of the form, Jan writes the date of the conference and title of the book. Next, she records any miscues the student makes, writing both the actual word from the text and what the student said. In the third column, Jan notes the skills or strategies that she teaches, then checks the student's level of fluency and comprehension. This simple form of miscue analysis can be used with readers of all ability levels. You can track progress over time, since you can record information from four conferences on one sheet.

Some of you may want to use the Reading Strategies I Use (Form 9.3), the Reading Conference Record (Form 9.6), or the Reading Conference Notes (Form 9.7) described earlier for most of your students, and use the Informal Miscue Analysis (Form 9.10A) only with students having reading difficulties. Others may want to administer the Informal Miscue Analysis to all students in the fall for baseline information and again in the spring to show growth. The better you become at analyzing students' miscues, the better you'll be able to provide appropriate instruction for each reader. Once you develop an "ear" for miscues, it's much easier to move from simply recording miscues and strategies to looking at patterns and making decisions for instruction. In Figure 9.6, we've outlined a simple procedure for administering the Informal Miscue Analysis.

You may want to begin using this technique by tape recording one student as you record the child's miscues. You may have to replay the tape a few times before you catch all the errors. It gets easier with practice! Most teachers supplement the miscue analysis technique with retelling, which we describe in the next section of this chapter. It's vital to examine comprehension along with fluency and accuracy.

Lisa Norwick uses the Informal Running Record (Form 8.2) with her beginning readers in order to look closely at their miscues and examine their strategies. For her more fluent readers, Lisa wanted a form where she could record only the miscues instead of placing check marks for every word the child reads correctly. Lisa also wanted to focus on meaning making at a sentence level, rather than at the word level. Let's take a look at each of the sections on the Informal Miscue Analysis (Form 9.10A).

In the first column, record the date and the title of the book the child selects to read. In the second column, you can write the word from the text next to the child's

Directions for Informal Miscue Analysis

1. Ask the student to choose a passage from a textbook or literature book that is somewhat challenging.
2. Photocopy the selection or use the miscue analysis sheet (Form 9.10). You may want to attach a copy of the text.
3. Ask the student to read the passage aloud. (It's also helpful to tape record the reading, especially if this assessment technique is new for you.) Tell the student that you can't provide any help.
4. Record the student's miscues on the photocopy of the text or miscue analysis form as you listen to the child read.
5. Ask the student to retell the passage to determine comprehension.
6. Afterward, analyze the information to determine the student's strengths and needs.
7. Based on the results, develop instructional strategies to help the student become a more proficient reader.

Figure 9.6: Directions for Informal Miscue Analysis

miscue. At other times, you may wish to record more general notes about the reader's strategies. You can note the strategies you've introduced in the third column, along with tallies to show whether each sentence made sense or not. If the student makes a miscue that doesn't disturb the meaning of the text, place the tally mark in the "Yes" section. Similarly, if the reader's miscue interferes with meaning, place the tally in the "No" column. You can quickly calculate the percentages for both categories. In the last columns, you can record information about fluency and comprehension. Lisa often discusses what she learns with the student at the end of the conference, emphasizing the reader's use of effective strategies.

Let's look at an example. In Figure 9.7, the Informal Miscue Analysis provides a record of Blake's growth over time. In the fall, the majority of the sentences Blake read maintained the meaning of the story. For instance, when he read *Stone Fox* (Gardiner, 1980), in the fall, 77 percent of his sentences made sense. In December, when he read *Pirate's Promise* (Bulla, 1994), 91 percent of his sentences made sense and he reread and self-corrected more often. When he read a nonfiction book about Monet in January, 100 percent of the sentences kept the meaning of the passage. As Blake improved in reading for meaning, his retellings became more thorough. He was increasingly able to retell both factual and inferential information as the year progressed. Rather than keeping all this information in your head or on "Post-it" notes, the Informal Miscue Analysis form provides an easy way to capture the specific steps a student makes along the path to reading proficiency.

INFORMAL MISCUE ANALYSIS

Name Blake

Date and Title	Miscues and Comments Text vs What student read	Skills/Strategies Taught	Fluency	Comprehension	
				Factual	Inferred
9/20 Stone Fox	Stopped when he came to a difficult word. Didn't reread	Reread when the text doesn't make sense. Does the sentence make sense? Yes: ~~||||~~ ~~||||~~ ~~||||~~ ~~||||~~ ~~||||~~ || No: ~~||||~~ |||	✓ % 77 % 23	✓+	✓
10/15 George's Marvelous Medicine	Hesitating w/ diff. words. Struggles w/ sounding out difficult words	Replace unknown word w/ a word that makes sense Does the sentence make sense? Yes: ~~||||~~ ~~||||~~ ~~||||~~ ~~||||~~ ~~||||~~ ~~||||~~ No ~~||||~~ |	✓+ % 83 % 17	✓+	✓
11/17 Mayflower text	Difficult nonfiction text Used background knowledge	Look for a smaller word inside a larger word Does the sentence make sense? Yes: ~~||||~~ ~~||||~~ ~~||||~~ ~~||||~~ ~~||||~~ || No: ||||	✓ % 87 % 13	✓+	✓+
12/7 Pirate's Promise	Strong retelling, able to connect w/ main character	Reread when the text doesn't make sense → making progress Does the sentence make sense? Yes: ~~||||~~ ~~||||~~ ~~||||~~ ~~||||~~ ~~||||~~ |||| No: |||	✓+ % 91 % 9	+	+
1/19 Monet	Nonfiction Strong retelling No miscues	Does the sentence make sense? Yes: ~~||||~~ ~~||||~~ ~~||||~~ ~~||||~~ ~~||||~~ | No:	+ % 100 % 0	+	+

Figure 9.7: Informal Miscue Analysis

The second variation of this form, the Informal Miscue Analysis Record (Form 9.10B) provides room to record the same information found on the Informal Miscue Analysis from just one conference, with more room to write comments. There's also a column for analysis of the cueing systems students used for each miscue (MSV). You may want to use this version with students who read too fluently to use a running record, but who still make a significant number of miscues. When they become more fluent, you could use the Informal Miscue Analysis (Form 9.10A).

It's important to remember (and to remind parents) that the primary focus of reading is to gain meaning. Pronouncing words correctly does not guarantee that a child has understood the words or passage. One reader may not make any miscues, but have poor comprehension. Another child will make several miscues, but maintain a clear understanding of what was read. Your instruction should be quite different for these two children. What types of miscues does each reader make? Are they primarily nonsense words? Are the miscues graphically similar to the text? Most importantly, do the miscues affect meaning? If students correct their own miscues or go back to search for more cues, it shows they are focusing on making sense of what they read. In the next section of this chapter, we'll look at assessment tools that specifically address comprehension.

Here we've presented ten techniques for diagnosing reading strategies. No one can possibly use more than one or two of these ideas. Which technique will work best for you?

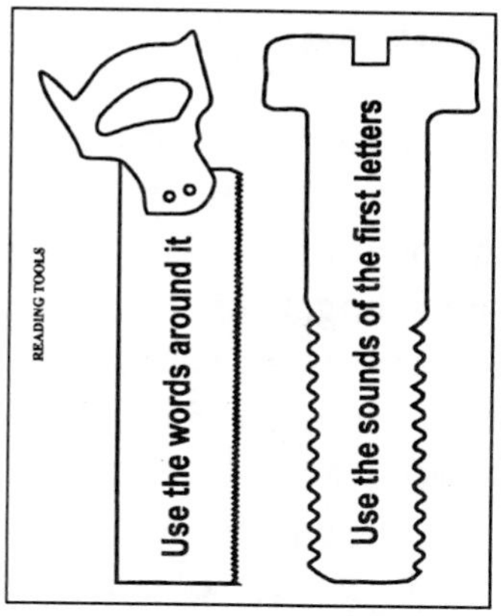

Form 9.1: Reading Tools

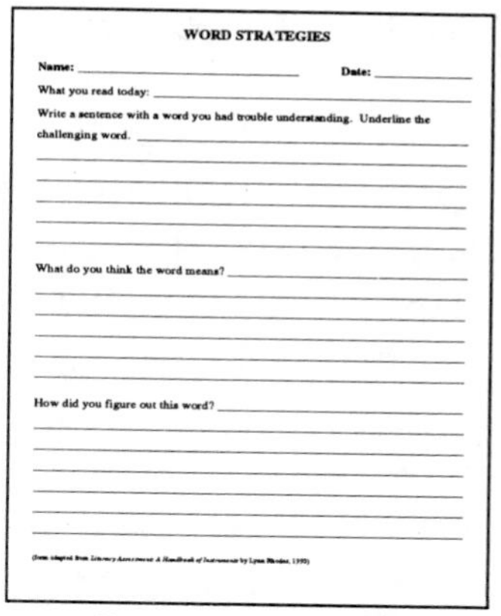

WORD STRATEGIES

Name: ______ Date: ______

What you read today: ______

Write a sentence with a word you had trouble understanding. Underline the challenging word. ______

What do you think the word means? ______

How did you figure out this word? ______

Form 9.2: Word Strategies

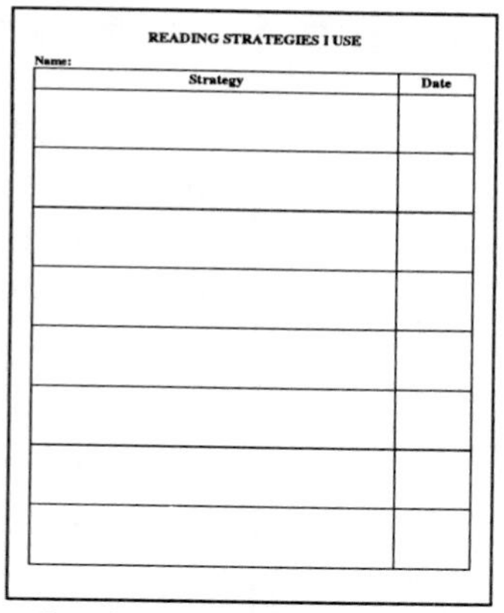

READING STRATEGIES I USE

Name:

Strategy	Date

Form 9.3: Reading Strategies I Use

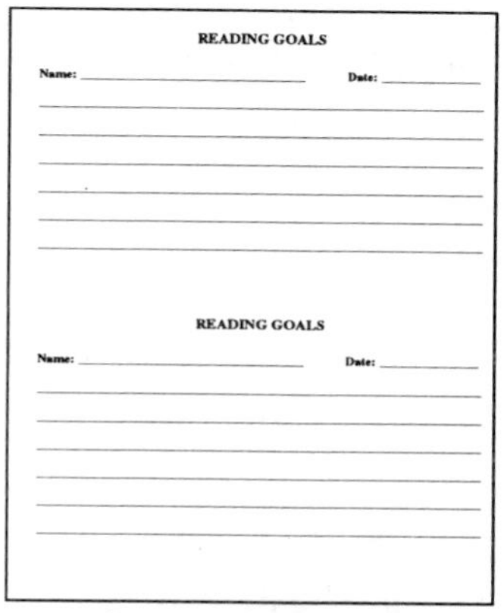

READING GOALS

Name: ______ Date: ______

READING GOALS

Name: ______ Date: ______

Form 9.4: Reading Goals

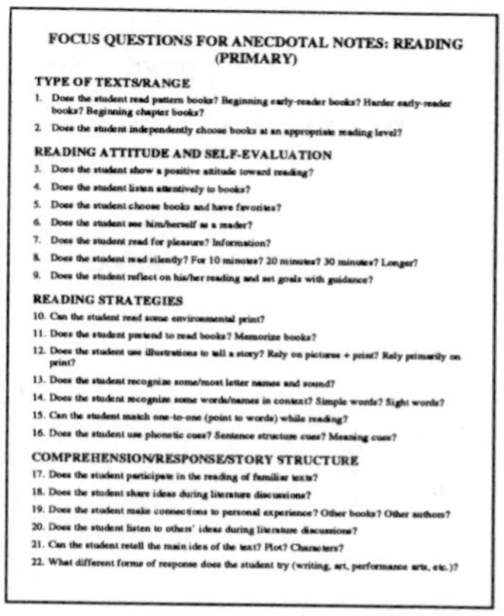

FOCUS QUESTIONS FOR ANECDOTAL NOTES: READING (PRIMARY)

TYPE OF TEXTS/RANGE

1. Does the student read pattern books? Beginning early-reader books? Harder early-reader books? Beginning chapter books?
2. Does the student independently choose books at an appropriate reading level?

READING ATTITUDE AND SELF-EVALUATION

3. Does the student show a positive attitude toward reading?
4. Does the student listen attentively to books?
5. Does the student choose books and have favorites?
6. Does the student see him/herself as a reader?
7. Does the student read for pleasure? Information?
8. Does the student read silently? For 10 minutes? 20 minutes? 30 minutes? Longer?
9. Does the student reflect on his/her reading and set goals with guidance?

READING STRATEGIES

10. Can the student read some environmental print?
11. Does the student pretend to read books? Memorize books?
12. Does the student use illustrations to tell a story? Rely on pictures + print? Rely primarily on print?
13. Does the student recognize some/most letter names and sound?
14. Does the student recognize some words/names in context? Simple words? Sight words?
15. Can the student match one-to-one (point to words) while reading?
16. Does the student use phonetic cues? Sentence structure cues? Meaning cues?

COMPREHENSION/RESPONSE/STORY STRUCTURE

17. Does the student participate in the reading of familiar texts?
18. Does the student share ideas during literature discussions?
19. Does the student make connections to personal experience? Other books? Other authors?
20. Does the student listen to others' ideas during literature discussions?
21. Can the student retell the main idea of the text? Plot? Characters?
22. What different forms of response does the student try (writing, art, performance arts, etc.)?

Form 9.5:
Focus Questions for Anecdotal Notes

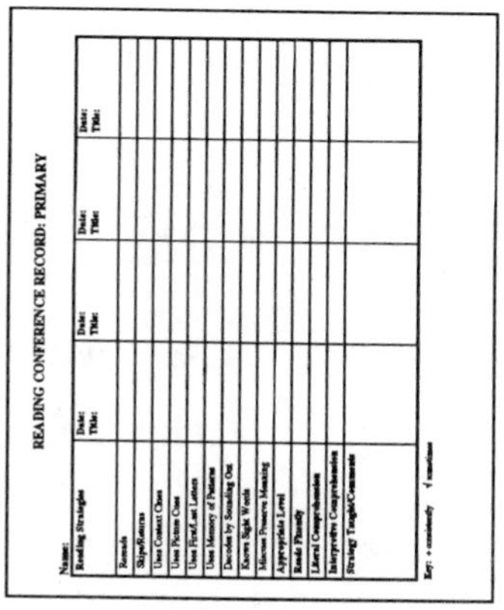

Form 9.6:
Reading Conference Record Form

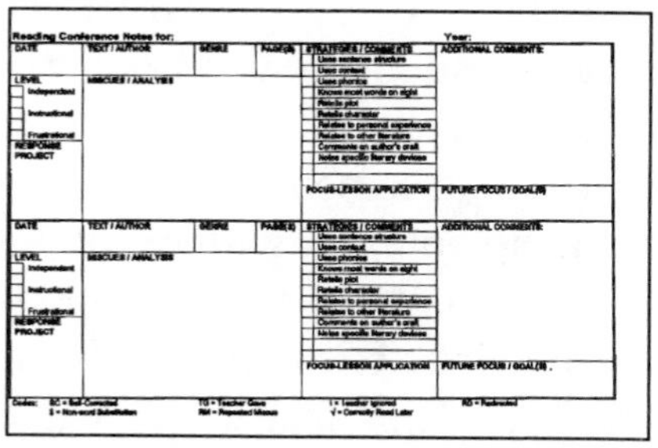

Form 9.7: Reading Conference Notes

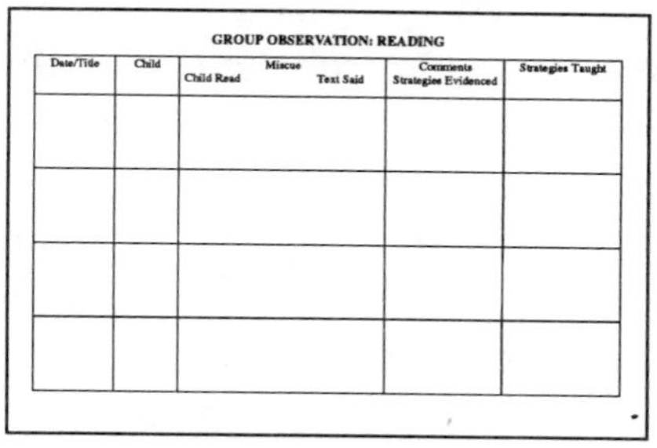

GROUP OBSERVATION: READING

Date/Title	Child	Miscue: Child Read	Miscue: Text Said	Comments Strategies Evidenced	Strategies Taught

Form 9.8: Reading Observation

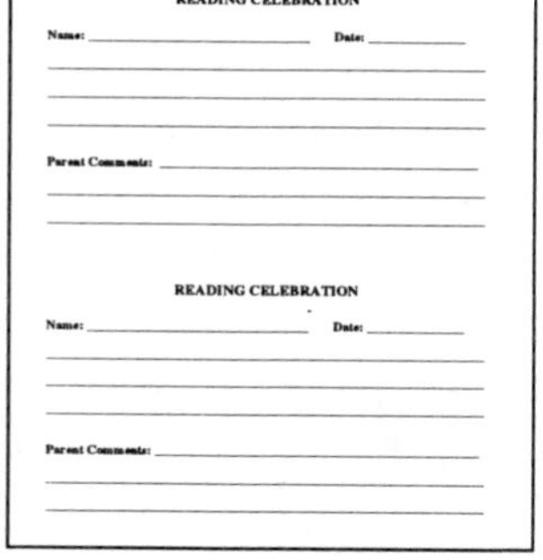

READING CELEBRATION

Name: ______ Date: ______

Parent Comments: ______

READING CELEBRATION

Name: ______ Date: ______

Parent Comments: ______

Form 9.9: Reading Celebration

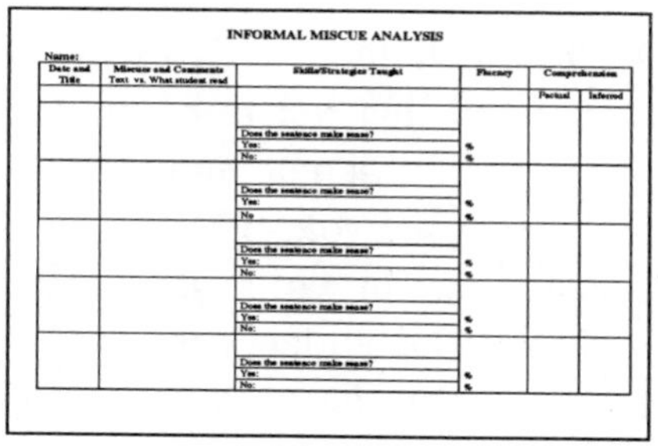

Form 9.10: Informal Miscue Analysis

Section Two: Assessing Reading Comprehension

When you were in school, how did you respond to what you read? If you're over the age of 30, you probably recall color-coded SRA kits, filling in the blanks on multiple-choice tests, or writing the answers to comprehension questions. Others may remember book reports all too well. If you are younger or were fortunate to have had some creative teachers, you may have performed an occasional play or constructed a diorama. Teachers assessed comprehension primarily through the use of pencil and paper tests. We know, however, that there are many more effective ways to assess comprehension besides short-answer, literal level questioning. Individual reading conferences, as described in the last section, provide one of the best opportunities to assess comprehension. In this section, we describe how you can also catch glimpses of students' understanding as you listen to literature discussions or examine their written and artistic responses to literature. We also show how you can use rubrics, retelling, and student self-evaluations to assess comprehension.

Assessing Oral Response to Literature

1. Anecdotal Notes

How can you document evidence of comprehension that you observe during discussions about books? We've found the most effective assessment method is to take anecdotal notes during student-led discussions. If you're facilitating or leading the discussion, you may want to tape record the conversation or jot down a few notes "after the fact." Other teachers take anecdotal notes as they listen in on a group. Although we provided a list of focus questions for reading earlier in this chapter, we also wanted to include the specific focus questions we use when we listen to literature circle discussions (Form 9.11).

Literature circles often begin with a focus lesson about a particular ingredient of effective discussions, such as backing up opinions with examples from the text. Teachers can then use their anecdotal notes to record evidence of students who apply that strategy during discussions. Literature circles often end with a whole-class conversation about what went well and problems that arose. These focus lessons and oral debriefings can help students learn how to conduct effective and independent discussions about literature.

For instance, Cindy Flegenheimer at Brighton School in Lynnwood, Washington noticed that her third graders would share a response, then the group would move on without responding to the idea. To illustrate more effective discussion strategies, she used role-play to demonstrate the difference between parallel conversations and one in which students respond to each others' ideas. After practicing this technique, the students added "Piggyback off each others' ideas" to their class chart of the characteristics of quality discussions. Cindy then used her anecdotal notes to record when children responded by linking onto others' ideas or asking questions. She shared her observations during the debriefings at the end of each literature circle discussion. As students learned to sustain the conversation for longer periods of time, Cindy was able step back and listen to the discussions in order to assess comprehension.

2. Literature Discussion Self-Evaluation

Many teachers find it helpful to periodically use written self-evaluation forms. Patti Kamber from Bainbridge Island developed the Literature Discussion Self-Evaluation (Form 9.12A). Students write about what they did well and how they could improve the next time. Anne Klein adapted the form to include room for students to give feedback to other members of their discussion group (Form 9.12B). In Figure 9.8, you can see an example of Jeff's self-evaluation for his first round of literature circle discussions and the compliments from his peers.

The information you learn from oral and written reflections can help you plan your next focus lessons. In addition, these listening and speaking skills carry over into discussions and collaborative projects in other areas.

3. Discussion Rubric

In *Literature Circles and Response* (Hill, Johnson and Noe, 1995), Anne Klein describes how she weaves discussions, writing, and responding to literature around a theme, genre, or topic. As her students meet to talk about a book they are reading in common, the class creates a chart of the criteria for quality discussions. Anne and her students then develop a rubric based on the criteria. At the beginning of the year, Anne refers to the rubric before and after discussions, so students can become more familiar with her expectations. In addition, the rubric provides a focus for Anne's anecdotal notes.

For example, during their first literature discussion, Anne told students that she would be looking to see if they were making eye contact with the person in their group who was speaking. Anne used her anecdotal notes to share her observations during the post-discussion debriefing. Later in the year, Anne watches for more sophisticated skills, such as drawing out quiet group members or making connections to other books and authors. The Discussion Rubric (Form 9.13) contains descriptors for being prepared for the meeting, contributing to the discussion, keeping the conversation going, listening well, and responding thoughtfully. Anne alternates between using the rubric and more open-ended self-evaluation forms to evaluate both participation and comprehension.

Assessing Written Response to Literature

Dialogue or response journals are often used in conjunction with novel studies or literature circles. Students may sometimes write spontaneous reactions as they read; other times the teacher may provide a focus for written responses. These journal entries reveal a great deal about students' comprehension and can provide a springboard for literature circle discussions.

Discussion Summary
Group Feedback
Anne Klein
Edmonds School District

Name: Jeff Linton **Date:** 11/4/97
Book: Night of the Twisters
Author: Ivy Ruckman

Please summarize what **you** did and/or learned today during your literature discussion group I talked mostly about tornados and if I was the kids in the book. I learned that the auther realy likes to use suspencful words to get you all jumpy. I thought the book was great.

Comments from other group members:

Adam. Kept us on track at all times and asks lots of question[r]

2. Ashley. Jeff, you did very good! I think you did a good disishion on some topick discussion and you stayed on track more than most of us.

Figure 9.8: Discussion Summary

In her first-grade classroom, Christy Clausen meets with small groups on Monday and Tuesday to talk about the books students read. On Wednesday, her students write in their journals. Their conversations provide the scaffolding for their written responses. At the beginning of the year in first grade, the journal entries are quite brief, sometimes consisting of a picture and caption or a short sentence. As students become more comfortable writing and talking about books, their journal entries increase in quality and length.

In Anne Klein's intermediate classroom, students write more extensively in their journals as they read and students often refer to their entries during literature circle discussions. Students often respond to what they read and jot down questions to raise in their discussions. Some students record favorite lines, interesting words, or new vocabulary. In classrooms like these, reading, talking, and writing are intertwined. As mentioned in Chapter 7, however, journal entries are not assessment tools. How can you actually assess students' written responses?

Lisa Norwick introduces response logs in the fall with a discussion about purpose and quality. In September, students tell Lisa that a good entry should say something about the events and characters, be written neatly, and should have some color. As she reads aloud and shares effective journal entries, students add to the class list. As you can see in Figure 9.9, after many conversations and demonstrations, the list of criteria in the spring shows greater depth in terms of both content and quality. You may want to construct a similar chart with your students and add to the list throughout the year. The criteria on this chart become a guide for students to select quality journal samples to include in their portfolios, along with written reflections. Lisa also uses the criteria on the chart as a focus for her anecdotal notes about students' journal responses.

FALL	**SPRING**
	Depth/Content
Include what happened	Go beyond retelling
Describe the characters	Reflect on the book and share your feelings
Write neatly	Tell why the scene was important to you
Add color to your pictures	Compare the book to your own life, someone you know or another book
	Imagine another point of view. If you were one of the characters, what would you do?
	Quality/Packaging
	Write neatly
	Pay attention to color, line, space, and texture
	Put details into your pictures
	You may want to add a border

Figure 9.9: Response Journal Criteria

4. Assessing Response to Literature

Once you've identified the characteristics of effective written response, how can you assess comprehension and document growth? Lisa Norwick and Bonnie Campbell Hill developed the Assessing Response to Literature checklists (Form 9.14A and 9.14B) several years ago. This form evolved through many drafts and has been a useful lens for assessing the developmental progression of students' written response to literature.

Let's take a look at four children's journal responses after reading *The Canada Geese Quilt* (Kinsey-Warnock, 1989). At first, young children's responses tend to be very concrete and literal: "The Canada Geese quilt is neat. I like the geese. They are neat. I like geese." At the next stage, students begin to understand the text at a deeper level as they summarize, make personal connections, respond to the author's craft, and support their opinions. For instance, Carissa responded, "A picture in this book makes my heart warm." Andrew wrote with feeling, "Ariel's mother is having a baby! Her grandma has a stroke! She does not like it! She wants to be an only kid! I know how she feels!" These students are just beginning to move beyond simple retellings. As these students mature and see examples of quality responses, they will begin to examine alternative viewpoints, comment on the author's craft, and evaluate texts.

Lisa Norwick keeps a copy of the primary Assessing Response to Literature page (Form 9.14A) in each child's section of her Teacher Notebook to show growth over time. When she taught sixth grade, she used the intermediate version (Form 9.14B). At first, she tried assessing each journal entry, but found she couldn't keep up with the paperwork and was becoming overwhelmed. Now she only uses the form at the end of each literature circle set. Lisa looks through each student's journal and chooses one representative entry to assess using the form. This sampling method was much more manageable. Based on what she learns, she may ask students to share exemplary work or provide more samples of responses that move beyond retelling. Lisa finds that this periodic assessment captures student growth and shapes her instruction.

Let's look at another example. In Figure 9.10, you can see by glancing at the form how much progress Bryce made during the year. In October, his written response to *Pioneer Cat* (Hooks, 1988) was very literal, consisting mainly of a picture and summary of the scene from the book:

> Kate has to move to Oregon. She is struggling to stay. She has a best friend in Mississippi. She found a cat. She named the cat Snuggles. She tries to bring the cat. She was in a panic. Then she finds Snuggles and puts the cat in the box which her mom said you can put anything in the box that will fit. I feel like she is desperate to take Snuggles.

In March, Bryce created a character mobile with a description of the characters' thoughts and feelings from *Sarah Plain and Tall* (McLaughlin, 1985). His written response was more sophisticated than earlier in the year. You can also see the improvement in his sentence structure and word choice:

> Caleb likes Sarah but I think he is also worried that Sarah won't be staying with them. He worries that Sarah doesn't like the flat prairie and wants to go back to Maine where her home was and the sea was. Caleb worries too much. Maine and the prairie are two different things and Caleb wants the sea to be where the prairie is. Caleb hopes Sarah will marry Pa. Pa and Sarah are both shy of each other, Caleb thinks. He wants to get Sarah and Pa together so they will get so fond of each other they will get married. Then Caleb would have someone to take care of him and teach him new things. He really likes Sarah!

Bryce not only summarized the story, but he also included his personal reaction and supported his ideas by including important information from the book. He was also able to write about Caleb's point of view; it's evident from reading his response that Bryce understands what Caleb was thinking and feeling about Sarah. In Figure 9.10, you can see how the Assessing Response to Literature form is simple to use and clearly reflects growth over time. Lisa finds this form particularly helpful to share with students and parents.

ASSESSING RESPONSE TO LITERATURE: PRIMARY

Name: Bryce

Date / Title	Literal Level	Personal Reaction	Prediction	Summarizes Retells	Supports Justifies	Other Points of View	Evaluates	Discusses Author's Craft	Comments
9-27 The Chalk Box Kid	✓								Picture with a short description of the scene
10-29 Pioneer Cat	✓			✓					Picture with a retelling of the story
11-25 On My Honor		✓		✓					Character Interview - Voice is evident
1-28 Stone Fox		✓		✓	✓				Pamphlet - aesthetic response
3-12 Sarah, Plain and Tall		✓	✓	✓	✓	✓			Character Mobile - elaborates on Caleb's feelings - complex sentences

Figure 9.10: Assessing Response to Literature

5. Reading Journal Rubrics

In the Tahoma school district in Washington, Emilie Hard developed a four-point rubric for response journal entries. She shows examples of journal entries for each level to her students. In her classroom, students often write two response journal entries each week. Emilie scores one of them using the Response Journal Rubric (Form 9.15A) and writes a brief response. As the year progresses, students are able to score their own journal entries and those of their partners. Emilie says that her students like the clear targets and are very honest in their self-evaluations.

Anne Klein, in Edmonds, Washington, created a more detailed rubric for journal entries with her intermediate students. Students at the expert level on the Journal Response Rubric (Form 9.15B) respond thoughtfully, summarize, evaluate, make connections to other books and discuss elements of literature. At the beginning of the year, Anne uses the rubric to respond to every journal entry in order to provide feedback and guidance. During focus lessons, she shares entries that support the reader's opinion and examine other perspectives. As the year progresses, Anne uses the rubric only at the end of a literature circle set to evaluate each journal as a whole. She also includes a narrative summary on the Journal Comments page (Form 9.15C). In Figure 9.11, you can see Anne's comments about Jeff's journal responses to *Night of the Twisters* (Ruckman, 1984). Students include their response journal, the rubric, and Anne's comments in their portfolios. Anne finds that when she provides models and helps students develop criteria for effective journal responses, the quality of students' written responses increases dramatically. She also notices that some children who rarely contribute during literature discussions may demonstrate comprehension in their written responses.

We want to interject a few warnings about journal entries. For primary students, the physical act of writing is hard work. We don't want the written response to become too time consuming or painful. Most primary teachers show quality examples of response and focus on building fluency, but do not use rubrics to evaluate students' journals. Rubrics at all levels are most effective when they are developed by students, used sparingly, and continually connected to instruction.

6. Artistic Response Rubrics

In any classroom, you'll find some students who shine during discussions and others who excel in written responses. Other children blossom when give opportunities to respond to literature through the arts. Students can show their understanding of a book through murals, talk show interviews with characters, and alphabet books based on novels. Lisa Norwick's chapter in *Literature Circles and Response* (Hill, Johnson and Noe, 1995) provides a rich menu of ways to respond to literature through music, drama, and art. Barry Hoonan, a sixth-grade teacher in Redmond, Washington, also wrote a chapter in the book on responding through the arts.

When you step into Barry's classroom, you can see evidence of literacy in every corner and on every wall. Students cluster at tables and on the floor, adding final

Journal Comments

Student Name: Jeff Linton Date: 11/3/97

Book Title: Night of the Twisters **Author:** Ivy Ruckman

Cover (title, author, student name, illustration & page #, neat)
Completed - dramatic scene of twister!
Includes all items

Entries (dated, varied, comments supported with examples/details, neat)
① Great Red letter Day Writing! And Black letter Day
② Clear prediction 10/15
③ Great sentences 10/20
④ Jeff - you did a very complete job of giving examples and reasons on 10/27 and 11/3!

Vocabulary (*at least* 10 words completed, correct definition, neat)
19 Words Completed!

Overall Score Based on the Literature Circle Scoring Guide: 5+
Super 1st Journal

Figure 9.11: Journal Comments

touches to their literature response projects. It's evident by listening to the rehearsal for a play or watching a group prepare a slide show that these students work hard and that expectations are high. Over the past few months, Barry helped the class develop a list of the criteria for quality response projects. When students share their projects with the class, the audience provides feedback based on the list of criteria by sharing "two stars and a wish," an idea Carolyn Burke uses in her graduate classes. The stars represent two things from the list of criteria that students think the group did well. The wish is a nudge for how the project could be improved. Barry explains that the wish should reflect what the audience thinks the group could have done differently or better. In this classroom, reactions are given orally after each presentation. In other classrooms, each group chooses two students to provide written feedback using the half-page form called Two Stars and a Wish (Form 9.16A), while other audience members share their compliments and suggestions orally.

We included a primary Presentation Rubric (Form 9.16B) which Trilby Cohen, Heidi Hanson, and Melissa Sargent developed for sharing final response projects in their second-grade classrooms at Syre Elementary in Seattle, Washington. They develop these criteria with their students and use the rubric as guidelines for creating response projects more than as an evaluation tool.

Anne Klein's intermediate students also create response projects using drama, art, or music after they complete a literature circle book. As in Barry's class, the projects are then shared with the whole class. Anne and her students developed a Response Project Rubric (Form 9.16C) and a Presentation Rubric (Form 9.16D). Students complete these forms after they share their projects with the rest of the class. Anne videotapes the presentations and completes the rubric, adding personal notes at the bottom of the form. Later in the day, each group watches the videotape of their presentation and individually completes the rubric. Students immediately notice if they turned their back to the audience or spoke too softly. The rubrics provide guidelines and reminders of quality as the students create new projects. As students present their projects, the rubrics also provide an evaluation tool for assessing comprehension. Response projects should require students to delve deeper into a novel.

For instance, one group of students spent hours scanning through *Walk Two Moons* (Creech, 1994), discussing story events and poring over maps as they created their own map of Salamanca's cross-country journey to find her mother. When they explained the story and shared the map, complete with illustrations of story events, there was no question about their understanding of the book.

Anne's students have an assessment section in their binders that go home and back to school each day. Anne gives each student a copy of the continuums, self-evaluation forms, and rubrics the class developed. She makes reference to the assessment tools in her newsletters. For instance, when students practice at home for their literature response projects, Anne mentions that families may want to refer to the rubrics to clarify expectations.

Retelling

7. Retelling Guides

Laura chatters about the latest Nancy Drew book she finished and takes half an hour to retell every single event, complete with phrases about faithful Hannah and George's boyish manner. There's no question about her comprehension! Retelling is an effective way to assess students' understanding of what they read. Many forms, however, are too cumbersome to use easily in the classroom. In addition, when students don't have experience with this technique, you are actually assessing their ability to retell rather than their comprehension.

Megan Sloan models both effective and ineffective retellings with her second graders in Snohomish, Washington. The class next develops criteria for a good retelling. Megan then asks her students to read a picture book or short story with a partner. The children take turns retelling the story, then they each complete the Retelling Self-Evaluation (Form 9.17A). After practicing this strategy, Megan uses the teacher version, called the Retelling Evaluation (Form 9.17B), to assess comprehension more meaningfully. She also finds that as students use the Retelling Self-Evaluation, they become more aware of literary elements which, in turn, impacts their writing.

Lisa Norwick developed a Fiction Retelling Guide (Form 9.17C) and a Nonfiction Retelling Guide (Form 9.17D) with her students. Lisa chooses five or six short fiction and nonfiction passages from a literature anthology or the *Qualitative Reading Inventory* (Leslie & Caldwell, 1995). During individual reading conferences, Lisa asks each child to select one of the passages. As the student reads the selection, Lisa uses the Informal Running Record (Form 8.2) or Informal Miscue Analysis (Form 9.10) to assess reading strategies, fluency, and accuracy. She then asks the student to retell the passage. Lisa uses the Fiction or Nonfiction Retelling Guide to assess comprehension. She created two columns on the form to note whether children could retell aspects of literary elements independently or needed prompting.

8. Retelling Rubrics

Lisa uses retelling guides with primary students but uses rubrics with older students, particularly when she is required to give letter grades on a report card. Grades in isolation have very little meaning. Rubrics, however, provide one way for students and parents to understand the criteria used to determine grades if letter grades are required at your school. Lisa transposed the criteria from the retelling guides into a Fiction Retelling Rubric (Form 9.18A) and a Nonfiction Retelling Rubric (Form 19.18B). The criteria on the rubric reflect the specific strategies Lisa teaches in her focus lessons. Rubrics and other assessment tools become most effective when conscious connections are made between assessment and instruction.

Retelling can take on a more playful air when it becomes part of storytelling. A prompt such as "Tell me what this story is about," often elicits of a string of "and then's." In Chapter 7 of *Looking, Listening, and Learning*, Carl Braun (1993) suggests that teachers will find an entirely different level of response when they begin with a storytelling rather than an assessment stance. In addition to assessing comprehension through storytelling, he raises other intriguing possibilities for assessing phonics through poetry cloze techniques and assessing oral fluency through verse and Reader's Theatre.

Self-Evaluation: Comprehension

9. Comprehension Strategies and Cloze Techniques

Another way to assess comprehension is to ask students to reflect on their own strategies. Based on the ideas in *Literacy Assessment: A Handbook of Instruments* (Rhodes, 1993), Lisa Norwick created a simple Comprehension Strategies survey (Form 9.19) with just two questions: What are 2–3 key ideas you remember from what you just read? What strategies did you use to help you understand what you read? Lisa guides several discussions about comprehension strategies and models how to fill out the form before she asks students to complete it independently.

For instance, when her class was studying the life cycle of salmon, Lisa copied a one-page nonfiction passage for each child. After they read the selection silently, Lisa asked the children to write down two or three key ideas they remembered or learned from the article. On the second half of the form, they listed the comprehension strategies they used while reading. Some students said they made predictions and then read to see if they were right. Others reread to check meaning or made connections to what they already knew about salmon. The Comprehension Strategies questionnaire and the discussions help Lisa assess the strategies students use to make sense of what they read. She finds this open-ended form works particularly well with nonfiction and content area reading and could be used by students at any level.

Another technique for assessing reading strategies is the cloze procedure (Pikulski and Tobin, 1982), in which every fifth or seventh word from a passage is omitted and students fill in words that would make sense. A more effective approach is to omit words based on parts of speech (two nouns, two adjectives, two adverbs, etc).

> In our view, the best use of cloze is as a classroom assessment/instructional procedure in which the teacher decides what words to leave out on her own. The teacher chooses to omit words that students can fill in if they are following semantic and syntactic cues within the text. (Rhodes and Shanklin, 1993, p. 191)

Regie Routman suggests having students work in pairs when using cloze activities so that they can share their choices and strategies. This technique, which may also be done orally, can spark conversations about effective reading strategies such as prediction, confirming, reading ahead, and self-monitoring.

10. Reading Self-Evaluation

Lavon Vigil-Johnson, a primary teacher from Salt Lake City, Utah developed the Reading Self-Evaluation (Form 9.20) for students to evaluate three aspects of reading: reading strategies, oral fluency, and comprehension. Students use the first part of the form after several weeks of discussions about reading strategies. Lavon then spends the next few weeks focusing on oral reading fluency and students tape record themselves as they practice reading smoothly. At this point, she explains the second portion of the form, which students use to evaluate their own oral reading. When she introduces the idea of retelling, students complete all three parts. This form helps students see the components of reading and learn to evaluate themselves.

We've focused on ten ways to assess student comprehension. Take a minute to look through this section and determine which forms might be most helpful in your classroom.

FOCUS QUESTIONS FOR ANECDOTAL NOTES:
LITERATURE DISCUSSIONS

1. Is the student prepared for the literature discussion?
2. Does the student use the text to share passages? To support ideas and opinions? How effectively?
3. Does the student listen actively to others?
4. Does the student ask questions? What kinds?
5. Do the questions get a thoughtful response? Which are most effective?
6. Does the student contribute thoughtful ideas?
7. Does the student make predictions? How effectively?
8. Does the student build on other people's comments?
9. Does the student keep the group on task?
10. Does the student discuss unknown or interesting words?
11. Does the student make personal connections to his/her life? At what levels?
12. Does the student make connections to other books, authors, and experiences?
13. Does the student discuss the author's craft and word choice?
14. Does the student discuss literary elements (plot, setting, character)?
15. Can the student reflect on literature circle participation and set goals?

Form 9.11: Focus Questions for Anecdotal Notes

LITERATURE DISCUSSION SELF-EVALUATION

Name: ______ Date: ______
Title: ______ Author: ______

What did I do well during our literature discussion? (asked good questions, listened actively, responded to others, supported my ideas using the book, took a risk, compared the book to my life or other books)

What could I do better next time?

Form 9.12: Literature Discussion Self-Evaluation

DISCUSSION RUBRIC

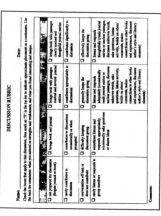

Form 9.13: Discussion Rubric

ASSESSING RESPONSE TO LITERATURE: PRIMARY

Form 9.14: Assessing Response to Literature

RESPONSE JOURNAL RUBRIC

Name: ______ Date: ______
Title of Book: ______

4 In addition to a precise plot summary, the writer makes inferences, predictions, comparisons, or evaluations and supports ideas with evidence from the story. The writer makes connections with his/her life, other books or other events. The writer demonstrates fluency.

3 The plot is accurately summarized with specific details. The writer shares one or more personal reflections and gives examples to support his/her interpretations.

2 The plot is summarized in a general way but lacks detail or support. The writer may share a general personal response.

1 The writer retells minimal details from the story.

Form 9.15: Response Journal Rubric

TWO STARS AND A WISH

Name: ______ Project: ______
Reviewer: ______ Date: ______
☆ ______
☆ ______
WISH ______

TWO STARS AND A WISH

Name: ______ Project: ______
Reviewer: ______ Date: ______
☆ ______
☆ ______
WISH ______

Form 9.16: Response Project Rubric

RETELLING SELF-EVALUATION

Name: ______ Date: ______
Title: ______

- ❑ I told when and where the story took place.
- ❑ I told about the main character.
- ❑ I told about other characters.
- ❑ I told the main problem in the story.
- ❑ I told some of the details from the story.
- ❑ I told how the problem was solved.
- ❑ I used some of the language from the book.
- ❑ I made connections to my life or other books.
- ❑ I told what I thought of the book.

Form 9.17: Retelling Self-Evaluation

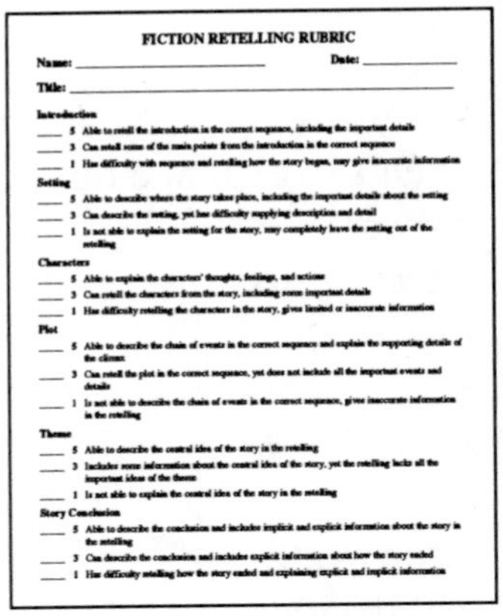

FICTION RETELLING RUBRIC

Name: ____________ Date: ________

Title: ______________________

Introduction

____ 5 Able to retell the introduction in the correct sequence, including the important details

____ 3 Can retell some of the main points from the introduction in the correct sequence

____ 1 Has difficulty with sequence and retelling how the story began, may give inaccurate information

Setting

____ 5 Able to describe where the story takes place, including the important details about the setting

____ 3 Can describe the setting, yet has difficulty supplying description and detail

____ 1 Is not able to explain the setting for the story, may completely leave the setting out of the retelling

Characters

____ 5 Able to explain the characters' thoughts, feelings, and actions

____ 3 Can retell the characters from the story, including some important details

____ 1 Has difficulty retelling the characters in the story, gives limited or inaccurate information

Plot

____ 5 Able to describe the chain of events in the correct sequence and explain the supporting details of the climax

____ 3 Can retell the plot in the correct sequence, yet does not include all the important events and details

____ 1 Is not able to describe the chain of events in the correct sequence, gives inaccurate information in the retelling

Theme

____ 5 Able to describe the central idea of the story in the retelling

____ 3 Includes some information about the central idea of the story, yet the retelling lacks all the important ideas of the theme

____ 1 Is not able to explain the central idea of the story in the retelling

Story Conclusion

____ 5 Able to describe the conclusion and includes implicit and explicit information about the story in the retelling

____ 3 Can describe the conclusion and includes explicit information about how the story ended

____ 1 Has difficulty retelling how the story ended and explaining explicit and implicit information

Form 9.18: Retelling Rubric

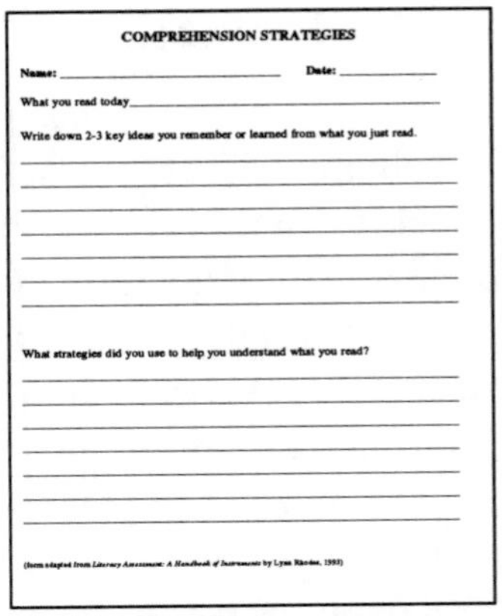

COMPREHENSION STRATEGIES

Name: ____________ Date: ________

What you read today____________________

Write down 2-3 key ideas you remember or learned from what you just read.

What strategies did you use to help you understand what you read?

(form adapted from *Literacy Assessment: A Handbook of Instruments* by Lynn Rhodes, 1993)

Form 9.19: Comprehension Strategies

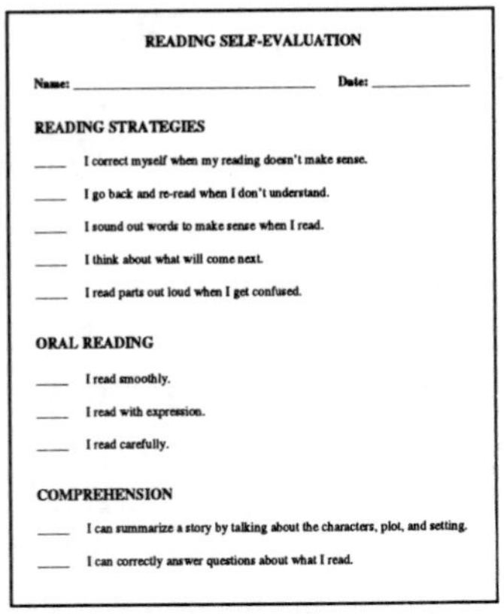

READING SELF-EVALUATION

Name: ____________ Date: ________

READING STRATEGIES

____ I correct myself when my reading doesn't make sense.

____ I go back and re-read when I don't understand.

____ I sound out words to make sense when I read.

____ I think about what will come next.

____ I read parts out loud when I get confused.

ORAL READING

____ I read smoothly.

____ I read with expression.

____ I read carefully.

COMPREHENSION

____ I can summarize a story by talking about the characters, plot, and setting.

____ I can correctly answer questions about what I read.

Form 9.20: Reading Self-Evaluation

Section Three: Reading Range

John has read almost every *Goosebumps* book written by R.L. Stine. Devon knows an amazing amount of details from each of Brian Jacques' action-packed fantasy novels. Michelle loves stories about dogs, especially ones that make her cry, like *Murphy and Kate* (Howard, 1995) and *Toby* (Wild, 1994). Maya and Tony prefer *Eyewitness* books and browsing through the encyclopedia on CD-ROM. Do you know what kinds of materials each of your students likes to read? How do you help them find new authors and invite them to try new genres? We need to help students learn to assess their own reading patterns and set goals for their reading. In this section, we'll look at six different ways you and your students can record and assess the types of materials they read.

In this book, we differentiate between reading response journals and reading logs. In the last section, we talked about response journals, in which students respond through writing and art to the books they read. In this section, we'll discuss reading logs as useful tools for keeping track of the amount and range of texts that children read. Although many assessment books describe journals that are often referred to as reading logs, very little mention is made of ways in which to assess students' reading patterns. Ironically, reading logs are probably the most familiar and most commonly used of any of the reading assessment techniques we've presented in this chapter. In this section, we hope to take a fresh look at the purpose and types of reading logs teachers have developed. All too often, reading logs become dreaded tasks or dead-end roads. Who is the audience for the reading log? How can the information become a springboard for conversations with other readers? How can a log become a manageable and informative assessment tool?

In the primary grades, a reading log might simply be a list of books. At the intermediate level, reading logs can include the author, the date when the book was started and completed, and a rating of the book on a numerical scale. You might also want students to record the genre, the number of pages in the book, and possibly a brief reaction statement or comment. Children can also note their favorite books and authors. As adults, you might record the titles and authors of children's books, professional books, and adult novels you read. What's important is that the purpose for keeping a log is clear and the expectations reasonable.

Reading logs may be used specifically for reading at home, reading in school, or a combination of both. You may wish to use the logs periodically or ask students to record only completed or favorite books. *It's important to encourage extensive reading without allowing students to become competitive about the number of books they are reading.* The focus should never be on quantity. Completing logs should not be a burdensome task that detracts from a child's pleasure in reading. You certainly don't want filling out the log to take more time than reading the book! Younger children might want to record just a few of their favorite books for the week, rather than all the books they read.

Reading logs can become an assessment tool when you and your students step back periodically to look for patterns. By recording the amounts and types of materials students read, you can catch a glimpse of children's interests, as well as the quantity and range of their reading. By knowing what students choose to read, you can match instruction to their abilities and interests. Information from the logs can also be shared with parents during conferences and in narrative comments on progress reports. Some of you may want to respond to students after they have read a number of books. You can write a brief note or recommend other titles and authors. The log then becomes a tool for a written conversation between you and your students.

As an adult, you probably have trouble remembering what you've read recently. We've found it helpful to keep our own reading log of chapter books, adult novels, and professional books. You may even want to use one of the reading logs in this section for yourself. Parents in your room may also be interested in trying out one of the reading logs for their own adult reading. We find that our logs help us keep a balance in our reading and celebrate how much reading we manage to squeeze into our busy lives. We share our logs with students as a way to show how much we value reading outside as well as inside of school.

Lisa Norwick finds that a rating scale on a reading log is also much more meaningful when the class talks about the criteria. In the fall, the class list about the qualities of a good book is quite simplistic. According to her class, a good book is fun, interesting, and not too hard. Throughout the year, the class adds to the list whenever Lisa finishes reading picture books or novels aloud. The increasing sophistication of the criteria list reflects students' increasing competence as readers and writers as well as the effectiveness of Lisa's focus lessons.

In Figure 9.12, you can see how the spring list reflects more specificity as they extend their criteria for a good book. Of course, you would want to create a similar chart with your own students and add to it throughout the year.

FALL	SPRING
Fun to read	Fun to read
Interesting writing	Holds your interest through the entire book
Interesting characters	You have strong feelings about the book
Not too hard	Exciting parts
	Steals your brain
	Sad and happy parts
	You know what the characters think and feel
	You learn new and interesting information

Figure 9.12: Criteria for a Good Book

Reading Logs and Records

1. Reading Log Variations

We have included four reading logs (Form 9.21A–D), ranging from the simplest version to more detailed logs for more proficient readers. You'll have to decide which form would be most appropriate for the ages of your students and if students will record books they finish in school, at home, or both. Of course, the rating scale will be more meaningful if students first develop the criteria for the rating.

We also wanted to include a variation that shows how you can adapt reading logs for specific themes or genres. Carrie Holloway's literature circles at Blakely Elementary on Bainbridge Island, Washington sometimes revolve around nonfiction texts. She developed a specific Marine Science reading log (Form 9.21E) where her students recorded the informational materials they read independently on the topic. You can adapt this form to fit your own themes or inquiry projects.

Julie Ledford's class in Lynnwood, Washington created a bulletin board labeled "Hooked on Books." Instead of reading logs, students record individual titles on paper "fish." Each child's set of "fish" is collected on a metal ring and hung on the child's hook on the bulletin board (Form 9.21F). As you can see in Figure 9.13, students record the title, author, date, and rating for each book. The children love this visual display of how much they read and enjoy sharing this creative variation of reading logs with each other.

2. Home Reading Logs

The Daily Reading Log (Form 9.22A) provides room to record what and how much students read at home each day. We have mixed feelings about this version. On the one hand, as adults, we would rebel if we had to record the number of pages in a book we read each night. On the other hand, holding students and their families accountable for reading together on a regular basis has substantial merit. Research clearly demonstrates the powerful effect of reading. "Research also shows that the

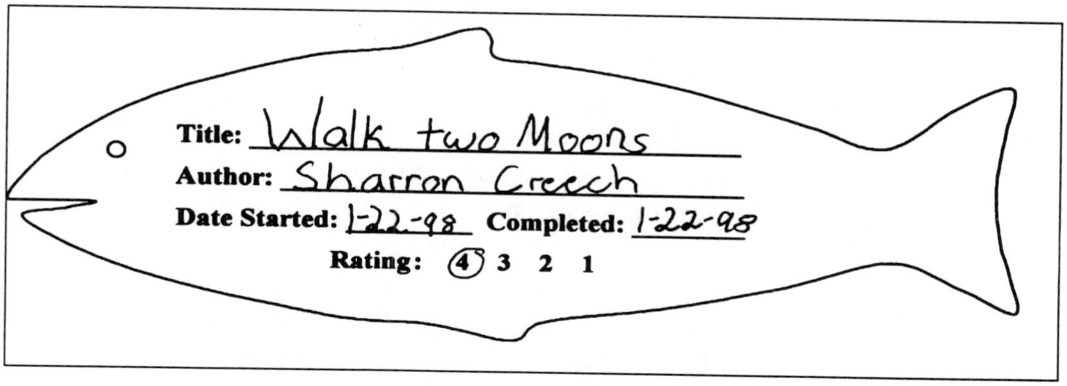

Title: Walk two Moons
Author: Sharron Creech
Date Started: 1-22-98 Completed: 1-22-98
Rating: 4 3 2 1

Figure 9.13: Hooked on Books

amount of reading students do outside of school is consistently related to gains in reading achievement" (Anderson, Hiebert, Scott and Wilkinson, 1985). Yet reading together is rarely as much a part of family life as watching television, particularly after third grade, when students become more independent readers. We've been amazed at the number of parents who have told us that weekly or monthly reading logs have been the impetus for making time each night to read together as a family. You may want to use this form periodically or only at the beginning of the year.

Christy Clausen developed a home reading program based on ideas from *Highlight My Strengths* (Traill, 1993), *Reading To, With, and By Children* (Mooney, 1990), and *Invitations* (Routman, 1991, 1994). At the end of each day, her first graders record the title of the book they take home on their library card and place it in their pocket on the Home Reading Chart. The next morning, the children check in their book on the library card and place their Home Reading Log (Form 9.22B) on Christy's desk.

At Curriculum Night and again in parent newsletters, Christy explained three ways to read a book. A book could be read to the child, with the child, or by the child. We've included a slight modification of the form in *Highlight My Strengths* (Traill, 1993) to include columns where parents could record the date and title of the book, how the book was read (to, with, or by), as well as comments to Christy. She gets about one third of the logs back each morning. During lunch or recess, she takes time to simply check the parent comment or give a quick response. She can give quick tips and answer parent concerns informally through her notes. Christy encounters fewer questions about early reading, since this technique provides an avenue for ongoing conversations about reading.

At Villa Academy in Seattle, Washington, Mary Davey sends home a monthly reading log (Form 9.22C) with her first graders each month. Parents record the books they read with their child each night. At the end of the month, students draw pictures of their favorite book from that month. Later in the year, students add written reactions to their illustrations (Form 9.22D). Monthly book responses are displayed in the room or in the hallway, then added to each child's portfolio. We've also included a Monthly Reading Reflection (Form 9.22E) for intermediate students. This self-evaluation form encourages students to look back at the quantity and range of their reading, record favorite books, and set goals for the next month. These monthly logs capture a picture of the student's reading outside of school and emphasize the value we place on voluntary reading.

Another way to get a broad picture of students' reading range is to use reading logs intensively for a short period of time. At Newport Heights Elementary School in Bellevue, Washington, everyone in the school keeps a reading log for a two-week "Reading Sweep" in the spring (Valencia, 1998). A letter is sent home asking families to help children remember to record everything they read at home and at school. At the end of two weeks, students use a survey (Form 9.22F) to examine the quantity, quality, and frequency of their reading. The log, along with the survey and a generic explanation of the reading sweep is attached to the reading log, included in each student's portfolio, and linked to goal setting. Like the daily or monthly reading logs described previously, this sampling reveals information about a child's reading patterns and emphasizes the value a school places on reading at home as well as at school.

In some communities, home reading logs may be overwhelming. Mary Ann Brown is a librarian at a school for at-risk youngsters in Urbana, Illinois. Instead of a form, Mary Ann makes 11" × 2" strips of paper in different colors for each class. When students come to the library to check out books, she gives them a colored strip on which their parents record the child's name, teacher and the title and author of the book they read. When the students bring completed strips back to school, Mary Ann adds a link to a paper chain that loops around the library. Some children start requesting two or three links each week and Mary Ann has seen a significant increase in family reading as a result of using this simple technique.

3. Range of Reading

Do you have students who only read *Babysitter's Club* or *Goosebumps* books? Do other students read only nonfiction or mysteries? Older students might want to conduct a survey about the types of materials adults read for pleasure and for work. Your class could design a checklist or open-ended survey and compile the results. Margaret Mooney, in her work with Washington state, claims that 80 percent of what adults read in real life is informational and only 20 percent is fiction. School, on the other hand, reverses that percentage, with students reading 80 percent fiction, 50 percent of which is fantasy! Even the prestigious Caldecott award for picture books has been awarded to authors of fiction or folktales 93 percent of the time (Duthie, 1996, p. 6). We are not adequately preparing students for the future if we don't provide a wider range of reading genres and materials. What about starting a bulletin board in the hallway for favorite cartoons? Recipes? Letters to the Editor? In our classrooms, we need to include maps, lyrics, schedules, brochures, lists, postcards, menus, and manuals, as well as poetry, fiction, and nonfiction. In addition, we also have to purposefully teach children how to read and write a wider range of genres.

Some students don't know much about different genres. You could create separate logs for each genre (poetry, historical fiction, nonfiction, etc.), along with a list of key characteristics and sample titles. After finishing a book, students can record the title and author on the appropriate genre list. Many intermediate teachers have developed genre wheels in order to encourage (or require) students to read a wider range of materials. One of the problems we found was that it is hard for students to record more than one title in a category. It's also challenging to print in the narrow pie-shaped slice of the wheel. We wanted to create a more flexible and visual way to see the patterns of students' reading. The Reading Genre Log (Form 9.23A) can be used with primary students. Intermediate teachers may want to use both the primary and the intermediate logs (Form 9.23A and B). The information that they gain from keeping these logs can help students balance their reading diet.

For instance, Laura was captivated by the stories in the *Orphan Train* series by Joan Lowry Nixon. This series is based on true events about the orphans from the East Coast who were shipped West between 1854 and 1929 and adopted by farm families. Her teacher knew that Laura's interest in this historical event was strong enough that she would be interested in *Orphan Train Rider* (Warren, 1996), a nonfiction account of a rider on the orphan trains, even though nonfiction was not Laura's favorite genre. Reading logs and genre forms can help you match children's interests with wonderful books and materials in a variety of genres.

4. Favorite Books

As students begin to increase the amount and range of their reading, it's helpful to know their reading preferences and interests. Kathy Egawa, a librarian at Madrona Elementary in Seattle, Washington, asked her intermediate students to write her a letter about themselves as readers (Egawa, 1988). She suggested that one way to begin was: "If you want to know me as a reader, you need to know that . . ." Together, they talked about what might be included in such a letter. Students wrote about where they like to read, favorite books or authors, and how they learned to read.

The responses were delightful. For instance, one student wrote, "If you want to know me as a reader, you need to know that I LOVE to read. Reading the Baby Sitter's Club is practically my life." Another student said, "If you want to know me as a reader, you need to know that I ADORE poetry. It is my passion. I read it, I write it, I live off it. My soul consists of poetry!" Most of the 400 students who wrote shared intriguing and personal information about themselves. The letters and her responses enable her to connect more meaningfully with the many students who visit the library each month. The letters also help in her search for good read-aloud books, book recommendations, and new titles to order for the library.

Earlier in the year, Kathy had asked the same intermediate students to create a timeline of the most important books in their lives. Working in pairs, students listed all the books they loved. Then, using a strip of 4¼ × 14" paper, they organized the books into a timeline. Some included one book for each year of their lives. Others sectioned off their timeline into periods. The 400 timelines, which were posted in the library, gave Kathy a great deal of information about these young readers. Classes took turns walking around and reading them, then students added the most commonly occurring titles to a "Madrona Students Recommend" list that was mounted for parents to see. As a further extension, students could interview their families about the favorite books their parents read as children. Would any of the books be the same for both generations? Data could be collected from all the intermediate grades and students could decide how to share the results in a school or class newsletter. These timelines and letters provide a great deal of information about young readers.

We created a form where students can record the title and author of their Favorite Books (Form 9.24), along with an illustration and brief comment. Like the Monthly Reading Reflection described earlier, a record of Favorite Books would be fun to share with students in other classrooms, pen pals, and parents. This would also be an informative piece to pass on to a student's next teacher.

5. Book/Movie Comparison

Sometimes we despair when students see the movie version in lieu of reading the book. Yet in our visual society, viewing *is* one of the language arts. Why not capitalize on the growing list of movies based on literature and help students learn to view and read critically? In the last few years, filmmakers have produced movies based on well-loved children's books such as *A Little Princess* (Burnett, 1905), *The Secret Garden* (Burnett, 1909), *Matilda* (Dahl, 1988), *James and the Giant Peach* (Dahl, 1961), *Charlotte's Web* (White, 1952), *Heidi* (Spyri, 1884), and *Sarah, Plain and Tall* (MacLachlan, 1985).

Have your students choose a novel to read that has been made into a movie. You can then ask students to compare the book and movie versions using the Book and Movie Comparison (Form 9.25). This activity might be an interesting homework assignment for students to do with their families. What decisions did the film director have to make when adapting the book? What is missing? What was added? What works better on film? How close is the dialogue to the text? What do you think the author would think of the film? Students can compare the positive and negative aspects of the film and written versions.

Cindy Flegenheimer read the novel *Shiloh* (Naylor, 1991) to her third-grade students at Brighton School in Lynnwood, Washington, then the students watched the movie and completed the Book and Movie Comparison (Form 9.25). The discussion in which students compared the book and movie was very lively. Students were asked to write whether they preferred the book or the movie and to justify their answer. Elizabeth replied, "I like the movie more than the book because I think the parts they added made it more dramatic and touching. I also liked the movie because it showed the characters in person. And in the beginning, when Judd was out hunting and when they were showing the scenery, I thought the music fit perfectly!" When asked what she liked better about the book, Elizabeth said, "The only parts I liked better about the book are how they explained more about the characters and how they described Judd. I also think Marty's language explained a lot about him and I personally like the language." The Book and Movie Comparison provides a springboard for conversations as students make connections between literature, movies, and their lives.

6. Books to Read

Do you write the titles and authors of books you want to read or buy on scraps of paper or worn-out "Post-it" notes? The last form in this chapter, Books to Read (Form 9.26) provides a place for you and your students to keep a running list of books to buy, borrow, or check out from the library. Students can keep this ongoing record in their reading folders to take to the library and share with their families. They can add to the list during reading conferences, response project presentations, and as peers share their reading logs and talk about their favorite books and authors. You can use this form as you attend conferences and workshops. You could even use this form to record titles as you read this book!

We've suggested six possible ways to assess the range of student reading. Which type of reading log would work for your students? Will you respond to their logs? Will they be shared with peers? How will you use the information you gain by looking at their logs? If one of our goals is to spark a love of reading in our students, then reading logs can provide a powerful way to assess what and how much students are reading.

In this chapter, we've described many ways to assess reading strategies, reading comprehension, and the range of students' reading. Take some time and scan back through this chapter before reading on. If you are feeling overwhelmed, you might want to select just one assessment tool from each of the three sections. Remember, these are ideas gathered from many different teachers. Be selective: don't overwhelm your students with forms! In the next chapter, we'll extend the ideas we've presented to content area learning.

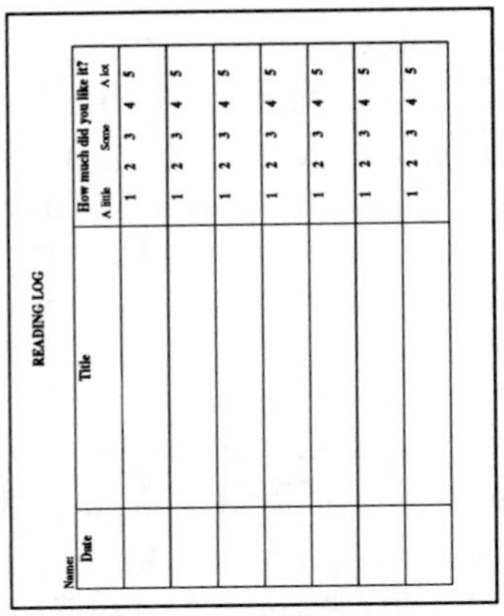

READING LOG

Name:

Date	Title	How much did you like it? A little / Some / A lot
		1 2 3 4 5
		1 2 3 4 5
		1 2 3 4 5
		1 2 3 4 5
		1 2 3 4 5
		1 2 3 4 5
		1 2 3 4 5

Form 9.21: Reading Log

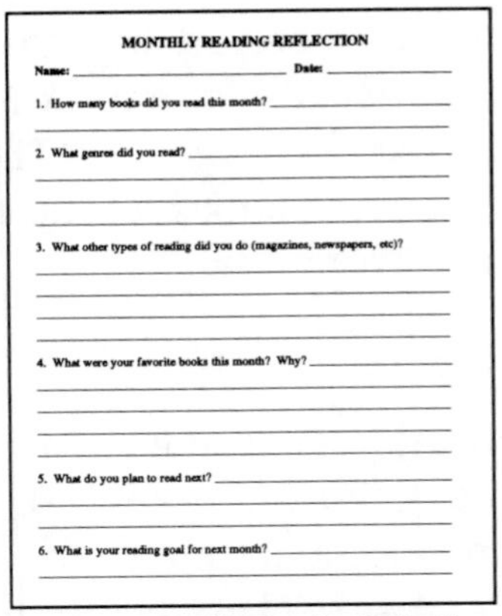

MONTHLY READING REFLECTION

Name: ______ Date: ______

1. How many books did you read this month? ______
2. What genres did you read? ______
3. What other types of reading did you do (magazines, newspapers, etc)? ______
4. What were your favorite books this month? Why? ______
5. What do you plan to read next? ______
6. What is your reading goal for next month? ______

Form 9.22: Monthly Reading Reflection

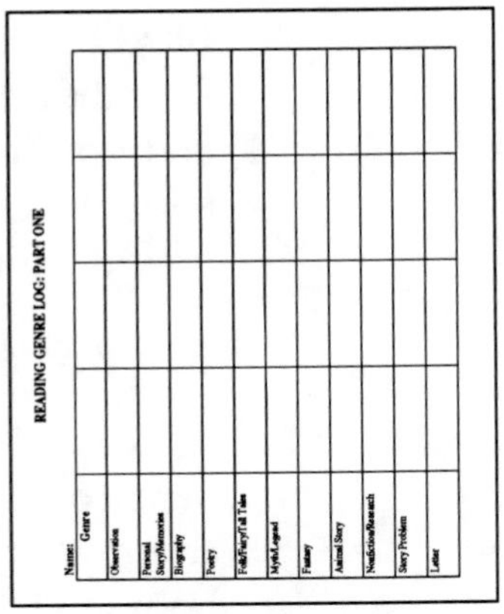

READING GENRE LOG: PART ONE

Name:

Genre: Observation, Personal Story/Memories, Biography, Poetry, Folk/Fairy/Tall Tales, Myth/Legend, Fantasy, Animal Story, Nonfiction/Research, Story Problem, Letter

Form 9.23: Reading Genre Log

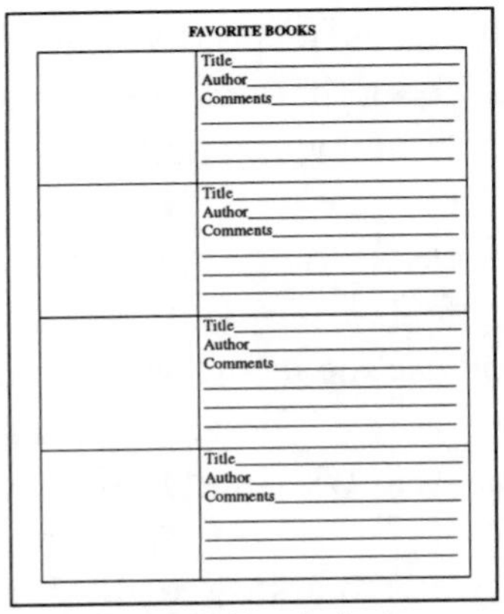

FAVORITE BOOKS

Title______
Author______
Comments______

Title______
Author______
Comments______

Title______
Author______
Comments______

Title______
Author______
Comments______

Form 9.24: Favorite Books

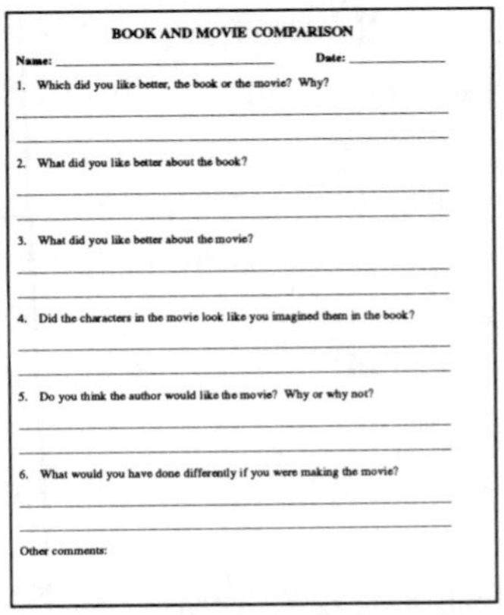

BOOK AND MOVIE COMPARISON

Name: ______ Date: ______

1. Which did you like better, the book or the movie? Why?
2. What did you like better about the book?
3. What did you like better about the movie?
4. Did the characters in the movie look like you imagined them in the book?
5. Do you think the author would like the movie? Why or why not?
6. What would you have done differently if you were making the movie?

Other comments:

Form 9.25: Book and Movie Comparison

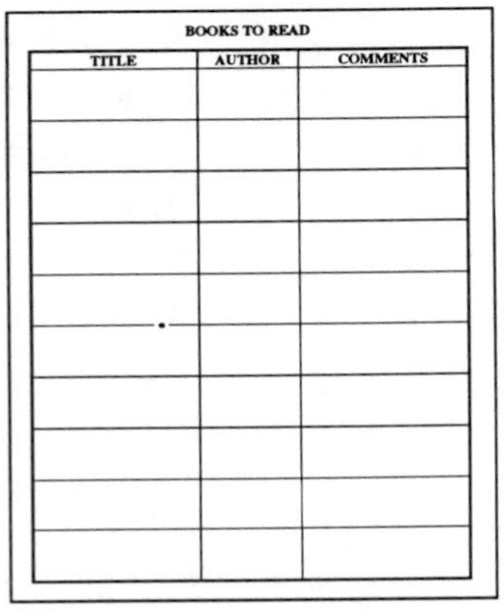

BOOKS TO READ

TITLE	AUTHOR	COMMENTS

Form 9.26: Books to Read

Professional Growth

Shelley Harwayne, a principal at the Manhattan New School in New York City, tries to connect reading in school with reading in the outside world. For instance, one of the things she does is to open her mail each day in a different classroom instead of in her office. Students see her modeling reading for real purposes, ask questions about her mail and see her toss some letters and respond to others. What a simple but powerful way to model functional reading!

The teachers at Shelley's school sometimes chose a topic to study in depth for a year or two. Last year, for instance, her school focused on struggling readers. Teachers read articles, visited each other's classrooms, and shared ideas. Teachers at your school might want try a similar focus. You could each select a student about whom you are concerned and each week tell classroom stories, share running records, and discuss response samples. You might bring your anecdotal notes and share what you are learning and the questions that still puzzle you.

At Brighton School, in Lynnwood, Washington teachers started a literature circle group of their own. They met for 30 minutes before school once a week for six weeks to talk about an adult novel. Just like their students, they read, wrote, and responded to the novel. In the process, they gained many insights about the challenges and rewards of literature circles. In addition, they enjoyed the camaraderie and sharing that occurred as they read and talked together about a book.

Your staff may want to start each faculty meeting with book talks about new picture books, chapter books, adult novels, and professional books. You could create a bulletin board in the staffroom or hallway for staff recommendations and reviews of current books. Once a month, a different class might be in charge of a similar bulletin board for students. Compile a list of Best Sellers or Student Book Recommendations each month in your classroom and publish the list in a school newsletter. Go hear children's authors speak at conferences. Students love hearing about the "story behind the story." Invite parents, staff, and community members to read their favorite picture book or chapter from a children's novel to your students. Develop interview questions students can ask guests about what they like to read and how they use reading as adults. Compile the findings in a class Guest Reader book along with photographs of the visitors and their books. Have a reading night at your school where students and families come in pajamas with stuffed animals and a stack of books to read together. You might want to have a storyteller or children's author as part of the evening. Your librarian could display new titles. Consider connecting the reading night with a book fair or workshop about reading.

If our goal is to create lifelong readers who read for information and pleasure inside and outside of school, these activities can help connect reading in school with reading at home and in the wider community. These activities also provide a chance for your school to demonstrate effective reading instruction and a commitment to ongoing communication with parents and the community.

Recommended Readings about Reading

Our favorite book about teaching reading and writing is *Invitations* (1991, 1994) by Regie Routman. We continue to refer to portions of this book as we grow and change as teachers. Two other books voted "most helpful and inspirational" by teachers are Shelley Harwayne's *Lasting Impressions: Weaving Literature into the Writing Workshop* (1992) and *In the Company of Children* (1996) by Joanne Hindley.

For more information on response journals, you may want to read *Expanding on Response Journals* (Parsons, 1994), *Reading Response Logs* (Kooy and Wells, 1996) or the section in *Invitations* (Routman, 1991, 1994) on pages 103–122. If you'd like to know more about retelling, Hazel Brown and Brian Cambourne's book, *Read and Retell* (1987), provides a wealth of information on this technique as both an instructional and diagnostic tool. *Portfolios and Beyond* (Glazer & Brown, 1993) and *Windows Into Literacy* (Rhodes & Shanklin, 1993) also contain helpful sections on retelling.

Christine Duthie's book, *True Stories: Nonfiction Literacy in the Primary Classroom* (1996) is an exciting book about widening the range of reading for young readers and writers. Her book includes a great annotated bibliography of nonfiction books.

We've found the following six books on literature circles informative and practical: *Lively Discussions! Fostering Engaged Reading* (Gambrell and Almasi, 1996); *Literature Study Circles in a Multicultural Classroom* (Samway and Whang, 1996); *Literature Circles and Response* (Hill, Johnson and Noe, 1995); *Literature Circles: Voice and Choice in the Student-Centered Classroom* (Daniels, 1994); *Talking About Books: Creating Literate Communities* (Short and Pierce, 1990); and *Grand Conversations: Literature Groups in Action* (Peterson and Eeds, 1990). Two other more general books about response are *Booktalk and Beyond: Children and Teachers Respond to Literature* (Roser and Martinez, 1995) and *Journeying: Children Responding to Literature* (Holland, Hungerford and Ernst, 1993).

Shirley Dodson is a parent who found it difficult to talk to her teenage daughter. Her book, *The Mother/Daughter Book Club* (1996), describes how she and nine other mothers set up book discussions with their daughters. You might start similar book clubs for families at your school.

Chapter 10

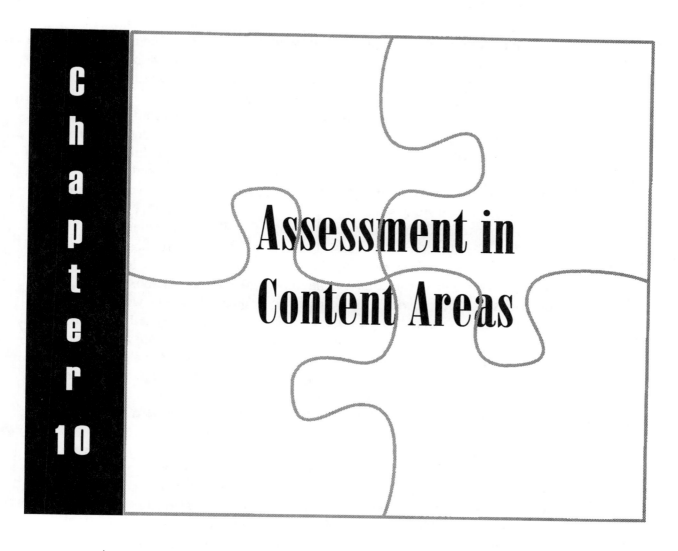

Assessment in Content Areas

"Listen!" Jimmy whispers to Tejas, "It's fizzing!" After verifying that his partner's observation is correct, Tejas makes a new column on the "Vinegar Test" table he has constructed in his science log. Above his table he has listed the materials he is using and has written that he plans to put a few drops of vinegar on each of his rocks to see what happens. Now, to the categories of "Changes Color," "Gets Shiny," and "No Change," Tejas adds "Fizzes" and makes a check in the box on the line for his "jagged gray rock."

Across the table, Maaro and Lee are also testing rocks, using a magnet. They are sorting their rocks into two piles—tested and not tested. When asked what they are doing, they respond that they are trying to see if rocks are magnetic; however, they have created no written record of their work. When prompted to record some of their findings, Maaro writes, "Some rocks are magnetic, but some are not."

Both pairs of lab partners are conducting experiments, but their sense of scientific methods is not the same. What is significant about the differences in these children's work? How do we evaluate the level of understanding that each of them exhibits? How should our instruction be modified to meet the needs of each of these students? When students work in pairs or groups, how can we assess the performance of each individual? How can we measure the many-faceted aspects of learning that result from thematic and collaborative projects?

With active project work, we can see and feel that the learning is taking place, but we need to be able to document it in a way that others can understand as well. How do we make sense of the flurry of activities and accomplishments we witness daily in our classrooms? How do we convey our appraisals of students' work when report cards often have room for only a grade, number, or check in content areas like science and social studies?

As our teaching becomes more integrated and student-centered, the artificial lines between the curricular areas of language arts, social studies, science, mathematics, and the arts begin to fade. The movement toward active learning, whether it is called thematic, project-based, inquiry-approach, constructivist, or just "hands-on/minds-on," brings with it the necessity to evaluate children's work in new ways.

Objective tests are easy to score, but how much can they tell us about what a child really knows? Multiple-choice and other forms of short-answer tests demonstrate simple short-term recall of facts. However, the emphasis in all curricular areas has shifted from information gathering and memorization to higher-level tasks that involve conducting experiments, solving problems, making decisions, and posing solutions. Conventional testing methods are not enough. Where can we look for additional, more appropriate tools that will help us evaluate and substantiate children's growth in the content areas?

In the 1970s, Mary Baratta-Lorton introduced new methods to engage children in learning mathematics through *Math Their Way* (1976). She encouraged teachers to observe students in an ongoing, focused manner. She also advocated assessment that was embedded in instruction. Marilyn Burns (1991, 1992) and Kathy Richardson (1984) expanded on Baratta-Lorton's innovations. Their new assessment methods in the area of mathematics included both formative (collecting information during instruction) and summative (collecting information after a unit or project) evaluation of specific concepts and skills.

In the late 1980s, the science community also began to examine ways to interpret children's work. Discovery-based programs had been in use since the 1960s. An assessment component was needed in order to move science education beyond investigative play to true teaching and learning of scientific methods and concepts. The updated science programs of the 1990s (*Science and Technology for Children, Full Option Science Systems/FOSS, GEMS, Insights*) include ideas for assessment of children's ability to apply specific components of the scientific method. These programs provide us with a new lens for viewing science education.

At the same time, Howard Gardner (Gardner, 1983) and David Perkins (Perkins, 1986; Perkins and Simmons, 1988) developed theories about "minds-on" education that encouraged children to interact with ideas and experiences through multiple intelligences in order to promote higher-level thinking. For the first time, children were asked to write about their understandings and the relationship of new learning to what they already knew.

For example, to insure that her students will acquire a deep understanding of the relationship between plants and bees, a teacher would read an assortment of nonfiction books about insects, but she might also have the students memorize a poem about bees. After viewing a videotape about pollination, students could conduct experiments to observe what happens to unpollinated plants compared to some that they "pollinate with bee sticks" as outlined in the Science and Technology for Children unit on plant growth and development. The class might play games in which children act out the "dance" that scout bees perform to lead other members of the hive to a field of flowers, while a recording of Bobby McFerrin's rendition of "The Flight of the Bumblebee" plays in the background. She might also read Patricia Polacco's book, *The Bee Tree* (1993), and have the students act out the cumulative tale. Students could perform a shadow puppet play to show others what they have learned about the life cycle of the honeybee. The products and reflective writing that children do after such a multi-faceted exploration of a topic show a deep level of understanding of the topic. In addition, learning spills over from one content area to another as the curricular areas flow together.

In the last ten years, it has become increasingly common to find social studies, mathematics, and science taught through thematic units of study. In theme-based classrooms, children are encouraged to make the connections essential for deep understanding and long-term learning. Learning through inquiry is fostered in a way that addresses the individual interests of the child (Short, Harste and Burke, 1996). Integration of writing, reading, and content occurs in a way that seems natural for teachers and students. How can we demonstrate to parents and the school community the advantages of these new approaches?

Many teachers encourage students to include a wide range of content area work in their portfolios. What other evidence can embody the rich learning that takes place in the classroom? George Hein and Sabra Price (1994) propose that:

> Anything students do can be used for assessment purposes. If we limit our thinking about assessment to ideas derived from traditional testing, we often end up with paper-and-pencil exercises. If, however, we consider assessment as using our senses to find out what someone else is thinking, we more readily comprehend the diverse forms available to us. (p. 13)

Assessment in the content areas may be focused on observations of experiments or group discussions, unstructured work like brainstorming, as well as asking students to write reflectively about their learning. Some activities and products that provide rich contexts for assessment include:

- brainstorming and other lists
- group interaction
- conversations
- first/last lab reports

- problem solving exercises
- written explanations and observations
- folders with work samples
- drawings, especially labeled ones
- process logs
- reports, stories, or poems
- demonstrations or expositions
- student constructed tables and graphs
- video and audio tapes

Although this list looks familiar, an emphasis on more reasoning and reflective learning requires a shift in focus. In order to provide evidence of true understanding of content, videotapes of projects must be more than mere recordings of memorable moments. Graphs and tables must clearly indicate the student-generated questions behind the data presented. Reports must go beyond information gathering to include interpreting, connecting, predicting, and /or posing solutions to problems.

For instance, a common practice is to ask students to collect facts about an animal on note cards in order to produce reports "in their own words." Students change a few words so they don't sound like the encyclopedia, then spend hours on maps and illustrations. In contrast, using an inquiry approach, students generate their own topics of study, consult multiple sources, and access current events through the Internet in order to produce authentic products for real audiences.

Let's look at an example. Teachers at Osaka International School in Japan worked with a group of multiage primary students who were fascinated by the size of whales and wanted to learn more. As the children consulted many books, magazine articles, and on-line encyclopedias, they were appalled to discover how many whales are still endangered. They continued to research various types of whales and environmental preservation groups that are committed to protecting these animals. As a result, the children decided to raise money to "adopt" a whale. They wrote announcements for the school bulletin explaining their goal, made posters advertising their fundraising sale of recycled products, and corresponded with the Pacific Whale Foundation in Maui, Hawaii to make arrangements for sending their contribution. Later, they organized a contest to name the whale they were supporting and began compiling a "baby book" for the whale based on the information supplied by the Pacific Whale Foundation. The fact that they could actually make a difference gave these students a real reason for their research, rather than merely copying facts out of the encyclopedia. The extensive reading and writing resulting from this highly motivating project provided rich material for assessment of students' true abilities.

Ongoing assessment provides two types of information. First, it helps you determine what concepts students understand deeply enough to apply in new situations. In addition, the assessment provides feedback on your teaching. What is missing from your instruction that would help students in the learning process?

For instance, during the whale study mentioned above, the teachers asked each other questions such as, "Have we provided enough support in helping these children learn how to research a topic like whales? Have we provided adequate samples of persuasive letters?" As the research process evolved into an environmental action project, the teachers continually monitored and modified their instruction based on the insights they gained as they assessed student learning.

Organized, ongoing assessment is just as important in other content areas as in the areas of reading and writing. When we embed reading and writing throughout the curriculum, some of the same assessment tools we have discussed earlier can be applied to the content areas. Nevertheless, evaluation for mathematics, science, and social studies must also reach beyond literacy assessment to appraisal of processes, skills, knowledge, and attitudes.

We divided this chapter into three sections. In the first part, we discuss ways to assess students as you observe them in action and examine their written work. In the next section, we explore ways to document growth over time. Finally, we provide some examples of checklists, rubrics, and rating scales. Cynthia Ruptic and Lisa Norwick provided most of the forms and examples since they are both deeply interested in content integration, inquiry, and their connection to assessment.

Observing Students and Their Written Work

1. Anecdotal Notes

Once you become a "kid watcher," it is a natural step to extend observation and anecdotal note taking to all areas of the curriculum. It's helpful to focus your observations on specific behaviors and skills tied to your unit or theme. You can then adjust your instruction based on the information you glean as you watch students at work.

As her students measured and recorded the height of their plants, Cynthia noticed that many children were placing the zero point of their centimeter rulers at the top of the pot, rather than at the base of the plant. She gathered the children together and they discussed why it was important to be consistent in measuring the entire plant from the same spot each day. Students who understood the concept then paired up with those who needed help and demonstrated how to measure properly.

At the end of a unit of study, the behaviors you note about each child become a very specific record of their ongoing growth in skills and knowledge. Such specific information is invaluable when writing evaluations and reporting to parents.

We've discussed the power of focused anecdotal notes in each of the previous chapters. Anecdotal notes can provide helpful information about collaborative projects, mathematical thinking, and scientific processes. We've developed Focus Questions for Anecdotal Notes about mathematics at the primary level (Form 10.1A) and intermediate level (Form 10.1B). We also included Focus Questions for Anecdotal Notes about science in the primary grades (Forms 10.1C) and intermediate grades (Form 10.1D). You will probably want to generate your own focus questions for social studies as you plan units on specific topics or themes.

2. Student-Constructed Tables, Graphs and Labeled Drawings

As with writing, samples of student work from content areas also provide us with information about what students know. In Chapter 5, we alluded to what may be learned from looking carefully at children's drawings. Nowhere is this more pertinent than in the content areas. Do your students use pictures and diagrams to show how they solved a math or logic problem? Are the drawings they include in their science logs stereotypic or are they carefully drawn renditions of what they have observed? At first glance, the map of Europe that George added to his portfolio may look crudely drawn, but more careful scrutiny reveals that he correctly placed and labeled every river and mountain range on the continent (Figure 10.1). George's work is evidence of his very accurate knowledge of geography.

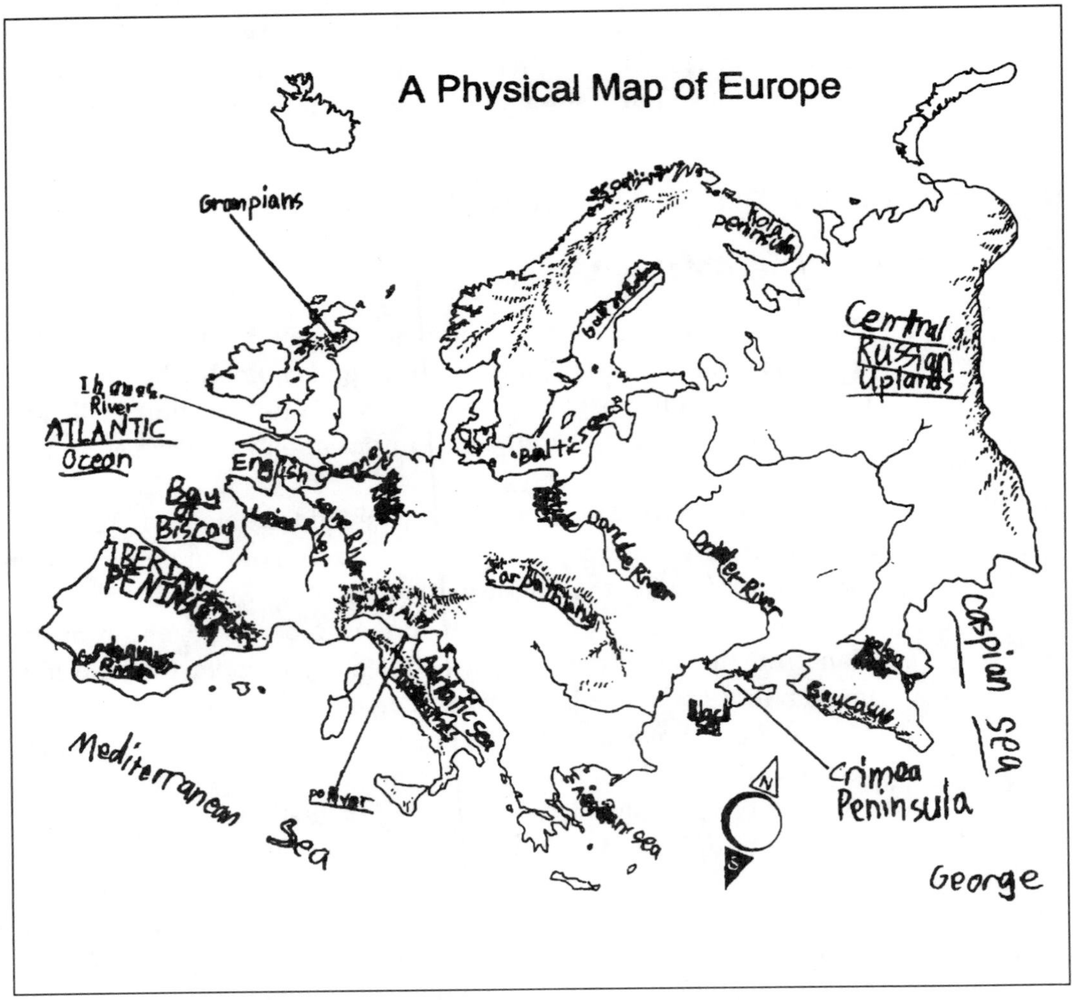

Figure 10.1: Student-Labeled Map

Any student-constructed table, graph, or labeled diagram is a rich source for evaluating skills and knowledge levels. When students become adept at reading graphs and filling in charts and tables, it is time to withdraw the templates and see how they construct their own method of conveying information. Can your students apply what they have learned about tables, graphs, and charts in order to communicate their ideas? Can they draw diagrams or pictures that show what they know in a visual way? If so, the children's performances become evidence of their ability to take learning beyond the knowledge level to application and synthesis. The students' graphics become artifacts that they often choose to include in their portfolios.

One of the challenges of collaborative projects is assessing individual children's understanding of a concept. For instance, in many classrooms, students graph weather patterns for several weeks. In order to assess each child's understanding of graphing, you can ask students to each chart the weather for the next few weeks on their own. Students can then display their results, along with a written explanation of what the graphs show. Students often include their graphs and explanations in their portfolios to share at conference time. Although it's important to assess the work students do collaboratively, assessment is most meaningful at the level of individual application.

3. Double Entry Journal

Lisa's students are busily working at math centers. Some are working on strategies for addition and subtraction facts. Another group is using manipulatives to explore the concept of regrouping when adding large numbers. Other students are writing in their double entry math journals. In Figure 10.2, you can see how Ashley used pictures to show the concept of regrouping on the left side of the page. She also solved the problem symbolically, using numbers. On the right side of her journal entry, Ashley wrote an explanation of her work. You can clearly see from Ashley's work that she understands the concept of regrouping. Lisa uses the double entry journals as an assessment tool. When children are able to successfully solve a problem and explain their thinking, Lisa knows they are ready to move on to a new concept. Students often chose samples from their math journals to include in their portfolio. Ashley selected this page to include and wrote in her reflection, "I picked this to put in my portfolio because I think I did a great job explaining how I solved this and most of what I did was mental math."

4. Project Check-Up

When children reflect upon their learning and communicate their knowledge in writing, we gain a clearer view of what they understand. Rather than trying to get the "correct answer," students begin to think metacognitively about what they are doing and learning. The Project Check-Up (Form 10.2) provides assessment information "in process" and can be used with a variety of activities or assignments. Students reflect on what they learned, list areas in which they need help, and set goals. Since

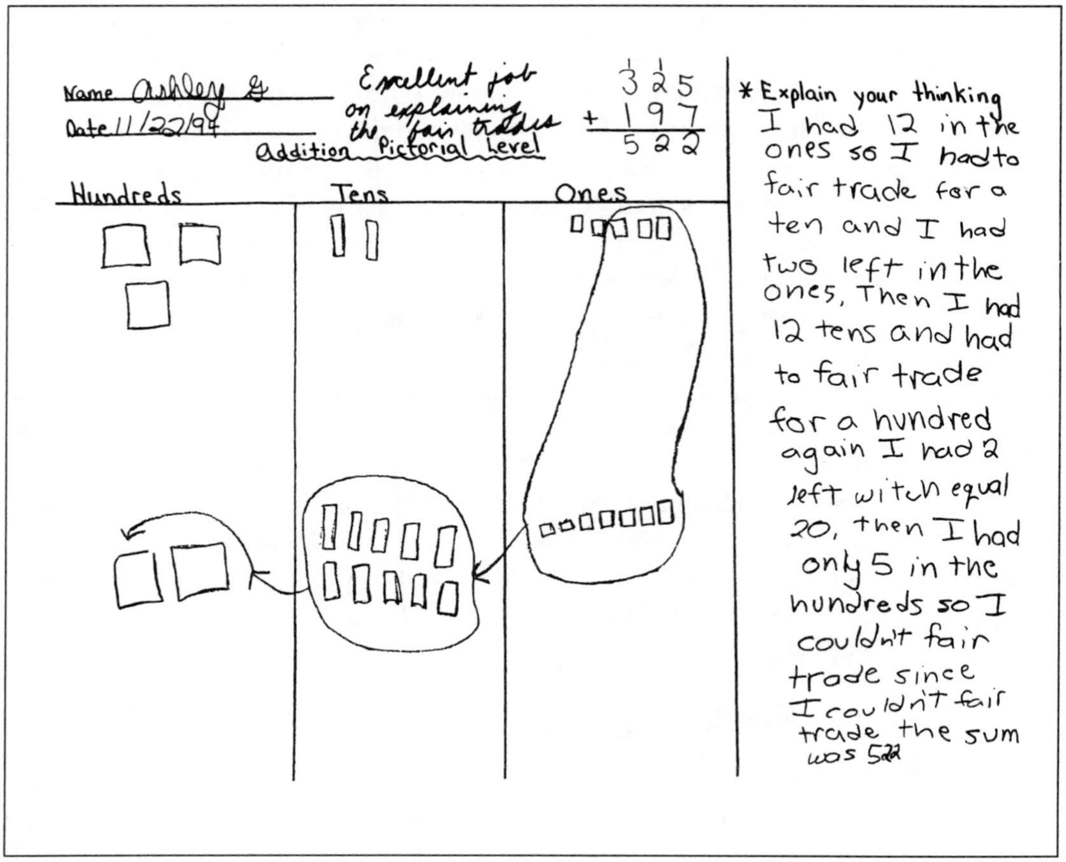

Figure 10.2: Double Entry Journal

it is used before the project is complete, students are able to ask for specific help along the way. This tool can help you assess process in order to adjust your instruction. If used periodically for comparison purposes, it's easy to see students' growing ability to explain their strategies and procedures.

5. Problem Solving Evaluation and Rubric

The NCTM standards have helped educators recognize the importance of problem solving in mathematics. In fact, Gerald Kulm (1994) writes,

> The primary reason for changing the direction of assessment has been to focus on problem solving as a key part of the mathematics curriculum. Continued efforts are aimed at moving beyond simple word problems toward evaluating the processes that students should learn and use in a variety of situations. (p. 25)

The Problem Solving Evaluation provides another glimpse into the learning process. This form is especially suitable for mathematics, but could also be used in science or cooperative learning activities. This assessment tool works well with materials from the Exemplars publications (for more information, see the Recommended Readings at the end of this chapter). We've included a primary version (Form 10.3A) as well as an intermediate adaptation (Form 10.3B). This form helps students articulate their own strategies during problem solving by asking, "What strategies did you use to solve the problem?" and "What are some things that might have made it easier for you?"

Lisa uses the Problem Solving Evaluation (Form 10.3A) with open-ended story problems in mathematics. Her second graders work on math story problems each week. Twice a month, Lisa introduces three different open-ended story problems. Her students select one, write their solutions, then complete the Problem Solving Evaluation form. Lisa learns a great deal about their thinking from this form. For instance, Jay was working on the following problem:

> Sandra was out for her morning bike ride. She started at the park and rode 4 miles south on the bike path. Then she stopped to take a rest. When she got back on her bike, she rode 5 more miles south. When a storm came up, she turned around and rode 3 miles north in the other direction to find shelter. After the storm, she rode 5 miles south to the end of the bike path. How many miles did Sandra ride?

Jay drew a diagram in order to solve this problem and arrived at the correct answer. In response to the first question on the Problem Solving Evaluation about his strategies, Jay replied,

> I drew a line that showed north and south. I put four marks down which stood for four miles south. Then I made 5 more marks south. Then I counted back 3 marks to show where the shelter was. Then I made 5 marks south to the end. When I counted all the marks, there were 11.

When asked about what would have made the problem easier, Jay answered, "I want to learn how to solve this problem by adding and subtracting the numbers like T.J. did." Jay's response provided Lisa with valuable information. She learned that Jay was able to explain his strategy and his labeled diagram. He chose a concrete approach to the problem, but his answer to the second question revealed that Jay is ready to move to a more abstract level. The next day Lisa worked with Jay and a group of students at the same level and taught them how to write a number sentence to solve similar problems.

Lisa Norwick also developed a Problem Solving Rubric (Form10.3C) to use with her sixth graders several years ago. The class felt it wasn't fair to receive a low score if they were able to identify the question and important information in the problem and successfully implemented the correct strategy, and made only a small computational error. Lisa and the students developed a rubric with three categories: understanding the problem, choosing and implementing a strategy, and answering the problem correctly. In that way, if a student made a minor computational error but got everything else correct, the score would be 13 out of 15 possible points. Since she was required to give letter grades on the report card, Lisa needed a clear way to evaluate math. Students and parents were highly concerned about grades since placement in junior high mathematics was based on the grades from sixth grade. Once a month, students completed a challenging open-ended problem and used the Problem Solving Rubric to tabulate their scores for the problem solving part of the mathematics grade. By using the rubric that the students helped develop, the criteria for grading became clear.

Asking students to write about "how they know what they know" is a powerful assessment tool, particularly in the content areas. In science, Lisa often asks her students to explain what they learned after an experiment. For instance, Lisa's students were studying density. Each team of two scientists tested four different-colored solutions. Each solution had a different amount of salt in it. The children were using test tubes and eyedroppers to test the liquids, not knowing which solutions had the most salt. The students were trying to build "parfaits" by floating one solution on top of another. The solution with the least amount of salt would float on the top and the heaviest solution would sink to the bottom. After the students had tested all four solutions and categorized them according to density, Lisa asked her young scientists to explain their findings. It was apparent from reading their explanations that they were able to justify their conclusions. Writing is a tool for learning in all subject areas. Writing about how they solve a math problem or justifying their conclusions in a science experiment helps students gain a deeper understanding of a concept. Next, we'll examine how written reflections can show growth over time.

Observing Growth Over Time

1. Know-Wonder-Learned-Wonder (K-W-L-W)

Donna Ogle (1986) developed the K-W-L technique to determine students' prior knowledge about a topic (what they Know), the focus for further research (what they Wonder), as well as findings (what they Learned). We added a fourth column (for further Wonderings) at the end. This last column demonstrates how research, although it provides answers to questions, can also lead to new questions and levels of inquiry. The technique can be used as ongoing assessment for units of study in almost any subject area.

Before exploring a topic, students create a chart with the four K-W-L-W vertical columns. In the first column, children individually list everything they know about the topic. In the second column, students record questions and wonderings about the topic. To pool knowledge from the whole class, conduct a meeting in which children combine their knowledge and questions in the first two columns on a large class chart. Post the chart in the classroom so that it can be viewed and updated throughout the duration of the unit as new information is learned and new questions arise.

If your students keep learning logs, they can create a four-column K-W-L-W chart in their notebooks. Throughout the unit, they add to the columns as they encounter new information. If students record new ideas or facts using different-colored pencils, the chart becomes a visual representation of new learning. In Cynthia Ruptic's classroom, students include their K-W-L-W charts in their portfolio, along with a formal written reflection at the end of a unit.

The K-W-L-W technique provides three types of information. First, the growing list of information provides a graphic record of how much each child learned. Second, the questions in the "Wonder" column also provide direction for further inquiry and instruction. The notion of continued inquiry offers a great opportunity to emphasize the importance of persevering in our research about things that intrigue us. Finally, the technique itself provides a structure for children's early steps in learning how to do research. What do they want to learn? How will they locate information? In fact, Margaret Mooney suggests adding a fifth column on the chart so that after students decide what they know and want to learn, they can record "How" they intend to gather information. It may be too hard to remember K-W-H-L-W as a sequence, but you might want to incorporate some of these ideas during classroom investigations.

K-W-L-W charts help students organize their thoughts about a topic. The technique also provides helpful information for instruction. Based on what you learn about your students' understandings and interests, you may have to adjust your instructional goals. For instance, as you watch their early steps at locating information, you may find you need to teach several focus lessons on how to find information on the Internet or how to organize notes into chapters. As we demonstrated with the Möbius strip in Chapter 2, instruction and assessment are truly intertwined.

2. "Fix-it" Strategies

Like the "Fix-it" strategy suggested in the Chapter 7, the next assessment technique gives students an opportunity to show what they have learned by changing or adding to an earlier piece of work. What Is Subtraction? (Form 10.4A) is a tool that Cynthia Ruptic created after reading Mary Montgomery Lindquist's article "Assessing for Learning: Assessing through Questioning" (1988). Before learning how to subtract large numbers by regrouping, Cynthia's third graders complete as much of the form as they are able, leaving any confusing sections blank. At the end of the subtraction unit, Cynthia gives the children their original forms and the students make corrections and complete the sections they first left blank. Using a different-colored pencil on the second attempt makes it easy to see how children have expanded their understanding or corrected misconceptions. You could devise similar "before and after" forms to assess specific skills or concepts in any curricular area.

Lisa Norwick uses a variation of this technique. Before she introduces multiplication, Lisa gives her students a questionnaire called What is Multiplication? (Form 10.4B). On the form, Lisa asks students to explain what multiplication is, using pictures and words. She then asks them to write an explanation of their picture. During the year, students spend time exploring multiplication at the concrete level (using manipulatives such as counters), pictorial level (using pictures to show groups of objects), and symbolic level (using numbers and symbols such as $3 \times 4 =$

12). At the end of the unit, students complete the What is Multiplication? form again. Using the two samples, you could also ask your students to write a reflection about what they've learned. For instance, at the beginning of the unit, Megan wrote, "I do not know how to explain multiplication." A month later, you can clearly see Megan's new understanding of the concept of multiplication in Figure 10.3.

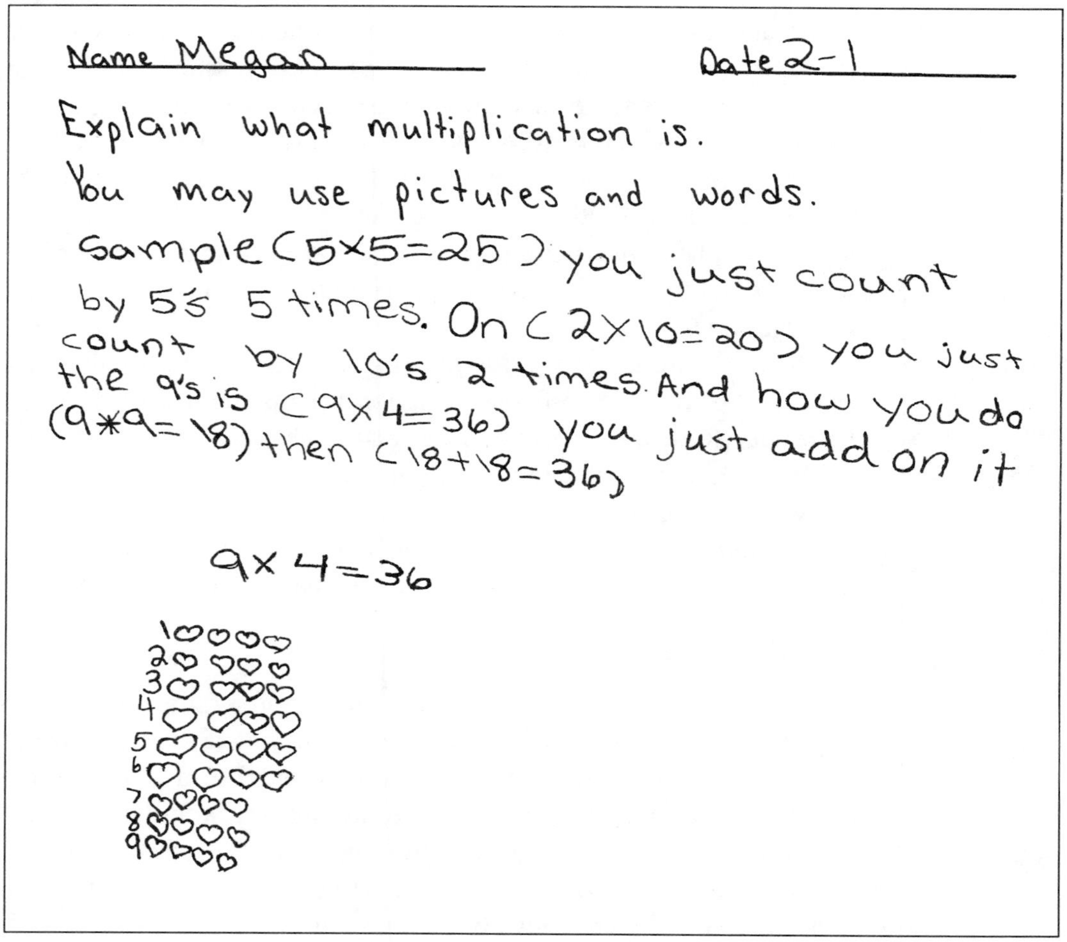
Name Megan Date 2-1

Explain what multiplication is.
You may use pictures and words.
sample (5×5=25) you just count
by 5's 5 times. On (2×10=20) you just
count by 10's 2 times. And how you do
the 9's is (9×4=36) you
(9*9=18) then (18+18=36) just add on it

9×4=36

Figure 10.3: What is Multiplication?

In her *Math by All Means* replacement units, Marilyn Burns (1991) includes many ideas for embedding assessment throughout the learning process as "check-ups" of children's growing knowledge. Her multiplication unit for third grade includes a variation of the questioning strategy that Lisa uses. You may want to look at her materials for more examples. Of course, such "before and after" reflections could be used for learning in any area.

3. First/Later Comparisons

Another way to compare prior knowledge and skills with acquired learning is by giving students similar tasks throughout a unit of study. In science, students could conduct related experiments at the beginning, middle, and end of the unit. The later experiments could be less structured and therefore reveal each student's knowledge and application of the scientific method.

Let's look at an example. For their first experiments with mystery powders in science class, Cynthia provided detailed instructions for the procedures that students should follow, as well as charts on which to record their results. Later, at the end of the unit, students were expected to devise their own plan to identify an unknown substance and record their observations and results. Cynthia could then ascertain whether or not they could apply the methods and skills they had practiced and generalize what they had learned about mystery powders during their earlier experiments. She also noted whether her students had improved their abilities to record and summarize data in an accurate, detailed way. For instance, in Figure 10.4, Lindsey's first lab report is purely descriptive. Her final report also includes description, but is organized into categories, processes, and results. Students place photocopies of their first and later samples side by side in their portfolios, along with their written reflection and Cynthia's written comments.

Checklists, Rubrics, and Rating Scales

1. Checklists

Checklists can be used for many things: to record attitudes, opinions, processes, understanding of content, and progress on a multi-step task. Some checklists even include rating scales for the purpose of comparison. Numbers or symbols, however, are not meant to be totaled or averaged to produce a single number to represent a composite of a student's performance. Rather, each score should be considered as a separate rating of the discreet skill or aspect being evaluated.

The Primary Math Evaluation (Form 10.5) is a checklist that was developed by a group of first-grade teachers from the Bainbridge Island School District. Teachers use a different-color pen each time they assess a student, as noted on the key at the top of the form. They write the date at the top of the form, then check what skill each child can do. Teachers mark the form as they observe a child's performance (counting, sorting shapes, identifying coins, and constructing patterns).

The Primary Math Evaluation is not used as a screening tool, but rather as an ongoing chronicle of the child's acquisition of fundamental skills in mathematics. Teachers, parents, and students appreciate the specificity of the benchmarks. Beyond second grade, math skills are not as discrete and the math strands become more intertwined. At the primary level, however, the skills listed on this form are the prerequisite building blocks from which further math learning is constructed. The advantage of a checklist is that it's quick and easy to use. Since primary teachers

Date 4-7

Red:
Smell: A little sweet and like soap

Sight: Grainy, like little squares.
Feel: Hard, like little rocks.

Yellow:
Smell: Oderless.
Feel: Soft and crumbley.
Sight: Packy, like snow.

Green:
Sight: Powerdery and Packy.
Feel: ~~Very~~ soft
Smell: Soapy.

Blue:
Smell: Oderless
Feel: A little grainy.
Sight: Very little particlas

Orange:
Sight: Very little particals.
Feel: Very soft and packy.
Smell:

Date 6.10

PREDICTONS	M.: Flour and water W.: Nothing I.: I think it will turn redish-orange.		
	Why	Results	Results
WATER	We want to do it becuase it's symple	1. Softer 2. Softer 3. Softer 4. Softer 5. Mushy	6. More mushy 7. Mushier 8. Creamy 9. Creamier 10. Very creamy
IODINE	We want to find out what happens.	1. Turned purple 2. Marble color 3. Darker 4. Easy to mix 5. Darker marble	6. Liquidley, Sliny 7. " 8. Very liquidly 9. Wartery 10. A liquid
CONCLUSION	I think turned we added	it is cornstarch purple and iodine	because it black when

Figure 10.4: First/Later Lab Reports

have little time to write extensive anecdotal notes, a checklist like the Primary Math Evaluation can provide a quick way to note accomplishments during the busy hum of math centers.

Cindy Flegenheimer and Linda Horn, third-grade teachers at Brighton School in Lynnwood, Washington, give students the Human Body Poster Checklist (Form 10.6) at the beginning of their study of the systems of the body. The children use the list as a guideline when they create their posters on whatever system they choose, such as the muscular or skeletal system. When they finish the assignment, students write a self-evaluation and hand it in with the completed posters. Cindy and Linda then evaluate the posters using the checklist to give specific feedback without having to write extensive comments about each child's work. The checklists clarify criteria and expectations and provide a framework as students work on a project by breaking the task down into manageable components. The checklists are also helpful in teaching students organizational strategies as they begin the research process. In addition, the results will shape instruction for the next research project later in the year.

Sometimes checklists are useful for keeping track of an entire class on one page to indicate that a piece of work has been completed or to note students' progression through a set of skills. Other checklists can include more room to write brief anecdotal comments. You can use this type of form to note a goal or how you plan to help a child with a specific aspect of a project.

We have included two checklists that Cynthia Ruptic uses with her class as they prepare for their Invention Convention. Cynthia posts the first form, Inventor's Checklist: Class Profile (Form 10.7A), in the room so she and her students can keep track of progress toward completing a particular project. Cynthia simply places a check in the appropriate box to show when a component (like the survey or working model) has been completed. With so many students working on different inventions, the checklist serves both as an assessment and an organizational tool. You could easily tailor this form to fit your particular project or unit.

George Hein and Sabra Price (1994) advocate making checklists with only a few students per page in order to provide room for narrative comments. Cynthia use the second form, Inventor's Checklist (Form 10.7B) on a clipboard. As she confers with each child, she notes materials she needs to provide, a reference to find, or a student's comments or questions. Cynthia uses these "process notes" as she writes up her final evaluations for the project. Students include Cynthia's final evaluation, along with their own reflection and photographs of their invention in their portfolios. You can easily develop similar checklists to match the topics you explore in your classroom.

During her first year of teaching, Lisa Norwick learned the value of creating a checklist to monitor students' progress. The day her students were presenting their inquiry projects to the class, she was shocked to discover that three projects were unorganized and missing important information. She realized she had not met with these children along the way to assist them with their projects. These three children

INVENTORS' CHECKLIST: CLASS PROFILE

	Name	Inventor Report	Survey	Description of Invention	Two View Sketches	Patent Signatures	Working Model	Invention Defense	Advertisement	Inventor's Log
1	Ayumi	✓	✓	✓						
2	Chris		✓	✓	✓					
3	Evan	✓	✓	✓	✓	✓	✓			
4	Flordeliz		✓	✓						
5	Haeng Nam		✓	✓						
6	Jacinta		✓	✓						
7	Jegaan		✓	✓						
8	Johanna	✓	✓	✓	✓	✓	✓			
9	Jyongri	✓	✓	✓	✓	✓	✓			
10	Kazuma	✓	✓	✓						
11	Ken		✓	✓						
12	Kwang	✓	✓	✓	✓					
13	Lee	✓	✓	✓	✓	✓				
14	Lisa	✓	✓	✓	✓	✓	✓			
15	Madeline	✓	✓	✓	✓	✓				
16	Marie	✓	✓	✓	✓	✓	✓			
17	Meelad	✓	✓	✓	✓	✓	✓			
18	Paul	✓	✓	✓	✓					
19	Sameera	✓	✓	✓	✓					
20	Sara	✓	✓	✓	✓	✓	✓			
21	Sean		✓	✓	✓					
22	Shi Hua	✓	✓	✓	✓	✓				
23	Shotaro	✓	✓	✓	✓	✓				
24	Stephen		✓	✓	✓					
25	Yatsu	✓	✓	✓	✓	✓	✓			
26	Thelma	✓	✓	✓	✓					
27	Tyler	✓	✓	✓	✓	✓	✓			
28	Yoko	✓	✓	✓	✓	✓				

INVENTOR'S CHECKLIST

STUDENTS	Meelad	Paul	Sameera
Inventor Report	Galileo	Ben Franklin	Kellogg
Survey	✓	✓	✓
Description of Invention	Toy/Game w/ ball/recycled goods	Turtle feeder	Lemonade making dispenser
Two-View Sketches	✓	✓	✓
Patent Signatures	✓	✓	call Mom to help remember
Working Model	needs a little bit of chicken wire? custodians?	Needs to solve stop/start problem	
Invention Defense	pair w/ Jegaan for practice and feedback		
Advertisement			
Inventor's Log			
Other			

Figure 10.5: Inventors' Checklists

needed specific focus lessons on note taking and organization. The next year Lisa created a checklist to help her monitor her interactions with each student. She now structures four different conferences with each student during the inquiry process. She first meets with children before they began their research to look over their planning sheet. For the second conference, Lisa and the students look over the research notes to make sure that all the important information is included. At the third conference, students share their drafts with Lisa. She has one last conference for a final editing of the project. Checklists can provide a way to make your assessment intentional and consistent. Rather than a final evaluation at the end of the project, the ongoing assessment throughout the process provides many teaching opportunities and prevents students from "slipping between the cracks."

Checklists are helpful for keeping track of day-to-day accomplishments on specific projects, like the Human Body Checklist or Inventor's Checklist described in this section. They can also be used for a series of skills you can observe and "check off," such as counting to 100 by 2's on the Primary Math Evaluation. Checklists, particularly when supplemented with anecdotal notes, are also helpful in team teaching situations as a means of communicating with each other about student progress on many different skills.

2. Rubrics

In Chapter 7, we described how you can use rubrics to evaluate writing in specific genres. Content area rubrics must also be specific to a particular project or product. Rubrics for science, social studies, mathematics, and other curricular areas, while sometimes including writing criteria, should primarily address specific content learning. Some may also focus on process and communication skills.

A rubric is like a ruler. The accuracy of its measurements will depend on the markings used. Even though the same descriptive levels may be used (e.g., novice, apprentice, practitioner, expert), a rubric must be set up in terms of the explicit set of tasks and concepts to be taught and experienced. Then, the criteria for each level of performance must be defined.

The Presentation Rubric (Form 9.16B) was briefly described in Chapter 9 and could be applied to content area project sharing as well as reading response project presentations. This simple form helps children develop an awareness of audience as they share projects in class. This form could be enlarged as a chart so primary students could be aware of the criteria for good oral presentations. Primary students can informally evaluate their presentation and set a goal based on the criteria for their next oral performance.

The next two rubrics are more specific and can be used with older students. Cynthia uses the Science Log Scoring Rubric (Form 10.8) to evaluate her students' application of scientific methods as evidenced in their science log. This type of rubric is helpful when conducting the "First-last lab reports" assessment suggested earlier. During the unit, she scans through their entries periodically to check how well they understand and apply the ideas, as well as to check if the entries meet the criteria on the rubric. Cynthia sometimes asks students to show their entries as exemplars for the four categories: observation skills, process skills, communication skills, and general understanding. At the end of the unit, students go through their logs and write a final reflection about their growth and learning. They also use a "Post-it" note to mark an entry to photocopy for their portfolios. Cynthia looks through their science journals specifically to find evidence of growth in each area. She fills out the rubric by checking the appropriate boxes, then writes a very brief summative comment (usually 1–3 sentences) to the child on the side or back of the rubric. By looking through the science journals both during and after the unit, Cynthia can support learning and evaluate growth.

For instance, at the end of their unit on plants, Cynthia was struck by the growth in her third graders' scientific drawings. Early entries in their logs had been sloppy, without labels or dates. Later entries were better-organized, with a standard format (date in the same corner, observations at the bottom) and more realistic drawings. She could tell by these detailed sketches that her students were really looking closely at their plants and taking the time to add details. Cynthia uses the information to give students feedback on their work and to check off specific skills on each child's report card. She also uses the sample and the rubric to show growth at parent conferences.

Cynthia Ruptic and Jodi Bonnette used the Cultural Museum Evaluation (Figure 10.6) to evaluate their third/fourth multiage students' exhibitions in their Japanese cultural museum at Osaka International School. Working as individuals or pairs, the children research some aspect of Japanese culture and prepare museum displays, brochures, and interpretive presentations. When they open their museum to the public (their parents as well as peers and teachers at their school), the students serve as docents. The evaluation form was used by the students, their peers, and the teacher to evaluate the docents and their displays during the museum exhibitions.

Each child has two or three peers they are assigned to evaluate. At various times during the three-day museum exhibition, a few students "close their museum" and visit their peers to evaluate their display. The teachers also observe the students giving their talk to visitors and ask the student questions about the exhibit. By the end of the project, each student has their self-evaluation, as well as feedback from two teachers and three peers. After the museum closing ceremonies, students reviewed their evaluations and reflected upon their performance. They comment on how they plan to improve as docents the next year when they participate in similar exhibitions.

The teachers developed the criteria for this assessment form. However, after using this form, the students made suggestions about changes that would make it more effective. In light of this feedback from their students and their own ongoing study of rubrics, Cynthia and Jodi continue to refine this tool to better reflect students' suggestions and the quality of their students' performances.

CULTURAL MUSEUM EVALUATION

Name______________________________ DATE:__________

Rate each category from 1-5. Use the "COMMENTS" areas to write your reasons.

MYSELF	PROCESS LOG	TEACHER
1 2 3 4 5	Contains explanations of what you did/how you did it	1 2 3 4 5
1 2 3 4 5	Makes connections	1 2 3 4 5
1 2 3 4 5	Includes questions related to your research	1 2 3 4 5
1 2 3 4 5	Includes research notes	1 2 3 4 5
1 2 3 4 5	Includes sketches	1 2 3 4 5
1 2 3 4 5	Includes written drafts	1 2 3 4 5
1 2 3 4 5	Ends with final reflection about project/experience	1 2 3 4 5
	COMMENTS	

MYSELF	BROCHURE	TEACHER
1 2 3 4 5	Includes narrative information about the exhibit	1 2 3 4 5
1 2 3 4 5	Includes visuals	1 2 3 4 5
1 2 3 4 5	Includes a quiz or puzzle	1 2 3 4 5
1 2 3 4 5	At least three sources in bibliography	1 2 3 4 5
1 2 3 4 5	Interesting, creative format	1 2 3 4 5
1 2 3 4 5	Neatly done	1 2 3 4 5
1 2 3 4 5	Correct use of writing conventions	1 2 3 4 5
	COMMENTS	

MYSELF	DISPLAY	TEACHER
1 2 3 4 5	Interesting, creative format	1 2 3 4 5
1 2 3 4 5	Informative	1 2 3 4 5
1 2 3 4 5	Clear interpretive signs aid understanding	1 2 3 4 5
1 2 3 4 5	Has eye appeal; is colorful	1 2 3 4 5
	COMMENTS	

MYSELF	PRESENTATION	TEACHER
1 2 3 4 5	Shows knowledge of subject	1 2 3 4 5
1 2 3 4 5	Organized and focused	1 2 3 4 5
1 2 3 4 5	Helpful in understanding exhibit	1 2 3 4 5
1 2 3 4 5	Maintains audience interest	1 2 3 4 5
1 2 3 4 5	Speaker uses clear, audible voice	1 2 3 4 5
	COMMENTS	

Figure 10.6: Cultural Museum Evaluation

3. Rating Scales

Rating scales provide feedback in graphic form. They can be used by teachers to evaluate students and are also useful for peer evaluations and self-evaluations. Each concept or skill is presented as a continuum. Students mark an "X" to indicate their approximate level of proficiency. Although commonly used in the past for opinion scales, these mini-continuums can be adapted to communicate a degree of competence for specific skills and to show progress over time.

Cynthia Ruptic uses the Simple Machines Rating Scale (Form 10.9) as a quick evaluation. At the end of the unit, students each use a pencil to rate their effort on the simple machine project. Using a pen, Cynthia evaluates each student using the same continuum. Although teachers sometimes worry that students might rate themselves too highly, Cynthia finds that most children are very realistic in their self-evaluations. If anything, some tend to be very hard on themselves and underrate their achievements. Cynthia confers with each student to discuss the rating scales and compare results. The rating scale should be supported by anecdotal notes taken as students are engaged in a task or process.

Cynthia Ruptic and Lisa Norwick agree that anecdotal notes are the most important assessment tool for assessing learning in the content areas. They both use checklists, rubrics, and rating scales, along with their anecdotal notes, to evaluate final projects, to mark specific items on the report card, and to write brief narrative comments about content area learning to share with students and their parents.

Planning for Assessment

It's important to build in opportunities for assessment throughout the unit of study. When planning for a unit, determine what you hope students will learn and do and how they can show what they know. Identify areas of learning and the behaviors or activities that will provide clear evidence that learning has occurred. Wendy Binder of The National Science Resource Center in Washington, D.C., advises teachers to "look for activities and experiences that you feel will give the children enough richness so that an assessment at that point would give you a lot of feedback" (Hein and Price, 1994, p.71).

As much as possible, embed assessments in what you already do. What will your students be doing that could double as an assessment tool? To get beyond mere recall of facts, identify activities in which students must apply the concepts, strategies, and skills they have learned. In the example given at the beginning of the chapter, Tejas is clearly able to create his own table to record his observations in science. Maaro, on the other hand, may use a teacher-made table when provided, but has not yet internalized this step of the scientific method enough to record data appropriately. Teaming Tejas and Maaro on a future experiment will help Tejas articulate his "knowing" as he assists Maaro in learning how to organize and record his own data.

Determine how you will verify and record the learning that is evident. What is the best technique for assessing acquisition of a specific concept or skill? Will anecdotal note taking be an appropriate method? Can you formulate focus questions that might guide your observations? Would a checklist or rubric be more efficient? How can you incorporate student self-evaluation into the project?

As you create your own assessments, it is important to pilot the new tool, reflect upon the quality of the information it provides you, revise it, and then try the tool again. It is usually helpful to collaborate with colleagues as well as to involve your students as you invent and refine your assessment tools.

Reporting Results

Once you have developed a plan of assessment, you must also determine how you will use the information you obtain. How will you use it to organize and adjust instruction? How might you interpret outcomes in order to communicate their significance to your students and their parents? Reducing the results of assessments to numeric scores, grades, or other symbols often dilutes the significance of the information you gained. Even words like excellent, fair, and poor take a child's endeavors and wrap them with our own values rather than holding them out and discerning their fundamental message. A grade, score, or comment like "good work" reveals little about a child's learning.

Often, the most effective method of communicating what has been learned is to examine the child's product or performance and write down what we notice. We can also share our insights during individual conferences with students and parents. Cynthia's students meet as a class to determine what to share at student-led conferences. Cynthia has input, but she tries to "keep a light touch," as Carol Avery (1993) suggests. While Cynthia prefers the "First/Later" and "Fix-it" samples, her students often choose their "very best work" or samples of projects they found particularly exciting or enjoyable. As educators, we must help children and parents recognize and interpret the evidence of learning inherent in students' work. We have included a variety of very specific techniques that you can adapt to fit your specific topics or projects.

It's not enough to "teach a unit." We must also set the criteria, then collect evidence that students understand and can apply to what they have learned. As you choose and design assessments, consider what information each might tell you about what a child knows, can do, or needs to learn, and how that knowledge will improve your teaching.

In this chapter, we presented several assessment strategies that do not have forms, such as the student-constructed graphics, double entry journals, K-W-L-W or the first/later comparisons. In addition, we included seven other content area assessment tools, many of which are specific to a particular unit or concept. We hope these ideas serve as springboards for your own thinking as you create assessment tools that fit your specific topics, projects, and group of students.

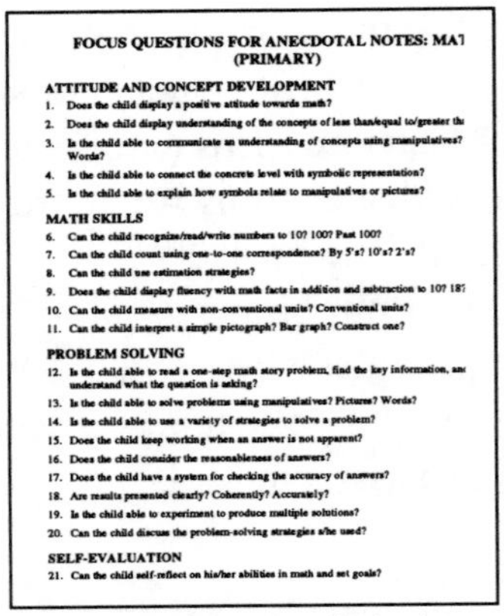

FOCUS QUESTIONS FOR ANECDOTAL NOTES: MA1 (PRIMARY)

ATTITUDE AND CONCEPT DEVELOPMENT

1. Does the child display a positive attitude towards math?
2. Does the child display understanding of the concepts of less than/equal to/greater th
3. Is the child able to communicate an understanding of concepts using manipulatives? Words?
4. Is the child able to connect the concrete level with symbolic representation?
5. Is the child able to explain how symbols relate to manipulatives or pictures?

MATH SKILLS

6. Can the child recognize/read/write numbers to 10? 100? Past 100?
7. Can the child count using one-to-one correspondence? By 5's? 10's? 2's?
8. Can the child use estimation strategies?
9. Does the child display fluency with math facts in addition and subtraction to 10? 18?
10. Can the child measure with non-conventional units? Conventional units?
11. Can the child interpret a simple pictograph? Bar graph? Construct one?

PROBLEM SOLVING

12. Is the child able to read a one-step math story problem, find the key information, an understand what the question is asking?
13. Is the child able to solve problems using manipulatives? Pictures? Words?
14. Is the child able to use a variety of strategies to solve a problem?
15. Does the child keep working when an answer is not apparent?
16. Does the child consider the reasonableness of answers?
17. Does the child have a system for checking the accuracy of answers?
18. Are results presented clearly? Coherently? Accurately?
19. Is the child able to experiment to produce multiple solutions?
20. Can the child discuss the problem-solving strategies s/he used?

SELF-EVALUATION

21. Can the child self-reflect on his/her abilities in math and set goals?

Form 10.1: Focus Questioning for Anecdotal Notes

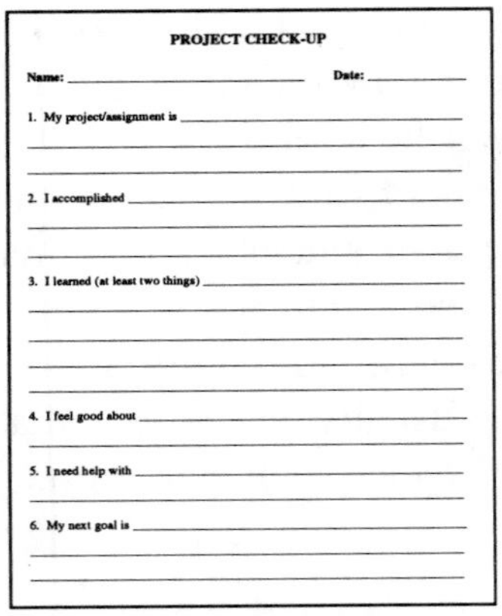

PROJECT CHECK-UP

Name: ____________ Date: ________

1. My project/assignment is ____________
2. I accomplished ____________
3. I learned (at least two things) ____________
4. I feel good about ____________
5. I need help with ____________
6. My next goal is ____________

Form 10.2: Project Check-up

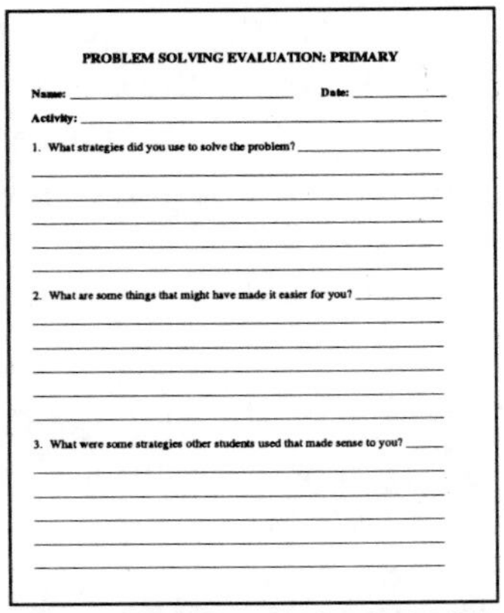

PROBLEM SOLVING EVALUATION: PRIMARY

Name: ____________ Date: ________

Activity: ____________

1. What strategies did you use to solve the problem? ____________
2. What are some things that might have made it easier for you? ____________
3. What were some strategies other students used that made sense to you? ______

Form 10.3: Problem Solving Evaluation

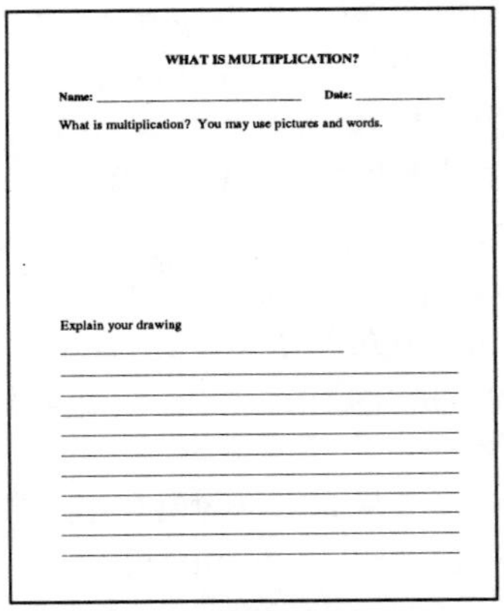

WHAT IS MULTIPLICATION?

Name: ____________ Date: ________

What is multiplication? You may use pictures and words.

Explain your drawing

Form 10.4: Fix-It Strategy

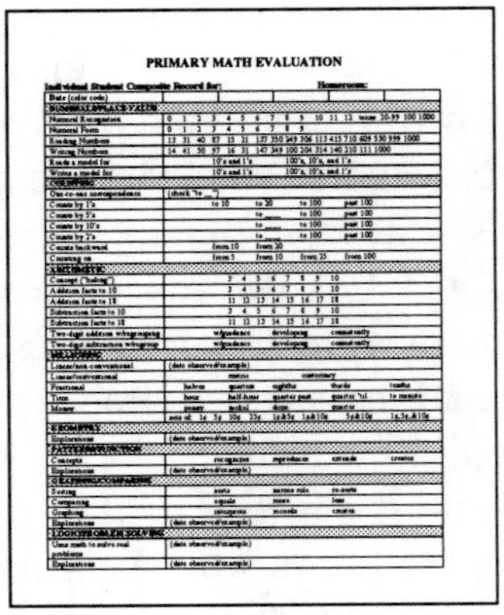

PRIMARY MATH EVALUATION

Form 10.5 to Form 10.7: Checklists

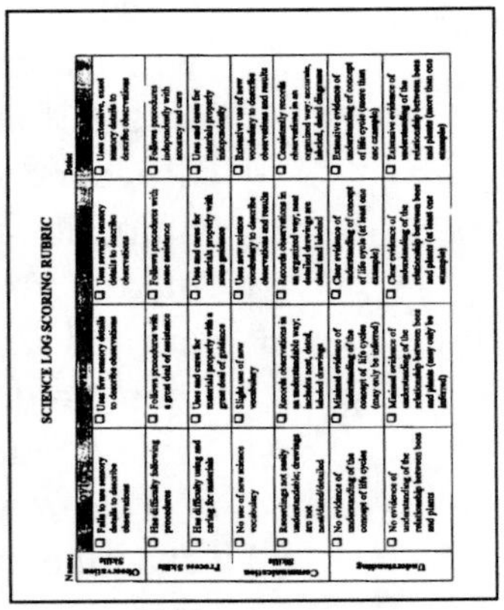

SCIENCE LOG SCORING RUBRIC

Form 10.8: Rubrics

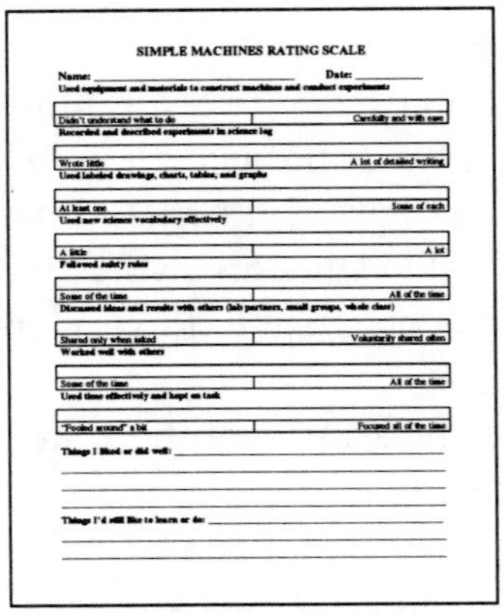

SIMPLE MACHINES RATING SCALE

Name: ____________ Date: ________

Used equipment and materials to construct machines and conduct experiments

Didn't understand what to do — Carefully and with ease

Recorded and described experiments in science log

Wrote little — A lot of detailed writing

Used labeled drawings, charts, tables, and graphs

At least one — Some of each

Used new science vocabulary effectively

A little — A lot

Followed safety rules

Some of the time — All of the time

Discussed ideas and results with others (lab partners, small groups, whole class)

Shared only when asked — Voluntarily shared often

Worked well with others

Some of the time — All of the time

Used time effectively and kept on task

"Fooled around" a bit — Focused all of the time

Things I liked or did well: ____________

Things I'd still like to learn or do: ____________

Form 10.9: Rating Scales

Professional Growth

Jean Moon and Linda Schulman, in *Finding the Connections* (1995), suggest an activity where you imagine that one of your students is moving away. What would you want to tell the child's new teacher about the child's mathematical abilities and understanding? They suggest that you will probably draw on a wealth of sources of information. This activity might provide a good introduction to a workshop on assessment in all content areas. You may want to meet as a staff or grade level team to brainstorm all the sources of information, as well as assessment forms and tasks you've found helpful. When these are held up next to the NCTM and NCTS standards, you can see where assessment aligns and where gaps still exist.

Jean Moon's recent book, *Developing Judgment: Assessing Children's Work in Mathematics* (1997) can be used as a focus for a study group on mathematics. She states, "It is through these guided conversations that you will build a common language for diagnosing student work, build an analytic framework for judging student work, reflect on your teaching, and determine mathematical lessons that will provide the best opportunities for students to demonstrate district and state outcomes" (p. 15).

Everett Kline, who works with Grant Wiggins as a senior associate at The Center on Learning, Assessment and School Structure (CLASS), suggests a collaborative model for creating rubrics. Working with colleagues from the same grade level, draft possible criteria for evaluating a task, specifying four to six levels of performance. Over the next week, gather as many samples of student work as possible. At the next meeting, use the criteria to rate the samples, using "Post-it" notes on the back of the samples. When all the samples have been scored, collect the ones for which everyone scored the same. Discuss why those samples fit the criteria for each level. Fine-tune the descriptors to make a rubric based on the discussion. This process could be used to develop tools to assess performance in any subject area. The ensuing discussions are as valuable as the tools any group creates.

Recommended Readings about Content Area Assessment

One of the best books on assessment in mathematics is *Finding the Connections: Linking Assessment, Instruction,* and *Curriculum in Elementary Mathematics* (1995) by Jean Moon and Linda Schulman. Their book is rich with examples of a variety of assessment tools that align with the new National Council of Teachers of Mathematics Standards. They frame the assessment in a larger context of current research and practices. A similar book that's equally practical is Gerald Kulm's *Mathematics Assessment: What Works in the Classroom* (1994).

Cynthia Ruptic has found the Exemplars (1996) materials particularly helpful. *Exemplars* is a monthly publication of math tasks meant to be used as rich contexts for assessment purposes. It is published by a group of educators from Vermont who have field-tested the benchmarks and tasks in classrooms. Everything you need is on a disk in Hypercard format, including a scanned student work sample for each level or benchmark. For information about a yearly subscription, write to: Exemplars, RR1, Box 7390, Underhill, VT 05489. She used some of the ideas for her invention unit by Beth Amer. For more information, write to Interact, 1825 Gillespie Way, #101, El Cajon, CA 98020 (1-800-359-0961).

In the area of science, we've found *Active Assessment for Active Science: A Guide for Elementary Teachers* (Hein and Price, 1994) to be readable and informative. George Hein and Sabra Price discuss the limitations of paper and pencil tests for assessing science and provide a wide variety of practical alternatives with examples from various published science programs. This compact book also contains sensible tips about developing and managing assessment in the context of "hands-on" science.

For those who have access to the Internet, the Center on Learning, Assessment and School Structure (CLASS) in Princeton, New Jersey has a website at www.classnj.org that is constantly updated with information about current projects and research in the area of school reform. One interesting feature called "Ask Dr. Rubric" allows the user to input and receive answers to questions about rubrics, portfolios, and other forms of authentic assessment. You can also download documents such as a rubric sampler or an extensive bibliography on assessment. By subscribing, you can also access a task and rubric database.

Chapter 11

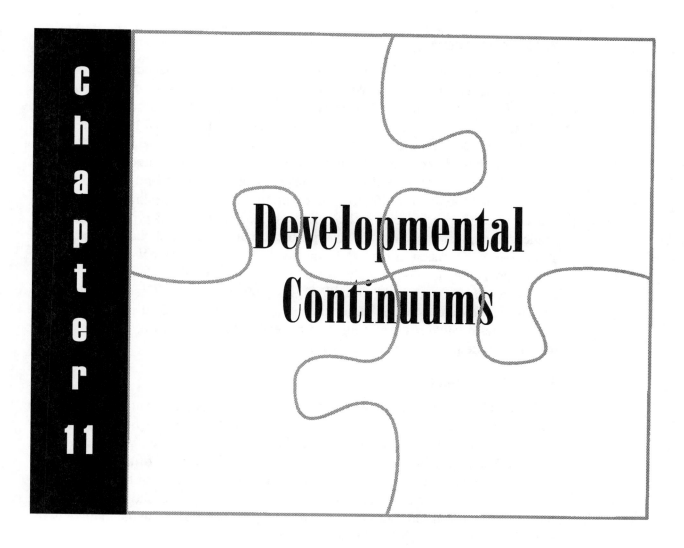

Developmental Continuums

Lisa Norwick's first baby was born as we were working on the final drafts of this book. Between phone calls about running records and rubrics, Lisa asked questions about colic and rejoiced over being able to sleep through the night. Like many new parents, Lisa and her husband talk to friends, look through baby books for advice, and mark developmental milestones on Blake's baby calendar. They are beginning to develop their own roadmap of child development.

Parents take their children in for check ups and watch with interest as the doctor plots where their children fall on growth charts. Some parents record developmental milestones for their children such as walking and starting to say single words at around 12 months, and losing baby teeth in first grade. As children grow and siblings are born, however, parents refer to books less often. They rely upon their growing experience as they internalize the benchmarks for their children's normal growth and development. When they watch their child in the herd of six-year-olds clustered around a soccer ball or shivering with friends on the edge of a swimming pool, parents develop a sense of social and physical benchmarks.

Parents' Concerns

When children enter school, parents want to know the educational benchmarks. When should students learn to read? When do they learn cursive? At what age should they know their multiplication facts? Parents need assurance that their child is growing academically at an appropriate rate. If not, parents want a plan of how to help their child at home and at school.

In the past, benchmarks have not been clearly communicated to parents. All too often students "slip between the cracks" or parents don't find out about problems until it's too late for effective intervention. Parents need to know the expectations for learning and receive a clear picture of how their child is progressing. Letter grades have not always been the straightforward answer they appear at first glance. What does a "C" mean in reading? Does the "C" reflect average work compared to other students in the class or in the district? Is the grade based on test scores, attitude and participation, or growth? Grant Wiggins (1994) suggests, "Grades rarely represent what the parent thinks: achievement" (p. 30). If traditional report cards and letter grades do not provide families with meaningful information, what can we use to report student progress and areas for growth?

Teachers' Concerns

Teachers also need clear benchmarks for growth in each content area. What are widely held expectations for seven-year-olds in mathematics? What types of revision can we expect from most ten-year-old writers? Of course, we will always see a range of behaviors, but we also need a big picture of the range of normal developmental growth in each area. Most of us develop an internal set of benchmarks primarily through experience. For instance, if you've taught second grade for more than five years, you can spot second graders at the grocery store, at the mall, or at the park. You develop an eye for books you know your second graders would like, and learn to appreciate second-grade humor. You internalize an understanding of what most seven- and eight-year-olds can do as readers, writers, scientists, and mathematicians. Unfortunately, your accumulated experience and knowledge is not always acknowledged or valued. The irony is that no matter how experienced we are, when confronted with new tests or materials, we inevitably begin to doubt our own professional knowledge. Districts deluge us with more and more information on what and how we are to teach, some of which is in direct conflict with what we know about the students with whom we work.

In the first ten chapters of this book, we provided a daunting amount of possible assessment tools. We hope you will use some of the ideas and forms as you collect information, make observations, jot down notes, and examine work samples. But what do you do with all the information you collect? Samples collected over time clearly show growth, but how do you know your students are growing at a rate that's appropriate for their age? How can you be assured they will do well on high-stakes tests? What are your goals for where your students should be at the end of the year?

Students' Concerns

Students also need clear benchmarks. How can students meet our expectations when they don't know what they are? How clear are the learning targets and the criteria for grading? How can we help students learn to evaluate their own progress and set goals for their next steps as learners?

All these questions point to the need for clearly articulated benchmarks. Is it possible to create a shared framework that could be understandable and helpful to teachers, parents, and students? Surely all of you have been plagued on road trips with the incessant question, "Are we there yet?" The question is not unreasonable from a youngster who can barely see out the window and who has no perspective on how far the family has come or how much farther to go remains. Similarly, the perennial question—"So how's my child really doing?"—is perhaps a wish for a shared roadmap of learning.

In the last decade, educators around the world have constructed just such benchmarks for student learning. In Canada, these standards are referred to as "widely-held expectations." In Australia, they are called "progress maps" or "profiles." We use the term "developmental continuums" in the United States. These benchmarks have been the missing corner piece of the assessment puzzle. Classroom based assessment provides signposts to document growth. The continuums provide the roadmap to show where we're going.

We'll first describe continuums, then explore seven reasons why we believe that the continuums provide an important framework for assessment, evaluation, and reporting.

Description of Continuums

A continuum is a visual representation of the stages of learning development in a particular area. Specific descriptors provide a framework for assessing individual growth. The literacy continuums (Forms 11.1 and 11.2) in this book paint a picture of how readers and writers develop in kindergarten through eighth grade. In *Book Two*, we'll also explore the challenge of constructing continuums in other content areas.

Stages of the Continuums

The ten stages for the reading and writing continuums are listed as follows:

Preconventional	(ages 3–5)
Emerging	(ages 4–6)
Developing	(ages 5–7)
Beginning	(ages 6–8)
Expanding	(ages 7–9)
Bridging	(ages 8–11)
Fluent	(ages 9–12)
Proficient	(ages 10–13)
Connecting	(ages 11–14)
Independent	

Each of the ten stages contains between six and fifteen specific descriptors. The reading and writing continuums also contain strands that build horizontally. For instance, the first descriptors on the reading continuum represent the types of texts students read, starting from books with simple patterns, to early readers, chapter books, young adult literature, and adult novels. Light bulbs go on when teachers realize that that there aren't ten discrete stages, but that the indicators build upon one another from stage to stage in order to document growth.

Ages on the Continuums

Despite national proclamations, teachers know that there's no such thing as a third-grade reader. In any one classroom, there is a wide range of reading ability levels. For instance, at the beginning of third grade, some students are still reading "I Can Read" books, some are reading beginning chapter books, such as *The Amber Brown* series by Paula Danzinger, while others have launched into reading medium-level chapter books by Judy Blume and Beverly Cleary. If you look at the stages on the reading continuum (Form 11.2), these eight- and nine-year-olds in the Beginning, Expanding, and Bridging stages are right where they should be. We also know that in any one classroom, there may be a two- or even three-year age span. This is particularly evident in kindergarten when we see the physical differences and developmental gap between some students who enter kindergarten just barely five years old, those who turn six during the year, and those with spring or summer birthdays who waited a year and turn seven by the end of kindergarten.

The continuum stages are therefore defined by chronological ages rather than grade levels. This makes the continuum particularly useful in multiage classrooms where the concept of grade levels blurs and the age range is even greater than in other classrooms. The ages of the continuum stages overlap, so that most students' behaviors fall into two or three stages. We recognize that no student's behaviors will fall neatly into one stage and that children grow at different rates. However, there is a general sequence and pattern of literacy development that we can use as guideposts.

Understanding the Continuums

The continuums are based on four basic tenets. First, they focus on what students *can do* by stating descriptors in a positive way. For instance, rather than stating that a student's writing is disorganized, teachers provide focus lessons on paragraphing, then note when a child "Begins to use paragraphs to organize ideas."

Second, the emphasis is on what students learn, rather than on how we teach. The strength of this approach is that the focus is on the learner. New textbooks and the latest methods are meaningless if they don't improve student learning. The continuums can be used by all classroom teachers. The continuums are not based on any particular teaching methodology, but reflect both the cumulative knowledge of classroom teachers and current research about literacy development.

Third, as we mentioned earlier, no child fits neatly into one stage. Children's behaviors fit mostly into one stage, but they may be still consolidating one or two strategies from the previous stage and may be stretching into the next level in one or two other areas. Progress is also uneven as students take developmental leaps, then spend time solidifying new strategies.

Finally, as you start using the continuums, it's important to understand our intentional use of three terms in the descriptors. When students learn something new, the descriptor indicates that the child performs the skill or strategy "with guidance." This indicates that the child would probably not show evidence without adult support and encouragement. For instance, very few primary students would voluntarily revise their work. However, with modeling and focus lessons on six traits of writing and revision strategies, students may be able to revise for specific qualities "with guidance." In the next stage, you'll often see that a student "begins to" show evidence of revision some of the time or with minimal assistance. A student may revise independently on some pieces, but not on others, or a child may try a few changes, but still need adult support. At the next stage, the student should demonstrate these strategies consistently and independently. These three modifiers ("with guidance," "begins to," and "independently") are important to understanding the developmental flow of the descriptors.

Marking the Continuums

In many schools around the country, teachers highlight specific descriptors on the continuum, using different colors for each grading period. For instance, at Brighton School in Lynnwood, Washington, teachers document growth using a yellow highlighter in the fall, a blue highlighter in the winter, and a pink highlighter in the spring. Parents can see growth by looking at the color coding on the descriptors. We've tried using different symbols for each quarter and three boxes by each descriptor for each grading period, but the continuums soon become so cluttered that they lose the visual impact. Time and again we've returned to color highlighting because it's such a visible way to show growth to teachers, students, and their parents.

Support Documents

As we shared the literacy continuums with colleagues, we developed supplementary materials to help students and parents, as well as teachers. We've included so many assessment ideas and forms that we were worried about the length of this book if we included all the continuum materials as well. These continuums and the support materials outlined in Figure 11.2 will be included in *Book Two: Developmental Continuums*. We have, however, included the reading and writing continuums in the Appendix.

- Narrative Portraits of Readers/Writers
- Glossary
- Books by Continuum Levels
- Student Version of Continuum
- Student Self-Evaluations by Stages
- Chart Versions of Continuums
- Family Support Document
- Version with Color-Coded Strands
- Version with State Standards
- Continuums in Other Content Areas

Figure 11.1: Continuum Support Materials

Rationale for Continuums

1. Creating a Common Language

The continuums provide a common language about reading and writing development for teachers, students, and parents. Instead of a three-inch-thick curriculum document, reading and writing K–8 development is presented on two pages. Rather than vague terms like "writes well" or "reads at grade level," the continuums contain specific and concise language. In some districts, teachers are re-shaping their curriculum guides with the continuums and their state standards as a framework. These districts are making a conscious effort to use the terminology from the literacy continuums to align philosophy, goals, curriculum, assessment, evaluation, and reporting.

In any school, there's a wide range of teaching styles. Sharon's classroom is filled with literature and she centers her curriculum around several broad themes for the year. Mark teaches at the same grade level and uses a basal for his reading groups. Both are excellent teachers, but their teaching beliefs and styles sometimes make it appear that they are going in different directions. One of the greatest strengths of the continuums is that they can provide a common framework for teachers like Sharon and Mark so that they can work toward common goals.

2. Capturing the Big Picture

Do you remember feeling overwhelmed and unsure of what you were supposed to teach your first year? Were you filled with anxiety the first time that you changed grade levels? Like new parents, many beginning teachers don't have the big picture.

If you are new to a grade level or are a first-year teacher, well-meaning colleagues probably handed you stacks of curriculum guides, worksheets, and manuals. How can you possibly wade through all that material? What new teachers first need is a broad picture of what students generally learn at a particular age. Many teachers have told us that the continuums were particularly helpful their first year in a new job or grade level.

Have you ever had students who are so far behind or so far ahead of their peers that you felt a bit inadequate in meeting their needs? When Phyllis Keiley-Tyler worked with middle school teachers in Washington state, she found they often complained that their students "couldn't read." However, when she handed the teachers the reading continuum and asked for specific examples, they realized that their students actually did demonstrate many reading strategies listed on the continuum. Since middle school teachers rarely have had training in the developmental nature of early reading, the continuum provided a new lens for assessing their students and planning instruction. The continuums show "what comes before" for readers and writers.

After having taught intermediate grades for several years, when Lisa Norwick first taught second grade, the continuums helped her gain a picture of literacy development in the primary grades. Sandra, one of Lisa's students, was struggling with reading and writing. Lisa sat down in early November with all of her classroom based assessment tools and anecdotal notes. As she filled out the continuums, her hunch that Sandra was significantly below the range of normal development in both areas was confirmed. This information prompted Lisa to have an early conference with Sandra's parents and to recommend that a team of specialists do further assessments and take a closer look at Sandra's specific learning needs. The continuums provided clear information as well as a starting point for planning how to meet her individual needs.

Teachers are also sometimes equally at a loss about how to meet the needs of students who are clearly farther ahead of other students. The same year, Lisa learned that Tom was far above the normal range of developmental growth in reading and writing as she collected assessment information and filled out his continuums. The information helped Lisa understand Tom's individual needs and design specific activities that would challenge him and encourage his growth as a reader and writer. For instance, even as a second grader, Tom consistently added description and detail to his writing. His pieces had a clear beginning, middle, and end. Tom was already beginning to use paragraphs to organize his ideas. Lisa looked at the next stage on the writing continuum as a guide for developing appropriate lessons for Tom. For instance, during an individual conference, Lisa showed him how to try a variety of leads to his stories. The continuums provided a structure for Lisa to meet the needs of both Sandra and Tom.

One of the biggest challenges in education is trying to meet the needs of the wide range of readers and writers in our classrooms. Whether you're a new or veteran teacher, the continuums can provide the big picture. It also helps to know that the continuums are based on current research about literacy acquisition. The continuums help make the connection between research, curriculum, assessment, and evaluation.

3. Providing Information about Students

Parking lots are usually full the nights before parent conferences as teachers gather their anecdotal comments and student work, then finish filling out their report cards. Most conferences are a pleasure and it's exciting to be able to show growth to families. However, there are two types of conferences that teachers dread. One is with the family of the child about whom you are most concerned. These conversations can be emotional and draining. The other type is with the "high maintenance parents." These are the parents, usually of good students, who have high expectations for their children and are very invested in their child's success. These parents want assurance that their child is being challenged. When you meet with both types of parents, you may feel as if you need to come "armed" with answers. Sometimes, you end up feeling inadequate or defensive.

The best response to both of these challenges is better assessment. Teachers often say that the classroom based assessment tools, especially anecdotal notes, their Teacher Notebook, and the continuums, make a huge difference in how they feel about parent conferences. Over and over we hear teachers say, "I know my children better than I've ever known them before." This is true for experienced teachers as well as novices. They tell us that their Teacher Notebooks make them feel organized and make filling out the report card much easier, since all their assessment information is in one place. The anecdotal notes give specificity and voice to their narrative comments on report cards and at parent conferences. The continuums provide families with a visual portrait of what their children have learned and what their next steps should be.

4. Guiding Your Instruction

How do you know what to teach? How do you plan your lessons for next week? Most of us rely on a combination of intuition and experience, grounded in knowledge of our particular age group and curricular guidelines. As mentioned throughout this book, instruction should also be based on information we gather from our classroom based assessment. The continuums provide an additional framework for planning instruction. As teachers study the continuums at the beginning of the year, they often see new aspects of reading and writing they need to incorporate into their teaching. Assessment and instruction become even more closely aligned when teachers recognize that every descriptor on the continuums for their particular age group should become an intentional part of instruction. For instance, Megan Sloan and Christy Clausen have used the continuums for several years and now know what to assess. Megan has developed a whole series of focus lessons about revising for specific writing traits. Christy uses her guided reading lessons to model and discuss reading strategies. These teachers consciously make a connection between their instruction and assessment.

Continuums also serve as an observation guide for teachers. What strategies and behaviors should you be looking for and assessing? Once Megan and Christy introduce a particular strategy, they use anecdotal notes to record when students actually use the strategy in the classroom. By connecting their anecdotal notes to the continuums, teachers can also make a connection between assessment and evaluation.

How do you know when a student is "at grade level" in reading? In the past, most of us relied on our teaching experience at a particular grade level. Some of us also used "more objective" Informal Reading Inventories with graded passages or end-of-the-unit tests in published reading series. Isolated tests, however, rarely match the rich literacy behaviors we see every day in our classrooms. On the other hand, information from a variety of classroom based assessment tools can provide a great deal of valid information. This rich collection of data can then be measured against the age ranges on the continuums to ascertain if a child is progressing at an acceptable rate.

5. Communicating with Parents

By providing clear criteria for evaluation, the continuums place an emphasis on growth rather than competition. All too often, students (and parents) focus on "getting good grades" rather than on learning. "Developmental assessment shifts the focus in assessment from notions of 'passing' and 'failing' to the concept of growth: from an emphasis on comparing one individual with another, to an emphasis on students' developing skills, knowledge and understanding" (Masters and Forster, 1996, p. 8).

The information on the continuums provides much more information than a "B" in reading or writing. The specificity of the descriptors and the differentiation of the strands on the continuums provide significantly more information to teachers, parents, and students. However, as much as we dislike the competitive overtones of the question, many parents (particularly parents of high-achieving students) want to know how their child compares to others in the class. Although we flinch at the thought of comparing one student against others, we have to face the fact that many parents need a sense of what we mean by an "acceptable rate" or "widely-held expectations." If this is their first fourth grader, they don't have a broad perspective of what fourth graders can do as readers and writers.

One strategy that some teachers have used is to create a graph of the range of literacy behaviors in their classroom. For instance, Christy Clausen creates a graph to show the range of her students as readers and writers in the fall. She removes names when she shows the overhead at Curriculum Night. Christy draws an analogy to physical and oral language development. She explains that just as children learn to walk and talk at different ages, not every child will learn to read at the same time or in the same way. She also uses the graph (again, without names) during individual conferences if parents voice concerns about their child. Parents tell Christy that the graph and continuums helped them understand the developmental aspect of reading and writing. The age spans on the continuums show the normal range of literacy behaviors. "By mapping the achievements of a number of students it is possible to show parents how an individual is achieving in relation to other students of the same age or grade" (Master and Forster, 1996, p. 60). Another benefit of the continuums is that they clearly demonstrate to parents the complex nature of literacy acquisition.

6. Providing Clear Targets and Standards

In 1993, the Washington Legislature created a Commission on Student Learning whose task was to develop new academic standards. One of the advantages in Washington state has been that our standards were developed with teacher input and feedback from the community. The standards provide reasonable guidelines for reading and writing. With benchmarks and testing only at the fourth, seventh and tenth grades, teachers aren't locked into the specificity of grade level descriptors and can look at growth more developmentally. Unlike the standardized tests of the past, the new state tests were purposefully aligned with the standards. As the standards and tests were developed, conversations in schools, in the community, and in the media began to focus more on what students were learning than on curriculum. (Recent legislation in the state, however, threatens to turn the discussion back into a debate over methodology and materials.)

When we revised the continuums in 1996, we carefully wove the Washington state standards into the reading and writing continuums. Interest in the continuums rose significantly this year, when the results of the new fourth-grade tests were announced, since 80 percent of the fourth- and seventh-grade Washington state standards for reading and writing are reflected on the continuums. When the results of the tests were splashed across newspaper headlines, school boards, administrators, and principals suddenly wanted to know more about how the continuums were tied to the standards. In *Book Two: Developmental Continuums*, we'll include versions of the continuums which indicates the descriptors that match the fourth- and seventh-grade Washington state benchmarks. This version visually shows how state benchmarks are clearly a part of the reading and writing continuums. If teachers use the continuums to assess students on a regular basis, the results from the new state tests should mirror their findings. In addition, since the assessment tools we've described in the first 10 chapters of this book also match the continuums, you can see how all the pieces start to fit together.

Of course, not every state has connected high-stakes state tests with developmentally appropriate standards. You'll need to look at your own state tests and national standards and decide where they align and where there are gaps. We have included the reading and writing continuums on the CD-ROM so that you can make changes in order to match your own curriculum and standards. We ask that you send us a copy, along with a note about the changes so that we can see what directions the continuums take. We will continue to revise and modify our continuums as we read more, collect data about student performances, and receive feedback from other teachers.

7. Completing the Picture

In many schools and districts in the United States and Canada, the reading and writing continuums have become part of the reporting process. Teachers who are just starting to use the continuums often share them informally at conferences, without sending them home as part of the official report card. In some schools, the continuums are inserted as a supplement to the report card. In other schools or districts, the reading and writing continuums are copied back to back and actually become the reading and writing sections of the report card. Teachers mark the descriptors with colored highlighters to document growth and these continuums are shared at parent conferences. In all three scenarios, the continuums provide a connection between evaluation and reporting.

In Chapter 2 of this book, we presented a circle (Figure 2.1) that showed the connection between seven educational components: philosophy, goals/standards, curriculum, assessment, evaluation, reporting, and research. In the last few years, a great emphasis has been placed on assessment and evaluation, but the conversation seems to have come to a grinding halt when we reach the issue of reporting. Few books or articles have brought the circle to completion by examining how student growth and progress can be reported to families in a meaningful way. One of the most exciting aspects of our work with the literacy continuums has been seeing how all the pieces fit together. In *Book Four: Reporting Student Growth*, we'll tackle evaluation and reporting, the last and most challenging components of the assessment puzzle.

Reflections

We want to end this chapter with three lingering issues that have arisen out of our work with continuums. Our first concern is the tendency for teachers and parents to blame each other for gaps in a child's learning. We believe this adversarial relationship has arisen because of a lack of trust in schools, which is exacerbated by the current legislative and media backlash against education. The only possible way to combat the highly charged accusations is to become more knowledgeable about current research, more politically proactive, and more articulate about what we do and why. We also need to create avenues for parents to become involved alongside us as partners in their child's learning.

What do you do when a student is not showing growth? It's important to look closely at possible causes. Is it a developmental issue and progress will merely be a matter of time? Are issues outside of school interfering with learning? Is there a significant learning problem about which we should be concerned? Or is the lack of growth in a particular area due to gaps in instruction? This last concern is one that warrants further contemplation by teachers. We hope that teachers use the continuum to critically examine their own teaching, as well as student learning.

Finally, there is a basic conflict inherent in the use of continuums between a developmental philosophy and the concept of standards. The President of our country declares on network television that all students will read by third grade. As teachers, we want to ask, "Read what? How well?" We want to know how this can happen when some students come to school with widely different language, cultural values, economic pressures, and opportunities. What if a law was passed that all children must walk by twelve months? We all know that, despite modeling, coaxing, and bribery by siblings and doting grandparents, toddlers walk when they are ready. Some of us had babies who walked around ten months, some who walked at around a year, and others who took their first steps at thirteen or fourteen months, yet they're all walking today! Learning to read and write are also developmental processes. Unlike walking, however, the process is more gradual and more complex. As states move from benchmarks to large-scale promotion policies and graduation requirements, the emphasis on standards seems to overshadow the acknowledgement of individual differences and the developmental nature of learning.

Most of us would agree that there should be some sort of standard in order to know where we're heading. The developmental sequence and age ranges on the continuums provide the roadmap for literacy development. At the same time, we need to allow for individual differences and celebrate growth. The collection of classroom based assessment information and the highlighting of specific descriptors on the continuums show how far a student has come and what's next along the road. Continuums also provide the corner piece that connects classroom based assessment, student portfolios, and methods for reporting student growth.

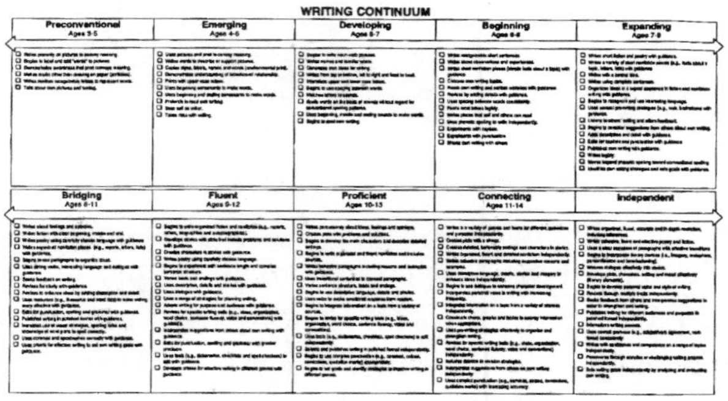

Form 11.1 Writing Contiuum

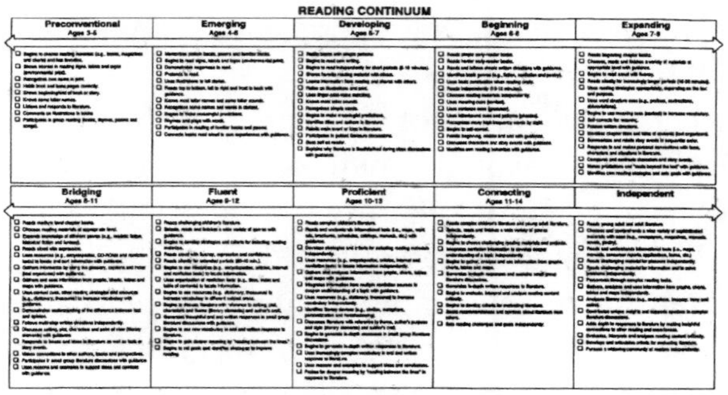

Form 11.2 Reading Contiuum

Professional Growth

One of the most effective and memorable ways to explain a continuum is to use a visual demonstration during a workshop. Ask 8–10 volunteers from the group to come up to the front of the room, explaining that they will not be required to do anything that will be intellectually or physically challenging. Explain that everything in life is on a continuum. Choose a topic, such as cooking. Facing the audience, explain that any of the volunteers who absolutely hate to cook should go stand to your far right. Next to them will be the people who like to cook when they have time, but never have time. In the middle will be people who like to cook and actually make time to create lovely meals. People who pride themselves on their cooking and those who read cookbooks for fun will be at the far left end of the continuum. Give the volunteers a chance to move to where they feel they would fit on the "cooking continuum." Next, follow a similar process with two or three other topics such as gardening, a specific sport, singing, or using computers. When you ask what people notice, the audience will probably comment that there was a great deal of movement. You can point out that there is some topic at which one person would be to your far left, and other topics at which someone would be on your far right. The point is that there's no good or bad place, but rather that people have different strengths and abilities. What's important is to decide the topic, articulate the criteria, set goals, and document growth. We've found this simple five-minute activity has tremendous power as an introduction to continuums for teachers, parents, and students.

If a group of teachers decide to use the literacy continuums, we've found the most helpful staff development activity is to mark the reading or writing continuum together, using actual student work. For instance, at Audubon Elementary in Redmond, Washington, a teacher from each grade-level team brought four samples of writing from one student, including drafts as well as the final published pieces. The teachers made enough copies so that each team member had a set of the samples. Together, the team looked at the student's work and marked the writing continuum. The teams did a similar activity the next month by looking at one child's reading. One teacher brought an audiotape or videotape of the student reading orally, along with a running record, reading conference notes, and a response journal sample. The team marked the reading continuum based on that evidence. These activities sparked wonderful conversations about literacy and helped teachers see how to fill out the continuum at a very concrete level. In order for the continuums to become a successful assessment and evaluation tool, teachers need time to share ideas and talk together as they use the continuums in order to develop consistency and a common understanding.

Recommended Readings on Continuums

There's very little published information about developmental continuums. In the past several years, there have been three resources available from mainstream publishers in this country. Geoff Master and Margaret Forster's magazine *Developmental Assessment* (1996) from Australia provides a helpful overview of continuums around the world. This resource and the accompanying video are now available through Christopher-Gordon Publishers.

A few years ago, Heinemann published a series of continuums, called *First Steps*. This program was first researched by Education Department of Western Australia. Their program includes resource books and developmental continuums for Oral Language, Reading, Writing, and Spelling, as well as a wonderful parent booklet. They offer staff development for instruction and assessment based on their continuums. You may also want to look at *The American Literacy Profile Scales: A Framework for Authentic Assessment* (Griffin, Patrick, Smith and Burrill, 1995), which is also published by Heinemann and based on the Australian literacy continuums.

Other materials are published primarily by school districts or divisions, or government agencies. For instance, the literacy continuums published by the Juneau, Alaska schools have also been extremely helpful. The *Language Arts Portfolio Handbooks* (1994) include developmental literacy continuums for primary and intermediate grades. They include instructional suggestions and guidelines for assessment techniques, in addition to the literacy continuums. For more information, call the Juneau School District at 1-907-463-1700.

Supporting Learning: Understanding and Assessing the Progress of Children in the Primary Grades RB0018 (1995) is a small booklet which provides an overview of curriculum and assessment in British Columbia and is a useful reference for parents and teachers. The focus is on the whole child - on academic, social, physical, and emotional growth. The continuums in this booklet are outstanding. The book is accompanied by two larger documents, the *Primary Program Resource Document* RB0008 (1994) and the *Primary Program Foundation Document* CG0279 (1990). These two volumes include specific forms and explanations of many tools, techniques and ways to assess learning. The literacy continuums are included in the booklets called *Evaluating Writing Across the Curriculum* RB0020 (1996) and RB0021 (1995) *and Evaluating Reading Across the Curriculum* RB0034 (1996). For more information, call Crown Publications at 1-250-386-4636 or the Ministry of Education at 1-250-356-2500.

As the interest in developmental continuums grows, we hope there will be more books and published materials on this topic.

Chapter 12

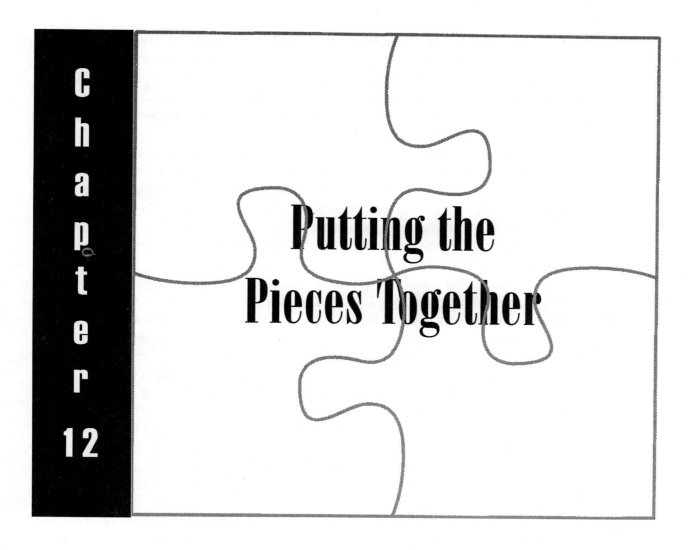

Putting the Pieces Together

Julie Ledford balances her coffee mug on the dashboard as she places her Teacher Notebook and anecdotal clipboard on the seat next to her, then pulls out of the school parking lot. As she heads home through the Seattle rain, she mentally runs through her "To Do" list. Spring is always a bit hectic, but this year she has her master's degree project to complete on top of the class trip to Camp Orkila, report cards, and parent conferences. For the first time in years, however, she won't be frantically checking endless boxes on report cards at midnight the night before they're due. Her Teacher Notebook, anecdotal notes, assessment forms, and the continuums made the process of preparing for conferences and filling out the report card more manageable and meaningful. Tonight she plans to transfer her latest "Post-it" notes into her Teacher Notebook and look over her narrative comments for a few children before she tucks all the report cards into envelopes to send home with students in the morning.

Julie realizes that she knows her students better this year than any other year she has taught. Yesterday, as she transferred her reading and writing conference forms into her Teacher Notebook, she marveled at how much information she had collected on each child and how organized she feels. The challenge has been finding enough hours in the day to make new forms, respond to student projects, and read her assignments for graduate classes, to say nothing of life outside of school!

Although Julie is still somewhat dissatisfied with small parts of her assessment program, she has great hopes for making some changes next year. She plans to tie her anecdotal notes more specifically to the district frameworks and state standards for science and social studies. Julie also wants to experiment with some different self-evaluation forms and find a way to make student goals a formal part of the report card. Over the summer, she looks forward to having time to read the professional books on portfolios that are gathering dust by her bed and on the dining room table. Although this year has been a lot of work, it's also been a year of new ideas and professional growth.

We hope that this first volume of the *Corner Pieces* assessment series helps you see how classroom based assessment fits in the big picture. As we collected ideas from teachers, created forms, and examined student reflections, we continually asked ourselves how assessment can lead to better teaching on our part, and to improved learning on the part of our students. We tried to make connections among assessing, teaching, and learning come alive through the classroom vignettes woven throughout the text, for it's at the classroom level that we discover what works. We believe that it's only through focused and intentional assessment that we can discover each student's needs and areas for growth. These discoveries must inform and guide our teaching. Lucy Calkins (1994) echoes this belief: "In the end, a classroom is student centered if and only if our teaching happens in response to individual students. Assessment allows us to be truly student-centered in our teaching" (p. 314).

You have to balance the goal of quality assessment with what's realistic and manageable in the busy world of your elementary classroom. As you've read about the many possible assessment techniques in various content areas, we hope that you haven't become overwhelmed by all you're *not* doing. You need to give yourself credit for all you are doing well. The examples we've included in *Classroom Based Assessment* were gathered from many teachers in many different classrooms. No one can possibly use more than a handful of these ideas and still have time to teach. We hope you will select a few assessment ideas, combine them with what you already use, then try a form or technique with your students. How does this idea fit with your philosophy and goals? Does it provide helpful information that will improve your instruction? Will you use a form directly from the book, or will you modify or create a new assessment form? We hope that your copy of *Classroom Based Assessment* is full of "Post-it" notes as you mark ideas to try right away, as well as some to try down the road.

As Julie Ledford compiles information about her students in her Teacher Notebook, how can she hold their growth up against state and national standards? How can she be sure that they will do well on the new statewide fourth-grade test? How can she be confident that her students are not only learning, but that they are growing at a rate that's appropriate for their age? In *Book Two: Developmental Continuums*, we'll focus on how developmental benchmarks can answer these questions and support the rich information you've collected in your Teacher Notebook.

Like Julie, we're eager to take another look at student portfolios by reading the wealth of new books on the topic and talking with teachers from around the world about the ways in which they involve students in the assessment and evaluation process. *Book Three: Student Portfolios* will show how classroom based assessment, developmental continuums, and portfolios can create a three-dimensional portrait of learners. We hope to pull all the pieces together in *Book Four: Reporting Student Growth* as we discuss ways in which the classroom based information you've gathered can be summarized and shared with parents on report cards. We'll demonstrate how students can share their portfolios during student-led conferences as evidence of progress toward the benchmarks outlined on the continuums.

Many teachers feel overwhelmed by the current barrage of standards, curriculum, and new materials. At the same time, there's heightened public scrutiny and criticism of education. How can you keep from burning out and still remain excited about teaching? A key to professional survival is to be able to articulate your beliefs, goals, and curriculum. It's equally important that your assessment and evaluation program is solidly in place. And the only way to keep from being overwhelmed by the changes and pressure in education is to set priorities and take one step at a time. It also helps when you can see how all the pieces fit together. We hope this first book in the series illuminates how classroom based assessment fits in the assessment puzzle. We also hope that the ideas provide a starting place for professional conversations and sharing.

Appendix

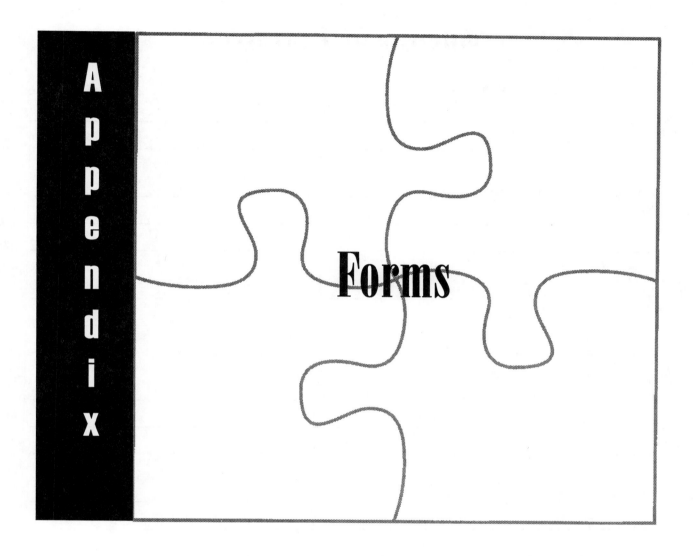

Forms

PHILOSOPHY AND GOALS

The goal of education should be to ____

____

____

I believe people learn best when ____

____

____

My role as a teacher is to ____

____

____

By the end of the year, I hope that my students will ____________________________

____

____

My broad curriculum goals for the year are __________________________________

____

____

Assessment and evaluation should ____

____

____

My professional goals for the year are ______________________________________

____

____

Form 2.1: Philosophy and Goals

CURRICULUM AND ASSESSMENT

Goal:	
Curricular Activities	**Assessment Tool**

ASSESSMENT PLANNING

NOW	NEXT	LATER

Form 3.1: Assessment Planning

ORGANIZATIONAL GRID

Assessment Tool/Strategy	SEPT	OCT	NOV	DEC	JAN	FEB	MAR	APR	MAY	JUN

Form 3.2: Organizational Grid

Anecdotal Records for:

Form 4.1A: Anecdotal Note Grid, 8 ½ X 11" (Photocopy at 120%)

Anecdotal Records for:

Form 4.1B: Anecdotal Note Grid, 8 ½ X 14" (Photocopy at 130%)

SPELLING CONTINUUM

Pre-writing (Preconventional) Ages 3-5 WORD = 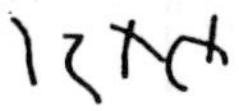	Pre-phonetic (Preconventional) Ages 3-5 WORD = BMTYZ	Semi-phonetic (Emergent) Ages 4-6 WORD = WD or YD	Phonetic (Developing & Beginning) Ages 5-8 WORD = W9d	Transitional (Expanding & Bridging) Ages 7-11 WORD = Werd	Conventional (Bridging & Fluent) Ages 8+ WORD = WORD
• Experiments with drawing and writing. • Uses scribble writing	• Understands that print carries meaning. • Writes random recognizable letters to represent words.	• Begins to recognize that letters represent specific sounds. • Uses beginning consonants to write a word. • Uses beginning and ending consonants to write a word. • May use letter names (e.g., u for you) as words. • Begins to take risks and write independently.	• Matches letters to sounds. • Spells some words by the sounds heard. • Spells some words by sight. • Uses beginning, middle, and ending sounds to write words. • Uses phonetic spelling to write independently. • Begins to notice common spelling patterns. • Begins to ask for correct spelling of words.	• Moves beyond phonetic spelling toward conventional spelling. • Spells simple common words correctly. • Relies on visual spelling patterns. • Uses vowels in all syllables. • Uses letter combinations when writing words (e.g., clusters, blends, diagraphs). • Experiments with various ways to spell words. • Begins to use resources to spell challenging words. • Begins to edit for spelling.	• Uses visual patterns and other strategies to spell most words correctly. • Spells prefixes and suffixes correctly. • Spells contractions correctly. • Spells most compound words correctly. • Begins to learn correct spelling for irregular words. • Identifies misspelled words. • Uses resources when spelling challenging words. • Edits for spelling in final drafts. • Chooses words to learn to spell.

Form 5.1: Spelling Continuum

SPELLING DEVELOPMENT: INDIVIDUAL PROFILE

Name:

Date	Writing Piece	Pre-Writing WORD=[illegible]	Pre-Phonetic WORD= BMTYZ	Semi-Phonetic WORD=WD or YD	Phonetic WORD=Wrd	Transitional WORD=Werd	Conventional WORD=WORD	Notes

SPELLING DEVELOPMENT: CLASS PROFILE

Student Name	**Pre-Writing** Makes letter-like marks WORD =	**Pre-Phonetic** Writes random strings of letters WORD = BMTYZ	**Semi-Phonetic** Beginning/ending consonants WORD = WD or YD	**Phonetic** Writes letters based on sounds WORD = WRd	**Transitional** Aware of spelling patterns and rules WORD = Werd	**Conventional** Spells most words correctly WORD = WORD

Form 5.2B: Spelling Development: Class Profile

SPELLING STRATEGIES I USE

Name:

Strategy	**Date**
I try to spell unknown words.	
I always do my best to spell correctly.	
I know how to spell words I use often.	
I am learning how to spell new words to use in my writing.	
I know how to spell the first (100, 200, 300, 400, 500) words.	
I know how to use capitals for proper names and titles.	
I know how to use apostrophes for contractions.	
I know how to use apostrophes to show possession.	
I use many strategies to spell new words:	
I use what I know about sounds to spell words.	
I think about what the word looks like to spell it.	
I use what I know about word patterns to spell.	
I use class lists, posters and books to help me spell.	
I use a dictionary to help me spell.	
I use a spell checker to help me spell.	
I can think of a base word and add a prefix or suffix.	
I know how to apply rules to add *–ed* and *–ing*.	
I can use rules for making plurals.	
I can use knowledge about word origins to spell.	
To prepare my final drafts, I edit my spelling.	
To prepare my final drafts, I ask someone to help me check my spelling.	
To prepare my final drafts, I use resources to check my spelling.	
I can choose words I want to learn to spell.	
I am interested in words and how they are spelled.	
I read a lot.	
I write a lot.	

Form 5.3: Spelling Strategies I Use

SPELLING 10 WORDS

Name: **Grade/Age:**

FALL	WINTER	SPRING

I noticed

____

____

Form 5.4A: Spelling 10 Words (Primary)

1	1	1
2	2	2
3	3	3
4	4	4
5	5	5
6	6	6
7	7	7
8	8	8
9	9	9
10	10	10

Form 5.4B: Spelling 10 Words

SPELLING 10 WORDS

1. ______________________	1. ______________________
2. ______________________	2. ______________________
3. ______________________	3. ______________________
4. ______________________	4. ______________________
5. ______________________	5. ______________________
6. ______________________	6. ______________________
7. ______________________	7. ______________________
8. ______________________	8. ______________________
9. ______________________	9. ______________________
10. ______________________	10. ______________________

Form 5.4C: Spelling 10 Words (Intermediate)

INDEX OF CONTROL

Name: **Date:**

Conventional Spelling	Constructed Spelling

A = # of total words
B = # of different words
C = # of different words spelled conventionally
D = # of constructed spellings
Index of Control = C divided by B x 100

Index of Control = ________________

(from *Spelling in Use* by Lester Laminack & Katie Wood, 1996)

"HAVE A GO" SPELLING

Name:

MY GUESS	TRY AGAIN	ASK FRIENDS	FINAL SPELLING

Form 5.6: "Have a Go" Spelling

SPELLING SURVEY

Name: ______________________________ **Date:** ______________

1. Are you a good speller? Why do you think so? ______________________

____

____

2. What do you do when you don't know how to spell a word? ____________

____

____

3. What are other ways to figure out how to spell a word? ______________

____

____

4. What kinds of words are hard for you to spell? ____________________

____

____

5. How do people get to be good spellers? ________________________

____

____

6. When is correct spelling important? ___________________________

____

____

WORDS I KNOW **Name:** **Date:**	**WORDS I KNOW** **Name:** **Date:**

(form adapted from *An Observational Survey of Early Literacy Achievement* by Marie Clay, 1993)

Form 6.1: Words I Know

EMERGENT WRITING DEVELOPMENT

Name:

Preconventional				Emerging	Developing	Beginning	Reading Own Writing		
Date	S = Squiggly	LL = Letter-like	RL = Random Letters	SP = Semi-Phonetic initial/end	P = Phonetic Sounds, vowels, spaces	T = Transitional vowels, patterns, sight words	Tells about it	Pretends to read	Reads & touches / matches

Form 6.2: Emergent Writing Development

WRITING TOPICS

Name:

Form 7.1: Writing Topics

PIECES I'VE WRITTEN

Name:

Began/Ended	Title

***Published**

Form 7.2: Pieces I've Written

WRITING GENRES: PART ONE

Name:

Genre				
Observation				
Personal Story/Memories				
Autobiography				
Poetry				
Folk/Fairy/Tall Tales				
Myth/Legend				
Fantasy				
Animal Story				
Nonfiction/Research				
Story Problem				
Letter				

Form 7.3A: Writing Genres: Part One

WRITING GENRES: PART TWO

Name:

Genre				
Realistic Fiction				
Adventure/Survival				
Biography				
Play				
Mystery				
Science Fiction				
Historical Fiction				
Sports Story				
Persuasive Writing				

WRITING STRATEGIES I USE

Name:

Strategy	Date

Form 7.4A: Writing Strategies I Use (Blank Form)

WRITING STRATEGIES I USE: PRIMARY

Name:

Strategy	**With Guidance ⟺ ndependently**
I date my work.	
I label my pictures with words.	
I write phrases and sentences.	
I use my sounds to write.	
I use spaces between my words.	
I use titles to tell my main idea.	
My writing has a beginning, middle, and end.	
I use different types of writing:	
personal stories/memories	
observations	
lists	
stories	
poems	
letters	
reports	
directions	
story problems	
I share my writing with others.	
I use capital letters for names.	
I use capital letters to begin sentences.	
I use periods correctly.	
I use question marks (?) correctly.	
I use exclamation marks (!) correctly.	
I use quotation marks in my writing.	
I correct my spelling on final drafts.	
I edit my work.	

WRITING STRATEGIES I USE: INTERMEDIATE

Name:

Strategy	**With Guidance ⟺ ndependently**
I use interesting titles that suit each piece.	
I use captivating leads.	
My writing has a clear beginning, middle, and end.	
I develop my ideas with details and vivid images.	
I use figurative language and interesting words.	
I use realistic dialogue and/or description.	
I use satisfying endings.	
I write in a variety of forms:	
lists	
personal stories/memories	
observations	
learning reflections	
stories	
poems	
letters	
reports	
directions	
story problems	
I share my writing with others.	
I give others feedback and advice about their writing.	
I use the feedback others give me about my writing.	
I use correct conventions for: paragraph indentation	
capital letters	
punctuation	
I correct my spelling on final drafts.	

Form 7.4C: Writing Strategies I Use (Intermediate)

WRITING GOALS

Name: ________________________ **Date:** ______________

____

____

____

____

____

WRITING GOALS

Name: ________________________ **Date:** ______________

____

____

____

____

____

Form 7.5: Writing Goals

FOCUS QUESTIONS FOR ANECDOTAL NOTES: WRITING (PRIMARY)

WRITING DEVELOPMENT

1. Does the student rely on pictures to convey meaning? Pictures plus print?
2. Does the student label pictures and add words?
3. Does the student copy names and familiar words?
4. Does the student interchange upper and lower case letters indiscriminately?
5. Does the student use beginning/ending sounds to make words? Middle sounds?
6. Does the student use invented spelling?
7. Does the student use spacing between words?
8. Does the student experiment with capitals and punctuation?

CONTENT, TRAITS, AND RANGE

9. Is the student able to choose a topic?
10. Does the student write noun-verb phrases? Short sentences? Paragraphs?
11. Does the student write pieces with a beginning, middle, and end?
12. Does the student write about experiences and observations?
13. Does the student add some description and detail?
14. What different types of writing does the student try?

WRITING PROCESS

15. Can the student tell about his/her writing? Pretend to read his/her writing?
16. Does the student share his/her own writing? Offer feedback to others?
17. Does the student listen to feedback from others?
18. Does the student revise by adding on?
19. Does the student edit for the correct use of capitals and punctuation?
20. Does the student put time and effort into publishing chosen pieces?

ATTITUDE AND SELF-EVALUATION

21. Does the student engage promptly in and sustain writing activities?
22. Does the student write independently? Show a positive attitude toward writing?
23. Can the student reflect upon his/her writing and set goals with guidance?

Form 7.6A: Focus Questions for Anecdotal Notes: Writing (Primary)

FOCUS QUESTIONS FOR ANECDOTAL NOTES: WRITING (INTERMEDIATE)

WRITING DEVELOPMENT

1. Can the student write a fluent draft in age-appropriate handwriting?
2. Does the student spell high frequency words correctly in drafts?
3. Does the student use effective strategies to spell difficult words correctly?

CONTENT, TRAITS AND RANGE

4. Does the student use interesting language?
5. Does the student use a variety of sentence structures?
6. Is the student's writing organized logically and cohesively? In paragraphs?
7. Does the student use literary devices (dialogue, figurative language, imagery, etc)?
8. Does the student use literary elements (plot, setting, character, conflict, etc.) effectively?
9. Does the student use resources to help with writing? (dictionary, thesaurus, etc.)
10. Does the student use a variety of styles and forms of writing?

WRITING PROCESS

11. Does the student use a pre-writing activity? If so, what type?
12. Can the student explain the audience and purpose for the piece of writing?
13. Does the student listen to feedback/advice and apply the information?
14. Does the student listen to the writing of others and give appropriate feedback?
15. Does the student make revisions during drafting or mostly focus on getting down ideas?
16. Does the student use revision strategies to clarify and elaborate?
17. Does the student carefully edit his/her writing for conventions (spelling, capitals, etc.)?
18. Does the student use resources to revise and edit? (dictionary, thesaurus, etc.)
19. Does the student put time and effort into producing a final product?
20. Is the final product neat, legible, and free of most errors?
21. How does the student share his/her final product with others?

ATTITUDE AND SELF-EVALUATION

22. Does the student engage promptly in and sustain writing activities?
23. Does the student write independently and display a positive attitude toward writing?
24. Can the student reflect upon his/her writing and set goals independently?

Form 7.6B: Focus Questions for Anecdotal Notes: Writing (Intermediate)

WRITING OBSERVATIONS

Child / Date	Title, Source, Activity, Comment:	Goals	Takes Risks	On Task

Form 7.7: Writing Observations

WRITING CONVERSATIONS

Name:

Date/Title	Which parts do you feel good about?	What is a struggle or frustration?	What have you learned?	What will you do next?

Form 7.8A: Writing Conversations (Student Form)

WRITING CONVERSATIONS

Name: **Title:** **Date:**

FIRST CONFERENCE (Ideas)	**SECOND CONFERENCE (Rough Draft)**	**FINAL CONFERENCE (Complete or Ready to Publish)**
What are you going to write about?	How is it going?	How do you feel about this piece?
Who will be your audience?	What are you struggling with?	What is your favorite part?
What are your goals for this piece?	What have you learned?	What was the audience's reaction?

Form 7.8B: Writing Conversations (Teacher Form)

WRITING CELEBRATION

Name: ______________________________ **Date:** _______________

____

____

____

____

Parent Comments: ____

____

____

WRITING CELEBRATION

Name: ______________________________ **Date:** _______________

____

____

____

____

Parent Comments: ____

____

____

STATUS OF THE CLASS

Student	Monday	Tuesday	Wednesday	Thursday	Friday

PW = Pre-writing
D1 = First Draft
D2 = Later Drafts
R = Revision

E = Editing
RR = Reading/Researching
P = Publishing
TC = Teacher Conference

PC = Peer Conference
AC = Author's Chair
* = See Anecdotal Notes
◯ = Off-task Behavior

Form 7.10: Status of the Class

SIX-TRAIT GUIDE TO REVISION

IDEAS

- ❑ Does my paper have a clear, focused idea?
- ❑ Did I use details to elaborate?

ORGANIZATION

- ❑ Does my piece have a clear beginning, middle, and end?

WORD CHOICE

- ❑ Did I use any interesting words?

SENTENCE FLUENCY

- ❑ Do my sentences sound smooth?

VOICE

- ❑ Does my piece have a spark, commitment, or that "nearly there" feeling?

CONVENTIONS

- ❑ Did I check my capitals, periods, and spelling (editing for conventions)?

(form based on the six-trait writing assessment model from the Northwest Regional Educational Laboratory)

SIX-TRAIT REVISION CHECKLIST

Name: ______________________________ **Date:** ____________

Title: ________________________________

Self Check:

❑ I have read it to myself.

❑ I have made at least one change.

My change was made for:

❑ Ideas
❑ Organization
❑ Word Choice
❑ Sentence Fluency
❑ Voice
❑ Conventions

Comments: ____

____

Partner Check:

❑ I told the author what I liked.

❑ I asked questions.

I made suggestions to help the author with:

❑ Ideas
❑ Organization
❑ Word Choice
❑ Sentence Fluency
❑ Voice
❑ Conventions

Comments: ____

____

Revising Partner:

____

(form based on the six-trait writing assessment model from the Northwest Regional Educational Laboratory)

REVISION CHECKLIST

Name:

DATE						DESCRIPTOR	STAGE
						Reads own writing and notices mistakes *with guidance.*	**Beginning**
						Revises by adding details *with guidance.*	
						Begins to consider suggestions from others about own writing.	**Expanding**
						Adds description and details *with guidance.*	
						Seeks feedback on writing.	**Bridging**
						Revises for clarity *with guidance.*	
						Revises to enhance ideas by adding description and detail.	
						Uses resources (e.g., thesaurus and word lists) to make writing more effective *with guidance.*	
						Revises for specific writing traits (e.g., ideas, organization, word choice, sentence fluency, voice, and conventions) *with guidance.*	**Fluent**
						Incorporates suggestions from others about own writing *with guidance.*	
						Begins to revise for specific writing traits (e.g., ideas, organization, word choice, sentence fluency, voice, and conventions).	**Proficient**
						Revises for specific writing traits (e.g., ideas, organization, word choice, sentence fluency, voice, and conventions) *independently.*	**Connecting**
						Includes deletion in revision strategies.	
						Incorporates suggestions from others on own writing *independently.*	
						Revises through multiple drafts independently.	**Independent**
						Seeks feedback from others and incorporates suggestions in order to strengthen own writing.	

Form 7.11C: Revision Checklist

REVISING AND EDITING GUIDELINES: PRIMARY

Name: ______________________________ **Date:** ___________

Title: ____

Genre: Observations, Personal Stories/Memories, Autobiography, Poetry, Folk Tale/Fairy Tale/Tall Tale, Myth/Legend, Fantasy, Animal Story, Nonfiction/Research, Story Problems, Letter

- ☐ I read my piece to myself.
- ☐ I read my piece to a partner.
- ☐ My writing makes sense.
- ☐ My name is on my writing.
- ☐ The date is on my writing.
- ☐ I used spaces between my words.
- ☐ This is my very best work.

REVISING AND EDITING GUIDELINES: PRIMARY

Name: ______________________________ **Date:** ___________

Title: ____

Genre: Observations, Personal Stories/Memories, Autobiography, Poetry, Folk Tale/Fairy Tale/Tall Tale, Myth/Legend, Fantasy, Animal Story, Nonfiction/Research, Story Problems, Letter

- ❑ I read my piece to a partner and myself.
- ❑ My writing makes sense.
- ❑ My name and the date are on my writing.
- ❑ I have a title.
- ❑ I numbered my pages.
- ❑ I used clear margins.
- ❑ I capitalized names.
- ❑ I used capital letters at the beginning of each sentence.
- ❑ I used periods, question marks, and exclamation marks correctly.
- ❑ My final work is neat and legible.
- ❑ This is my very best work.

REVISING AND EDITING GUIDELINES: PRIMARY

Name: ________________________________ **Date:** ____________

Title: ____

Genre: Observations, Personal Stories/Memories, Autobiography, Poetry, Folk Tale/Fairy Tale/Tall Tale, Myth/Legend, Fantasy, Animal Story, Nonfiction/Research, Story Problems, Letters

- ❑ I read my piece to two others (sign here).
- ❑ My writing makes sense.
- ❑ My name and the date are on my writing.
- ❑ I have a title.
- ❑ I numbered my pages.
- ❑ I used clear margins.
- ❑ I used capital letters for names and at the beginning of each sentence.
- ❑ I used periods, question marks, and exclamation marks correctly.
- ❑ My final draft is neat and legible.
- ❑ This is my very best work.
- ❑ I have a Dedication page (for books).
- ❑ I have an "About the Author" page (for books).

Form 7.12C: Revising and Editing Guidelines (Primary Spring)

REVISING AND EDITING GUIDELINES: INTERMEDIATE

Name: ______________________________ **Date:** ____________

Title: ____

Genre: Observations, Personal Stories/Memories, Autobiography, Poetry, Folk Tale/Fairy Tale/Tall Tale, Myth/Legend, Fantasy, Animal Story, Nonfiction/Research, Story Problems, Letter, Realistic Fiction, Adventure, Biography, Play, Mystery, Science Fiction, Historical Fiction, Sports Story

- ☐ I have an interesting title that suits the piece and a captivating lead.
- ☐ My writing has a clear beginning, middle and end.
- ☐ I developed my ideas with details and vivid images.
- ☐ I used figurative language (like similes) and interesting words.
- ☐ I used realistic dialogue and/or description.
- ☐ I indented each paragraph.
- ☐ My piece has a satisfying ending.
- ☐ I edited my work for capitals, spelling, and punctuation.
- ☐ I read my piece to two others:
- ☐ I incorporated suggestions from others:
- ☐ My final draft is neat and legible.
- ☐ This is my very best work.
- ☐ I have a Dedication page and an "About the Author" page.

Form 7.12D: Revising and Editing Guidelines (Intermediate Spring)

REVISING AND EDITING GUIDELINES: NONFICTION

Name: ______________________________ **Date:** ___________

Title: ____

- ❑ I have an interesting title that expresses my topic.
- ❑ My piece has an interesting/grabbing lead.
- ❑ My piece has a satisfying conclusion.
- ❑ I developed my ideas with details.
- ❑ I used paragraphs correctly.
- ❑ My paragraphs are connected logically.
- ❑ I used pictures and graphics to support my writing.
- ❑ I used information from more than one source.
- ❑ I listed my sources.
- ❑ I edited my work for capitals, spelling, and punctuation.
- ❑ I read my piece to two others:
- ❑ I incorporated suggestions from others:
- ❑ My final draft is neat and legible.
- ❑ This is my very best work.
- ❑ I have a Table of Contents and an "About the Author" page

Form 7.12E: Revising and Editing Guidelines: Nonfiction

REVISING AND EDITING CHECKLIST: FALL

Name: ______________________________ **Date:** ____________

Title: ____

Revising Checklist

- ❑ I have included everything I want.
- ❑ My writing makes sense.
- ❑ I made changes to improve my writing.

Editing Checklist

- ❑ All my sentences begin with a capital letter.
- ❑ I used capitals for the word "I" and names.
- ❑ My sentences end with the right punctuation mark.
- ❑ I checked my paper for correct spelling.

REVISING AND EDITING CHECKLIST: WINTER

Name: ______________________________ **Date:** ___________

Title: ____

Revising Checklist

❑ I have included everything I want.

❑ My writing makes sense.

Please check which trait you worked on in order to improve your writing. Be prepared to talk about these changes at your conference.

❑ Ideas and Content

❑ Organization

❑ Word Choice

❑ Fluency

❑ Voice

Editing Checklist

❑ All my sentences begin with a capital letter.

❑ I used capitals for the word "I" and names.

❑ My sentences end with the right punctuation mark.

❑ I checked my paper for correct spelling.

(form based on the six-trait writing assessment model from the Northwest Regional Educational Laboratory)

REVISING AND EDITING CHECKLIST: SPRING

Name: ______________________________ **Date:** ___________

Title: ____

Revising Checklist

- ❑ I have included everything I want.
- ❑ My writing makes sense.

Please check which trait you worked on in order to improve your writing. Be prepared to talk about the changes at your conference.

- ❑ Ideas and Content
- ❑ Organization
- ❑ Word Choice
- ❑ Fluency
- ❑ Voice

Editing Checklist

- ❑ All my sentences begin with a capital letter.
- ❑ I used capitals for the word "I" and names.
- ❑ My sentences end with the right punctuation mark.
- ❑ I checked my paper for correct spelling.
- ❑ I used commas to separate words in a series.
- ❑ I used quotation marks to show when a character is talking.

(form based on the six-trait writing assessment model from the Northwest Regional Educational Laboratory)
)

WRITING PROCESS EVALUATION

Name: ________________________________ **Date:** ______________

During pre-writing, I ____

____

____

When I draft, I ____

____

____

I revise by ____

____

____

I get feedback from others by _______________________________________

____

____

The feedback I find most helpful is ___________________________________

____

____

When I edit, I look for ____

____

____

I have used these publishing formats: _________________________________

____

____

Form 7.14: Writing Process Evaluation

FOLKTALE CHECKLIST

Name: ______________________________ **Date:** __________________

Title of Folktale: ____

- ❑ Title reflects folktale theme
- ❑ Neat and colorful illustrations which match the story
- ❑ Interesting lead appropriate for folktale ("Once . . . Long ago . . . Far away . . .)
- ❑ Setting suitable for folktale (fantasy or ancient land . . . natural setting . . . in a culture)
- ❑ Developed plot with beginning, middle, and end appropriate for folktale (why/how something came to be; teaches a lesson; trickster tale)
- ❑ Developed with details and vivid images
- ❑ Includes one or more "stock" character/s (hero, villain, wise person, sorcerer, magical person)
- ❑ Lively, realistic dialogue used to further the plot
- ❑ Correct spelling in final draft
- ❑ Correct paragraphing in final draft (including dialogue if used)
- ❑ Correct use of capital letters and punctuation in final draft (including quotation marks if used)
- ❑ Storytelling voice (sounds like a retelling from long ago; sounds like it should be told more than read)
- ❑ Satisfying ending appropriate for folktale (. . . and so that is why/how; Remember . . .; and from that day on . . .)

Form 7.15: Folktale Checklist

FOLKTALE RUBRIC

Title of Folktale: ______________________ Date: __________

Author: ______________________ Evaluator: ______________________

Check the boxes that apply to this piece of writing, then mark an "X" in the top bar to indicate approximate placement on a continuum. Use the back for comments: what you noticed as strengths and weaknesses, and what you found interesting and unique.

NOVICE	APPRENTICE	PRACTITIONER	EXPERT
o has a title	o interesting title	o interesting title indicates folktale theme	o interesting title indicates folktale theme
o has illustrations	o neat and colorful illustrations	o neat and colorful illustrations complement the story	o neat and colorful illustrations with direct correlations to the story
o includes very few folktale elements, such as a folktale style lead, suitable setting, a folktale story line, "stock" characters, typical folktale ending	o includes many folktale elements, such as a folktale style lead, suitable setting, a folktale story line, "stock" characters, typical folktale ending	o includes all folktale elements, such as a folktale style lead, suitable setting, a folktale story line, "stock" characters, typical folktale ending	o has a storytelling tone in addition to other folktale elements, such as a folktale style lead, suitable setting, a folktale story line, "stock" characters, typical folktale ending
o plot may lack clarity or may not be fully developed, limited use of dialogue, details, and imagery	o plot is developed with clear beginning, middle, and end; details add interest	o Plot is well-developed with clear beginning, middle, and satisfying ending; details are used to further the plot; dialogue used by at least two characters	o plot is well-developed with clear beginning, middle, and satisfying ending; details are used to further the plot; dialogue is lively and realistic; exact language creates vivid images
o most common words spelled correctly, but may contain spelling errors	o most common words spelled correctly, but may contain a few spelling errors	o most words spelled correctly	o contains few/no spelling errors
o may contain errors in writing conventions such as: paragraphing, use of capital letters and punctuation	o may contain a few errors in writing conventions such as: paragraphing, use of capital letters and punctuation	o correct use of most writing conventions such as: paragraphing, use of capital letters and punctuation, except for dialogue	o correct use of most writing conventions such as: paragraphing, use of capital letters and punctuation, including most dialogue

RUBRIC

4 WOW! TERRIFIC!	
3 You've Got It!	
2 Not Yet	
1 Try Again!	

Form 7.17A: Rubric (Primary)

DRAWING RUBRIC

4 WOW! TERRIFIC!	• Pictures add new information to words • Unusual details • Details in background • 5 or more colors
3 You've Got It!	• Pictures match words • Accurate details • 5 or more colors • Space is filled
2 Not Yet	• Space not filled • Confusing details • 4 or less colors
1 Try Again!	• Pictures do not match words • No details • 1 color only

Form 7.17B: Drawing Rubric (Primary)

FICTION RUBRIC

4 WOW! TERRIFIC!	• Writing tells a story • Holds the reader's attention • Has a clear beginning, middle, and end • Uses description and details • Uses some interesting words • Uses complete sentences • Capitals and periods used correctly • Correct spelling in final draft
3 You've Got It!	• Includes a beginning, middle, and end • Includes some details • Includes a few interesting words • Uses complete sentences • Capitals and periods mostly used correctly • Mostly correct spelling in final draft
2 Not Yet	• Story is confusing • No clear beginning, middle, or end • Does not use interesting words • Very little description or detail • Capitals and periods used incorrectly • Short sentences or phrases • Many spelling mistakes
1 Try Again!	• Few sentences • Story doesn't make sense • Writing lacks interesting language • Printing and drawings are messy or incomplete • No capitals or periods • Many spelling mistakes

Form 7.17C: Fiction Rubric (Primary)

NONFICTION RUBRIC

4 WOW! TERRIFIC!	• All sentences written in own words • Pictures add new facets to writing • Exceptional printing and drawings • Capitals and periods used correctly • Correct spelling in final draft
3 You've Got It!	• Most sentences written in own words • All the pictures match the information • Neat printing and drawing • Capitals and periods used correctly most of the time • Most of the spelling in final draft is correct
2 Not Yet	• Few sentences written in own words • Few pictures match the information • Printing and drawings are often incomplete or messy • Capitals and periods used incorrectly • Many spelling errors
1 Try Again!	• Few sentences written • Pictures don't match the information • Printing and drawings are incomplete or messy • No capitals or periods • Many spelling errors

Form 7.17D: Nonfiction Rubric (Primary)

FICTION RUBRIC

Ideas and Content

_____ **5** Developed a sense of story, holds the reader's attention

_____ **3** Beginning to develop a controlling idea, yet parts of the story are not clear or focused

_____ **1** Story is difficult to follow, lacks a controlling idea

Organization

_____ **5** Writing includes an interesting lead and has a clear beginning, middle, and end

_____ **3** Story has a beginning, middle, and end but lacks smooth transition and good pacing

_____ **1** Writing has no sense of direction and no clear beginning or ending

Voice

_____ **5** Writing is lively and expressive

_____ **3** Writing is beginning to sound personal, yet ideas are repeated and expression is uneven

_____ **1** Story lacks energetic and personal phrases and uses dull language

Word Choice

_____ **5** Writer chooses words carefully and uses a precise vocabulary

_____ **3** Writing includes some interesting language, yet mostly includes ordinary words

_____ **1** Writing lacks interesting and new language

Fluency

_____ **5** Sentences begin in different ways, sentence structure is varied

_____ **3** Sentence structure is correct, but sentences are short and choppy

_____ **1** Story is hard to read, sentences are short and irregular

Conventions

_____ **5** Writing is edited carefully for spelling, punctuation, and capitalization

_____ **3** Evidence of proofreading, but still noticeable errors

_____ **1** Many errors and the story is difficult to read

Form 7.17E: Fiction Rubric (Intermediate)

POETRY RUBRIC

Ideas and Content

_____ **5** Poem has a controlling idea and includes description and detail

_____ **3** Poem lacks a controlling idea, description and detail are minimal

_____ **1** Poem lacks a controlling idea, description and detail are missing

Organization

_____ **5** Poem flows well, is organized and has a smooth transition from beginning to end

_____ **3** Poem has some effective phrases, no smooth transition from beginning to end

_____ **1** Poem does not flow and lacks a clear sequence

Voice

_____ **5** Poem is lively and expressive

_____ **3** Poem includes some expressive phrases

_____ **1** Poem lacks energetic and personal phrases and uses dull language

Word Choice

_____ **5** Writer chooses words carefully and uses a precise vocabulary

_____ **3** Writing includes some interesting language, yet mostly includes ordinary words

_____ **1** Writing lacks interesting and new language

Fluency

_____ **5** Author uses words that add bounce and rhythm

_____ **3** Some poetic and rhythmic phrases but writing sometimes flat

_____ **1** Poem is difficult to read

Conventions

_____ **5** Writing is edited carefully for spelling, punctuation, and capitalization

_____ **3** Evidence of proofreading, but still noticeable errors

_____ **1** Many errors and the poem is difficult to read

Form 7.17F: Poetry Rubric (Intermediate)

NONFICTION RUBRIC

Ideas and Content

_____ **5** Well-developed topic with support of relevant examples. Uses knowledge and personal experiences to enrich the topic.

_____ **3** Ideas are mostly clear. Begins to support ideas and content with some examples.

_____ **1** Ideas are difficult to follow and writing lacks a clear focus. Ideas and content are not supported by examples.

Organization

_____ **5** Information is presented in a logical sequence and writing flows. Ideas are grouped logically into paragraphs.

_____ **3** Information is presented adequately. Sequence does not always make sense. Some transitions needed to show how ideas connect.

_____ **1** Little direction or structure to writing. Ideas and information randomly sequenced.

Voice

_____ **5** Writing is engaging, lively, and expressive. Voice is consistent throughout the piece.

_____ **3** Writing sometimes flows but expressiveness is uneven. Some evidence of the author's voice.

_____ **1** Writing is flat with dull or weak phrasing. Little personal voice in the writing.

Word Choice

_____ **5** Writing is compelling and conveys meaning through precise vocabulary. Writer is selective about use of information yet provides sufficient details.

_____ **3** Writer begins to use engaging language to enhance the writing. Author includes some interesting details. Writing is inconsistent and some parts lack descriptive language.

_____ **1** Writing lacks interesting and new language. Sentences are simple with very little description.

Fluency

_____ **5** Sentences begin in different ways. Writing shows variation in sentence length and structure.

_____ **3** Sentence structure is mainly correct but most sentences are short and not consistently smooth. Writing shows some variation in sentence length and structure.

_____ **1** Writing is hard to read. Sentences are short and incomplete.

Conventions

_____ **5** No obvious errors in final draft. Writing is edited carefully for spelling, punctuation, and capitalization

_____ **3** Evidence of proofreading, but still noticeable errors

_____ **1** Many errors and writing is difficult to read

Form 7.17G: Nonfiction Rubric (Intermediate)

DUTHIE INDEX: LETTER RECOGNITION / SOUND ASSOCIATION

Name: ______________________ Birthdate: ______________

Date: Fall: ______________ Observer: ______________

Winter: ______________ ______________

Spring: ______________ ______________

1	Fall		Winter		Spring	
	R	S	R	S	R	S
B						
K						
P						
T						
V						
Z						
D						
J						

2		Fall		Winter		Spring	
		R	S	R	S	R	S
R							
H							
C	S						
	K						
O	˘						
	¯						
G	J						
	G						
U	˘						
	¯						
I	˘						
	¯						
Q							
A	˘						
	¯						

3		Fall		Winter		Spring	
		R	S	R	S	R	S
E	˘						
	¯						
W							
F							
M							
X							
N							
S							
L							
Y							

COLUMN KEY: R = Recognizes Letter S = Sound Association

ENTRY CODES: Correct Response = √ Incorrect Response = **blank** or child's spoken response

Comments: ____

____

____

Form 8.1A: Duthie Index (Upper Case)

DUTHIE INDEX: LETTER RECOGNITION / SOUND ASSOCIATION

Name: ______________________________ Birthdate: ______________

Date: Fall: ______________ Observer: ______________

Winter: ______________ ______________

Spring: ______________ ______________

1	Fall		Winter		Spring	
	R	S	R	S	R	S
b						
k						
p						
t						
v						
z						
d						
j						

2		Fall		Winter		Spring	
		R	S	R	S	R	S
r							
h							
c	s						
	k						
o	˘						
	¯						
g	j						
	g						
u	˘						
	¯						
i	˘						
	¯						
q							
a	˘						
	¯						

3		Fall		Winter		Spring	
		R	S	R	S	R	S
e	˘						
	¯						
w							
f							
m							
x							
n							
s							
l							
y							

COLUMN KEY: R = Recognizes Letter S = Sound Association

ENTRY CODES: Correct Response = √ Incorrect Response = **blank** or child's spoken response

Comments: ______________________________

ADMINISTERING THE DUTHIE INDEX

1. Assess the student in a quiet area with few distractions and no view of an alphabet. Complete data at the top of the upper case version of the Duthie Index (Form 8.1A).

2. Say to the child, "Today we are going to talk about the names of the letters the alphabet and the sounds the letters make. We are doing this so I can find out the best way to help you if you need to learn any of these letters or sounds. We'll start with this one (point to the "B") and do all these first (point to the first section).

3. Point to the "B" again and say, "Tell me the *name* of this letter." If the child seems confused, then re-phrase by saying, "Tell me what letter this is." If the child says the letter name, put a check in the box in the column for Recognizes (R). If a child responds incorrectly by saying, "D," then write the letter "D" in the box.

4. Next, say to the student, "Tell me what *sound* this letter makes as you point to the "B" again. Put a check in the Sounds (S) column if the child makes the correct sound. If the child answers incorrectly by telling you that the letter has the sound of "duh," then write "duh" in the box beside the letter "B." If a letter has two sounds, then assess as described, then add, "This letter also makes another sound. Do you know the other sound this letter makes?"

5. An empty box also means that a response was incorrect. Sometimes it's not possible to keep up with a child's pace and record every response. Stop if the child becomes frustrated or clearly does not know the letter names or sounds. If the child knows most of the letters, complete the first section before moving on to the second section.

6. If the child knows most letter names and sounds in upper case, repeat the process with the lower case version (Form 8.1B).

7. When you finish assessing, that the child for working so hard and end the conference with a positive comment. Take a few minutes to complete the comment section and make anecdotal notes about the child's behavior or attitude.

8. Children should be expected to show progress in acquiring letter/sound associations from one trimester to another. Children most often show a progression from the first and section sections before recognizing the sounds in the third section.

9. It's helpful to show the students and their parents the progression from one trimester to the next.

10. You may want to do more extensive testing if no new letters/sounds are acquired from one trimester to the next, or if a child knows some letters during one conference, and a different set the next time. You will want to supplement the information you gain from this index with observations, anecdotal notes and other assessment techniques.

Form 8.1C: Duthie Index (Directions)

INFORMAL RUNNING RECORD

Name: ____________ Title: ____________________ Page(s): ________ Date: __________

On each line, make a check for each word read correctly in that line or record miscues as read.

Text Line	Words	Errors				Self-corrections				Comments / Strategies Taught
		M	S	V	#	M	S	V	#	
1										
2										
3										
4										
5										
6										
7										
8										
9										
10										
11										
12										
13										
14										
	TOTAL									

Form 8.2: Informal Running Record

RUNNING RECORD SUMMARY

Name:

DATE	TITLE	SEEN OR UNSEEN	SELF-CORRECTS	COMMENTS

Form 8.3: Running Record Summary

READING TOOLS

Use the words around it

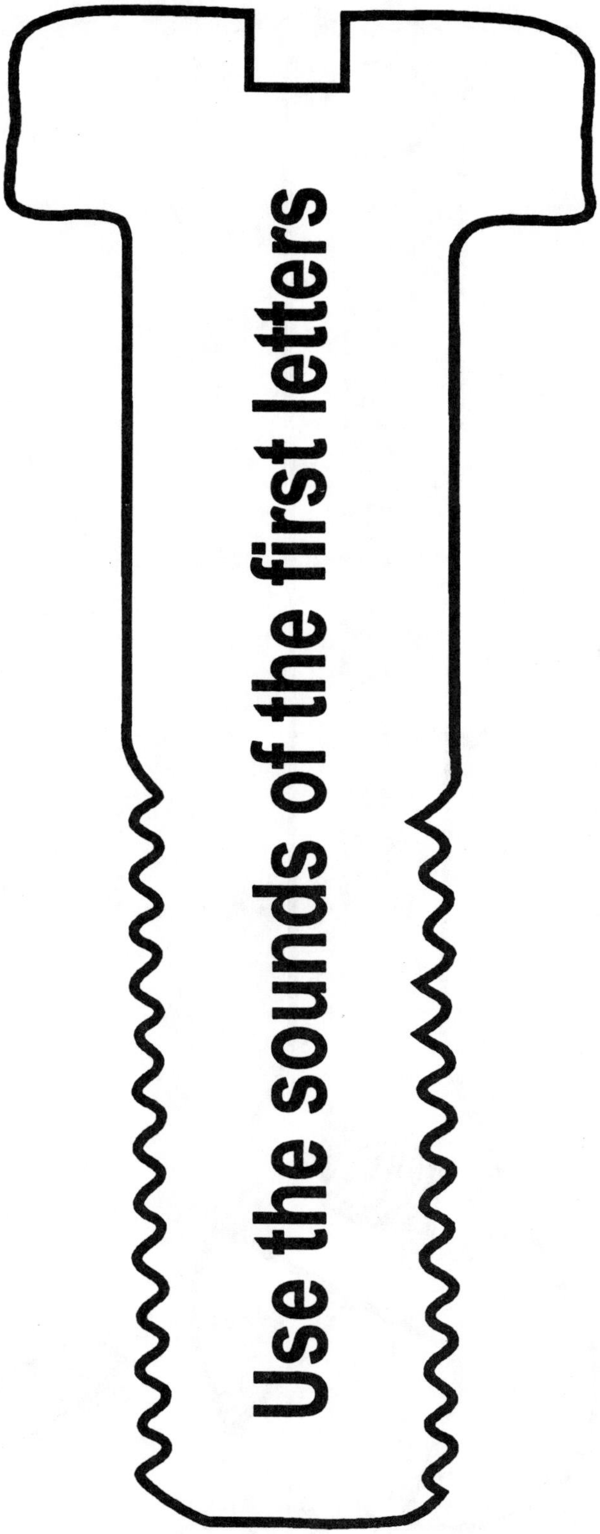
Use the sounds of the first letters

Form 9.1A and 9.1B: Reading Tools

READING TOOLS

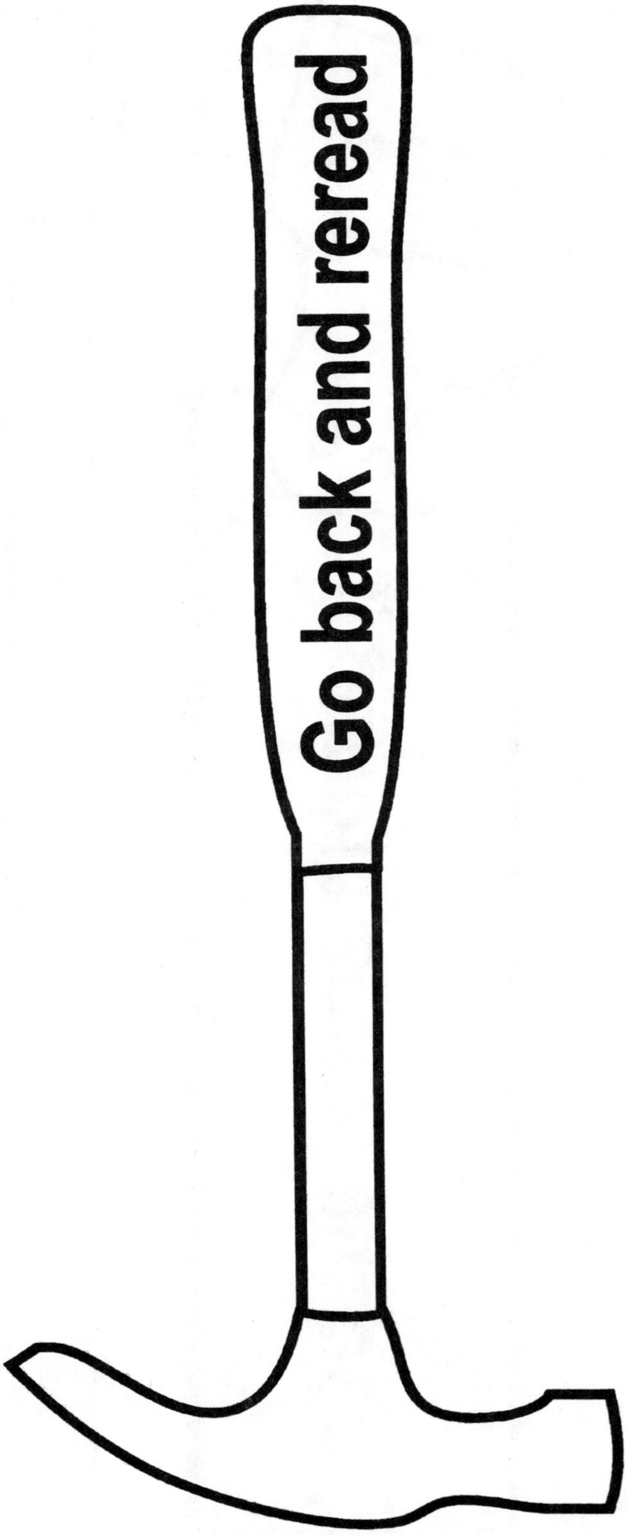

Form 9.1C and 9.1D: Reading Tools

READING TOOLS

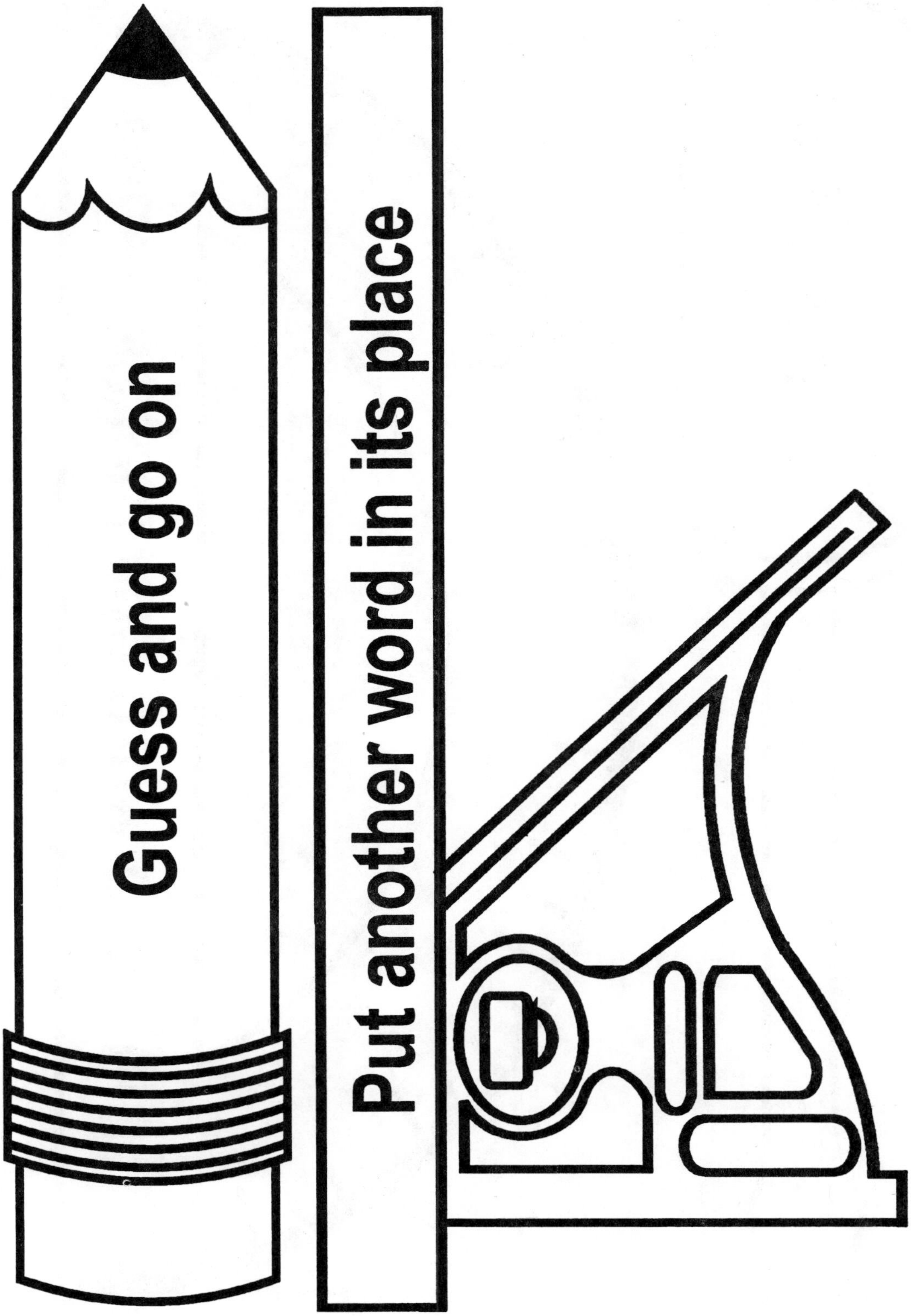
Guess and go on
Put another word in its place

Form 9.1E and 9.1F: Reading Tools

READING TOOLS

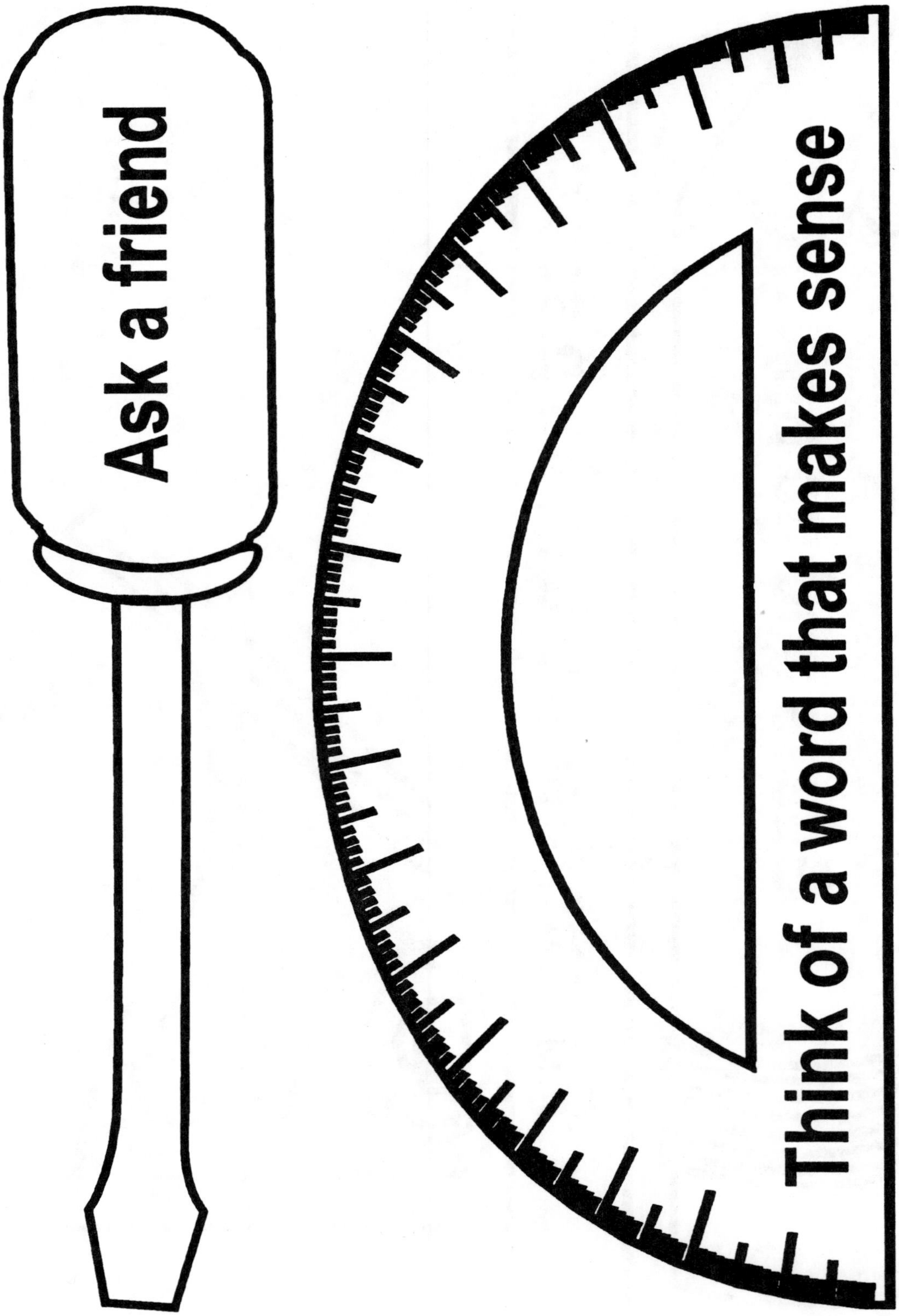
Ask a friend
Think of a word that makes sense

Form 9.1G and 9.1H: Reading Tools

READING TOOLS

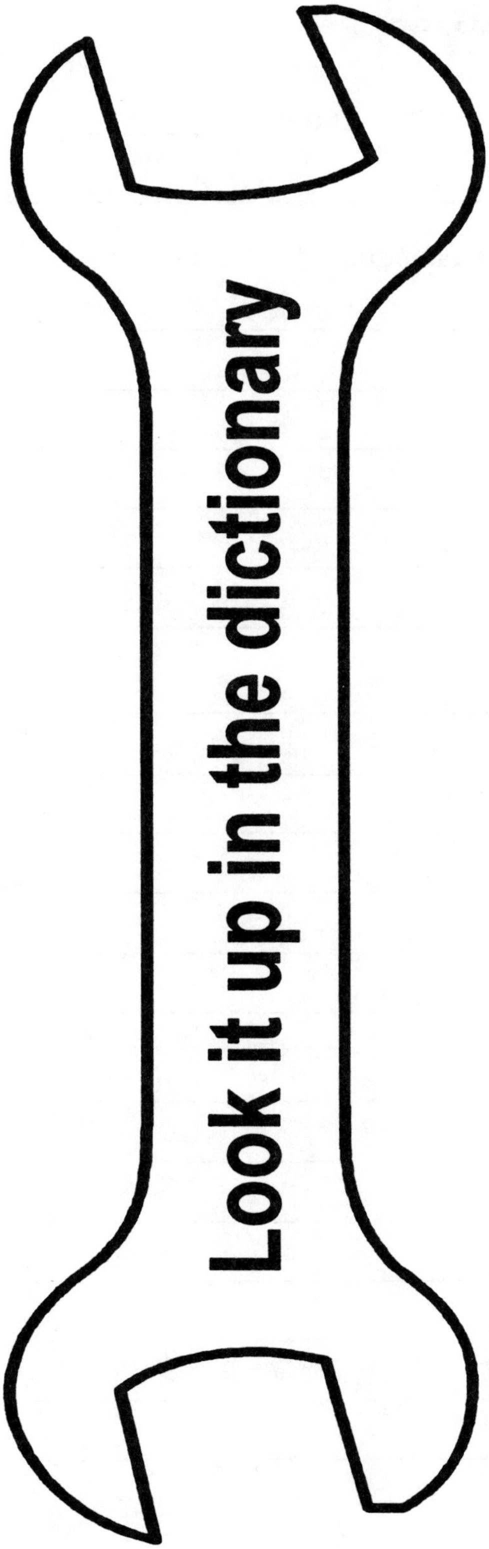
Look it up in the dictionary

Skip the word and keep going

WORD STRATEGIES

Name: ______________________________ **Date:** ______________

What you read today: ____

Write a sentence with a word you had trouble understanding. Underline the challenging word. ____

____

____

____

____

____

What do you think the word means? ____

____

____

____

____

____

How did you figure out this word? ____

____

____

____

____

____

____

(form adapted from *Literacy Assessment: A Handbook of Instruments* by Lynn Rhodes, 1993)

READING STRATEGIES I USE

Name:

Strategy	Date

Form 9.3A: Reading Strategies I Use (Blank Form)

READING STRATEGIES I USE: PRIMARY

Name: **Date:**

Strategy	**With Guidance ⟺ Independently**
I choose what to read by myself.	
I have favorite books and authors.	
I like to read.	
I can read by myself and stay focused.	
I use different reading strategies.	
I confirm my predictions.	
I read different types of texts:	
stories	
poems	
nonfiction	
letters	
directions	
biographies	
I can retell what I read.	
When I read, I make connections to my life.	
I think about what I learned or felt.	
I share what I read by talking to others.	
I write about what I read.	
I use the arts to share what I read.	
I read for fun.	
I read for information.	

Form 9.3B: Reading Strategies I Use (Primary)

READING STRATEGIES I USE: INTERMEDIATE

Name: **Date:**

Strategy	**With Guidance ⟺ Independently**
I choose reading materials at my reading level.	
I have favorite books, authors and genres.	
I like to read.	
I can read silently for long periods.	
I use a variety of effective reading strategies.	
I read a variety of texts:	
realistic fiction	
poetry	
nonfiction/informational	
historical fiction	
adventure stories	
mysteries	
biographies	
plays	
I read for fun.	
I read for information.	
I use the computer and resources to find information.	
I can summarize what I read.	
I can discuss the plot, characters, and ideas in a story.	
I gain deeper meaning by reading "between the lines."	
I share thoughtful responses when I talk about what I read.	
I write thoughtfully about what I read.	
I use the arts to share what I read.	
I make connections to my life, other authors, and books.	

Form 9.3C: Reading Strategies I Use (Intermediate)

READING GOALS

Name: ______________________________ **Date:** ______________

____

____

____

____

____

____

READING GOALS

Name: ______________________________ **Date:** ______________

____

____

____

____

____

____

Form 9.4: Reading Goals

FOCUS QUESTIONS FOR ANECDOTAL NOTES: READING (PRIMARY)

TYPE OF TEXTS/RANGE

1. Does the student read pattern books? Beginning early-reader books? Harder early-reader books? Beginning chapter books?
2. Does the student independently choose books at an appropriate reading level?

READING ATTITUDE AND SELF-EVALUATION

3. Does the student show a positive attitude toward reading?
4. Does the student listen attentively to books?
5. Does the student choose books and have favorites?
6. Does the student see him/herself as a reader?
7. Does the student read for pleasure? Information?
8. Does the student read silently? For 10 minutes? 20 minutes? 30 minutes? Longer?
9. Does the student reflect on his/her reading and set goals with guidance?

READING STRATEGIES

10. Can the student read some environmental print?
11. Does the student pretend to read books? Memorize books?
12. Does the student use illustrations to tell a story? Rely on pictures + print? Rely primarily on print?
13. Does the student recognize some/most letter names and sound?
14. Does the student recognize some words/names in context? Simple words? Sight words?
15. Can the student match one-to-one (point to words) while reading?
16. Does the student use phonetic cues? Sentence structure cues? Meaning cues?

COMPREHENSION/RESPONSE/STORY STRUCTURE

17. Does the student participate in the reading of familiar texts?
18. Does the student share ideas during literature discussions?
19. Does the student make connections to personal experience? Other books? Other authors?
20. Does the student listen to others' ideas during literature discussions?
21. Can the student retell the main idea of the text? Plot? Characters?
22. What different forms of response does the student try (writing, art, performance arts, etc.)?

FOCUS QUESTIONS FOR ANECDOTAL NOTES: READING (INTERMEDIATE)

TYPE OF TEXT/RANGE

1. Does the student read medium chapter books? Challenging children's literature? Young adult literature?
2. Does the student independently choose books at an appropriate reading level?
3. Does the student read a variety of genres with guidance? Independently?
4. Does the student use reference materials to locate information with guidance? Independently?

READING ATTITUDE AND SELF-EVALUATION

5. Does the student show a positive attitude toward reading?
6. Does the student select/read/finish a variety of materials with guidance? Independently?
7. Does the student read silently for 20 minutes? 30 minutes? Longer?
8. Does the student reflect on his/her reading and set goals independently?

READING STRATEGIES

9. Does the student read and understand most words?
10. Does the student self-correct for meaning?
11. Does the student use reading strategies appropriately?
12. What strategies does the student use when encountering a new word?
13. Does the student consult a dictionary when appropriate?

COMPREHENSION/RESPONSE/STORY STRUCTURE

14. Can the student retell the main idea of the text? Plot? Characters?
15. Does the student make connections to personal experience? Other books? Other authors?
16. Does the student discuss literature in terms of genre? Writer's craft?
17. Does the student interpret deeper meaning in literature with guidance? Independently?
18. Does the student share during literature discussions when asked? Voluntarily?
19. Does the student respond to/elaborate upon other's ideas during literature discussions?
20. Does the student evaluate/interpret/analyze literature critically?
21. What different forms of response does the student try (writing, art, performance arts, etc.)?

READING CONFERENCE RECORD: PRIMARY

Name:

Reading Strategies	**Date:** **Title:**	**Date:** **Title:**	**Date:** **Title:**	**Date:** **Title:**
Rereads				
Skips/Returns				
Uses Context Clues				
Uses Picture Cues				
Uses First/Last Letters				
Uses Memory of Patterns				
Decodes by Sounding Out				
Knows Sight Words				
Miscues Preserve Meaning				
Appropriate Level				
Reads Fluently				
Literal Comprehension				
Interpretive Comprehension				
Strategy Taught/Comments				

Key: + consistently √ sometimes

READING CONFERENCE RECORD: INTERMEDIATE

Name:

Reading Strategies	**Date:** **Title:**	**Date:** **Title:**	**Date:** **Title:**	**Date:** **Title:**
Rereads				
Skips/Returns				
Uses Context Clues				
Decodes				
Knows Sight Words				
Replaces Unknown Words				
Miscues Preserve Meaning				
Appropriate Level				
Reads Fluently				
Literal Comprehension				
Interpretive Comprehension				
Strategy Taught/Comments				

Key: + consistently √ sometimes

Form 9.6B: Reading Conference Record (Intermediate)

READING CONFERENCE RECORD: INTERMEDIATE 2

Name:

Reading Strategies	**Date:** **Title:**	**Date:** **Title:**	**Date:** **Title:**	**Date:** **Title:**
Rereads to Preserve Meaning				
Uses Context Clues				
Decodes Challenging Words				
Appropriate Level				
Reads Aloud Fluently				
Reads with Expression				
Reads with Confidence				
Literal Comprehension				
Interpretive Comprehension				
Strategy Taught/Goal				

Key: + consistently √ sometimes

Form 9.6C: Reading Conference Record (Intermediate 2)

Reading Conference Notes for: **Year:**

DATE	TEXT / AUTHOR	GENRE	PAGE(S)	STRATEGIES / COMMENTS	ADDITIONAL COMMENTS:
				Uses sentence structure	
				Uses context	
LEVEL	MISCUES / ANALYSIS			Uses phonics	
Independent				Knows most words on sight	
				Retells plot	
Instructional				Retells character	
				Relates to personal experience	
Frustrational				Relates to other literature	
RESPONSE				Comments on author's craft	
				Notes specific literary devices	
				FOCUS-LESSON APPLICATION	FUTURE FOCUS / GOAL(S)

DATE	TEXT / AUTHOR	GENRE	PAGE(S)	STRATEGIES / COMMENTS	ADDITIONAL COMMENTS:
				Uses sentence structure	
				Uses context	
LEVEL	MISCUES / ANALYSIS			Uses phonics	
Independent				Knows most words on sight	
				Retells plot	
Instructional				Retells character	
				Relates to personal experience	
Frustrational				Relates to other literature	
RESPONSE				Comments on author's craft	
				Notes specific literary devices	
				FOCUS-LESSON APPLICATION	FUTURE FOCUS / GOAL(S)

Codes: SC = Self-Corrected; $ = Non-word Substitution; TG = Teacher Gave; RM = Repeated Miscue; I = Teacher Ignored; v = Correctly Read Later; RD = Redirected

Form 9.7: Reading Conference Notes

GROUP OBSERVATION: READING

Date/Title	Child	Miscue Child Read / Text Said	Comments Strategies Evidenced	Strategies Taught

Form 9.8: Group Observation: Reading

READING CELEBRATION

Name: ______________________________ **Date:** ______________

____

____

____

Parent Comments: ____

____

____

READING CELEBRATION

Name: ______________________________ **Date:** ______________

____

____

____

Parent Comments: ____

____

____

INFORMAL MISCUE ANALYSIS

Name:

Date and Title	**Miscues and Comments** Text vs. What student read	**Skills/Strategies Taught**	**Fluency**	**Comprehension**	
				Factual	Inferred
		Does the sentence make sense?			
		Yes:	%		
		No:	%		
		Does the sentence make sense?			
		Yes:	%		
		No	%		
		Does the sentence make sense?			
		Yes:	%		
		No:	%		
		Does the sentence make sense?			
		Yes:	%		
		No:	%		
		Does the sentence make sense?			
		Yes:	%		
		No:	%		

INFORMAL MISCUE ANALYSIS RECORD

Name: ______________________________ **Date:** ________________

Title: ____

Does the sentence make sense?

Yes: ____ ______%

No: ____ ______%

Student	Text	Cues Used
		M S V
		M S V
		M S V
		M S V
		M S V
		M S V
		M S V
		M S V
		M S V
		M S V

Fluency________

Factual Comprehension ________

Higher Level Comprehension ________

Skills/Strategies Taught:

Skills/Strategies Used:

Comments:

Form 9.10B: Informal Miscue Analysis Record

FOCUS QUESTIONS FOR ANECDOTAL NOTES: LITERATURE DISCUSSIONS

1. Is the student prepared for the literature discussion?
2. Does the student use the text to share passages? To support ideas and opinions? How effectively?
3. Does the student listen actively to others?
4. Does the student ask questions? What kinds?
5. Do the questions get a thoughtful response? Which are most effective?
6. Does the student contribute thoughtful ideas?
7. Does the student make predictions? How effectively?
8. Does the student build on other people's comments?
9. Does the student keep the group on task?
10. Does the student discuss unknown or interesting words?
11. Does the student make personal connections to his/her life? At what levels?
12. Does the student make connections to other books, authors, and experiences?
13. Does the student discuss the author's craft and word choice?
14. Does the student discuss literary elements (plot, setting, character)?
15. Can the student reflect on literature circle participation and set goals?

Form 9.11: Focus Questions for Anecdotal Notes: Literature Discussions

LITERATURE DISCUSSION SELF-EVALUATION

Name: ______________________________ **Date:** _______________

Title: _______________________________ **Author:** ________________

What did I do well during our literature discussion? (asked good questions, listened actively, responded to others, supported my ideas using the book, took a risk, compared the book to my life or other books)

____

____

____

____

____

____

____

What could I do better next time?

____

____

____

____

____

____

Form 9.12A: Literature Discussion Self-Evaluation

DISCUSSION SUMMARY/GROUP FEEDBACK

Name: ______________________ **Date:** ______________

Title: ______________________ **Author:** ______________

Summarize what you did well and/or learned today during your literature discussion.

____

____

____

____

____

Comments from other group members:

1. ____

____

2. ____

____

3. ____

____

4. ____

____

DISCUSSION RUBRIC

Name: ______________________________ **Date:** ______________

Check the boxes that apply to this discussion, then mark an "X" in the top bar to indicate approximate placement on a continuum. Use the back for comments: what you noticed as strengths and weaknesses, and what you found interesting and unique.

NOVICE	APPRENTICE	PRACTITIONER	EXPERT
❑ not prepared for discussion (forgets journal or book)	❑ brings book and journal	❑ brings book with passages marked and several journal entries	❑ brings book with passages clearly marked and thoughtful journal entries
❑ rarely contributes to discussion	❑ contributes to discussions occasionally or when prompted	❑ contributes appropriately to discussions	❑ contributes significantly to discussion
❑ conversation off-task or does not contribute	❑ difficulty keeping discussion going	❑ generally keeps the discussion going	❑ effectively keeps the discussion going
❑ rarely listens or responds to group members	❑ sometimes listens and responds appropriately, occasionally asks questions or shares ideas	❑ listens and responds adequately (occasionally reads journal entries or unclear passages, discusses unknown words, asks questions, listens actively, builds on others' comments, makes connections to other books and experiences, discusses author's style and literary elements)	❑ listens and responds thoughtfully (reads journal entries or unclear passages, discusses unknown words, asks questions, listens actively, builds on others' comments, makes connections to other books and experiences, discusses author's style and literary elements)

Comments:

ASSESSING RESPONSE TO LITERATURE: PRIMARY

Name:

Date / Title	Literal Level	Personal Reaction	Prediction	Summarizes Retells	Supports Justifies	Other Points of View	Evaluates	Discusses Author's Craft	Comments

Form 9.14A: Assessing Response to Literature (Primary)

ASSESSING RESPONSE TO LITERATURE: INTERMEDIATE

Name:

Date / Title	Personal Reaction	Prediction	Summarizes Retells	Supports Justifies	Other Points of View	Evaluates Analyzes	Discusses Author's Craft/Theme	Discusses Literary Elements	Connects to Other Books and Authors	Comments

Form 9.14B: Assessing Response to Literature (Intermediate)

RESPONSE JOURNAL RUBRIC

Name: ______________________________ **Date:** ______________

Title of Book: ____

4 In addition to a precise plot summary, the writer makes inferences, predictions, comparisons, or evaluations and supports ideas with evidence from the story. The writer makes connections with his/her life, other books or other events. The writer demonstrates fluency.

3 The plot is accurately summarized with specific details. The writer shares one or more personal reflections and gives examples to support his/her interpretations.

2 The plot is summarized in a general way but lacks detail or support. The writer may share a general personal response.

1 The writer retells minimal details from the story.

JOURNAL RESPONSE RUBRIC

Name: ______________________ **Date:** ____________

Check the boxes that apply to this journal response, then mark an "X" in the top bar to indicate approximate placement on a continuum. Use the back for comments: what you noticed as strengths and weaknesses, and what you found interesting and unique.

NOVICE	APPRENTICE	PRACTITIONER	EXPERT
❑ little writing	❑ some writing (includes reactions, summaries, and connections to other books or experiences, evaluates and analyzes)	❑ adequate writing (includes occasional reactions, summaries, and connections to other books or experiences, evaluates and analyzes author's craft or elements of literature)	❑ thorough writing (includes thoughtful reactions, summaries, and connections to other books or experiences, evaluates and analyzes author's craft or elements of literature)
❑ includes no examples to support opinions	❑ includes occasional, incomplete or unclear examples to support opinions	❑ includes sufficient examples to support opinions	❑ includes clear, complete examples to support opinions
❑ no variation in forms of written response	❑ occasionally varies forms of written response	❑ clearly varies forms of written response	❑ skillfully and creatively varies forms of written response
❑ no attention to details (lacking in organization and neatness with many spelling and punctuation errors)	❑ slight attention to details (lacking in organization and neatness with some spelling and punctuation errors)	❑ adequate attention to details (somewhat organized and neat, with mostly correct spelling and punctuation)	❑ thorough attention to details (well organized and neat, with correct spelling and punctuation)

Comments:

JOURNAL COMMENTS

Name: ______________________ **Date:** ______________

Title: ______________________ **Author:** ______________

Cover (title, author, student name, illustration, page numbers, neat appearance)

____

____

____

____

Journal Entries (dated, varied format, comments supported with examples/details, neat appearance)

____

____

____

____

Vocabulary (*at least* 10 words completed, correct definition, neat appearance)

____

____

Total Score Based on Journal Response Rubric ______________

Form 9.15C: Journal Comments

TWO STARS AND A WISH

Name: ______________________ **Project:** ______________________

Reviewer: ______________________ **Date:** ______________________

☆ ____

____

☆ ____

____

WISH ____

____

TWO STARS AND A WISH

Name: ______________________ **Project:** ______________________

Reviewer: ______________________ **Date:** ______________________

☆ ____

____

☆ ____

____

WISH ____

____

Form 9.16A: Two Stars and a Wish

PRESENTATION RUBRIC

4 WOW! TERRIFIC!	• I spoke loudly all of the time • I faced the audience all of the time • I looked at the audience all of the time • I was serious all of the time • I followed along all of the time • I knew when it was my turn all of the time • I did my part well
3 You've Got It!	• I spoke loudly most of the time • I faced the audience most of the time • I looked at the audience most of the time • I was serious most of the time • I followed along most of the time • I knew when it was my turn most of the time • I did my part well most of the time
2 Not Yet	• I spoke loudly some of the time • I faced the audience some of the time • I looked at the audience some of the time • I was serious some of the time • I followed along some of the time • I knew when it was my turn some of the time • I did some of my part
1 Try Again!	• I did not speak loudly • I rarely faced the audience • I rarely looked at the audience • I was not serious • I did not follow along • I did not know when it was my turn • I did not participate

Form 9.16B: Presentation Rubric (Primary)

RESPONSE PROJECT RUBRIC

Name: ______________________________ **Date:** ______________

Check the boxes that apply to this response project, then mark an "X" in the top bar to indicate approximate placement on a continuum. Use the back for comments: what you noticed as strengths and weaknesses, and what you found interesting and unique.

NOVICE	APPRENTICE	PRACTITIONER	EXPERT
❑ project does not convey meaning of book	❑ project partially communicates meaning of book	❑ project adequately communicates meaning of book	❑ project clearly communicates meaning of book
❑ no organization evident	❑ lacks organization	❑ generally organized	❑ well organized
❑ lacks appeal	❑ some visual appeal	❑ visually appealing to audience	❑ visually creative and artistic
❑ little attention to details	❑ slight attention to details	❑ strong attention to details	❑ thorough attention to details
❑ minimal response from audience	❑ may or may not draw audience to book	❑ project somewhat attracts audience to book	❑ convincingly draws audience to book

Comments:

PRESENTATION RUBRIC

Name: ____________________ **Date:** __________

Check the boxes that apply to this presentation, then mark an "X" in the top bar to indicate approximate placement on a continuum. Use the back for comments: what you noticed as strengths and weaknesses, and what you found interesting and unique.

NOVICE	APPRENTICE	PRACTITIONER	EXPERT
❑ not prepared for presentation	❑ not fully prepared or rehearsed for presentation	❑ evidence of adequate preparation and rehearsal	❑ thoroughly prepared and rehearsed
❑ little eye contact with audience	❑ occasionally looks at audience	❑ eye contact with most of the audience most of the time	❑ eye contact engages all of the audience
❑ little voice inflection (too quiet, too loud, or monotone)	❑ occasional use of voice inflection and volume	❑ adequate use of voice inflection and volume	❑ skillful use of voice inflection, volume and expression

Comments:

RETELLING SELF-EVALUATION

Name: ______________________________ **Date:** _______________

Title: ____

- ❑ I told when and where the story took place.
- ❑ I told about the main character.
- ❑ I told about other characters.
- ❑ I told the main problem in the story.
- ❑ I told some of the details from the story.
- ❑ I told how the problem was solved.
- ❑ I used some of the language from the book.
- ❑ I made connections to my life or other books.
- ❑ I told what I thought of the book.

RETELLING EVALUATION

Name: ________________________________ **Date:** ______________

_____ Setting

____

____

_____ Plot
- _____ chain of events
- _____ story problem
- _____ supporting details
- _____ resolution/ending

____

____

_____Characters
- _____ main characters
- _____ supporting characters

____

____

_____Theme/Central Idea

____

____

Student Retelling: Comments:

_____ literal retelling

_____ supports with language from text

_____ summarizes logically

_____ connects to other books/authors/experiences

_____ evaluates

FICTION RETELLING GUIDE

Name: ______________________________ **Date:** __________________

Title: ____

Retelling	**Aided**	**Unaided**
Story introduction	_____	_____
Setting	_____	_____
Main character(s)	_____	_____
Supporting character(s)	_____	_____
Plot/chain of events	_____	_____
Plot/supporting details	_____	_____
Plot/climax	_____	_____
Theme/central idea	_____	_____
Story conclusion	_____	_____
Student Response		
Personal reflection	_____	_____
Supports with language from the text	_____	_____
Explicit information	_____	_____
Implicit information	_____	_____

Comments:

Form 9.17C: Fiction Retelling Guide

NONFICTION RETELLING GUIDE

Name: ______________________________ **Date:** __________________

Title: ____

Retelling	Aided	Unaided
Introduction of topic	_____	_____
States main idea	_____	_____
Sequences ideas	_____	_____
Includes important details	_____	_____
Draws conclusions	_____	_____
Student Response		
Demonstrates understanding of concept(s)	_____	_____
Uses key vocabulary	_____	_____
Understands cause & effect relationships	_____	_____
Explicit information	_____	_____
Implicit information	_____	_____

Comments:

FICTION RETELLING RUBRIC

Name: ______________________________ **Date:** _______________

Title: ____

Introduction

_____ **5** Able to retell the introduction in the correct sequence, including the important details

_____ **3** Can retell some of the main points from the introduction in the correct sequence

_____ **1** Has difficulty with sequence and retelling how the story began, may give inaccurate information

Setting

_____ **5** Able to describe where the story takes place, including the important details about the setting

_____ **3** Can describe the setting, yet has difficulty supplying description and detail

_____ **1** Is not able to explain the setting for the story, may completely leave the setting out of the retelling

Characters

_____ **5** Able to explain the characters' thoughts, feelings, and actions

_____ **3** Can retell the characters from the story, including some important details

_____ **1** Has difficulty retelling the characters in the story, gives limited or inaccurate information

Plot

_____ **5** Able to describe the chain of events in the correct sequence and explain the supporting details of the climax

_____ **3** Can retell the plot in the correct sequence, yet does not include all the important events and details

_____ 1 Is not able to describe the chain of events in the correct sequence, gives inaccurate information in the retelling

Theme

_____ **5** Able to describe the central idea of the story in the retelling

_____ **3** Includes some information about the central idea of the story, yet the retelling lacks all the important ideas of the theme

_____ **1** Is not able to explain the central idea of the story in the retelling

Story Conclusion

_____ **5** Able to describe the conclusion and includes implicit and explicit information about the story in the retelling

_____ **3** Can describe the conclusion and includes explicit information about how the story ended

_____ **1** Has difficulty retelling how the story ended and explaining explicit and implicit information

Form 9.18A: Fiction Retelling Rubric

NONFICTION RETELLING RUBRIC

Name: ______________________________ **Date:** __________________

Title: ____

Introduction of the Topic

_____ **5** Able to retell the introduction in the correct sequence, including the important details

_____ **3** Can retell some of the main points from the introduction in the correct sequence

_____ **1** Has difficulty with sequence and retelling how the text began, may give information that is not accurate

States the Main Idea

_____ **5** Able to retell the main idea of the text, including important details and cause and effect relationships

_____ **3** Able to retell some of the key events that make up the main idea, yet struggles with supplying all the important details about the text

_____ **1** Has limited information and is not able to support the retelling with important details and events from the text

Text Structures

_____ **5** Able to use precise vocabulary and retell the beginning, middle, and end of the text

_____ **3** Can retell the beginning, middle, and end of the text in the correct sequence but does not include all the key ideas or important facts

_____ **1** Has difficulty retelling the text in the correct sequence

Demonstrates Understanding on Concept(s)

_____ **5** Able to use accurate vocabulary and explain the concept(s) from the text

_____ **3** Can begin to explain the concept(s) from the text, yet struggles with clarifying ideas and details

_____ **1** Has restricted information about the text and struggles with explaining the concept(s) from the book

Draws Conclusions

_____ **5** Able to explain implicit information and draw conclusions from inferred meaning

_____ **3** Can draw some conclusions from explicit information, yet has difficulty with inferred meaning

_____ **1** Has difficulty drawing conclusions and explaining explicit and implicit information

COMPREHENSION STRATEGIES

Name: ______________________________ **Date:** ______________

What you read today ____

Write down 2-3 key ideas you remember or learned from what you just read.

____

____

____

____

____

____

____

What strategies did you use to help you understand what you read?

____

____

____

____

____

____

____

(form adapted from *Literacy Assessment: A Handbook of Instruments* by Lynn Rhodes, 1993)

Form 9.19: Comprehension Strategies

READING SELF-EVALUATION

Name: ______________________________ **Date:** ______________

READING STRATEGIES

_____ I correct myself when my reading doesn't make sense.

_____ I go back and re-read when I don't understand.

_____ I sound out words to make sense when I read.

_____ I think about what will come next.

_____ I read parts out loud when I get confused.

ORAL READING

_____ I read smoothly.

_____ I read with expression.

_____ I read carefully.

COMPREHENSION

_____ I can summarize a story by talking about the characters, plot, and setting.

_____ I can correctly answer questions about what I read.

READING LOG

Name:

Date	**Title**	**How much did you like it?** A little Some A lot
		1 2 3 4 5
		1 2 3 4 5
		1 2 3 4 5
		1 2 3 4 5
		1 2 3 4 5
		1 2 3 4 5
		1 2 3 4 5

Form 9.21A: Reading Log (Primary)

READING LOG

Name:

Date	Title	Author	How much did you like it? A little Some A lot
			1 2 3 4 5
			1 2 3 4 5
			1 2 3 4 5
			1 2 3 4 5
			1 2 3 4 5
			1 2 3 4 5

Form 9.21B: Reading Log (Primary)

READING LOG

Name:

Date	Title	Author	Genre	How much did you like it? A little Some A lot
				1 2 3 4 5
				1 2 3 4 5
				1 2 3 4 5
				1 2 3 4 5
				1 2 3 4 5
				1 2 3 4 5

Form 9.21C: Reading Log (Intermediate)

READING LOG

Name:

Date	Title	Author	Genre	Comments

Form 9.21D: Reading Log (Intermediate)

MARINE SCIENCE READING LOG

Name:

Date	Title	Author	Pages Read	Comments

Form 9.21E: Marine Science Reading Log

HOOKED ON READING

Title: ______________________________

Author: ______________________________

Date Started: ________ **Completed:** ________

Rating: 4 3 2 1

Title: ______________________________

Author: ______________________________

Date Started: ________ **Completed:** ________

Rating: 4 3 2 1

Title: ______________________________

Author: ______________________________

Date Started: ________ **Completed:** ________

Rating: 4 3 2 1

DAILY READING LOG

Name:

Day	Title	Author	How much did you like it? A little / Some / A lot
Monday			1 2 3 4 5
Tuesday			1 2 3 4 5
Wednesday			1 2 3 4 5
Thursday			1 2 3 4 5
Friday			1 2 3 4 5
Saturday			1 2 3 4 5
Sunday			1 2 3 4 5

Form 9.22A: Daily Reading Log (Primary)

HOME READING LOG

Name:

Date	Title	To	With	By	Comments

(form adapted from *Highlight My Strengths* by Leanna Traill, Rigby, 1993)

MONTHLY READING LOG

Date	Title	How much did you like it? A little Some A lot
		1 2 3 4 5
		1 2 3 4 5
		1 2 3 4 5
		1 2 3 4 5
		1 2 3 4 5
		1 2 3 4 5
		1 2 3 4 5
		1 2 3 4 5
		1 2 3 4 5
		1 2 3 4 5
		1 2 3 4 5
		1 2 3 4 5
		1 2 3 4 5
		1 2 3 4 5
		1 2 3 4 5
		1 2 3 4 5

Form 9.22C: Monthly Reading Log

MONTHLY READING FAVORITE

Name: ______________________________ **Date:** ______________

Form 9.22D: Monthly Reading Favorite

MONTHLY READING REFLECTION

Name: ______________________________ **Date:** ____________________

1. How many books did you read this month? ____________________________

____

2. What genres did you read? ____

____

____

____

3. What other types of reading did you do (magazines, newspapers, etc)?

____

____

____

____

4. What were your favorite books this month? Why? ______________________

____

____

____

____

5. What do you plan to read next? ____

____

____

6. What is your reading goal for next month? ____________________________

____

____

Form 9.22E: Monthly Reading Reflection

READING SWEEP

Name: ______________________________ **Date:** ____________________

1. How often did you read during the 2-week sweep?

   ❑ every day ❑ most days ❑ not very much

2. How many different types of books did you read?

   ❑ 3 or more types ❑ 2-3 types ❑ usually the same type

3. What do you know about yourself as a reader? What do you like to read? How much do you like to read? Where do you like to read?

____

____

____

____

4. What was your favorite thing to read? Why? ____________________

____

____

5. What would you like to read next? ____________________________

____

____

6. How would you rate the books you have been reading? Are they easy, medium, or hard for you? Why?

____

____

READING GENRE LOG: PART ONE

Name:

Genre				
Observation				
Personal Story/Memories				
Biography				
Poetry				
Folk/Fairy/Tall Tales				
Myth/Legend				
Fantasy				
Animal Story				
Nonfiction/Research				
Story Problem				
Letter				

READING GENRE LOG: PART TWO

Name:

Genre				
Realistic Fiction				
Adventure/Survival				
Autobiography				
Play				
Mystery				
Science Fiction				
Historical Fiction				
Sports Story				
Persuasive Writing				

Form 9.23B: Reading Genre Log: Part Two

FAVORITE BOOKS

	Title________________ Author________________ Comments________________ ________________ ________________ ________________
	Title________________ Author________________ Comments________________ ________________ ________________ ________________
	Title________________ Author________________ Comments________________ ________________ ________________ ________________
	Title________________ Author________________ Comments________________ ________________ ________________ ________________

Form 9.24: Favorite Books

BOOK AND MOVIE COMPARISON

Name: ______________________________ **Date:** ______________

1. Which did you like better, the book or the movie? Why?

____

____

2. What did you like better about the book?

____

____

3. What did you like better about the movie?

____

____

4. Did the characters in the movie look like you imagined them in the book?

____

____

5. Do you think the author would like the movie? Why or why not?

____

____

6. What would you have done differently if you were making the movie?

____

____

Other comments:

BOOKS TO READ

TITLE	AUTHOR	COMMENTS

Form 9.26: Books to Read

FOCUS QUESTIONS FOR ANECDOTAL NOTES: MATH (PRIMARY)

ATTITUDE AND CONCEPT DEVELOPMENT

1. Does the child display a positive attitude towards math?
2. Does the child display understanding of the concepts of less than/equal to/greater than?
3. Is the child able to communicate an understanding of concepts using manipulatives? Pictures? Words?
4. Is the child able to connect the concrete level with symbolic representation?
5. Is the child able to explain how symbols relate to manipulatives or pictures?

MATH SKILLS

6. Can the child recognize/read/write numbers to 10? 100? Past 100?
7. Can the child count using one-to-one correspondence? By 5's? 10's? 2's?
8. Can the child use estimation strategies?
9. Does the child display fluency with math facts in addition and subtraction to 10? 18?
10. Can the child measure with non-conventional units? Conventional units?
11. Can the child interpret a simple pictograph? Bar graph? Construct one?

PROBLEM SOLVING

12. Is the child able to read a one-step math story problem, find the key information, and understand what the question is asking?
13. Is the child able to solve problems using manipulatives? Pictures? Words?
14. Is the child able to use a variety of strategies to solve a problem?
15. Does the child keep working when an answer is not apparent?
16. Does the child consider the reasonableness of answers?
17. Does the child have a system for checking the accuracy of answers?
18. Are results presented clearly? Coherently? Accurately?
19. Is the child able to experiment to produce multiple solutions?
20. Can the child discuss the problem-solving strategies s/he used?

SELF-EVALUATION

21. Can the child self-reflect on his/her abilities in math and set goals?

Form 10.1A: Focus Questions for Anecdotal Notes: Math (Primary)

FOCUS QUESTIONS FOR ANECDOTAL NOTES: MATH (INTERMEDIATE)

ATTITUDE AND CONCEPT DEVELOPMENT

1. Does the child display a positive attitude towards math?
2. Is the child able to communicate an understanding of concepts using manipulatives? Pictures? Words?
3. Is the child able to connect the concrete level with symbolic representation? Is the child able to explain how symbols relate to manipulatives or pictures?
4. Can the child make connections between processes s/he has learned (e.g., the relationship between addition and subtraction)?

MATH SKILLS

5. Can the child read/write large numbers to 1000? 10000?
6. Is the child using mental math strategies?
7. Is the child using estimation strategies?
8. Does the child know the math facts or is non-fluency interfering with his/her ability to solve problems?
9. Can the child measure with accuracy?
10. Can the child interpret/construct bar graphs? Line graphs? Circle graphs?

PROBLEM SOLVING

11. Is the child able to read a math story problem, find the key information, and understand what the question is asking?
12. Can the child restate the problem in his/her own terms?
13. Is the child able to solve complex problems using manipulatives? Pictures? Words?
14. Does the child approach problem solving in an organized way?
15. Is the child able to apply his/her understanding of math concepts to solve problems (e.g., does s/he know when to use multiplication?
16. Does the child choose an appropriate and efficient procedure to solve the problem?
17. Does the child keep working when an answer is not apparent?
18. Does the child consider the reasonableness of answers?
19. Does the child have a system for checking the accuracy of answers?
20. Are results presented clearly? Coherently? Accurately?
21. Is the child able to experiment to produce multiple solutions?
22. Can the child discuss the problem-solving strategies s/he used?

SELF-EVALUATION

23. Can the child self-reflect on his/her abilities in math and set goals?

Form 10.1B: Focus Questions for Anecdotal Notes: Math (Intermediate)

FOCUS QUESTIONS FOR ANECDOTAL NOTES: SCIENCE (PRIMARY)

ATTITUDE

1. Does the child display a positive attitude and curiosity about science?
2. Does the child display care of equipment and materials?

OBSERVATION SKILLS

3. Does the child make observations using all senses?
4. Does the child make descriptive observations? ("It's round.") Comparative ones? ("It smells like powder.") Inferences? (It's crystally . . . it must be sugar!")

SCIENTIFIC PROCESS SKILLS

5. Does the child demonstrate skill in using materials?
6. Does the child make predictions?
7. Does the child follow simple procedures correctly?
8. Does the child measure carefully? Accurately?
9. Does the child record results using drawings? Words?
10. Does the child label the drawings?
11. Does the child look for patterns in results?
12. Does the child generalize information in new situations?

GROUP PROCESS AND COMMUNICATION SKILLS

13. Can the child describe objects and ideas clearly?
14. Does the child use new vocabulary to describe observations and/or results?
15. Can the child express in writing what s/he has observed?
16. Does the child work cooperatively with partner(s)?

FOCUS QUESTIONS FOR ANECDOTAL NOTES: SCIENCE (INTERMEDIATE)

ATTITUDE

1. Does the child display a positive attitude and curiosity about science?
2. Does the child display care of equipment and materials?

OBSERVATION SKILLS

3. Does the child make observations using all senses?
4. Does the child make descriptive observations? ("It's round.") Comparative ones? ("It smells like powder.") Inferences? (It's crystally . . . it must be sugar!")

SCIENTIFIC PROCESS SKILLS

5. Does the child demonstrate skill in using materials?
6. Does the child follow procedures correctly?
7. Does the child measure carefully? Accurately?
8. Does the child record results with diagrams? Words? Tables/charts?
9. Does the child draw accurate, understandable diagrams?
10. Is the child using a control for comparison of variables?
11. Does the child support predictions with test data?
12. Does the child look for patterns in the results?
13. Can the child draw valid conclusions based on test data?
14. Can the child devise testing strategies and solve problems by applying new knowledge/skills?

COMMUNICATION SKILLS

15. Can the child describe objects and ideas clearly?
16. Does the child use new vocabulary to explain observations and/or results?
17. Can the child express in writing what s/he has observed?
18. Does the child work cooperatively and efficiently with partner(s)?

Form 10.1D:Focus Questions for Anecdotal Notes: Science (Intermediate)

PROJECT CHECK-UP

Name: ________________________________ **Date:** ______________

1. My project/assignment is ______________________________________

____

____

2. I accomplished ____

____

____

3. I learned (at least two things) ____________________________________

____

____

____

____

4. I feel good about ____

____

5. I need help with ____

____

6. My next goal is ____

____

____

PROBLEM SOLVING EVALUATION: PRIMARY

Name: ______________________________ **Date:** ______________

Activity: ____

1. What strategies did you use to solve the problem? ____________________

2. What are some things that might have made it easier for you? ____________

3. What were some strategies other students used that made sense to you? _____

Form 10.3A: Problem Solving Evaluation (Primary)

PROBLEM SOLVING EVALUATION: INTERMEDIATE

Name: ______________________________ **Date:** ______________

Activity: ____

1. How did you approach the problem? What strategies and/or techniques did you use to get started? ______________________________________

____

____

2. What different ways did you organize all of your materials/information? _______

____

____

3. How did you solve the problem? What strategies/techniques made you feel successful? ______________________________________

____

4. What are some things that might have made it easier for you? ______________

____

____

5. What were some strategies other students used that made sense to you? _______

____

____

PROBLEM SOLVING RUBRIC

Name: ______________________________ **Date:** ________________

Activity: ____

Understanding the Problem

_____ **5** Able to highlight the question and important information. Completely understands the problem.

_____ **3** Misinterprets the question or important information.

_____ **1** Completely misinterprets the problem.

Choosing and Implementing a Strategy

_____ **5** Chooses a strategy and plan that leads to a correct solution.

_____ **3** Chooses a partially appropriate strategy.

_____ **1** No attempt to solve the problem or an inappropriate plan.

Answering the Problem

_____ **5** Correct solution

_____ **3** Copying error, computational error, partial answer for a problem with more than one solution, or a wrongly-labeled answer.

_____ **1** Incorrect answer based on an inappropriate strategy.

WHAT IS SUBTRACTION?

Name: ______________________________ **Date:** ____________

1. Would the answer to 594 - 268 be closer to 30 or 300? __________

2. Do as much as you can of these two problems:

A. 594	B. 94
-268	-68

3. What is the difference between these two problems?

____

____

____

____

4. Why do we begin with the units? What would happen if we began with the tens place in problem B? ______________________________

____

____

____

5. Why do we cross out the 9 and write an 8? What does the small 1 we write by the 4 mean? ______________________________

____

____

____

6. Why do we line up the digits as we do? ______________________

____

____

7. Why can we add to check subtraction problems? ____________________

8. Write the problem 523 - 76 vertically in these boxes.
Then solve the problem.

9. What would it tell us if someone got 553 for an answer to this problem?

10. Write the problem 300 - 73 vertically in these boxes.
Then solve the problem.

11. What is different about this problem which might make it more difficult to solve? ____________________

(form adapted from "Assessing for Learning: Assessing through Questioning" by Mary M. Lindquist in *The Arithmetic Teacher*, 1988)

WHAT IS MULTIPLICATION?

Name: ______________________________ **Date:** _____________

What is multiplication? You may use pictures and words.

Explain your drawing

____

____

____

____

____

____

____

____

____

____

____

PRIMARY MATH EVALUATION

Individual Student Composite Record for: **Homeroom:**

Date (color code)	
NUMERALS/PLACE VALUE	
Numeral Recognition	0 1 2 3 4 5 6 7 8 9 10 11 12 teens 20-99 100 1000
Numeral Form	0 1 2 3 4 5 6 7 8 9
Reading Numbers	13 31 40 87 15 21 137 350 249 306 113 415 710 609 530 999 1000
Writing Numbers	14 41 50 97 16 31 147 349 100 204 314 140 210 111 1000
Reads a model for	10's and 1's 100's, 10's, and 1's
Writes a model for	10's and 1's 100's, 10's, and 1's
COUNTING	
One-to-one correspondence	(check "to __")
Counts by 1's	to 10 to 20 to 100 past 100
Counts by 5's	to ____ to 100 past 100
Counts by 10's	to ____ to 100 past 100
Counts by 2's	to ____ to 100 past 100
Counts backward	from 10 from 20
Counting on	from 5 from 10 from 25 from 100
ARITHMETIC	
Concept ("hiding")	3 4 5 6 7 8 9 10
Addition facts to 10	3 4 5 6 7 8 9 10
Addition facts to 18	11 12 13 14 15 16 17 18
Subtraction facts to 10	3 4 5 6 7 8 9 10
Subtraction facts to 18	11 12 13 14 15 16 17 18
Two-digit addition w/regrouping	w/guidance developing consistently
Two-digit subtraction w/regroup	w/guidance developing consistently
MEASURING	
Linear/non-conventional	(date observed/example)
Linear/conventional	metric customary
Fractional	halves quarters eighths thirds tenths
Time	hour half-hour quarter past quarter 'til to minute
Money	penny nickel dime quarter
	sets of: 1¢ 5¢ 10¢ 25¢ 1¢&5¢ 1¢&10¢ 5¢&10¢ 1¢,5¢,&10¢
GEOMETRY	
Explorations	(date observed/example)
PATTERNS/FUNCTION	
Concepts	recognizes reproduces extends creates
Explorations	(date observed/example)
GRAPHING/COMPARING	
Sorting	sorts names rule re-sorts
Comparing	equals more less
Graphing	interprets records creates
Explorations	(date observed/example)
LOGIC/PROBLEM SOLVING	
Uses math to solve real problems	(date observed/example)
Explorations	(date observed/example)

Form 10.5: Primary Math Evaluation

HUMAN BODY POSTER CHECKLIST

Name: ______________________ **Date:** ____________

STUDENT EVALUATION	TEACHER EVALUATION
❑ I chose 8-10 important facts about my topic and included them on my cards.	❑ Important facts were listed on cards (8-10).
❑ I chose 5-7 of the most important facts to include on my poster	❑ 5-7 of the most important facts were included on the poster.
❑ At least one of my poster facts tells about the function or purpose of this body part.	❑ The poster explains the function of this body part.
❑ I used 2-3 sentences to explain each fact	❑ Facts were well explained using at least 2-3 sentences.
❑ I used neat handwriting.	❑ Handwriting is neat and careful.
❑ I added at least one quality illustration that is clear and neat.	❑ Illustration(s) shows quality work and is (are) clear and neat.
❑ My poster is organized and easy to understand.	❑ Poster is organized in an "easy to read" way.
❑ I attached the completed self-assessment.	❑ Completed self-assessment is attached.

OPTIONAL:

❑ I went beyond expectations!	❑ Expectations were exceeded.

INVENTORS' CHECKLIST: CLASS PROFILE

	Name	Inventor Report	Survey	Description of Invention	Two View Sketches	Patent Signatures	Working Model	Invention Defense	Advertisement	Inventor's Log
1										
2										
3										
4										
5										
6										
7										
8										
9										
10										
11										
12										
13										
14										
15										
16										
17										
18										
19										
20										
21										
22										
23										
24										
25										
26										
27										
28										

Form 10.7A: Inventors' Checklist: Class Profile

INVENTOR'S CHECKLIST

STUDENTS			
Inventor Report			
Survey			
Description of Invention			
Two-View Sketches			
Patent Signatures			
Working Model			
Invention Defense			
Advertisement			
Inventor's Log			
Other			

Form 10.7B: Inventor's Checklist

SCIENCE LOG SCORING RUBRIC

Name: **Date:**

	NOVICE	APPRENTICE	PRACTITIONER	EXPERT
Observation Skills	❑ Fails to use sensory details to describe observations	❑ Uses few sensory details to describe observations	❑ Uses several sensory details to describe observations	❑ Uses extensive, exact sensory details to describe observations
Process Skills	❑ Has difficulty following procedures	❑ Follows procedures with a great deal of assistance	❑ Follows procedures with some assistance	❑ Follows procedures independently with accuracy and care
	❑ Has difficulty using and caring for materials	❑ Uses and cares for materials properly with a great deal of guidance	❑ Uses and cares for materials properly with some guidance	❑ Uses and cares for materials properly independently
Communication Skills	❑ No use of new science vocabulary	❑ Slight use of new vocabulary	❑ Uses new science vocabulary to describe observations and results	❑ Extensive use of new vocabulary to describe observations and results
	❑ Recordings not easily understandable; drawings are not neat/dated/detailed	❑ Records observations in an understandable way; includes neat, dated, labeled drawings	❑ Records observations in an organized way; neat detailed drawings are dated and labeled	❑ Consistently records observations in an organized way: accurate, labeled, dated diagrams
Understanding	❑ No evidence of understanding of the concept of life cycles	❑ Minimal evidence of understanding of the concept of life cycles (may only be inferred)	❑ Clear evidence of understanding of concept of life cycle (at least one example)	❑ Extensive evidence of understanding of concept of life cycle (more than one example)
	❑ No evidence of understanding of the relationship between bees and plants	❑ Minimal evidence of understanding of the relationship between bees and plants (may only be inferred)	❑ Clear evidence of understanding of the relationship between bees and plants (at least one example)	❑ Extensive evidence of understanding of the relationship between bees and plants (more than one example)

Form 10.8: Science Log Scoring Rubric

SIMPLE MACHINES RATING SCALE

Name: ______________________________ **Date:** ___________

Used equipment and materials to construct machines and conduct experiments

Didn't understand what to do	Carefully and with ease

Recorded and described experiments in science log

Wrote little	A lot of detailed writing

Used labeled drawings, charts, tables, and graphs

At least one	Some of each

Used new science vocabulary effectively

A little	A lot

Followed safety rules

Some of the time	All of the time

Discussed ideas and results with others (lab partners, small groups, whole class)

Shared only when asked	Voluntarily shared often

Worked well with others

Some of the time	All of the time

Used time effectively and kept on task

"Fooled around" a bit	Focused all of the time

Things I liked or did well: ____

____

____

____

Things I'd still like to learn or do: ____

____

WRITING CONTINUUM

Preconventional
Ages 3-5

- ☐ Relies primarily on pictures to convey meaning.
- ☐ Begins to label and add "words" to pictures.
- ☐ Demonstrates awareness that print conveys meaning.
- ☐ Makes marks other than drawing on paper (scribbles).
- ☐ Writes random recognizable letters to represent words.
- ☐ Tells about own pictures and writing.

Emerging
Ages 4-6

- ☐ Uses pictures and print to convey meaning.
- ☐ Writes words to describe or support pictures.
- ☐ Copies signs, labels, names and words (environmental print).
- ☐ Demonstrates understanding of letter/sound relationship.
- ☐ Prints with upper case letters.
- ☐ Uses beginning consonants to make words.
- ☐ Uses beginning and ending consonants to make words.
- ☐ Pretends to read own writing.
- ☐ Sees self as writer.
- ☐ Takes risks with writing.

Developing
Ages 5-7

- ☐ Begins to write noun-verb phrases.
- ☐ Writes names and familiar words.
- ☐ Generates own ideas for writing.
- ☐ Writes from top to bottom, left to right and front to back.
- ☐ Intermixes upper and lower case letters.
- ☐ Begins to use spacing between words.
- ☐ Matches letters to sounds.
- ☐ Spells words on the basis of sounds without regard for conventional spelling patterns.
- ☐ Uses beginning, middle and ending sounds to make words.
- ☐ Begins to read own writing.

Beginning
Ages 6-8

- ☐ Writes recognizable short sentences.
- ☐ Writes about observations and experiences.
- ☐ Writes short nonfiction pieces (simple facts about a topic) with guidance.
- ☐ Chooses own writing topics.
- ☐ Reads own writing and notices mistakes with guidance.
- ☐ Revises by adding details with guidance.
- ☐ Uses spacing between words consistently.
- ☐ Forms most letters legibly.
- ☐ Writes pieces that self and others can read.
- ☐ Uses phonetic spelling to write independently.
- ☐ Experiments with capitals.
- ☐ Experiments with punctuation.
- ☐ Shares own writing with others.

Expanding
Ages 7-9

- ☐ Writes short fiction and poetry with guidance.
- ☐ Writes a variety of short nonfiction pieces (e.g., facts about a topic, letters, lists) with guidance.
- ☐ Writes with a central idea.
- ☐ Writes using complete sentences.
- ☐ Organizes ideas in a logical sequence in fiction and nonfiction writing with guidance.
- ☐ Begins to recognize and use interesting language.
- ☐ Uses several pre-writing strategies (e.g., web, brainstorm) with guidance.
- ☐ Listens to others' writing and offers feedback.
- ☐ Begins to consider suggestions from others about own writing.
- ☐ Adds description and detail with guidance.
- ☐ Edits for capitals and punctuation with guidance.
- ☐ Publishes own writing with guidance.
- ☐ Writes legibly.
- ☐ Moves beyond phonetic spelling toward conventional spelling.
- ☐ Identifies own writing strategies and sets goals with guidance.

Bridging
Ages 8-11

- ☐ Writes about feelings and opinions.
- ☐ Writes fiction with clear beginning, middle and end.
- ☐ Writes poetry using carefully chosen language with guidance.
- ☐ Writes organized nonfiction pieces (e.g., reports, letters, lists) with guidance.
- ☐ Begins to use paragraphs to organize ideas.
- ☐ Uses strong verbs, interesting language and dialogue with guidance.
- ☐ Seeks feedback on writing.
- ☐ Revises for clarity with guidance.
- ☐ Revises to enhance ideas by adding description and detail.
- ☐ Uses resources (e.g., thesaurus and word lists) to make writing more effective with guidance.
- ☐ Edits for punctuation, spelling and grammar with guidance.
- ☐ Publishes writing in polished format with guidance.
- ☐ Increases use of visual strategies, spelling rules and knowledge of word parts to spell correctly.
- ☐ Uses commas and apostrophes correctly with guidance.
- ☐ Uses criteria for effective writing to set own writing goals with guidance.

Fluent
Ages 9-12

- ☐ Begins to write organized fiction and nonfiction (e.g., reports, letters, biographies and autobiographies).
- ☐ Develops stories with plots that include problems and solutions with guidance.
- ☐ Creates characters in stories with guidance.
- ☐ Writes poetry using carefully chosen language.
- ☐ Begins to experiment with sentence length and complex sentence structure.
- ☐ Varies leads and endings with guidance.
- ☐ Uses description, details and similes with guidance.
- ☐ Uses dialogue with guidance.
- ☐ Uses a range of strategies for planning writing.
- ☐ Adapts writing for purpose and audience with guidance.
- ☐ Revises for specific writing traits (e.g., ideas, organization, word choice, sentence fluency, voice and conventions) with guidance.
- ☐ Incorporates suggestions from others about own writing with guidance.
- ☐ Edits for punctuation, spelling and grammar with greater precision.
- ☐ Uses tools (e.g., dictionaries, checklists and spell checkers) to edit with guidance.
- ☐ Develops criteria for effective writing in different genres with guidance.

Proficient
Ages 10-13

- ☐ Writes persuasively about ideas, feelings and opinions.
- ☐ Creates plots with problems and solutions.
- ☐ Begins to develop the main characters and describe detailed settings.
- ☐ Begins to write organized and fluent nonfiction and includes sources.
- ☐ Writes cohesive paragraphs including reasons and examples with guidance.
- ☐ Uses transitional sentences to connect paragraphs.
- ☐ Varies sentence structure, leads and endings.
- ☐ Begins to use descriptive language, details and similes.
- ☐ Uses voice to evoke emotional response from readers.
- ☐ Begins to integrate information on a topic from a variety of sources.
- ☐ Begins to revise for specific writing traits (e.g., ideas, organization, word choice, sentence fluency, voice and conventions).
- ☐ Uses tools (e.g., dictionaries, checklists, spell checkers) to edit independently.
- ☐ Selects and publishes writing in polished format independently.
- ☐ Begins to use complex punctuation (e.g., commas, colons, semicolons, quotation marks) appropriately.
- ☐ Begins to set goals and identify strategies to improve writing in different genres.

Connecting
Ages 11-14

- ☐ Writes in a variety of genres and forms for different audiences and purposes independently.
- ☐ Creates plots with a climax.
- ☐ Creates detailed, believable settings and characters in stories.
- ☐ Writes organized, fluent and detailed nonfiction independently.
- ☐ Writes cohesive paragraphs including supportive reasons and examples.
- ☐ Uses descriptive language, details, similes and imagery to enhance ideas independently.
- ☐ Begins to use dialogue to enhance character development.
- ☐ Incorporates personal voice in writing with increasing frequency.
- ☐ Integrates information on a topic from a variety of sources independently.
- ☐ Constructs charts, graphs and tables to convey information when appropriate.
- ☐ Uses pre-writing strategies effectively to organize and strengthen writing.
- ☐ Revises for specific writing traits (e.g., ideas, organization, word choice, sentence fluency, voice and conventions) independently.
- ☐ Includes deletion in revision strategies.
- ☐ Incorporates suggestions from others on own writing independently.
- ☐ Uses complex punctuation (e.g., commas, colons, semicolons, quotation marks) with increasing accuracy.

Independent

- ☐ Writes organized, fluent, accurate and in-depth nonfiction, including references.
- ☐ Writes cohesive, fluent and effective poetry and fiction.
- ☐ Uses a clear sequence of paragraphs with effective transitions.
- ☐ Begins to incorporate literary devices (i.e., imagery, metaphors, personification and foreshadowing).
- ☐ Weaves dialogue effectively into stories.
- ☐ Develops plots, characters, setting and mood effectively (literary elements).
- ☐ Begins to develop personal voice and style of writing.
- ☐ Revises through multiple drafts independently.
- ☐ Seeks feedback from others and incorporates suggestions in order to strengthen own writing.
- ☐ Publishes writing for different audiences and purposes in polished format independently.
- ☐ Internalizes writing process.
- ☐ Uses correct grammar (e.g., subject/verb agreement, verb tense) consistently.
- ☐ Writes with confidence and competence on a range of topics independently.
- ☐ Perseveres through complex or challenging writing projects independently.
- ☐ Sets writing goals independently by analyzing and evaluating own writing.

Form 11.1: Writing Continuum

READING CONTINUUM

Preconventional
Ages 3-5

- ❑ Begins to choose reading materials (e.g., books, magazines and charts) and has favorites.
- ❑ Shows interest in reading signs, labels and logos (environmental print).
- ❑ Recognizes own name in print.
- ❑ Holds book and turns pages correctly.
- ❑ Shows beginning/end of book or story.
- ❑ Knows some letter names.
- ❑ Listens and responds to literature.
- ❑ Comments on illustrations in books.
- ❑ Participates in group reading (books, rhymes, poems and songs).

Emerging
Ages 4-6

- ❑ Memorizes pattern books, poems and familiar books.
- ❑ Begins to read signs, labels and logos (environmental print).
- ❑ Demonstrates eagerness to read.
- ❑ Pretends to read.
- ❑ Uses illustrations to tell stories.
- ❑ Reads top to bottom, left to right and front to back with guidance.
- ❑ Knows most letter names and some letter sounds.
- ❑ Recognizes some names and words in context.
- ❑ Begins to make meaningful predictions.
- ❑ Rhymes and plays with words.
- ❑ Participates in reading of familiar books and poems.
- ❑ Connects books read aloud to own experiences with guidance.

Developing
Ages 5-7

- ❑ Reads books with simple patterns.
- ❑ Begins to read own writing.
- ❑ Begins to read independently for short periods (5-10 minutes).
- ❑ Shares favorite reading material with others.
- ❑ Learns information from reading and shares with others.
- ❑ Relies on illustrations and print.
- ❑ Uses finger-print-voice matching.
- ❑ Knows most letter sounds.
- ❑ Recognizes simple words.
- ❑ Begins to make meaningful predictions.
- ❑ Identifies titles and authors in literature.
- ❑ Retells main event or idea in literature.
- ❑ Participates in guided literature discussions.
- ❑ Sees self as reader.
- ❑ Explains why literature is liked/disliked during class discussions with guidance.

Beginning
Ages 6-8

- ❑ Reads simple early-reader books.
- ❑ Reads harder early-reader books.
- ❑ Reads and follows simple written directions with guidance.
- ❑ Identifies basic genres (e.g., fiction, nonfiction and poetry).
- ❑ Uses basic punctuation when reading orally.
- ❑ Reads independently (10-15 minutes).
- ❑ Chooses reading materials independently.
- ❑ Uses meaning cues (context).
- ❑ Uses sentence cues (grammar).
- ❑ Uses letter/sound cues and patterns (phonics).
- ❑ Recognizes many high frequency words by sight.
- ❑ Begins to self-correct.
- ❑ Retells beginning, middle and end with guidance.
- ❑ Discusses characters and story events with guidance.
- ❑ Identifies own reading behaviors with guidance.

Expanding
Ages 7-9

- ❑ Reads beginning chapter books.
- ❑ Chooses, reads and finishes a variety of materials at appropriate level with guidance.
- ❑ Begins to read aloud with fluency.
- ❑ Reads silently for increasingly longer periods (15-30 minutes).
- ❑ Uses reading strategies appropriately, depending on the text and purpose.
- ❑ Uses word structure cues (e.g., prefixes, contractions, abbreviations).
- ❑ Begins to use meaning cues (context) to increase vocabulary.
- ❑ Self-corrects for meaning.
- ❑ Follows written directions.
- ❑ Identifies chapter titles and table of contents (text organizers).
- ❑ Summarizes and retells story events in sequential order.
- ❑ Responds to and makes personal connections with facts, characters and situations in literature.
- ❑ Compares and contrasts characters and story events.
- ❑ Makes predictions and "reads beyond the text" with guidance.
- ❑ Identifies own reading strategies and sets goals with guidance.

Bridging
Ages 8-11

- ❑ Reads medium level chapter books.
- ❑ Chooses reading materials at appropriate level.
- ❑ Expands knowledge of different genres (e.g., realistic fiction, historical fiction and fantasy).
- ❑ Reads aloud with expression.
- ❑ Uses resources (e.g., encyclopedias, CD-ROMs and nonfiction texts) to locate and sort information with guidance.
- ❑ Gathers information by using the glossary, captions and index (text organizers) with guidance.
- ❑ Gathers and uses information from graphs, charts, tables and maps with guidance.
- ❑ Uses context cues, other reading strategies and resources (e.g., dictionary, thesaurus) to increase vocabulary with guidance.
- ❑ Demonstrates understanding of the difference between fact and opinion.
- ❑ Follows multi-step written directions independently.
- ❑ Discusses setting, plot, characters and point of view (literary elements) with guidance.
- ❑ Responds to issues and ideas in literature as well as facts or story events.
- ❑ Makes connections to other authors, books and perspectives.
- ❑ Participates in small group literature discussions with guidance.
- ❑ Uses reasons and examples to support ideas and opinions with guidance.

Fluent
Ages 9-12

- ❑ Reads challenging children's literature.
- ❑ Selects, reads and finishes a wide variety of genres with guidance.
- ❑ Begins to develop strategies and criteria for selecting reading materials.
- ❑ Reads aloud with fluency, expression and confidence.
- ❑ Reads silently for extended periods (30-40 min.).
- ❑ Begins to use resources (e.g., encyclopedias, articles, Internet and nonfiction texts) to locate information.
- ❑ Uses organization of nonfiction texts (e.g., titles, index and table of contents) to locate information.
- ❑ Begins to use resources (e.g., dictionary, thesaurus) to increase vocabulary in different subject areas.
- ❑ Begins to discuss literature with reference to setting, plot, characters and theme (literary elements) and author's craft.
- ❑ Generates thoughtful oral and written responses in small group literature discussions with guidance.
- ❑ Begins to use new vocabulary in oral and written response to literature.
- ❑ Begins to gain deeper meaning by "reading between the lines."
- ❑ Begins to set goals and identifies strategies to improve reading.

Proficient
Ages 10-13

- ❑ Reads complex children's literature.
- ❑ Reads and understands informational texts (i.e., maps, want ads, brochures, schedules, catalogs, manuals, etc.) with guidance.
- ❑ Develops strategies and criteria for selecting reading materials independently.
- ❑ Uses resources (e.g., encyclopedias, articles, Internet and nonfiction texts) to locate information independently.
- ❑ Gathers and analyzes information from graphs, charts, tables and maps with guidance.
- ❑ Integrates information from multiple nonfiction sources to deepen understanding of a topic with guidance.
- ❑ Uses resources (e.g., dictionary, thesaurus) to increase vocabulary independently.
- ❑ Identifies literary devices (e.g., similes, metaphors, personification and foreshadowing).
- ❑ Discusses literature with reference to theme, author's purpose and style (literary elements) and author's craft.
- ❑ Begins to generate in-depth responses in small group literature discussions.
- ❑ Begins to generate in-depth written responses to literature.
- ❑ Uses increasingly complex vocabulary in oral and written response to literature.
- ❑ Uses reasons and examples to support ideas and conclusions.
- ❑ Probes for deeper meaning by "reading between the lines" in response to literature.

Connecting
Ages 11-14

- ❑ Reads complex children's literature and young adult literature.
- ❑ Selects, reads and finishes a wide variety of genres independently.
- ❑ Begins to choose challenging reading materials and projects.
- ❑ Integrates nonfiction information to develop deeper understanding of a topic independently.
- ❑ Begins to gather, analyze and use information from graphs, charts, tables and maps.
- ❑ Generates in-depth responses and sustains small group literature discussions.
- ❑ Generates in-depth written responses to literature.
- ❑ Begins to evaluate, interpret and analyze reading content critically.
- ❑ Begins to develop criteria for evaluating literature.
- ❑ Seeks recommendations and opinions about literature from others.
- ❑ Sets reading challenges and goals independently.

Independent

- ❑ Reads young adult and adult literature.
- ❑ Chooses and comprehends a wide variety of sophisticated materials with ease (e.g., newspapers, magazines, manuals, novels, poetry).
- ❑ Reads and understands informational texts (i.e., maps, manuals, consumer reports, applications, forms, etc.)
- ❑ Reads challenging material for pleasure independently.
- ❑ Reads challenging material for information and to solve problems independently.
- ❑ Perseveres through complex reading tasks.
- ❑ Gathers, analyzes and uses information from graphs, charts, tables and maps independently.
- ❑ Analyzes literary devices (e.g., metaphors, imagery, irony and satire).
- ❑ Contributes unique insights and supports opinions in complex literature discussions.
- ❑ Adds depth to responses to literature by making insightful connections to other reading and experiences.
- ❑ Evaluates, interprets and analyzes reading content critically.
- ❑ Develops and articulates criteria for evaluating literature.
- ❑ Pursues a widening community of readers independently.

Form 11.2: Reading Continuum

References

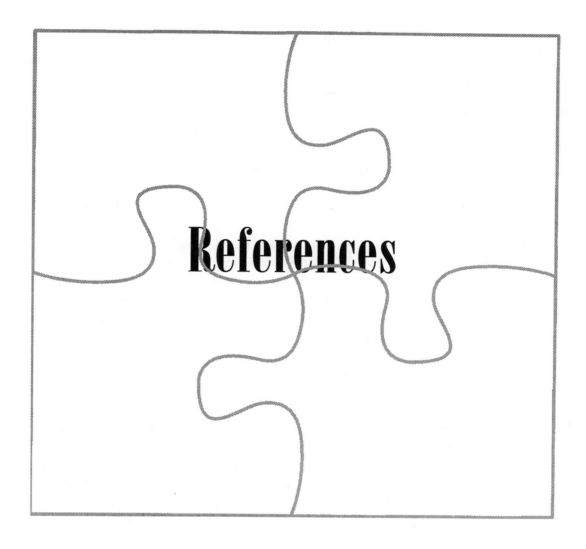

Anderson, R., Hiebert, E., Scott, J., & Wilkinson, I. (1985). *Becoming a nation of readers: The report of the commission on reading.* Washington, DC: National Institute of Education.

Armstrong, T. (1987). *In their own way.* Jeremy Tarcher.

Armstrong, T. (1994). *Multiple intelligences in the classroom.* Alexandria, VA: Association for Supervision and Curriculum Development.

Arner, B. (1996). *Invent.* El Cajon, CA: Interaction Publishers, Inc.

Atwell, N. (1987). *In the middle: Writing, reading, and learning with adolescents.* Portsmouth, NH: Heinemann.

Atwell, N. (1998). *In the middle: New understandings about writing, reading, and learning with adolescents.* (2nd ed.). Portsmouth, NH: Heinemann.

Avery, C. (1993). *And with a light touch: Learning about reading, writing, and teaching with first graders.* Portsmouth, NH: Heinemann.

Baratta-Lorton, M. (1976). *Mathematics their way.* Menlo Park, CA: Addison-Wesley.

Bialostok, S. (1996). *But will she read? A teacher's guide to helping parents understand whole language.* Winnipeg, Manitoba, Canada: Peguis.

Bird, L., Goodman, K., & Goodman, Y. (1994). *The whole language catalog: Forms for authentic assessment.* Columbus, OH: SRA/McGraw-Hill.

Braun, C. (1993). *Looking, listening, and learning: Observing and assessing young readers.* Winnipeg, Manitoba, Canada: Peguis.

Bridge, S. (1982). Squeezing from the middle of the tube. In T. Newkirk & N. Atwell (Eds.), *Understanding writing: Ways of observing, learning and teaching K–8* (pp. 68–75). Chelmsford, MA: The Northeast Regional Exchange.

Brown, H., & Cambourne, B. (1987). *Read and retell.* Portsmouth, NH: Heinemann.

Brown, M. W. (1947). *Goodnight moon.* New York: Harper.

Bulla, C. (1994). *Pirate's promise.* New York: HarperCollins

Burnett, F. H. (1905; 1963). *A little princess.* New York: Lippincott.

Burnett, F. H. (1909; 1962). *The secret garden.* New York: Lippincott.

Burns, M. (1991). *Math by all means: Multiplication.* White Plains, NY: Math Solutions Publishers, Cuisinaire Company of America.

Burns, M. (1992). *About teaching mathematics: A K–8 resource.* White Plains, New York: Math Solutions Publishers, Cuisinaire Company of America.

Calkins, L. (1994). *The art of teaching writing.* (2nd ed.). Portsmouth, NH: Heinemann.

Calkins, L. M., & Harwayne, S. (1991). *Living between the lines.* Portsmouth, NH: Heinemann.

Chittenden, E. (1991). Authentic assessment, evaluation, and documentation of student performance. In V. Perrone (Ed.), *Expanding student assessment* (pp. 22–31). Alexandria, VA: Association for Supervision and Curriculum Development.

Clay, M. (1972). *Sand.* Portsmouth, NH: Heinemann.

Clay, M. (1972). *Stones.* Portsmouth, NH: Heinemann.

Clay, M. (1993). *An observation survey of early literacy achievement.* Portsmouth, NH: Heinemann.

Clymer, T. (1996). The utility of phonic generalizations in the primary grades. *The Reading Teacher, 50* (3), 182–187.

Crafton, L. (1991). *Whole language: Getting started . . . moving forward.* Katonah, NY: Richard C. Owen.

Creech, S. (1994). *Walk two moons.* New York: HarperCollins.

Culham, R., & Spandel, V. (1993). *The student-friendly guide to writing with traits.* Portland, OR: Northwest Regional Educational Laboratory.

Culham, R., & Spandel, V. (1998). *Picture books: An annotated bibliography for use with the 6-trait analytic model of writing assessment and instruction* (4th ed.). Portland, OR: Northwest Regional Educational Laboratory.

Dahl, R. (1961). *James and the giant peach.* New York: Bantam.

Dahl, R. (1981). *The Twits.* New York: Knopf.

Dahl, R. (1983). *Witches*. New York: Viking.

Dahl, R. (1986). *Fantastic Mr. Fox*. New York: Knopf.

Dahl, R. (1988). *Matilda*. New York: Puffin.

Daniels, H. (1994). *Literature circles: Voice and choice in the student-centered classroom*. York, ME: Stenhouse.

Dodson, S. (1996). *The mother-daughter book club: How ten busy mothers and daughters came together to talk, laugh and learn through their love of reading*. New York: HarperCollins.

Drummond, M.J. (1994). *Learning to see: Assessment through observation*. York, ME: Stenhouse.

Duthie, C. (1996). *True stories: Nonfiction literacy in the primary classroom*. York, ME: Stenhouse.

Egawa, K. (1998). Children's voices: Responding to literature. *New Advocate, 11* (1), 70–71.

English: A curriculum profile for Australian schools. (1994). Victoria, Australia: Curriculum Corporation.

Ernst, K. (1994). *Picturing learning: Artists and writers in the classroom*. Portsmouth, NH: Heinemann.

Fein, S. (1993). *First drawings: Genesis of visual thinking*. Portsmouth, NH: Heinemann.

Fein, S. (1993). *Heidi's horse*. Portsmouth, NH: Heinemann.

First steps program. (1996). Education Department of Western Australia. Portsmouth, NH: Heinemann.

Fisher, B. (1991). *Joyful learning: A whole language kindergarten*. Portsmouth, NH: Heinemann.

Fletcher, R. (1993). *What a writer needs*. Portsmouth, NH: Heinemann.

Fletcher, R. (1996). *Breathing in, breathing out: Keeping a writer's notebook*. Portsmouth, NH: Heinemann.

Fountas, I., & Pinnell, G. (1996). *Guided reading: Good first teaching for all children*. Portsmouth, NH: Heinemann.

Fox, M. (1993). *Radical reflections: Passionate opinions on teaching, learning, and living*. New York: Harcourt Brace.

Full option science systems series (FOSS). Lawrence Hall Science. Berkeley, CA: University of California.

Gambrell, L., & Almasi, J. (Eds.). (1996). *Lively discussions! Fostering engaged reading*. Newark, DE: International Reading Association.

Gardiner, J. (1980). *Stone Fox*. New York: Harper.

Gardner, H. (1983). *Frames of mind: The theory of multiple intelligences*. New York: Basic Books.

Garmston, R. (1997). *The presenter's fieldbook: A practical guide*. Norwood, MA: Christopher-Gordon.

Great explorations in math and science series (GEMS). Lawrence Hall Science. Berkeley, CA: University of California.

Gentry, J. R. (1997). *My kid can't spell: Understanding and assisting your child's literacy development*. Portsmouth, NH: Heinemann.

Gentry, J. R., & Gillet, J. (1993). *Teaching kids to spell*. Portsmouth, NH: Heinemann.

Gentry, J.R. (1987). *Spel . . . is a four-letter word*. Portsmouth, NH: Heinemann.

Glazer, S.M., & Brown, C. S. (1993). *Portfolios and beyond: Collaborative assessment in reading and writing*. Norwood, MA: Christopher-Gordon.

Goodman, K. (1973). Windows on the reading process. In K. Goodman (Ed.), *Miscue analysis: Application to reading instruction*. Urbana, IL: National Council of Teachers of English.

Graves, D., & Hansen, J. (1983). The author's chair. *Language Arts*, *60* (8), 176–183.

Graves, D. (1983). *Writing: Teachers and children at work*. Portsmouth, NH: Heinemann.

Graves, D. (1994). *A fresh look at writing*. Portsmouth, NH: Heinemann.

Griffin, P., Smith, P. & Burrill, L. (1994). *The American literacy profile scales*. Portsmouth, NH: Heinemann.

Hall, N. (1987). *The emergence of literacy*. Portsmouth, NH: Heinemann.

Harp, B. (1996). *The handbook of literacy assessment and evaluation*. Norwood, MA: Christopher-Gordon.

Harste, J., Woodward, V., & Burke, C. (1984). *Language stories and literacy lessons*. Portsmouth, NH: Heinemann.

Harwayne, S. (1992). *Lasting impressions: Weaving literature into the writing workshop*. Portsmouth, NH: Heinemann.

Harwayne, S. (in press). *Spirits on high: Lessons in literacy and leadership from the Manhattan New School*. Portsmouth, NH: Heinemann.

Heard, G. (1989). *For the good of the earth and sun: Teaching poetry*. Portsmouth, NH: Heinemann.

Hein, G., & Price, S. (1994). *Active assessment for active science: A guide for elementary school teachers*. Portsmouth, NH: Heinemann.

Hill, B.C., & Ruptic, C. (1994). *Practical aspects of authentic assessment: Putting the pieces together*. Norwood, MA: Christopher-Gordon.

Hill, B.C., Johnson, N., & Noe, K.S. (Eds.). (1995). *Literature circles and response*. Norwood, MA: Christopher-Gordon.

Hindley, J. (1996). *In the company of children*. York, ME: Stenhouse.

Holland, K., Hungerford, R., & Ernst, S. (Eds.). (1993). *Journeying: Children responding to literature*. Portsmouth, NH: Heinemann.

Hooks, W. (1988). *Pioneer cat*. New York: Random House.

Howard, E. (1995). *Murphy and Kate*. New York: Simon & Schuster.

Hubbard, R., & Ernst, K. (Eds.). (1996). *New entries: Learning by writing and drawing*. Portsmouth, NH: Heinemann.

Hubbard, R. (1989). *Authors of pictures, draughtsmen of words*. Portsmouth, NH: Heinemann.

Insights. Dubuque, IA: Kendall Hunt Publishers.

Jacques, B. (1988). *Mossflower*. New York: Philomel.

Johnston, P. (1997). *Knowing literacy: Constructive literacy assessment*. York, ME: Stenhouse.

Karelitz, E. B. (1993). *The author's chair and beyond: Language and literacy in a primary classroom*. Portsmouth, NH: Heinemann.

Kinsey-Warnock, N. (1989). *The Canada geese quilt*. New York: Cobblehill.

Kooy, M., & Wells, J. (1996). *Reading response logs*. Portsmouth, NH: Heinemann.

Kulm, G. (1994). *Mathematics assessment: What works in the classroom*. San Francisco: Jossey-Bass.

Laminack, L. L., & Wood, K. (1996). *Spelling in use: Looking closely at spelling in whole language classrooms*. Urbana, IL: National Council of Teachers of English.

Lane, B. (1993). *After the end: Teaching and learning creative revision*. Portsmouth, NH: Heinemann.

Language arts portfolio handbook for the primary grades (1993). Juneau, AL: Juneau School District.

Leslie, L., & Caldwell, J. (1995). *Qualitative reading inventory* (2nd ed.). New York: Addison Wesley.

Lindquist, M. (1988). Assessing for learning: assessing through questioning. *The Arithmetic Teacher*, *35* (7), 16–18.

Lobel, A. (1971). *Frog and Toad together*. New York: HarperCollins.

MacLachlan, P. (1985). *Sarah, plain and tall*. New York: HarperCollins.

Martens, P., Goodman, Y., & Flurkey, A. (Eds.). (1995). Miscue analysis for classroom teachers. *Primary Voices K–6*, *3* (4).

Masters, G., & Forster, M. (1996). *Developmental assessment: Assessment resource kit*. Camberwell, Melbourne, Australia: Australian Council for Educational Research. In U.S., Norwood, MA: Christopher-Gordon.

Matthews, C. (1992). An alternative portfolio: Gathering one child's literacies. In D. Graves & B. Sunstein (Eds.), *Portfolio portraits* (pp. 158–170). Portsmouth, NH: Heinemann.

Ministry of Education, British Columbia, Canada. *Supporting learning: Understanding and assessing the progress of children in the primary grades* RB 0018. (1995). *Primary program resource document* RB0008 (1994) and the *Primary program foundation document* CG0279 (1990). *Evaluating writing across the curriculum* RB0020 (1996) and RB0021 (1995). *Evaluating reading across the curriculum* RB0034 (1996). Victoria, British Columbia, Canada: Crown Publications.

Moon, J., & Schulman, L. (1995). *Finding the connections: Linking assessment, instruction, and curriculum in elementary mathematics*. Portsmouth, NH: Heinemann.

Moon, J. (1997). *Developing judgment: Assessing children's work in mathematics*. Portsmouth, NH: Heinemann.

Mooney, M. (1990). *Reading to, with and by children.* Katonah, NY: Richard C. Owen.

Mooney, M. (1994). *Exploring new horizons in guided reading*. Worthington, OH: SRA/McGraw-Hill.

Mooney, M. (1994). *Exploring new horizons in shared reading*. Worthington, OH: SRA/McGraw-Hill.

Morrison, I. (1994). *Getting it together: Linking reading theory to practice.* Bothell, WA: The Wright Group.

Morrow, L. (1989). *Literacy development in the early years*. Englewood Cliffs, NJ: Prentice-Hall.

Murray, D. (1996). *Crafting a life in essay, story, poem.* Portsmouth, NH: Boyton-Cook.

Naylor, P. (1991). *Shiloh.* New York: Macmillan.

Newkirk, T. (1989). *More than stories: The range of children's writing*. Portsmouth, NH: Heinemann.

Ogle, D. (1986). K-W-L: A teaching model that develops active reading of expository text. *The Reading Teacher*, *39*, 564–570.

Parsons, L. (1994). *Expanding response journals in all subject areas*. Portsmouth, NH: Heinemann.

Patron, S. (1993). *Maybe yes, maybe no, maybe maybe*. New York: Orchard.

Perkins, D., & Simmons, R. (1988). An integrative model for science, math and programming. *Review of Educational Research*, *58*, 303–326.

Perkins, D. (1986). *Knowledge as design.* Hillsdale, NJ: Erlbaum.

Perrone, V. (Ed.). (1991). *Expanding student assessment*. Alexandria, VA: Association for Supervision and Curriculum Development.

Peterson, R., & Eeds, M. (1990). *Grand conversations: Literature groups in action*. New York: Scholastic.

Pikulski, J., & Tobin, A. (1982). The cloze procedure as an informal assessment technique. In J. Pikulski & T. Shanahan (Eds.), *Approaches to the informal evaluation of reading* (pp. 42–62). Newark, DE: International Reading Association.

Polacco, P. (1993). *The bee tree*. New York: Philomel.

Powell, D., & Hornsby, D. (1993). *Learning phonics and spelling in a whole language classroom*. New York: Scholastic.

Power, B. (1996). *Taking note: Improving your observational notetaking*. York, ME: Stenhouse.

Preece, A., & Cowden, D. (1993). *Young writers in the making: Sharing the process with parents*. Portsmouth, NH: Heinemann.

Rhodes, L., & Shanklin, N. (1993). *Windows into literacy: Assessing learners K–8*. Portsmouth, NH: Heinemann.

Rhodes, L. (Ed.). (1993). *Literacy assessment: A handbook of instruments*. Portsmouth, NH: Heinemann.

Richardson, K. (1984). *Developing number concepts using unifix cubes*. Menlo Park, CA: Addison-Wesley.

Roser, N., & Martinez, M. (Eds.). (1995). *Book talk and beyond: Children and teachers respond to literature*. Newark, DE: International Reading Association.

Routman, R. (1991, 1994). *Invitations: Changing as teachers and learners K–12*. Portsmouth, NH: Heinemann.

Routman, R. (1996). *Literacy at the crossroads: Crucial talk about reading, writing, and other teaching dilemmas*. Portsmouth, NH: Heinemann.

Ruckman, I. (1984). *Night of the twisters*. New York: HarperCollins.

Rylant, C. (1993). *Henry and Mudge and the wild wind*. New York: Bradbury.

Samway, K. D., & Whang, G. (1996). *Literature study circles in a multicultural classroom*. York, ME: Stenhouse.

Science and technology for children series. National Science Resource Center. Burlington, NC: Carolina Biological Supply Company.

Short, K., & Pierce, K. (1990). *Talking about books: Creating literate communities*. Portsmouth, NH: Heinemann.

Short, K., Harste, J., with Burke, C. (1996). *Creating classrooms for authors and inquirers* (2nd ed.). Portsmouth, NH: Heinemann.

Sitton, R. (1995). *Rebecca Sitton's spelling sourcebook*. Spokane, WA: Curriculum Associates.

Smith, D. B. (1973). *A taste of blackberries*. New York: HarperCollins.

Smith, F. (1988). *Joining the literacy club: Further essays into education*. Portsmouth, NH: Heinemann.

Snowball, D. (1996). Spelling strategies. *Instructor, 106* (1), 36–37.

Sowers, S. (1982). Six questions teachers ask about invented spelling. In T. Newkirk & N. Atwell (Eds.), *Understanding writing: Ways of observing, learning and teaching K–8* (pp. 47–54). Chelmsford, MA: The Northeast Regional Exchange.

Spandel, V., & Stiggins, R. (1997). *Creating writers: Linking writing assessment and instruction* (2nd ed.). New York: Longman.

Spandel, V. (1997). *Seeing with new eyes: A guidebook on teaching and assessing beginning writers* (4th ed.). Portland, OR: Northwest Regional Educational Laboratory.

Spyri, J. (1884). *Heidi*. New York: Messner.

Strickland, D., & Morrow, L. (1989). *Emerging literacy: Young children learn to read and write*. Newark, DE: International Reading Association.

Teale, W., & Sulzby, E. (1986). *Emergent literacy: Writing and reading*. Norwood, NJ: Ablex.

Traill, L. (1993). *Highlight my strengths: Assessment and evaluation of literacy learning*. Crystal Lake, IL: Rigby.

Tully, M. (1996). *Helping students revise their writing*. New York: Scholastic

Valencia, S. (1998). *Literacy portfolios in action*. New York: Harcourt Brace.

Vygotsky, L. S. (1978). *Mind in society: The development of higher psychological processes*. Cambridge, MA: Harvard University Press.

Warren, A. (1996). *Orphan train rider: One boy's true story*. Boston: Houghton Mifflin.

Waters, K. (1989). *Sarah Morton's day: A day in the life of a pilgrim girl*. New York: Scholastic.

Waters, K. (1993). *Samuel Eaton's day: A day in the life of a pilgrim boy*. New York: Scholastic.

Watson, D., & Henson, J. (1994). Reading evaluation—Miscue analysis. In B. Harp (Ed.), *Assessment and evaluation for student centered learning*, (pp. 67–96). Norwood, MA: Christopher-Gordon.

Weeks, B., & Leaker, J. (1991*). Managing literacy assessment with young learners*. Evanston, IL: McDougal, Littell and Co.

White, E. B. (1952). *Charlotte's web*. New York: Harper.

Wiggins, G. (1993). *Assessing student performance: Exploring the purpose and limits of testing*. San Francisco: Jossey-Bass.

Wiggins, G. (1994). Toward better report cards. *Educational Leadership*, *52* (2), 28–37.

Wild, M. (1994). *Toby*. New York: Ticknor & Fields.

Wilde, S. (1992). *You kan red this! Spelling and punctuation for whole language classrooms, K–6*. Portsmouth, NH: Heinemann.

Wilde, S. (1996). A speller's bill of rights. *Primary Voices K–6: Teaching writers to spell. 4* (4), 7–10.

Wilde, S. (1996). Reflections. *Primary Voices K–6: Teaching writers to spell, 4* (4), 36–41.

Wilde, S. (1997). *What's a schwa sound anyway? A holistic guide to phonetics, phonics, and spelling*. Portsmouth, NH: Heinemann.

Wood, D. (1984). *The napping house*. San Diego, CA: Harcourt Brace Jovanovich.

Yolen, J. (1980). *Commander Toad in space*. New York: Putnam and Grosset.

About the Authors

Bonnie Campbell Hill is a nationally known educational consultant in the areas of children's literature, writing, and assessment. She spent 10 years as a classroom teacher and continues to work closely with elementary students and teachers today. The co-author with Cynthia Ruptic of *Practical Aspects of Authentic Assessment: Putting the Pieces Together,* also published by Christopher-Gordon, her articles and poetry appear in well respected journals. She is currently working on the next three books in the Corner Pieces Series. Her Ph.D. in Reading/Language Arts is from the University of Washington.

Cynthia Ruptic is an educational consultant and teacher in Japan where she is a member of the multi-age intermediate team at Osaka International School. She has also taught at the primary and middle school levels in Illinois, Oregon, and on Bainbridge Island in Washington State. Co-author with Bonnie Campbell Hill of *Practical Aspects of Authentic Assessment: Putting the Pieces Together,* she received her Master's degree in Education from Northern Illinois University.

Lisa Norwick is currently teaching second grade in Bloomfield Hill, Michigan. She also taught sixth grade and a third/fourth multi-age classroom in Redmond, Washington for six years. Lisa received her Masters degree from Seattle Pacific University.

Author Index

A

B

C

D

Subject Index

A

Read Me file for CLASSROOM BASED ASSESSMENT CD-ROM

Install Adobe Acrobat Reader on your computer, if it is not already installed. You can download Adobe Acrobat Reader directly from the Adobe website or from this CD-ROM.

You must have Adobe Acrobat Reader in order to run this CD-ROM

Determine which operating system you are using: Windows or Macintosh

1. For Windows 3.1 users,
   a. In the file manager, select the directory "Acroread" from the CD-ROM disk
   b. Select the directory "WIN"
   c. Select the directory "Reader"
   d. Select the directory "16bit"
   e. Double click on the file "SETUP.EXE" to install Adobe Acrobat Reader

   OR

   a. In the program manager, Go to "File"
   b. Select "Run"
   c. Select "Browse" and go to the CD-ROM drive
   d. Follow instructions 1a–1e.

2. For Windows 95 users,
   a. In the file manager, select the directory "Acroread" from the CD-ROM disk
   b. Select the directory "WIN"
   c. Select the directory "Reader"
   d. Select the directory "32bit"
   e. Double click on the file "SETUP.EXE" to install Adobe Acrobat Reader

   OR

   a. Select "Start"
   b. Select "Run"
   c. Select "Browse" and go to the CD-ROM drive
   d. Follow instructions 2a

3. For Macintosh users,
   a. Select the directory "MAC"
   b. Select the directory "Reader"
   c. Select the subdirectory "Reader"
   d. Double click on "Reader 3.01 Installer" to install Adobe Acrobat Reader

Once you have had a successful installation of Adobe Acrobat Reader you will be able to start using this CD-ROM.

Go to the root directory of your CD-ROM drive.

Select the file BEGIN.PDF

You're on your way. Have fun.

If you would like to copy the word processing files (forms) from the CD-ROM disk onto either your hard disk or a floppy disk,

1. Go to the CD-ROM drive.
2. Select the "Forms" directory.
3. Select the appropriate sub directory (Word97, Word6, Word51, Works3, or PDF) in the word processing format you want.
4. Copy the files onto your hard disk or floppy disk. It is recommended that you create a separate directory of "forms" where all the forms should go in order to find them easily.
5. Open your word processing package and select the forms you wish to edit and print.

MINIMUM SYSTEM REQUIREMENTS

Windows
386, 486, or Pentium* processor-based personal computer Microsoft Windows 3.1, Windows 95, or Windows NT* 3.51 or later.
8 MB of RAM (16 MB for Windows NT)
CD-ROM drive

Macintosh*
Macintosh with a 68020 processor or Power Macintosh ®
3.5 MB of RAM (5 MB for Power Macintosh)
Apple System Software version 7.0 or later
CD-ROM drive